I0814347

INTEGRATION AT SECOND BASE

CARTER G. WOODSON INSTITUTE SERIES

Black Studies at Work in the World

Deborah E. McDowell, Shawn Leigh Alexander,
and Robert T. Vinson, Editors

INTEGRATION AT SECOND BASE

JACKIE ROBINSON AND THE QUEST FOR BLACK CITIZENSHIP

PETER EISENSTADT

UNIVERSITY OF VIRGINIA PRESS
Charlottesville and London

Published in association with the University of Virginia's
Carter G. Woodson Institute

The University of Virginia Press is situated on the traditional lands of the Monacan Nation, and the Commonwealth of Virginia was and is home to many other Indigenous people. We pay our respect to all of them, past and present. We also honor the enslaved African and African American people who built the University of Virginia, and we recognize their descendants. We commit to fostering voices from these communities through our publications and to deepening our collective understanding of their histories and contributions.

University of Virginia Press

Printed in the United States of America on acid-free paper

First published 2026

1 3 5 7 9 8 6 4 2

ISBN 978-0-8139-5500-1 (hardback)
ISBN 978-0-8139-5501-8 (ebook)

Library of Congress Cataloging-in-Publication Data is available for this title.

Cover art: Back cover of Jackie Robinson comic book, Fawcett Publications, ca. 1951.
(Library of Congress, LC-USZC4-6147)
Cover design: Joel W. Coggins

To Jackie Robinson's vision of full American citizenship
to all who need it and seek it, and, as always, to Jane

CONTENTS

INTEGRATION AT SECOND BASE

INTRODUCTION

The First

LET'S START WITH A baseball anecdote, but not one involving Jackie Robinson. Bill White was an all-star first baseman for several teams from 1956 to 1969, most notably with the St. Louis Cardinals, and was a remarkable baseball pathbreaker in his own right. In 1971 he became the first African American play-by-play announcer in the major leagues, calling games for the New York Yankees. In 1989, he became the first African American named president of the National League (and he is still the highest-tiered Black official in major-league history). In 1961, while playing with the Cardinals, he was excluded, along with every other Black player on the team, from an annual breakfast held by the St. Petersburg, Florida, chamber of commerce, where the Cardinals held their spring training. White spoke up about it, complained to a reporter. After some fuss, all the Cardinals were invited to the breakfast. Then, White turned down the invitation. "I hadn't wanted to eat with those bigots anyway. All I had really wanted, what all the black players wanted, was simply the opportunity to say no."[1] To be able to turn down an invitation, you first must be invited. There would've been no difference, in terms of his physical presence, between Bill White being barred from the breakfast or choosing not to attend the breakfast. But the meaning of White's nonattendance had been utterly changed. Rather than being excluded as a noncitizen, he'd chosen not to attend as a citizen—a Black citizen. This was a lesson in the meaning of integration that Bill White had learned, in part, from Jackie Robinson.

He was the first. The announcement of the signing of Jackie Robinson by the Brooklyn Dodgers on 23 October 1945 was an epochal event and one that has lost none of its momentousness with the passage of years, a taboo shattered with the force of a baseball bat reducing a pane of glass to shards. It was a victory in a war that was very old. Adam Clayton Powell Jr., the new congressman from Harlem elected in 1944, thought a better name for the conflict that began for the United States on 7 December 1941 was Civil War II. It was a war that began with the arrival of the first slave ship on North American shores. The war did not end with the victories over Germany and Japan.[2] On 18 August 1945, three days after Japan announced its surrender, the well-known novelist Fannie Hurst, speaking at a Harlem rally of the Committee to End Jim Crow in Baseball, told the crowd that, indeed, nothing seemed more important than ending Jim Crow in baseball, and if this did not happen in the immediate future, the war would have been fought in vain.[3]

Ten days after the rally, on 28 August 1945, Jackie Robinson had his famous meeting with Branch Rickey in the Montague Street offices of the Brooklyn Dodgers. The October announcement of his signing was the most celebrated indication that something profound and fundamental might be changing for Black people in America. About a month later, in a Manhattan recording studio, Charlie Parker, Miles Davis, Dizzy Gillespie, Max Roach, Curley Russell, and Sadik Hakim, jazz musicians and baseball fans, made the first recording of Parker's bebop anthem-in-the-making, "Now's the Time." If you had asked them, "Time for what?" they probably would've told you that if you had to ask, you wouldn't understand the answer.[4]

Jackie Robinson was far from being the first "First Negro." By 1940, the title had become such a cliche in the Black press that there were apologies for its overuse.[5] But there had never been and never would be another famous "first" story like Robinson's (Barack Obama's probably excepted). It was news that stayed news, throughout his 1946 season with the Montreal Royals and during his first season with the Dodgers in 1947. Everything that happened to him that season was extensively reported, starting with his spring training, the 151 regular-season games, and the seven World Series games he played. Sportswriters also wrote about the booing and the cheering, Black hopes and white fears, the name-calling, the beanballing, the threatened hate strikes by other teams, hotels that barred his admittance, and the 21,000 Dodgers fans who signed an antilynching petition while attending "Jackie Robinson Day" at Ebbets Field in late September.[6] If almost all the accounts of his season could be found in the sports pages, everyone knew that the Jackie Robinson story had, in the end, very little to do with baseball.

One of the reasons people love sports is that it reduces the ambiguities of life's successes and failures to a simple, definitive calculus of winning and losing. And Jackie Robinson was a winner. In 1947, he was the rookie of the year on a pennant-winning team, with a *Time* magazine cover story to his credit. Robinson's accomplishments came seven years before the *Brown/Briggs* decision, eight years before Rosa Parks, the Montgomery bus boycott, and the emergence of Martin Luther King Jr. as a leader of the civil rights movement.[7] Long before 1962, the year he joined his peers in Cooperstown, New York, in recognition of his baseball accomplishments, he was already a member of a far more exclusive Hall of Fame.

With all that, it's not surprising that some would argue, such as conservative *Washington Post* columnist George Will, that "Robinson's first major-league game was the most important event in the emancipation of black Americans since the Civil War."[8] Or that some would agree with the left-wing public intellectual Cornel West that "more than either Abraham Lincoln and the Civil War, or Martin Luther King Jr. and the Civil Rights movement, Jackie Robinson . . . personified the challenge to the vicious legacy and ideology of white supremacy in American history."[9] Or would nod approvingly with Negro Leagues great and baseball Hall of Famer Buck O'Neil that Robinson "changed the pattern for the black man" and "did more for integration than anything [else] did."[10]

These claims are pardonable exaggerations, but it's important to recognize that many people, both then and now, have believed them to be true. There seems little reason to challenge Jules Tygiel's assertion that "in the years before Martin Luther King Jr., Robinson, more than any individual, personified the era's liberal optimism and reaffirmed the possibility of racial integration."[11] This was King's own opinion as well. He said of Robinson that "back in the days when integration wasn't fashionable, he understood the trauma and the humiliation and the loneliness which comes with being a pilgrim walking the lonesome byways toward the high road of Freedom. He was a sit-inner before sit-ins, a freedom rider before freedom rides."[12]

Jackie Robinson helped usher in what we might call the "age of integration," an era that roughly coincided with his athletic and postathletic career, from about 1940 to 1972, the year of his untimely death. Integration originally was an effort by Black America to topple white supremacy and transform race relation in the United States. Integration has always had multiple meanings and has evoked many strong, contradictory emotions. For its supporters, integration was a watchword and a battle cry for civil rights. For its detractors on the right, it was a war against white people, a communist plot, little more than a modern-day slave revolt. For its left-wing detractors, it was too little and probably too late—weak medicine at best, a superficial ointment prescribed for a deep wound. In his last years, Robinson knew that the push for integration had lost much of its impetus. Robinson, says his biographer Arnold Rampersad, moved beyond the "misty dream of true racial integration in America in the 1930s."[13] But this is to misunderstand what integration had meant for Robinson and millions of other Black Americans. Integration had never been gauzy or nebulous. It was the immensely practical product of an intense, concentrated, and burning anger by Black Americans demanding their full rights as American citizens. It was not premised on white goodwill—though white allies were welcome to join the struggle—but on Black actions and activism.

Jackie Robinson played second base for most of his career. He is universally regarded as one of the best ever to play the position.[14] A second baseman needs swiftness of foot, sure hands, and great hand-eye coordination to play the position well. Robinson had these in abundance, along with certain other intangible qualities. "Never underestimate the power of intelligence," writes baseball analyst Bill James of Robinson, particularly when it's combined with "ability, determination, and a formidable competitive instinct."[15] James was of course writing of Robinson's baseball prowess.

But the same might be said of Robinson's contribution to what he liked to call the "Negro revolution," and the cause of integration.[16]

If Jackie Robinson is remembered as a second baseman, perhaps second base is where integration is as well, far from where it started and far from where it needs to go. This is a book about integration, and it is a book about Jackie Robinson. It attempts to provide a new perspective on both. But it's neither a full history of integration nor a complete biography of Robinson. It primarily focuses on Robinson's pre- and post-Dodgers years. It will attempt to tell the story of integration as illustrated and exemplified in the life of Jackie Robinson.

"Integration," like most complex ideas, has never had a single, specific meaning, nor has it remained unchanged over time. It is an example of what social theorist Raymond Willians called a "keyword," one of those admired/abhorred, misused/overused terms that form the building blocks of our political vocabulary.[17] It is a capacious term. This book will contrast two alternative visions of integration. There is integration as inclusion: the opening of all-white spaces, places, and institutions previously closed to racial minorities. And there is integration as effective Black citizenship: being able to lead lives unburdened by white strictures and demands.

Roughly analogous to these two views of integration are two different understandings of citizenship. Political scientists contrast citizenship understood as noninterference with citizenship understood as nondomination.[18] Integration as inclusion highlights noninterference as a goal. No institution should have the right to prevent persons from participating in their organizations solely because of their racial or ethnic backgrounds. Integration as inclusion tends to focus on individual attainments, not group advancement. Its adherents are often suspicious of government intervention to promote measures of social equality or leveling out of a fear that laws that prohibit actions by private individuals tend to violate the principles of noninterference. An underlying assumption of integration as inclusion is that by opening white institutions to qualified minorities, the problems of segregation could largely be solved. (This is often accompanied by the assumption of the superiority of white institutions to their alternatives.) This understanding of integration more or less matches that of Branch Rickey, the president of the Brooklyn Dodgers who signed Jackie Robinson in 1945. He felt segregation was wrong, and this deeply religious man saw it as a sin: no logical reason kept African Americans out of major-league baseball, and it would be good for the political and moral welfare of the nation to end segregation. It would benefit individual African Americans, like Robinson, and strengthen and broaden the white institutions they were entering, like the Dodgers. As a moderately conservative, anti–New Deal Republican, he wished to extend the principle of citizenship as noninterference to African Americans, something he fervently believed in for himself and for private businesses.

Jackie Robinson was sympathetic to Rickey's perspective on integration and deeply admired all he had done to advance it, but he viewed integration from a different vantage—that of effective Black citizenship, or integration as nondomination. Integration was not just about entering white institutions. It was about everything Black Americans wanted to do and could not. What Robinson sought to join was not white America but America itself. He sought the right to join white institutions *and* enter white spaces, but not the obligation to do so. What was critical was the *choice,* for Black Americans to be able to structure their lives without coercion or intimidation.[19]

In 1945, the eminent African American sociologist E. Franklin Frazier published a pamphlet, *The Integration of the Negro into American Life.*[20] For Frazier, integration was a possible remedy for almost all the myriad problems facing African Americans. This included urgent questions such as where people could live, where they could work (or join a union), whether they could vote (and, if they could, whether their votes would matter), who they could love or marry, and, more broadly, whether the American political system would protect them from arbitrary arrests and extralegal threats to their person. Integration was a demand for everything that white America denied them.

To overcome the constant threat and reality of white domination and white supremacy was Jackie Robinson's dream. It was Martin Luther King's dream as well. If the "age of integration" had a high-water mark, surely it was the 1963 March on Washington. (Jackie and Rachel Robinson, with son David, were in attendance.) The key sentences in King's famous speech are often overlooked. "There will be neither rest nor tranquility in America until the Negro is granted his citizenship rights. The whirlwinds of revolt will continue to shake the foundation of our nation until the bright day of justice emerges."[21] Citizenship was the dream. Interracial inclusion and comity, the "little black boys and little white girls" joining hands as "sisters and brothers" was only a potential consequence and by-product.

Integration, in all its forms, was opposed to segregation, but the two contrasting views of integration also had differing understandings of segregation. The idea of integration as inclusion saw segregation as racial separation: Black and white water fountains, Black and white churches, Black and white baseball leagues. End the separation, and end segregation. Integration as effective citizenship saw segregation as an assertion of racial dominance, controlling the options and alternatives available to Black people. The goal of integration as effective citizenship was, in every way, to end white supremacy and to end what African American religious thinker Howard Thurman called the "will to segregation" that infected every aspect of public and private life: the need for white America to demonstrate, at every turn, their control of Black America.[22]

Even at their height, segregation and Jim Crow were never really about separation of the races, just as slavery was not about racial separation. Whites always allowed African Americans in their immediate proximity if their subordinate or servile status was clear, but the goal was to limit their life possibilities. Segregation excluded them from the basic rights of society, such as the right to vote and the right to legal protection. Segregation was only incidentally spatial. And if Black Americans were often banned from white spaces, the reverse was rarely true. Benjamin Mays and Joseph Nicholson wrote in the 1930s that white Protestant churches almost always barred Blacks from worship, while on the other hand whites were often treated as honored guests.[23] In many neighborhoods, African Americans were prohibited, legally or extralegally, from living or purchasing property there. If a white neighborhood had few or no Black families, so-called Black neighborhoods in the interwar years were often racially mixed. On Southern buses, generally, Black passengers were limited in their seating options. Usually, especially if the bus was crowded, whites could sit anywhere. On

Southern trains, whites could move at will through the "colored cars," white crew members could sit anywhere and use any toilet facility. The reverse was not so.[24] In baseball, Sportsman's Park in St. Louis, home of the Cardinals and the Browns, was the last major-league ballpark to be desegregated (in 1944). Before then, African American fans were restricted to the bleachers and other sections of the outfield and were prohibited from seats in the grandstands or other areas close to the field. But if Black fans were restricted to the outfield, white fans who wanted to sit in the "colored seats"—perhaps to take advantage of the lower ticket prices—were free to do so.[25] And perhaps most tragically, everyone knew that so-called antimiscegenation laws were intended to prevent Black men from having liaisons with white women, not to prevent white men from forcing themselves on Black women. Black opposition to antimiscegenation laws, as its champions tirelessly explained, was not born out of a great desire to marry white people but from the insistence that Blacks should not be prohibited from doing so, as if there was something disgraceful in being married to an African American. This was certainly Jackie Robinson's view. African Americans are "more interested in being recognized as a brother by the white man than as a brother-in-law." But that said, any Black person has the right "to marry whomever he loves and whoever loves him."[26]

Integration understood as inclusion ultimately depended on the belief that existing white institutions could be extended to include racial minorities without changing their fundamental character. Integration understood as effective citizenship and nonexclusion, the right and opportunity to join American institutions as full equals, was at once an affirmation of American values and a radical critique of them. Integration as inclusion reserved the ultimate authority for change to the white institutional gatekeepers. Integration as nonexclusion gave the initiative to African Americans and was as much concerned with maintaining and transforming Black institutions as entering white ones. Integration was seen not as reducing or eliminating collective Black autonomy but through the empowerment it would bring, preserving or enhancing it.

Without alternatives, even something you wanted to do, something you loved to do, such as pray in a Black church or attend a Black college, was not free of the taint of coercion. Segregation robbed African Americans of choice. Integration restored it, with the aim to better shape one's future, to gain control over one's life, rather than let it be shaped by outside social factors that were indifferent or hostile to your fate. This was, as Jackie Robinson and every other African American knew, both an individual and collective task. Not every African American had the requisite athletic talent to play on a major-league infield, but as Jackie Robinson knew all too well, none were exempt from the pain of exclusion.

Black Americans had been demanding their American citizenship as early as 1776.[27] But as Stephen Kantrowitz has written, "Citizenship was a weak and poorly defined category in the early republic, less important than other criteria for determining status and membership, such as age, gender, race, and able-bodiness."[28] Before the passage of the Fourteenth Amendment, there was no requirement that states observe "equal protection of the laws," and the status of citizenship rights for Free Blacks varied widely from state to state. The trend was not positive. In 1860, with thirty-three states in the Union, fewer states allowed unrestricted Black voting than in 1789.[29] One of the most prominent "reform movements" in antebellum America involved colonization, which held that free Blacks had to return to Africa because there was no place for them as citizens in the United States. The possibility of national Black citizenship was decisively rejected in the infamous US Supreme Cout decision *Dred Scott v. Sanford* (1857.) It was then resoundingly affirmed with the guarantee of birthright citizenship with the ratification of the Fourteenth Amendment (1868).[30] But as citizenship rights were steadily whittled away after the destruction of Reconstruction, the meaning of "birthright citizenship" meant less and less.

Without full citizenship rights, many African Americans turned inward and found the sense of collective purpose and assertion that citizenship can provide by creating and living within their own institutions, their own churches, schools, businesses, and organizations. Booker T. Washington vaulted to the leadership of Black America by championing Black institutional life. There were some—notably W. E. B. Du Bois and many of the early leaders of the NAACP—who thought Washington's strategy of accommodationism was too comfortable with the sacrifice of equal citizenship. But Du Bois and the NAACP also supported the need for separate Black institutions. There was no alternative. A segregated Black school was a better alternative, if nothing else was possible, to no school at all. If Black athletes wished to play professional baseball on the highest level possible, they had to organize the games themselves.

By the 1920s and 1930s, the heyday of Washingtonianism had passed. Living within separate Black institutions might be a form of belonging to the United States on one's own terms, but it was far from equal citizenship. The hope, propounded by supporters of Washington, that a strong separate institutional base could provide a jumping-off point for full citizenship was not being realized. By the 1920s, E. Franklin Frazier was ridiculing the separate social worlds created by the Black bourgeoise as empty and pathetic imitations of their white models. Ralph Bunche and Abram Harris Jr., Howard University political scientist and economist, respectively, argued that financially and politically, Black institutions had failed Black America and could pave the way for charismatic charlatans.[31] With a new political mood in the 1930s, many younger Black intellectuals argued that some form of socialism or communism and cooperation with white workers was necessary for the transformation of American society that the Black masses desperately needed. It was at this time that the term "integration" entered America's racial vocabulary.

Howard University president Mordecai Wyatt Johnson agreed with Bunche and the others on the limitations of Black institutions—including his own university, widely recognized at the time as the preeminent Black campus for higher education. He said in 1938 that he would "support segregated institutions just as long as it was necessary to keep up the fight for the complete integration of the Negro in American life."[32] As a typical expression of this attitude, in 1939 the Black newspaper the *Philadelphia Tribune* printed an editorial, "Exclusion Wrong Policy for Negroes in America," that opened with the sentence: "Being a thing apart is too serious handicap for colored citizens to carry if they hope to win in their battle for full rights as American citizens."[33]

One paradox for Black institutions in the age of integration was that the best way to make the case for the inclusion of Black Americans in white institutions was to point to the strength of their Black counterparts. The intellectual eminence of Howard University demonstrated the absurdity of keeping African American scholars off the faculties of white universities. The athletic excellence of Satchel Paige and Josh Gibson underlined the irrationality of their exclusion from major-league baseball. Although at the same time, the stronger the Black institution, the more important it becomes to those within it and to its supporters. But this conundrum has always been at the heart of African American debates about integration, the tradeoff between what is lost and what is gained, trading what is familiar, however imperfect it might be, for a possibly better though uncertain future. For major-league baseball, the consequences of integration are clear. The Negro Leagues became the first major Black institution to collapse because of racially inclusive alternatives, more or less as a direct consequence of Robinson joining the Dodgers. (Rachel Robinson, his widow, dated it even earlier: "Jack's joining the Negro Leagues was the beginning of the end of black baseball.")[34] By the beginning of the 1949 season, by which time only three franchises—the Dodgers, the St. Louis Browns, and the Cleveland Indians—had fielded Black players, the Negro Leagues were no longer playing baseball at a major-league level.[35] The end of the Negro Leagues meant the elimination of opportunities not only for Black baseball players but also for on-field and off-field support staff, as well as the shuttering of Black businesses. Since it took twelve years after Robinson joined the Dodgers for every major-league franchise to field a Black player, and since there was often an informal quota limiting a franchise to no more than three Black players per team, many very talented Black ballplayers languished in the minor leagues if their talent was not on the level of a Willie Mays or a Henry Aaron. Black ballplayers found less opportunity in the 1950s than they had enjoyed during the heyday of the Negro Leagues.[36] If integration opened some possibilities for African Americans, then it closed others, in part because whites, as in the case of baseball, had more control over the pace and scope of integration than African Americans. This was another paradox of integration.

In many ways, the Black radicalism of the 1960s defined itself through its opposition to the idea and practice of integration, understood as integration as inclusion, integration as assimilation, integration as destroying Black institutional autonomy, integration as what was sometimes denounced as "cultural genocide."[37] In 1965, James Farmer wrote that "no word has served to epitomize the movement's goals for these past ten years as well as 'integration.'" Farmer was the longtime director of CORE, the Congress of Racial Equality, probably the civil rights organization most committed to the ideal of integration. But he was writing in part to demonstrate that he was not a "rabid integrationist." Regardless, shortly after writing this, he was forced from his position at CORE, in large part for his support of integration.[38]

Two years later, in his final book, *Where Do We Go from Here?,* Martin Luther King quoted the prominent African American novelist John O. Killens: "Integration has never been the main slogan of the revolution. The oppressed fights to free himself from his oppressor, not to integrate with him." King responded that he wanted Black people to be "integrated, with power, into every level of American life"; he wrote that "liberation cannot come without integration and integration cannot come without liberation."[39] There is evidence that throughout the 1960s, most African Americans, even if they did not support integration as an ideal, continued to do so as a practical matter because they thought that they and their families night benefit from closer proximity to whites. Nonetheless, on this issue, King's opponents would largely carry the day. Since the 1960s, there has been talk of "integration exhaustion," as if the problem was integration itself rather than the exhausting and seemingly intractable problems of racial inequality in this country.[40] Integration continued, and continues, to have passionate defenders along with detractors just as passionate. The debate over integration will continue because the idea is central to the very concept of a democratic society, a society without a hierarchy of more favored and less favored classes of persons.

Jackie Robinson became a symbol of integration when he joined the Dodgers, and he embraced this role for the remainder of his life. During his career and after 1956, when his career with the Dodgers ended, he pioneered another role: the famous athlete who used their celebrity to advance the political causes most important to them—especially the realization of full and effective citizenship, a model that others, from Bill Russell to Kareem Abdul-Jabbar to Billie Jean King, would make their own. He remained a popular hero, especially to the masses of average African Americans, while becoming an advisor to presidents and would-be presidents. His understanding of integration was intuitive, something he first learned on the streets of Pasadena, on its infields, basketball courts, and gridirons. But it was also an intellectual as well as an experiential understanding, something he was taught in church, something that was expressed in the hundreds of speeches and actions he undertook for civil rights and expounded on in a decade's worth of newspaper columns. He understood integration's complexities. Believers in integration adhere to a complex faith. His politics are not easily pigeonholed. If his affirmation of American values can at times seem comfortably mainstream, they were at the same time utterly radical, at once loving American possibilities while loathing American realities.[41]

Jackie Robinson's faith in America was not free from dark nights of the soul. Unfortunately, such was the mood of Jackie Robinson's last days. He certainly thought in 1972, in the last year of his life, that the United States was headed in the wrong direction. He wrote in his autobiography *I Never Had It Made,* published that year: "I cannot say that I have made it when our country drives full speed ahead to deeper rifts between men and women of varying colors, speeds along toward a course with more and more racism." He continued, "There was a time when I deeply believed in America. I have become bitterly disillusioned."[42] Still, he hoped and believed that "someday the pendulum will swing back to the time when America seemed ready to make an effort to be a united state." To unite is to integrate; to integrate is to make a whole of diverse parts. For those who remain committed to Jackie Robinson's vision of integration, there still are dark nights. Let us hope that Jackie's pendulum will continue to swing.

ONE

Coming of Age in Pasadena

IN THE SECOND DECADE of the twentieth century, it would have been difficult to find two places in the continental United States more different than Cairo, Georgia, and Pasadena, California. Cairo was the town or small city in southern Georgia where Jackie Robinson was born in January 1919. Pasadena was the city where he moved, with his mother and four siblings, in mid-1920. On the opposite side of the United States, Pasadena might as well have been on the far side of the moon. Cairo lay in the deepest South, a place of tenant farming, debt peonage, turpentine camps, and convict labor. The boll weevil first made its unwanted appearance in the area's cotton fields in 1915. By 1919, the area was in dire straits, barely getting by, an economic backwater. Cairo was the county seat of Grady County, and in 1920 African Americans comprised about 36 percent of the county's approximately twenty thousand residents. This area of southern Georgia also had one of the highest rates of lynching in the United States. In 1919, the NAACP reported that between 1889 and 1918, there were 386 documented lynchings in Georgia, of which 119 took place in sparsely populated south Georgia.[1] In 1918, in nearby Brooks County, there was a brutal pogrom, a lynching of thirteen Black men and women.[2]

Pasadena, by contrast, was prosperous and bustling, proudly self-promoting, growing rapidly in both size and stature. It offered opportunities for the Robinson family that weren't possible in Georgia, and Jackie and his siblings greatly benefited from the move. But in some ways, the choice between Cairo and Pasadena was a choice between Jim Crow Georgia and Jim Crow California, two different species of white supremacy. Pasadena had a different demographic mix. In 1920, its population of about 45,000 was over 95 percent white; the other 5 percent was made up of African American, Mexican, and Japanese residents. Racial discrimination was less overt and less legally mandated (generally) but just as ubiquitous and just as painful. Jackie Robinson's life and racial attitudes were shaped by stories of what had been left behind in Georgia and by what he daily faced in California.

Jack Roosevelt Robinson was born on January 31, 1919, about three months after the end of World War I and about three weeks after the death of Theodore Roosevelt.[3] Jackie Robinson and Theodore Roosevelt are perhaps an unlikely duo, but in some ways Robinson was a Black version of the former president. Both were outspoken in their patriotism, both were progressive Republicans who came to intensely dislike their party's conservatives, and both, in a huff and on principle, abandoned the party. They both practiced a strenuous, sometimes bellicose and muscular Christianity that merged the body and the spirit. If Mallie Robinson's choice of her son's middle name had any other significance, perhaps it also reflected the widespread sentiment among African Americans that the recently concluded war that Roosevelt had so stridently supported would mark a turning point in the status of Black Americans. As Howard University professor Kelly Miller said in September 1918: "The chief beneficiary of the war is the Negro, and . . . the outlook for becoming a real American is more hopeful than ever before."[4]

This was wishful thinking. The year of Jackie's birth would be one of the most notorious in the country's sordid history of violence against African Americans. In April 1919, in Jenkins County, Georgia, four Black men were lynched and several churches and Masonic lodges burnt. This initial act of collective white violence against Black Americans would later give the forthcoming season the grim sobriquet the "Red Summer." But red summers and red seasons were nothing new in south Georgia.[5]

Raised in Cairo, Mallie McGriff, Jackie's mother, had been born into this violent world as the seventh of fourteen children of Wash and Edna McGriff, who had both been enslaved before emancipation in 1865. Jackie was the fifth and final child of the deteriorating marriage of Mallie McGriff and Jerry Robinson. The McGriffs were members of a class of respectable Black farmers who tilled their own land and had enjoyed a modicum of financial success. Black-owned farms during the Jim Crow era were more common than many people realize—a quarter of all Black agricultural workers in the South in 1910 worked farms they owned—and though Georgia had a lower rate than most other states, the area around Cairo was an exception. Mallie and her family seem to have absorbed an ethos typical of independent Black farmers. Owning land, in the words of the most thorough students of the subject, gave turn-of-the-century Black farmers "a decades-long psychic and material refuge from the most vicious attacks and insults of the Jim Crow Era, a base for developing the social capital of community and community institutions, including decent rural black schools, and an invisible launching pad towards the urban black middle class. African Americans' sustained quest for land represented an alternative vision of a more equitable, democratic society, even if it was never fully realized."[6] Mallie Robinson was raised with these ideals and aspirations, and she imparted them to her children after she moved her family to California.

Like many Black landowners, the McGriffs lived by the code of hard work, self-improvement, and education, qualities that were instilled in Mallie from her earliest years.[7] She attended school through the sixth grade, no small accomplishment for a Black girl in rural Georgia at the turn of the twentieth century. She learned in school, at home, and at church about the evils of personal improvidence, the saving grace of divine providence, and the importance of retaining your dignity before white people; you should neither needlessly antagonize nor cravenly defer to them. The McGriffs attended the Rocky Hill African Methodist Episcopal Church, a denomination steeped in Black pride and one that had greatly expanded in postemancipation Georgia, thanks in part to the efforts of its presiding bishop, Henry McNeal Turner, an outspoken nationalist and advocate of Black emigration to Africa.

Mallie probably married down when, in 1909, at the age of seventeen, she wed Jerry Robinson, an illiterate laborer on a plantation near Cairo.[8] The marriage was relatively happy at first, though Mallie wanted her husband to be more assertive and pushed him to get work as a sharecropper rather than working as a laborer for $12 a month. She also threw herself into raising produce and farm animals. Jerry, however, was a restless soul and a serial philanderer, straying and then returning. His departure some six months after Jackie's birth left Mallie determined to end the marriage, get off the farm where her husband had been sharecropping, get out of Cairo, and get out of Georgia. Jerry Robinson dropped out of their lives, his whereabouts unknown, his ultimate fate of little interest to the Robinsons, perhaps especially Jackie, who never knew him. "To this day," Robinson wrote in his autobiography, "I have no idea of what became of my father. Later, when I became aware of how much my mother had to endure alone, I could only think of him with bitterness. He, too, may have been a victim of oppression, but he had no right to desert my mother and five children."[9]

By 1920, the Great Migration was at its first high tide. In 1920 alone, about fifty thousand Black Americans migrated from Georgia to other parts of the United States. Most moved North, to cities like Philadelphia, Chicago, or New York. Relatively few at the time followed Mallie's path from Georgia to California.[10] But like many folks deciding where to move during the Great Migration, her choice of destination relied on a personal connection. Mallie's half-brother, Burton Thomas, returned home for a visit full of tales about the (relatively) good life in Southern California, where he worked as a gardener tending to the region's great estates. He encouraged Mallie to follow.[11]

White Southerners were alarmed by the scope of the Great Migration and made some efforts to staunch the outflow of such a cheap and easily exploitable labor force, but for the most part this proved unavailing. Although Mallie encountered some hostility from white policemen at the Cairo train station, she and her family (along with her sister Cora Wade and her family) departed without major incident. In late June 1920, the party arrived in California and started to make new lives for themselves in Pasadena.[12]

Jackie was of course too young to have any direct memories of life in Georgia. His grandmother, Edna Sims McGriff, born into slavery in the late 1850s, came to live with her relatives in Pasadena after the death of her husband in 1927. Young Jackie remembered sitting next to her, looking at what he thought was her impossibly aged face with "a thousand wrinkles" in a dim light as she told him: "When the slaves were freed, they wanted no part of freedom. They were afraid of it." We don't know what prompted Robinson's grandmother to offer this generalization, but it stuck with young Jackie, who later wrote, "Can you imagine anyone born in the United States being afraid of freedom?"[13] He could not. Perhaps her words later stimulated his convictions about integration. The first adherents of integration were conscious of being standard-bearers for their generation, and they believed that their parents' and grandparents' generations had been too easily cowed and intimidated into meekness. A sharp break with the past was urgent. Robinson sometimes described himself as a "'refugee' from Georgia," and for him Georgia represented not only a place but a way of life that he spent his life trying to leave behind.[14]

This is not to say that the Robinsons ever viewed Pasadena through rose-colored glasses. Though it was proclaimed by a Columbia University study in 1939 as the most livable city in the United States,[15] that same year the WPA's *Guide for California* described it as being "something of a paradox."[16] The paradoxes of the Robinsons' Pasadena were not those cited by the guide's authors, yet paradoxes abounded. The guide claimed it was "the richest city, per capita, in America," and evidence of this could be glimpsed in the "pretentious homes" that lined "Millionaire's Row," with their lush private gardens and estates. Incorporated in 1886, probably no city in America had more ardent or determined boosters. The first Tournament of Roses parade was held only four years after incorporation; the first Rose Bowl game was played in 1902. Two decades later, Pasadena opened its most iconic attempt at self-monumentalizing, the Rose Bowl stadium itself. During Robinson's Pasadena years, the city was burgeoning, more than doubling its population from 43,000 residents in 1920 to 97,000 in 1940. Even though the full impact of the Great Migration would not affect California until World War II, the Black population of Pasadena doubled from about 2.5 percent to about 5 percent during the interwar years—still a relatively small minority, but a growing one.[17] They were not welcomed to their new home: the city was aptly described as "rich, reactionary, and Republican."[18]

When the Robinsons arrived in Pasadena, they experienced poverty and food insecurity, sometimes only having two meals a day. Things did not get easier during the Depression years. Their first apartment in Pasadena was a ramshackle flat without hot water or a kitchen sink, in which Mallie and her five children slept in a single room.[19] If they had left legal Jim Crow and overt mob violence behind, they still had to abide by a series of formal and informal onerous restrictions, including being relegated to movie theater balconies and being refused service in restaurants and stores. Most of white Pasadena did not want the city's Black residents in their workplaces, their neighborhoods, or their schools. In almost every arena of public life, Pasadena's Black residents were reminded, sometimes subtly and sometimes not so subtly, of their civic inferiority.

In the words of a thorough sociological study from 1941 (thus toward the end of Robinson's Pasadena years), it was a city where whites fretted about what to do about the growing "Negro Problem"—that is to say, the problem of too many of them too near. For Black residents, "the constant and all-powerful impact of white dominance is probably the strongest influence on their lives."[20] The same survey collected anonymous comments from white residents. Those who stated that we "are all God's children" or voiced similar aspirations to racial equality were a distinct minority.[21] More common were grumbles to the effect that with the "liberties granted them they become too officious and domineering, in fact unbearable," because if you "give an inch to a Negro, they will demand a foot, and expect a yard." Pasadena had been too welcoming: "If we weren't doing so much for the Negroes here, we wouldn't have so many of them coming to the city and causing this problem." As an alternative, one respondent offered the time-honored expedient of "sending them back to Africa."[22]

In Pasadena, Black Americans were largely limited to jobs as servants, janitors, and common laborers; Mallie Robinson found employment as a maid soon after her arrival in the city. The local schools were not segregated but did their best to keep Black students from entertaining higher ambitions. Jackie's sixth-grade transcript included a comment that he would be well suited for the occupation of gardener.[23]A 1940 study published under the auspices of the City of Pasadena suggested that Black residents needed to avoid an "overemphasis on entrance into the ranks of the professions."[24] Most unions did not allow African American members, and labor and management continued to conspire to do so even as the war effort greatly expanded available factory work. In 1941, one nearby aircraft plant didn't have "a Negro in the entire plant." Most of Pasadena's retail establishments had a "no-Negro" hiring policy as well, and the City of Pasadena limited its employment of Black workers to a strict quota, confining them, as one man complained, to the "street-cleaning, sewage-disposal, and garbage can divisions."[25]

In 1936, Jackie's older brother Mack Robinson won the silver medal in the two-hundred-meter dash at the Berlin Olympics, runner-up to Jesse Owens. (Speediness ran in the family.) If Hitler is remembered for snubbing that year's African American Olympians, the city fathers of Pasadena did little better, ignoring Mack's triumph though later offering to employ its Olympic champion as a street sweeper on the night shift. Despite much subsequent success as a college athlete at the University of Oregon, the snub rankled for the remainder of his life.[26]

Discrimination in housing was as pervasive as it was in employment. In 1922, a few years after their arrival in Pasadena, Mallie Robinson and her sister Cora Wade purchased a house on Pepper Street. The Wades moved away a few years later, and Mallie, on a servant's salary, often was pressed to make ends meet. Her children were often forced to do without or to make do with very little. Pepper Street, at the time, was predominantly white, and the Robinsons were not welcomed. A petition was circulated to force them from their new house, and attempts were made to buy them out. Willa Mae Robinson, Jackie's sister, later said that "we went through a sort of slavery, with the whites, slowly, very slowly, getting used to us."[27]

Mallie told her sons to do chores, without pay, to ingratiate themselves with some of their neighbors. This helped, but it did not prevent other neighbors from calling the police when they thought the Robinson boys were too noisy in their roller skating or were trespassing on their property by walking on their sidewalks. A cross was burned on their front lawn. Multiple fires, possibly of a suspicious nature, plagued the Robinsons at 121 Pepper Street. When Jackie was eight, a young girl in a neighboring house taunted him, calling him "nigger, nigger, nigger." He in turn called her a "cracker," and when her father came out, he and Jackie got into an argument that soon degenerated into a "pretty good stone-throwing fight."[28]

White Pasadenans who worried about what they called "the infiltration of Negro families" into their working-class neighborhoods wanted them to move elsewhere. They looked enviously at nearby communities such as Glendale and Burbank that had been successful, more or less, in keeping out Black residents, towns that had been centers for the Ku Klux Klan and later the John Birch Society.[29] Pasadena's problem was that the city was far wealthier than some of the surrounding areas. Its prosperous families required servants to maintain things, and, for practical reasons, employers wanted the hired help "to live close, but not too close."[30] Rachel Robinson later recalled that during the years she was dating Jackie, "Pasadena was not integrated," yet "there were no Black neighborhoods there." Perhaps not, but the Robinsons moved into the area in northwest Pasadena that was becoming the primary area of residence for Black Pasadenans.

Like many interwar "Black" neighborhoods, the population of the Robinsons' working-class Pasadena neighborhood was more mixed than postwar Black neighborhoods, and other nonwhite ethnicities, especially Mexican and Japanese families, lived alongside some white families. The area, which did not acquire a specific name during Jackie's time there, was originally outside the city limits and offered little in the way of services and amenities. But by the 1930s, it had been incorporated into Pasadena proper and was surrounded by wealthier neighborhoods. To its west, the Arroyo Seco area, site of the Rose Bowl and various golf courses and country clubs, reminded Pepper Street residents of Pasadena's vertiginous divides between its haves and have-nots.[31]

In 1939, white residents organized the Pasadena Improvement Association to "persuade and assist property owners to place restrictions on their property to members of the White or Caucasian races"—that is, to bar the sale of houses to nonwhites. Similar measures had been tried in the city before. In 1900, Pasadena had passed a local ordinance banning African Americans from residing in the city. This was not entirely successful, and after 1917, once the US Supreme Court banned formal neighborhood segregation, Pasadena, like many localities, used restrictive covenants to the same ends. The Pasadena Improvement Association, the culmination of those efforts, was created because, as one supporter stated, there were "too many nigger lovers in the city." By 1941, there were active restrictive covenants on 7,500 lots, or 60 percent of all the residences in Pasadena, with special attention paid to constructing a "cordon sanitaire" around the more mixed neighborhoods. A whopping 89 percent of white residents surveyed that year were in favor "of a regulation requiring Negroes to live in a section of the city by themselves."[32] As one respondent, who wrestled a little with his conscience before abandoning it, wrote, "Property rights make one favor injustice at times."[33] As in many cities, Black and white Americans viewed this situation asymmetrically. If most white Americans definitively did not want Black Americans as neighbors, colleagues, or schoolmates, most Black Americans either welcomed or were indifferent to the prospects of closer contacts with white people. These contrasting attitudes starkly illustrate the difference between segregation understood as separation, segregation as exclusion, and segregation as the institutionalization of social inferiority.

In Pasadena, as elsewhere, educational and housing patterns were closely linked. As was the case for housing, the city's schools were not segregated but were far from fully integrated. On the whole, Black students were not particularly welcome. Although some of the white parents surveyed in 1941 said they would, at most, tolerate "a few" Black students in their children's schools, many were afraid of what became known as "tipping points" and wanted to avoid the nonwhite student population rising to dangerous percentages. The 1941 survey reported that a majority of white residents were opposed to any African American students in their schools. Often, one Black child was one Black child too many, and several respondents said they would move to avoid this possibility. In the same survey, almost half the city's teachers—all of whom were white—expressed a preference to have no Black students in their classes.[34] Over 90 percent of Black respondents answered negatively when asked, "Do you believe that Negro students in local schools are given a fair chance?"[35]

Young Jackie attended two elementary schools. He first attended Cleveland Elementary, but after the second grade, he was transferred to Washington Elementary (followed by Washington Junior High) as part of an effort to prevent Cleveland Elementary from acquiring too many Black students. (A few years after his attendance, the three schools had, respectively, Black enrollments of 43 percent, 10 percent, and 16 percent in a school system that was, in 1939, 4 percent African American; Mexican and Asian students raised the nonwhite percentage to about 11.5.)[36] At the same time, some schools clustered Black and minority students to preserve white majorities elsewhere.[37] Attitudes to the Robinsons, and to Black students in general, were mixed. Some teachers befriended the Robinsons and helped them out, slipping Mallie's hungry brood the occasional extra sandwich, offering some encouraging words, and creating enduring friendships. Others were less forthcoming.[38] In the words of Yoshi Hasagawa, who attended high school two years behind Robinson, "Discrimination against the blacks and Japanese was obvious, though it was a subtle statement. And there was nothing you could do about it. You felt it from the teachers."[39] As one Pasadena teacher described her attitude toward Black students, "Tolerance is the desired end, not race equality." That was just how Robinson and his siblings felt in Pasadena's schools. At best, they were tolerated.[40]

But there was one area in which Jackie was more than tolerated. It was his luck to come of age in sports-mad Pasadena. As he discovered when he was about eight years old, sports were "the one sector of life in southern California I was free to compete with whites on equal terms."[41] Many, though by no means all, of the city's abundant athletic facilities were open to him and other Black participants. And he was not alone among Pasadena's young Black men who found recompense for rejections elsewhere by winning on its playing fields. There they girded their loins for bigger battles ahead. Recreation, like most aspects of public life in Pasadena, was largely racially separated but not entirely segregated. The local YMCA had no Black members, but it did sponsor boys' clubs in local churches and other organizations, many of which were either all white or all Black, and the clubs occasionally came together for city-wide athletic tournaments. The tournaments director told a researcher in 1941: "One problem which attends this program is the fact that Negro teams [representing about a fifth of the participants, way out of proportion to the African American population of Pasadena] consistently win the greater portion of the athletic contests. This is true to such an extent that white boys sometimes become discouraged." The director of the club activities identified two factors for this trend: "The first of these is natural ability, and the second, compensation for a lack of a real chance to compete with whites in other lines."[42]

The comment about "natural ability" was a damnable stereotype, a way of reducing Black athletic skill to mere brawn. But young Black athletes did come to the tournaments with the intention of proving something to their white peers. No doubt this was Jackie Robinson's attitude. He was one of the most extraordinarily gifted athletes of his generation, and his abilities soon became apparent to everyone. His third-grade soccer team beat the sixth graders. In the cruel childhood sport known as dodgeball, Jackie was always the last person left standing. (He was from his earliest years a great dodger.)[43] From elementary school to the "jockocracy" of the playground to more organized athletic competitions, Robinson excelled in "any kind of game with a ball," including tennis (lawn and table) and golf, to say nothing of his prowess in badminton and in track and field.[44] Possessed of great speed, agility, and remarkable hand-eye coordination, he was versatile enough to excel in every athletic endeavor he tried. In addition to his success in track, he excelled in the triumvirate of team sports that, then and now, stand at America's athletic apex—baseball, football, and basketball.

Robinson entered Pasadena Junior College in the fall of 1937. He set a national collegiate record in the long jump: 26 feet, 6½ inches, breaking a record set by his older brother Mack. He was a standout on the basketball and baseball teams as well and won a few tennis tournaments. But the collegiate sport that really mattered was football. His talent soon attracted national attention in the Black press. In 1939, the *Pittsburgh Courier,* employing the adjective-clotted sportswriter-ese characteristic of the era, described him as a "cyclone-gaited hellion," who had performed his "razzle-dazzle hocus-pocus" before appreciative crowds of thirty to sixty thousand in the Rose Bowl, where Pasadena Junior College played its home games. According to one account, "Ninety-nine percent of those present were there because they wanted to see Robinson."[45] Yet the *New York Times* called "dusky Jackie Robinson" the "Midnight Flash," and the *Los Angeles Times* insisted on describing the speedy Robinson's football exploits as the ability to "run with the ball like it was a watermelon and the guy who owned it was after him with a shotgun." Meanwhile, the Black press praised him for "riding prophetic winds across gridiron domains" and recognized him as someone whose future "glory [was] secure."[46] The *Cleveland Call and Post* called him perhaps "the greatest junior college athlete ever developed on the coast."[47]

Ater two years, it was time to move on. Several schools vied for his services. Stanford didn't have Black athletes, but a Stanford booster was willing to pay for his education as long as he went east for college and didn't attend a Stanford rival.[48] The University of Southern California (USC), the area's dominant sporting power, was interested, but Robinson was afraid that its prejudiced coach would leave him riding the bench. He chose UCLA, a school that was going out of its way to improve its sporting results, in part by recruiting Black athletes. However, ULCA was a very white place: of its 9,600 students, only about 50 were African Americans, along with a smattering of Japanese and Mexican students. Racial minority students were excluded from the school's social life and could not live in the community of Westwood, where the UCLA campus was located.

Throughout college and until he was drafted into the military in 1942 (and thereafter more sporadically), Jackie continued to call Pepper Street home until his marriage and first season in the Dodgers organization in 1946. Needless to say, UCLA had no Black professors, instructors, or coaches. The UCLA Bruins played their home games at the Los Angeles Coliseum, which had been the site of the 1932 Olympics. What made the 1939 UCLA Bruins team unique was that three members of the starting backfield were African Americans, and the three "sepia horsemen" broke whatever informal quota UCLA had about Black athletes in important starting positions on the football team.[49]

Robinson's backfield mates, Kenny Washington and Woody Strode, did their own breaking of the color barrier of the National Football League by joining the Los Angeles Rams in 1946; Strode also had a significant career as an actor.[50]As for Robinson, his role was primarily as a halfback, but as the *Atlanta Daily World* put it he was also a "needle-threading passer, coffin-corner punter, and vicious tackler and blocker on the football field."[51] The Bruins had a great season in 1939, good enough that it had "twelve million Negroes hoping UCLA will receive a Rose Bowl bid," but alas, a scoreless tie against crosstown rival USC ended that dream.[52] The University of Tennessee, which had threatened not to play against UCLA because it fielded Black players, was off the hook. Adam Clayton Powell Jr., with whom Robinson would later have a complex relationship, commended the "three terrors in black" in the UCLA backfield and condemned the "bunch of morons" who led the "intellectual gutters" of white Southern universities.[53]

Off the gridiron, Robinson continued to impress observers, Black and white. There was speculation about his possible participation in the never-to-be held 1940 Summer Olympic games. His basketball coach thought he had a chance to become one of the all-time greats.[54] With his jumping ability, he was one of the first basketball players to dunk as a part of his game.[55] And although by general consensus, baseball was the weakest of his three team sports, in September 1941 the football coach of Washington State raved that Robinson was "the best athlete I ever saw. Why he could play shortstop on a major-league team right now, and he's uncanny on a basketball floor."[56] Yet, of course, in September 1941, Jackie Robinson could not have played shortstop on an all-white major-league team.

As early as March 1940, the *Atlanta Daily World* reported speculation that Jackie Robinson, UCLA's "baseball wizard," would "turn his attention to the professional diamond" once his college days were over.[57] This would of course have been in the Negro Leagues, but given the likely meager financial compensation, it probably wasn't worth the opportunity to pass up the chance to play big-time collegiate sports at UCLA. However, if Robinson had been white, it's entirely possible that he would have been offered a minor-league contract out of high school in 1938, and Robinson, thinking of his family's needs, probably would have signed. Thus, by September 1941, he could well have been a member of a major-league infield long before 1947. These were, as his major biographer has suggested, the years of "the lost baseball youth, never to be recovered, of Jackie Robinson."[58]

By the end of his second year of football at UCLA, in December 1940, the *Chicago Defender* hailed Robinson as one of the greatest African American athletes "in all history." But no encomium, however glittering, could spare him from his likely future.[59] With his college career coming to an end, the question of what to do next was becoming more pressing, with the knowledge that big-time professional athletics (with the partial exception of boxing, perhaps the only sport there is no record of Robinson trying) was closed to him. This sense of futility contributed to a decision—opposed by his family, friends, and fiancée, Rachel Isum—to leave UCLA after his last basketball game, short of credits for his degree. Despite a good season, as a headline put it, "Robinson Wins Title but Needs Dough."[60] He certainly wanted to earn money to help Mallie. But his reasons for leaving college went deeper. The "plight of the educated Negro" unable to use an advanced education as a marketable skill was a much-discussed phenomenon in the interwar years. He dropped out because, as he later wrote, "I was convinced that no amount of education would help a black man get a job." After all, his brothers had studied hard and ended up as "porters, elevator operators, taxi drivers, bellhops."[61] He worked at various jobs and played semipro basketball and football.[62]

College baseball, then and now, took a back seat to college football and basketball, but Robinson would later write that because he knew he could play on interracial semipro California basketball and football leagues, he "didn't put as much effort into baseball as I did the other sports. Like most Negro athletes, I just assumed that baseball was a sport without a professional future." As a result, he played baseball "just for the fun of it."[63] On the other hand, in March 1941, the *Pasadena Star-News* reported that after dropping out of UCLA, he "planned to step into professional baseball."[64] Reconciling these statements is not easy, and it seems that while Robinson might have considered the possibility of playing in the Negro Leagues, he likely assumed his future would be as a coach at a historically Black college, and for that career, football and basketball were more useful than baseball.[65]

There would be a last college hurrah of sorts in September 1941, when, after leaving UCLA, he played on the college all-star team against the Chicago Bears before nearly a hundred thousand people at Chicago's Soldier Field. The mighty Bears had defeated the Washington Redskins in a legendary 73–0 drubbing in the NFL title game the previous December. The college all-stars were not shut out, though, and halfback Jackie Robinson scored a touchdown. Many observers regarded him as his team's best player. The point of the game, besides filling seats, was to allow pro scouts to examine the best graduating college seniors. But of course, Robinson was taboo. Jackie Robinson was "exhibit A," wrote the *Pittsburgh Courier*, of the "inviolate proscriptions practiced against us sons of Ham in professional football" and of the limitations of America's "so-called democracy."[66]

The *Los Angeles Examiner* called him probably "the greatest colored athlete of all time" but lamented that because of the color bar, "the future holds no riches for Robinson."[67]

This was an old story. While at Pasadena Junior College, he had played baseball on the Pasadena Sox, an interracial team sponsored by the Chicago White Sox, who held their spring training in Pasadena in the 1930s and 1940s. In 1938, when the Pasadena Sox won the California State Amateur Baseball Championship,[68] the *California Eagle,* a Black newspaper, wrote that the success of Robinson and his teammates was "the biggest argument for the participation of the Negro in major-league baseball."[69] As for the parent club, the White Sox provided more examples of Robinson's frustrating and fruitless encounters with big-time professional sports. While training in Pasadena, the White Sox would occasionally play a few demonstration games against local baseball talent. In 1938, this included a game in which a White Sox squad played a game against some Pasadena youngsters. Robinson played shortstop for the Pasadena squad and started a sparkling double play against future Hall of Famer Luke Appling, got some hits, and stole a few bases. This led Jimmy Dykes, the White Sox manager, to exclaim that Robinson was "worth $50,000 in anybody's money" and "if that kid was white I'd sign him right now."[70]

Four years later, on 18 March 1942, Robinson and another Black player, Nate Moreland, showed up at the White Sox training facility, along with a reporter from the *Pittsburgh Courier,* asking for a tryout. Dykes, still the manager, turned them down but also said that there was no clause in the bylaws of the major leagues "which prevents Negro ballplayers from participating in organized baseball. Rather it is an unwritten law. The issue is out of our hands as us managers. We are powerless to act and it's strictly up to the club owners and Judge [Kenesaw Mountain] Landis [commissioner of baseball and staunch defender of baseball's racial status quo] to get the ball a-rolling. Go after them! Personally, I would welcome Negro players on the White Sox and I believe that every one of the other fifteen league managers [of the sixteen major-league teams] feel likewise. As for the players, they'd get along."[71] By the mid-1940s, it had become easy for people like Dykes to acknowledge the abstract right of Black ballplayers to play in the major leagues at some future date, without doing anything to make it more likely, evading responsibility by passing the task onto others. Dykes's remarkable statement was largely ignored in the mainstream press, though Commissioner Landis was evidently quite displeased to have Dykes publicly discuss baseball's unwritten laws and summoned him to a meeting in the commissioner's office, in which he supposedly told Dykes to "keep his trap shut."[72]

Robinson and Moreland complained to Dykes about the "utter unfairness of the situation," to which, according to the reporter from the *Courier,* he "heartily agreed." Moreland told Dykes: "I can play in the Mexican National League, but I must fight to defend this country where I can't play!"[73] Robinson was quoted as saying that he "expects to enter the army to 'fight for democracy.'" Although the reporter provided the scare quotes, it likely represented Robinson's own sentiments. After the encounter with Dykes, a photographer for the *Pittsburgh Courier* captured a somber looking Moreland and Robinson, described as "a couple of grim, disgruntled, unwanted baseball outcasts."[74] A few months later, the *New York Amsterdam News* wrote that Jackie Robinson was a "star dimmed by bias," lamenting that this "colorful and gifted halfback in his college days," who "found the opportunity of making a living at that which he is best suited, closed to him as tightly as if Adolf Hitler himself were in control."[75]

As was the case for millions of other young American men in the early 1940s, Hitler played a crucial role in determining Robinson's immediate vocational future. After leaving UCLA, Robinson briefly worked for Lockheed in nearby Burbank, a job that probably only opened to him when, earlier that year, President Franklin D. Roosevelt, under pressure from A. Philip Randolph and other civil rights leaders, had signed Executive Order 8802 banning racial discrimination in the defense industry. But after 7 December, Robinson knew that his next job was likely to be in the military.

Pasadena was a challenging place to grow up, and the experience gave him a sharp sense of what was possible and what was deemed impossible for young Black men to achieve in America. This hard lesson was reinforced many times, including one afternoon, probably when he was still in high school, when he and some buddies decided to take a swim. But because African Americans were barred from the municipal swimming pool, they took their dip in the city's reservoir. Unfortunately, they were spotted, arrested, and escorted to jail at gunpoint.[76] The episode perhaps sparked a political awakening in the young Robinson, as he told students at Howard University in 1960. Reflecting on his least favorite word, "patience," he said: "It seems to me that I have been hearing that word all my life. As a boy in Pasadena, California, I heard it from local officials at the YMCA who told us that it would take time before we could use their swimming pool to have patience and wait."[77] A slightly odd aspect of this incident is that, in later years, swimming was one of his least favorite activities. Rachel Robinson writes that "Jack couldn't tolerate cold water" and that "swimming was not his thing."[78] Perhaps cold water was not the only thing he couldn't tolerate about swimming.

Robinson and his cronies weren't the only African American residents in the city who had problems with their access to the municipal pool. Black residents were permitted to swim in the municipal pool, the Brookside Plunge, one day a week, Wednesday afternoon from 2 to 5, after which the pool was drained and refilled. By 1937, the local Communist Party was protesting discrimination at the pool, and the NAACP also took up the cause.[79] In 1939, the NAACP lodged a legal complaint against the City of Pasadena. The city attorney complained that outside agitators were behind the protests. He argued that African Americans only comprised about 5 percent of Pasadena's population but had one-seventh of the swimming time allocated to their exclusive use; thus, they "really have more than equal facilities or rights guaranteed under the law." According to him, the Fourteenth Amendment guaranteed "equal *political* and *civil* rights, but not equal *social* rights."[80] Beyond the reality that having access to the pool on one weekday was in no way equivalent to having access on the weekend, the city attorney's crabbed reading of the Fourteenth Amendment followed a skewered interpretation still predominant among racists: The words of the amendment couldn't possibly mean what those words state unambiguously—that no state can deny to any citizen the "equal protection of the law," which in this case meant the right to choose to fully participate in any and all of its public institutions.

City officials offered to build a separate pool for Black Pasadenans, though both Black and white residents of the city knew the real issue was not whether Black residents could swim in their own pool but whether they could swim alongside white residents. (Because bathing suits showed more flesh than any other permissible public attire, interracial swimming was often a flashpoint for racial controversies.)[81]

Such bad-faith offers often divided the opinions of Black Americans. Some were willing to take the (usually not quite) half a loaf for the want of an alternative, while others angrily rejected the offer. A 1941 survey recorded 42 percent in favor of the "equalization" deal, 40 percent opposed, with the remainder undecided.[82] Another survey recorded complaints that Black Pasadenans were split between those making "extreme demands for separate existence" and those making demands for "social equality in all community activities."[83] In the end, a Black community center was not built, the result due less to Black disunity than white hostility and indifference: "The main drawback in the proposal for a recreational center is the unwillingness of the municipality or the school district or both combined to finance the project," and this was because a substantial group of white Pasadenans were "opposed to giving the nonwhite groups any kind of recognition or comfort. They are even attempting to penalize them and make it unpleasant for them to live in the community."[84]

The consensus among Black Pasadenans around 1941 was that things were bad in their city and getting worse. In answer to the question of "how the position of the Negroes in Pasadena compares with other cities in the country," the majority felt that it was either "worse than most" or "among the worst." Only 4 percent of Black respondents gave the city high marks. When asked about the trend of race relations in the city over the previous five years, over 70 percent said they had "become more strained."[85] Jackie Robinson remembered that "Pasadena regarded us as intruders" and that "in certain respects Pasadenans were less understanding than Southerners and even more openly hostile."[86] James Crimi, the author of the 1941 study of Pasadena, concluded that many young Black residents "feel that only by fighting every step of the way will their race receive recognition" because "any other arrangement" is a "needless and dangerous curtailment of their liberty."[87]

Surely Jackie Robinson was among their number. Integration was often understood instinctively before it was grasped intellectually. It was a boast—and a challenge. It was about winning and ending Black America's losing streak. A friend from a Black family remembered Jackie's excellence at another childhood game. "There was nothing he could not do. When marble time came, he played marbles. . . . Boy, that dude Jackie, he cleaned us out. He could concentrate. He could concentrate better than any of us."[88] Concentration, the ability to focus with unblinking intensity, the ability to ignore irrelevancies and see only what was important and crucial, was another aptitude of both the great athlete and the unswerving fighters for Black citizenship and integration. They played for all the marbles.

TWO

Karl Downs and the Cause of Integration

Babe Ruth opened his as-told-to autobiography with the memorable line: "I was a bad kid. I say that without pride, but with a sense that it is better to say it."[1] In the opening pages of *I Never Had It Made,* Jackie Robinson says something similar after discussing the incident at the Pasadena city reservoir. If things had continued as they had been going, he speculates, "I suppose I might have become a full-fledged juvenile delinquent."[2] A key involvement on this path was the Pepper Street Gang. He was a member and perhaps its ringleader.

Robinson tells of their mischief-making and larcenies: throwing clods of dirt at passing cars, robbing fruit from grocers and other kinds of petty shoplifting, stealing golf balls from the roughs of local courses, and the like. One former Pepper Streeter remembered the group as mainly a "sports gang," taking on all comers in pickup games, with Jackie always the star.[3] There were run-ins, almost weekly, with local police authorities, some of them involving arrests.[4] Robinson's gang members were Black, Mexican, and Japanese Americans. (There is a difference of opinion as to whether there were any white members.)[5] During the probable heyday of the Pepper Gang, there were complaints in the Black press about "the number of boys and girls loitering in the streets" in Pasadena, a situation attributed to the lack of a youth center where young people could, without the fear of being barred from other facilities, find more wholesome ways of discharging their excess teenage energy. Alienation no doubt contributed to the Pepper Street Gang's delinquencies.[6]

The interactions of the three main groups of nonwhites in Pasadena followed their own complex racial etiquette and rules. Because people of color were generally excluded by white Pasadenans, they found themselves lumped together, whether they wanted to be or not. Yoshi Hasagawa told an interviewer that in his high school "there weren't a lot of Blacks. There were six or seven in a class and sometimes less. When we ate lunch, the Blacks sat on one side of the table and the Japanese on the other, and we monopolized the whole area. We were friendly, but we each knew our place." And though Jackie had Japanese friends who lived on Pepper Street, for the most part, he "hung out with all the blacks. My friends were Japanese. At the time, that's the way it was."[7] Nonetheless, it seemed to be all-for-one and one-for-all in the Pepper Street Gang, whose activities were animated by, Robinson wrote, the "growing resentment at being deprived of some of the advantages the white kids had."[8]

At some point, probably by the time he graduated from high school, he put the activities of the Pepper Street Gang behind him. But this did not make things easier for a proud Black man in Pasadena. On 25 January 1938, while a first-year student at Pasadena Junior College, Robinson and a friend, Jonathan Nolan, were walking home from a movie when Nolan started singing a popular novelty song, "Flat Foot Floogie." A passing policeman thought the cryptic and nonsensical lyrics were meant as an insult to him. They weren't. But perhaps he thought anything two Black men said to one another that he couldn't understand was taunting the ofays.[9] (During his major-league career, Robinson occasionally would have to refute the accusation that he and other Black players spoke to one another using a secret antiwhite code.)[10] The ensuing confrontation culminated in Robinson's arrest. He spent a night in the Pasadena city jail and was sentenced to ten days in prison. The sentence was suspended, in part because this was Robinson's first arrest and in part because he was already a football and basketball star at Pasadena Junior College. The episode has become wrapped up in the mythology of Robinson's supposed brawling with the cops and an example of the indiscriminate nature of his explosive temper, but this fight is unlikely to have happened. Robinson always had enough self-composure to avoid slugging a police officer, whatever the verbal provocation, and it misunderstands the combination of racial pride and racial prudence that always governed his actions.[11]

The following September, Robinson was arrested again. In the words of the *Los Angeles Times,* he "assertedly resisted the officer's attempt to disperse a group of negroes who were threatening a white man." The white man in question had called Robinson and his friends "niggers." When a crowd of Black men gathered and a Pasadena motorcycle cop told them to break it up, Robinson, who found himself "up against the side of my car with a gun barrel pressed unsteadily into the pit of my stomach," was "scared to death" and arrested.[12]

Coming just before classes started and he started playing football at UCLA, the Bruins coach convinced Pasadena authorities to smooth over the incident, though it cast a cloud on Robinson at the school: "The thing followed me all over and it was pretty hard to shake off."[13] Robinson knew that his athletic prowess, and the determination of powerful white boosters to protect their investment in him, had led to milder treatment than he otherwise would have faced. But these episodes disclosed the true face of Pasadena. As he later said, "I always thought Pasadena was a great place until I got more experiences of life."[14]

In his serious run-ins with the police, there is little doubt that racist officers were the main source of the confrontations. Still, these episodes, and his time with the Pepper Street Gang, raise questions about his temperament during his Pasadena years. To what extent was he "acting out" an adolescent rebellion, an angry response to his sense of alienation from his home city? How did he reconcile the accolades of athletic stardom with the knowledge, that, off the field, he was just another unwanted Black man? How haphazard and how inappropriate were the targets of his anger? He was seen as a problem. He was befriended by Hugh D. Morgan, a white policeman who was head of the youth division. A former football player from Louisiana State University, Morgan was more of a social worker than a strict disciplinarian.[15] He gave public talks defending Pasadena's Black teenagers, in which he "expressed the opinion that Negro youth give less trouble than the whites."[16] A local African American car mechanic, Carl Anderson, told Robinson that his activities with the gang were embarrassing to his mother and to Black Pasadena and that he could do better things with his life.[17]

No doubt the biggest worrier about Jackie's wayward behavior was Mallie Robinson. She was a devoutly religious person, someone to whom God spoke without intermediaries, sometimes through intense prayer, sometimes in dreams. "I would always live so close to God till he would tell me things, what would happen."[18] Her God was an active God, one that she turned to for help in all the travails of her life: surviving her failed marriage, the courageous decision to move from Georgia to California, and making a living for herself and raising her family in Pasadena. "Take one step toward God, and he'll take two toward you" was a favorite saying.[19] She was a regular churchgoer. In Georgia, she had been active in the African Methodist Episcopal Church. (Her Christianity was tinged with racial pride; for example, she told her children that Adam and Eve were originally Black, but they "turned pale" out of fright when God confronted them after eating the apple.)[20] In Pasadena, she joined the Scott United Methodist Church, a Black congregation in the Methodist Episcopal denomination. She made her children attend, but when the minister at the Methodist church wanted to baptize Jackie and he was reluctant, Mallie didn't force the issue. "Jack's got to be sincere. He's got to understand what this means and believe in it."[21]

Jackie was eventually baptized, and Robinson acquired a good deal of religion from his mother. He wrote in 1949 that "besides having faith in my mother, I came to realize through her that I had a lot of faith in God. I came to know that for sure when I was still pretty young. There's nothing like faith in God to help a fellow who gets booted around once in a while."[22] It's not easy to determine the precise depth of Robinson's faith. He could write in 1949 that he wasn't "ashamed to admit that I often get down on my knees to pray. It's the best way to get close to God and a hard hit ground ball."[23] He missed going to church when the demands of baseball got in the way. Robinson's solution was to suggest that "a little chapel could be built at Ebbets Field."[24] Without doubting Robinson's sincerity, it is likely that his statement in an unpublished document is probably closer to his true opinions: "I am not the most religious person in the world. I believe in God, in the Bible, and trying to do the right thing as I understand."[25]

Mallie's concern for her son's soul and his social adjustment led her to act as intermediary between him and the new pastor of Scott United Methodist Church, Karl Everette Downs, who assumed his position in January 1938, the same month as the "Flat Foot Floogie" incident. She evidently asked Reverend Downs to have a chat with her son. Downs soon became Robinson's mentor and, later, his good friend. The fatherless and perhaps somewhat rudderless Robinson, like many young men in his situation, often looked to male authority figures, from policemen to car mechanics to teachers and coaches, as substitute fathers. Downs became the most important of these male mentors and probably enacted the biggest influence on young Robinson other than his mother. It was Downs who helped Robinson move beyond his Pepper Street Gang juvenile hooliganism and other confrontations with the law. He also assisted him in dealing with the vagaries of athletic stardom. Downs provided Robinson with a usable Christianity, both comfortable and challenging. And Downs helped Robinson come to terms with his inchoate feelings of rage toward white America and to deal with his equally strong desire to enter its institutions on his own terms. He helped Robinson sort out his multiple loyalties: to his family, his people, and his country. Downs gave this old dilemma a new name: integration.

In the 1930s, many young African Americans increasingly saw religion as less a rock in a weary land than an obstacle that had blocked the path of the Black freedom struggle. The Black church, many argued, was more concerned with individual salvation in the world to come rather than collective social and political advancement in their actual lives. Benjamin Mays, an ordained Baptist minister, and Joseph Nicholson concluded in *The Negro's Church* (1933) that the Black church's social program "except in rare instances, is static, non-progressive." Ministers preached sermons that were "imbued with a magical conception of religion."[26] Mays and his colleagues at Howard University were in the forefront of influencing a rising generation of Black ministers to break with old models of the Black ministry. Adherents to both Protestant modernism and the Social Gospel, they were pioneers of a new Christianity who saw in their ministry a particular outreach to that generation's growing crowd of "learned despisers." The ranks of the despisers included many rebellious young Black women and men who, influenced by socialism, communism, Black nationalism, or other ideologies, found in the Black Church only the musty, failed piety and ineffectuality of an older generation, a generation whose deep faith in God and Jesus had done little or nothing to change the abysmal status of Black Americans.[27]

These new ministers were hip, religious, and spiritual but also worldly and tough-minded. They tried to address what Mays called the "failure of American Christianity in the realm of race-relations" in the most direct way possible—by making the mission of the Black Church to smash Jim Crow. One of these newly minted ministers in the 1930s was Karl Everette Downs, who was only seven years older than Jackie Robinson. He was born in Abilene, Texas, in 1912.[28] He attended high school in Waco and college at Samuel Huston College, a historically Black college in Austin.[29] The son of Methodist minister John Wesley Downs, Karl decided to follow his father's path and entered Gammon Theological Seminary in Atlanta, the Black seminary for the Methodist Episcopal Church. After graduating in 1936, he studied at Boston University School of Theology, in many ways the flagship seminary of the Methodist Episcopal Church. Karl Downs considered several paths, including that of an African missionary, before deciding to become minister of the Scott United Methodist Church in early 1938.[30] Wherever he went, he made a name for himself. He was tall, slender, and athletic, with his prowess in basketball noted in the press.[31] Downs was a musician, too, and gave up a potential career as bandleader for the ministry; he remained a good enough trumpeter to entertain students at "intercollegiate musicales."[32] An article from 1941 effused that if other Black clergy in Southern California were "hidebound," Downs was "ultra-modern."[33] Jackie Robinson learned many things from Karl Downs, among them how to be a modern, if not an ultramodern, Christian, and how to be ultramodern in the fight for full Black citizenship. In Atlanta, Downs had been a leader in the Education for Citizenship campaign, fighting for voting rights for Black Georgians. He is credited with coining a well-known catchphrase: "A voteless people is a hopeless people."[34]

It is likely that Jackie Robinson attended Scott Memorial Church for the annual Lincoln Day service in February 1941, when Downs persuaded the great bandleader Duke Ellington to preach the sermon on the text, "I, Too,

Sing America," the famous poem by Langston Hughes. Ellington spoke of African American patriotism throughout history and stated that the country was calling on Black Americans once again in a time of national emergency.[35] He also said that the "the Negro is the creative voice of America" and that when America sings, Black Americans take the melody, are the sopranos and the violins, whereas white Americans, if they have the voices, only fill in the harmony, because "this kicking, yelling, touchy, sensitive, scrupulously-demanding minority" had "recreated in America the desire for true democracy."[36] And given his closeness to Downs, Robinson either attended or heard about Ellington's return that fall with his orchestra to perform a full-length concert, which included songs from their new anti–Jim Crow musical, *Jump for Joy*.[37]

After speaking to Jackie, Downs made a convert, and soon the younger man was a regular at services, attending dances at the church and playing badminton on a newly installed court. Downs became a confidant, offering pastoral advice on questions that troubled Robinson, such as his inability, despite his collegiate stardom, to give more financial support to his overworked mother. Soon, the "Reverend Downs watched me play football on Saturday and then made sure that I taught my Sunday-school class the following morning," regardless of his bone-weariness from a gridiron pounding.[38] For Robinson, Downs was someone who "knew how to listen" and "had the ability to communicate with you spiritually, and at the same time was fun to be with."[39]

Downs had much to teach Robinson about growing up and the responsibilities of adulthood; about religion; about how to successfully channel and repurpose his anger; and especially about how to conduct himself with white Americans without demeaning himself. If Robinson had to work this out on the streets of Pasadena and on assorted playing fields of Southern California, Downs had been navigating his way through similar challenges at the highest levels of student Christian interracial organizations. "Interracial" was a word and idea that had come into fashion during the interwar years. After the horrible riots of 1919, Southern racial moderates, white and Black, had formed the Commission on Interracial Cooperation. This organization was committed to friendship and harmony between the races and worked to ameliorate the worst of American race relations, such as lynching, without directly challenging the foundations of white supremacy.[40] The idea of interracialism was particularly prevalent in the church and Christian organizations like the YWCA and the YMCA. In the early 1920s, the Federal Council of Churches started to promote "Race Relations Sundays." In 1921, the governor of Georgia and the Southern Baptist Convention proclaimed an "Interracial Sunday" dedicated to developing "more patience and self-control, growing out of the spirit of the Christ, in the association of the two races." This was a laudable, if wan, goal—"more even justice in the courts, better housing and sanitary conditions . . . better school facilities, better traveling conditions"—but ending segregation was not on the agenda.[41] This high-minded talk by persons who were basically upholders of the racial status quo left a number of Black participants unimpressed. Marion Cuthbert, an official in the YWCA, complained in 1933 that "for some people the inter-racial experience has become one so inept, so futile, and so sentimental that they have become nauseated."[42]

For Cuthbert, and for many other African American intellectuals like Karl Downs, the dilemma was that these organizations did provide forums in which Black Americans were treated with a modicum of respect, where they wielded influence, and where some whites were trying to give voice to the perspectives of African Americans beyond formal inclusion.[43] Yet Black Americans often confronted a combination of sincere concern and paternal ignorance about African American life in these interracial settings. Participation at least provided a venue in which Black opinions would be disseminated in influential venues not otherwise open to Black participants. But it was no longer enough to speak up in such settings. Those who spoke had to be listened to.

In 1936, Downs, then at Gammon Theological Seminary in Atlanta, published an article in *The Crisis,* the journal of the NAACP, "Timid Negro Students," which lamented the "deplorable timidity prevalent among Negro college students as a result of their own faintheartedness." This reflected what he saw as the general fearfulness and pusillanimity among Black churches, historically Black colleges, and Black institutions in general. Although he praised the possibility of genuine interracial cooperation, it would only work if Black Americans were not overly deferential to their white counterparts. Although "racial adjustment must be made through fearless, rational comprehensive and cooperative ventures of both races," all too often, Black participants "become overly enthusiastic and overly cautious lest they make a slip and the dream of racial equality will fade away." Some suffer from "figments of self-glorification" and place themselves above the masses of Black people; others sacrifice "racial pride" for often gossamer-thin "racial goodwill."[44] "Racial respect" could not be won by half measures. Downs preached "courage instead of timidity."[45]

Robinson wrote later of Downs that he showed him that "a person can be quite religious and at the same time militant in defense of his ideals." He added that "like Reverend Downs, I believe in doing to others the things they have done to me." Robinson acknowledged that he at times could "do too much to others," and his aggressive, eye-for-an-eye version of the Golden Rule sometimes "left him out a limb." And while Robinson would always have occasional intemperate outbursts, his model remained Downs, a "militant Christian who diplomatically induced others to do what he wanted them to do by his powers of persuasion."[46] In 1938, the *Baltimore Afro-American* called Downs perhaps the "most promising and potent minister today" and gave readers notice of a forthcoming sermon, "Wanted, Revolutionists."[47] In the 1930s, lots of people were talking about revolution and the need for revolutionary change, whether with the structures of capitalism, the need to challenge imperialism in Africa and elsewhere, or the revolution that was closest to Downs's heart: the overthrow of white supremacy to create full Black citizenship and racial integration.

"Integration" was just entering America's racial lexicon in the mid-1930s. It was an unlikely word to become a racial rallying cry. The word entered the English language in the early seventeenth century as part of a flood of Latinate neologisms. A definition from 1658 stated that without integration, "there are only parts and pieces."[48] Integration has always concerned making wholes out of parts. For the first two centuries of English usage, "integration" was generally used as a technical term, primarily in logic and mathematics, especially in calculus. The modern use of "integration" largely began with the English philosopher and polymath Herbert Spencer (1820–1904), who during his heyday was probably the best-known philosopher in the English-speaking world. Spencer saw integration not simply as conglomeration: It was the simultaneous increase in complexity and incorporation, in specialization and differentiation. This was central to his "theory of evolution," first formulated in outline before the publication of Darwin's *On the Origin of Species* (1859.)[49] In Spencer's theory of evolution, everything evolved, from plants and animals to the stars and the planets to languages and societies, following a preordained formula and order, or, in Spencer's famous words, "from an indefinite incoherent homogeneity to a definite, coherent heterogeneity through continuous differentiations and integrations."[50] Integration was the touchstone of Spencer's evolutionary edifice, explaining how increasing complexity would lead to greater order rather than chaos.

Spencer is best remembered as the theorist behind the heartless social philosophy known as social Darwinism, though "social Spencerism" might have been more apt. Whatever his intellectual sins, Spencer encouraged his readers not to be afraid of complexity and modernity—another notion he helped popularize—and to be comfortable with heterogeneity. Crucially, for our purposes, his writings greatly broadened the use of "integration" as a term in the sciences and the social sciences. Its use was by no means limited to adherents of his laissez-faire ideology. By the early twentieth century, every respectable social science used the idea of integration for its own purposes, from psychology (the integration of the personality and mental functioning), to anthropology and sociology (the integration of cultures and societies), economics (the vertical and horizontal integration of businesses), to pedagogical theory. (An exasperated reviewer of a book in the latter field complained that "integration is one of those words which one must accept with blank and non-committal patience until the user explains what he means.")[51]

The phrase "racial integration" appeared as early as 1895. Israel Zangwill, the Anglo-Jewish author who coined the term "melting pot," wrote of the plight of the emancipated Jew, "dazed in the sunlight of the wider world without, his gabardine half off and half on," groping and grappling with "problems of racial integration and disintegration."[52] But it would not be until the 1930s that the idea of "racial integration" came into wider use, especially in connection to the situation of African Americans. This was a response to the decade's convulsive economics and politics.

The adage about Black workers, "last hired, first fired," was devastatingly true during the Great Depression. By 1932, African American unemployment was over 50 percent in most large cities, twice that of whites; and those unemployed Black workers were surrounded by a larger circle of the underemployed, all with plummeting incomes.[53] There was a widespread feeling, as expressed by a shopkeeper in Mariana, Florida, that a Black man "hasn't got the right to have a job when there are white men who can do the job and are out of work."[54] Some Black leaders recommended that Black workers leave the Northern cities to which so many had recently migrated and return to the farm, where at least they would not starve.[55] If incomes were down, lynchings were up: 1933 was one of the worst years of the Depression for the economy, and it was also a year that experienced what the *Norfolk Journal and Guide* called a "lynching epidemic," the article pointedly adding that the high totals did not include "the murders of Negroes by police without provocation, an almost daily habit in southern and some northern cities."[56]

The Depression underlined Black powerlessness, as the *Pittsburgh Courier* lamented in May 1932: "It must be remembered, also, that Negroes, least of all people, are to be charged with the responsibility of the present financial depression. Negroes have nothing to do with the financial structure of our country. . . . Negroes have no voice in fixing tariffs, or of levying taxes. The machinery of government, so far as this country is concerned, is beyond the reach of Negro participation. The Negro did not bring on the depression. . . . We rise each morning, not knowing what will be thrust upon us during the day." As undercapitalized Black banks and businesses failed, "one by one," the *Courier* lamented, "the landmarks of economic progress have fallen before a relentless and soulless condition."[57]

"Progress" was a key word for Black Americans, especially for the middle class after Emancipation. And if, after Reconstruction's demise, political advancement was at best in stasis, there was demonstrable progress in many other areas. Between 1865 and 1930, as reported by the *Negro Year Book* (published annually by the Tuskegee Institute), the literacy rate for Black Americans had increased from 10 to 80 percent. There were now thousands of schools for Black students, over fifty thousand Black teachers, over one hundred Black colleges, hundreds of Black newspapers, over forty thousand

Black churches, and the collective wealth of Black America was over $2.5 billion.[58] These were impressive figures, all the more so because every Black person knew how hard-won every advance had been. But this was progress within the Black world, within Black institutions African Americans had largely built themselves, progress that had taken place without equal gains in political rights.

Yet now, during the Depression, talk of Black progress sounded stale and irrelevant. In 1932, the *Pittsburgh Courier* said it was time to face facts and time to stop listening to the myriad "platform orators, ministers, educators, and columnists [who] have been telling us of the rapid strides of the Negro group. . . . [It] has become so common until it has grown monotonous, even in the ears of Negro listeners."[59] In 1933, W. E. B. Du Bois wrote that "we have imbibed from the surrounding white world the childish idea of Progress." Not everything gets better. "We have no assurance this twentieth century civilization will survive. We do not know that American Negroes will survive."[60]

There were two main ways to try to ensure African American survival. The first was to double down on Black institutional life, strengthening it, rendering it more impervious to either the unfair demands or the corrupting blandishments of white America while also trying to insulate Black economic life from the chutes and ladders of the business cycle. The other was to argue that building a network of separate Black institutions had accomplished little to increase Black power elsewhere, and doing more of the same was likely to have the same result. Only by working with white Americans, especially on shared economic concerns, could Black people advance their situation. Although there were Democratic and Republican versions of this argument, in this "red decade" the most influential and pervasive versions, certainly among Black intellectuals, were socialist, Trotskyist, and communist and focused on the hope that after "the reduction of both Negro and white labor to the lowest common denominator of present-day industrialization," a common oppression would bring the races together.[61] This was the hope of the Second Amenia Conference held in upstate New York in August 1933, where a stellar group of young, left-leaning though non-communist African American intellectuals gathered, including Ralph Bunche and E. Franklin Frazier. The conference resolutions included stating that "it is the opinion of the conference that the welfare of the white and black labor are one and inseparable and that the existing agencies working among and for Negroes have conspicuously failed in facing a necessary alignment of black and white workers."[62] W. E. B. Du Bois was present as one of the leaders of the Second Amenia Conference. His politics, like that of so many, had moved leftward during the Depression. But he thought seeking common ground with white unionists and leftists as a waste of time and an impossibility. Instead, he believed Black Americans had to build stronger separate institutions that could better block and fend off the persistent inevitability of white racism.

It was in this context that, in 1934, the word "integration" entered America's racial vocabulary. Du Bois was Black America's most venerated intellectual. He was editor of the NAACP's magazine *The Crisis,* a position he had held since the journal's founding in 1910. Every month thousands of readers awaited the next issue of *The Crisis,* which contained his insights and verdicts on the vast array of topics that interested him, and nothing interested him more than the parlous state of Black America. In January 1934, what most concerned Du Bois was his strong conviction that the world's economic and political crises were leaving Black America more vulnerable than ever and that something drastic, something radical, had to be done. Black Americans had to embrace segregation.

For regular readers of *The Crisis,* this notion came as a shock, but it shouldn't have been a surprise. For several years Du Bois had been increasingly skeptical of the NAACP's approach to Black advancement, with its emphasis on ending segregated, separate, and unequal facilities and institutions. He equally questioned the NAACP's heavy reliance on fighting segregation in the courts, in national political contexts, and in the realm of public opinion, rather than focusing on strengthening Black institutions. In September 1933, he wrote that "there seems no hope that America in our day will yield in its color or race hatred any substantial ground" and that Black Americans had "no physical or economic power" or any fruitful alliances with those who did, "to effect any significant change in the foreseeable future."[63] Like so many Black Americans, he was disgusted by the decade's civil rights cause célèbre, the case of nine young African American men arrested on a false rape accusation in Scottsboro, Alabama, in March

1931. As the young men's fate hung in the balance through a seemingly never-ending series of court trials, their treatment demonstrated, Du Bois wrote in January 1934, "the blood lust of a sadistic people." He was convinced that white Southerners would continue to act this way "until the South becomes civilized, and no one living is going to see that day."[64]

In January 1934, Du Bois wrote an editorial in *The Crisis* simply titled "Segregation." It argued that the status of Black Americans since the end of Reconstruction had been a history of steady deterioration and that in 1934 segregation was "more insistent, more prevalent, and more unassailable by appeal or argument" than ever.[65] Any attempt to work with white Americans was rendered "almost impossible by petty prejudice, deliberate and almost criminal propaganda, and various survivals from prehistoric heathenism."[66] Black Americans lacked a firm economic base. Without it, they would always be at the mercy of white America. Du Bois suggested that Black people develop their own cooperative economy, a very popular "third way" alternative between capitalism and socialism in 1930s America.[67] He concluded that "the thinking colored people of the United States must stop being stampeded by the word segregation" and that it would "be idiotic simply to sit on the sidelines and yell: 'No Segregation' in an increasingly segregated world."[68] In response to the furor the original article created, Du Bois allowed in the next issue of *The Crisis* that, in the abstract, integration might be a good idea and might even be "the great end toward which humanity is tending." But only very, very slowly. "Not for a century, and more probably not for ten centuries, will any such consummation be reached." For the next thousand years, the only choice Black Americans faced was navigating between "varying degrees of segregation."[69]

Du Bois's campaign to rehabilitate "segregation" was a failure. The word was simply too tainted and soiled to be used neutrally, even for ardent Black nationalists. Decades later, Malcolm X, while a minister of the Nation of Islam, would say, "Segregation is that which is done to inferiors by superiors, separation is done voluntarily by two peoples. . . . We are not for segregation but we are for separation."[70] One consequence of the segregation controversy for Du Bois was that by directly challenging the policies of the NAACP, his quarter-century tenure as editor of *The Crisis* came to an end in July 1934, a loss for both parties. But if his intention was to provoke a serious discussion on the future of Black America, it succeeded beyond his imagining.

Although some supported Du Bois's newfound enthusiasm for segregation—primarily Garveyites (followers of Black nationalist Marcus Garvey's Universal Negro Improvement Association), who reminded Du Bois of his former crusade against their movement. However, most of the comments were lacerating in their hostility toward Du Bois's editorial. Many thought the sixty-six-year-old Du Bois was suffering from "mental sterilization" or that he had become a "quitter," a "coward," or even a "race traitor," and some offered very premature eulogies: "My Du Bois is dead."[71] Although Du Bois had tried to make clear that he was in favor of voluntary, unforced, segregation, many of his readers didn't acknowledge the distinction or thought it a distinction without a difference, one that white segregationists would employ to their advantage. Typical of these critics was William Hastie, a Howard University School of Law graduate then working at the Department of Interior and later to be the first African American federal judge, who felt that whatever rationale Du Bois provided for the defense of segregation, he was giving aid and comfort (and the imprimatur of his distinguished name) to the enemy: "William Edward Burghardt Du Bois himself—or not himself—making a puny defense of segregation and hair splitting about the difference between segregation and discrimination. Oh, Mr. Du Bois! How Could You?!"[72]

If Du Bois did not yet require an obituary, then had he somehow transformed into his longtime ideological opponent Booker T. Washington? The *Chicago Defender* featured a picture of Washington under the caption, "Was He Right After All?," somewhat tendentiously paraphrasing Du Bois as saying, "Since we can do nothing to get rid of this evil [segregation] we might as well make the best of it."[73] Indeed, the eminent historian Carter G. Woodson thought the comparison was unfair to Washington, since Washington, for all of his pussyfooting, had never as baldly as Du Bois hailed segregation as a positive good; Woodson found a nice quote to the point from Washington: "Whenever a form of segregation exists, it will be found that it has been administered in such a way as to embitter the Negro."[74]

Walter White, the executive secretary of the NAACP, argued in his response to Du Bois—the two men detested one another—that Du Bois was correct that the fight against segregation had been a wearying struggle of attrition, with many defeats and only the occasional victory. Nonetheless, "the mere difficulty of the road should not and will not serve as a deterrent" to persisting. White insisted that voluntary segregation by "submerged, exploited and marginal" groups meant "a distinctly inferior position in national and communal life" and would only lead to "spiritual atrophy." Acknowledging the challenges, he claimed that "the Negro must, without yielding, continue the grim struggle for integration, and against segregation, for their bodies and the souls, and the spiritual well-being of America, and of the world."[75] As used by White and others, "integration" in this moment emerged in the Black press as the opposite and alternative to segregation and Du Bois's notion of voluntary self-separation. Although there had been a few earlier uses of integration in a racial context, it was only after the Du Bois controversy that the term became popular in the Black press, with 1934 as the breakthrough year. In four widely circulated Black newspapers (*Pittsburgh Courier, Chicago Defender, New York Amsterdam News, and Baltimore Afro-American*) the word "integration" appeared a total of 13 times before 1930, 14 times from 1930–33, 34 times in 1934, and 48 times in 1935–36. By 1937–40, it achieved ubiquity with 261 uses, and rose to 1,227 appearances from 1941 to 1945. By contrast, in the *New York Times* there were 42 articles that included the words "Negro" and "integration" through 1940, with 98 articles during the war years. Its regular use in a racial context only took off after the war.

The most significant and searching response to the Du Bois segregation controversy was by Du Bois's friend James Weldon Johnson, the former executive secretary of the NAACP—Walter White's predecessor—and the only other possible claimant to the title of grand old man of African American letters. In a book-length response, *Negro Americans, What Now?* (1934), Johnson considered several political alternatives for Black Americans, rejecting a return to Africa or a Marxist-inspired revolution as unfeasible and unlikely to change white prejudice. This left only two real options: "isolation or integration." This, he argued, had been the basic tension in Black political and intellectual opinion from the outset, between fighting for "the common rights and privileges, as well as duties, of citizenship" versus "an acknowledgement of our isolation and the determination to accept and make the best of it."[76]

This was not an easy choice. There were times, wrote Johnson, "when the most persistent integrationist becomes an isolationist, when he curses the White world and consigns it to hell." There were times when fighting for equal citizenship seemed futile, an exercise in wishful thinking, "shooting at the stars with a pop-gun." But to point out the reality of prejudice was to make the isolationists "apostles of the obvious." Calling on Black Americans to "realize that prejudice is an actuality" was to place an "emphasis on what has never been questioned." Johnson concluded that the problem was not a failure to acknowledge "that we are segregated, but in acknowledging it too fully." Of course, Johnson added, Black Americans needed to make their separate institutions, their schools, their business enterprises, their newspapers, as strong as possible. But Johnson urged Black people to consider them "as a means, not an end." The strength gained from them "should be applied to the objective of entering into, not *staying out* of the body politic." Integration did not mean "suddenly doing away with voluntary groupings in religious or secular organizations or of abolishing group enterprises." It meant following the fraught path that "leads to equal rights."[77]

For Johnson and others, the Depression was both a catastrophe and an opportunity in a country whose basic institutions now seemed newly contestable and malleable. For Black New Dealers, what President Franklin Roosevelt promised was a reordering of America in which Black Americans would be treated as equals. In January 1937, Mary McLeod Bethune, one of the most respected figures in Black America, granted a VIP seat for Roosevelt's second inaugural, heard him invoke his responsibilities to the "one-third of a nation" that was "ill-housed, ill-clad, ill-nourished." While the speech made no explicit references to Black Americans, she was satisfied that Roosevelt was speaking to their plight. She wrote that "as I looked into the smiling, beaming face of our president, lighted with a spiritual torch, and saw his head pointed toward God, I realized that thirteen million Negroes of America were included in that oath and received great hope for the protection, for the integration, for the participation of my people into the American way of living."[78] As she emphasized, integration now seemed possible.

But as Bethune knew only too well, the Roosevelt administration was at best cautious on racial issues, still largely beholden to the Democratic Party's white Southern segregationist base. If there were a few promising developments, the president had taken few, if any, forthright initiatives to end segregation. From the outset, some Black critics of integration thought that, at best, it might lead to a few middle-class Black Americans taking positions with important sounding titles but no real power, dulling them to the needs of those not similarly privileged and leading them into the divide-and-conquer trap so often used by the powerful to keep the powerless at bay. Those with a Marxist-nationalist perspective often took great exception to the idea of integration, such as the Harlem Renaissance writer Claude McKay. Participating in a 1937 debate about integration in New York City, McKay acknowledged that "we all want integration" but noted that "a few Negroes here and there employed in white institutions" was not integration and that to integrate into a hostile majority was to let one's guard down. For McKay, the "Negro leaders who run away from the practical issues of group organization and development to shibboleth the empty slogan of 'integration' . . . are not betrayers but lynchers of the soul of the race."[79]

McKay felt that integration meant superficial inclusion in mainstream white institutions that changed nothing—what a later generation would call tokenism. For others, integration meant something far more fundamental. In the 1930s, Cheraw, South Carolina, had a population of around 3,500; about 30 percent of its residents were African American. Like everyplace else in South Carolina, white supremacy was enforced by law and fear. In 1931, Cheraw's soon-to-be-most-famous son, the musician John Birks "Dizzy" Gillespie, then fourteen years old, was frightened when the trombonist in his first band suddenly vanished. His disappearance was never solved, but Gillespie and his bandmates were sure that he had been murdered by whites. Gillespie took this as a sign to "get the hell out of Cheraw, that was all we could do," and he did just that, on the road to bebop glory.[80]

In 1933, Cheraw resident Levi Byrd, the town plumber, investigated the circumstances of a man who was beaten by a white mob. He, in turn, was severely beaten by a group of white thugs. This only stiffened his resolve to investigate similar incidents. He started corresponding with Walter White, complaining that "hear for the last 6 are 8 months we Had 5 are 6 Brutal Beaten hear bye the whites and there has not one of them bee eaven arressted for it." He added, "We are treated as Slaves hear in Cheraw. They have no law hear to protect our race at all." Thanks to Byrd's doggedness, a chapter of the NAACP, an organization then largely moribund in South Carolina, was established in Cheraw in 1938. Its founding manifesto read in part:[81]

> To be set aside as a subject group by social prejudice and government sanction, subject to the domination of all and any who many assume authority to command, is to be robbed of the same native rights which others demand and for which they barter their lives. . . . What the Negro needs is integration, instead of segregation. These conditions are exact opposites. They are to each other as plus is to minus. The one affirms, the other denies. All the blessings of life, liberty, and happiness are possible in integration, while in segregation lurk all the forces destructive of their values.

Integration in Cheraw was not a call for race mixing, for placing a few middle-class Blacks into management positions in white institutions, or ending the system of separate schools, things not possible in the South Carolina of 1930s. Rather, at no little personal risk to Byrd and his colleagues, it was a call for sweeping, radical change. Unlike assimilation, integration summoned and demanded racial pride. Integration was the opposite of segregation. At its core segregation was not about Black separation from whites but Black separation and exclusion from the powers, privileges, and responsibilities of citizenship, of which the most important was the right to live without constant fear. Integration was life. Segregation was death. Integration was a call for the life that was only possible as an equal citizen.

A few years later, in September 1941, Rebecca Stiles Taylor, the women's columnist for the prominent *Chicago Defender,* reported on a recent lexicographical trend in "Integration Versus Disintegration Is Question of the Hour." She wrote that "the word *integration* has become so popular today it has almost become a byword." Indeed, "if for Shakespeare 'To be or not to be' was the question," she wrote, the new question for Black America was "to integrate or to disintegrate." But, she concluded, this was not a real choice: "There can be but one choice and that is to integrate."[82]

What did integration mean for Taylor? She provided a definition: "To integrate is to bring together the parts of; to pass from a complex and unstable state to one relatively simple and stable." But this simplicity required not Black assimilation but Black assertion. First, Black Americans had to internally unite and integrate. "There can be no full integration into the governmental set-ups in the face of the disintegration that exists among group members themselves." Integration for Taylor, and for a rising generation, meant both strengthening Black institutions and entering the mainstream of American society as a coherent political and social presence.

Integration, it needs to be stressed, was never the sole option for Black politics in the 1930s and early 1940s. Given the utter lack of effective Black political power in the mid-1930s—one Black member of Congress against 534 whites; no Black federal judges; no Black cabinet secretaries, assistant secretaries, or undersecretaries—unlikely political alternatives were all Black Americans had. But every alternative had the same drawback. It was far easier to make the case that they would fail than to make the case for their possible or probable success. In December 1933, a month before Du Bois's article on segregation in *The Crisis,* Henry Lee Moon, an NAACP official and civil rights activist, wrote a negative review of a recent novel, which he criticized on the basis that all Black novelists have "a special duty" to "indicate some means of meeting the problems of the race." The reviewer indicated five possible solutions: "Acceptance and promotion of the principles of Marxism; the building of the racial economy; back to Africa; social and cultural integration in American life; amalgamation."[83] The idea of "integration" was in the air at the time—and it was distinct from "amalgamation," that is, the elimination of dark skin color and characteristic cultural traits through intermarriage and merging with whites. In other words, in the 1930s for Moon, Black Americans had the option of communist revolution, racial isolation at home or in Africa, disappearance via amalgamation, or fighting for full citizenship via integration.

All these alternatives had passionate advocates. The Communist Party USA had, at its late 1930s peak, about seven thousand Black members, but its penumbra of support and sympathizers was much wider.[84] The 1930s is sometimes seen as a fallow decade for Black nationalism, after the spectacular rise and fall of Marcus Garvey and the Universal Negro Improvement Association, but the UNIA lingered, if a shadow of its former self, and was serving as an incubator for many smaller, often under-the-radar organizations, such as the nascent Nation of Islam.[85] In the 1930s in the Black press there was much talk—and little else—of establishing an all-Black "forty-ninth state" somewhere in the South. Those behind the idea were pillars of the African American establishment in Chicago, promoting it because they "were deeply concerned about the plight in which our folks found themselves, with no prospects of improvement."[86]

Racial amalgamation had few open advocates, though Thomas H. R. Clarke took to the pages of the *Pittsburgh Courier* in 1934 to urge everyone sufficiently light-skinned enough "to walk across to the other side of the line into the sunlight of economic and political opportunity—into the land of Freedom. There are at least two millions of us who can do this," thereby "sloughing off Negroism," suggesting that those too dark-skinned to take advantage of this could at least stop thinking of themselves as Negroes when this meant "remoteness from social and political influence, economic power and prestige."[87] More commonly, "passing" was something one did quietly rather than write about and announce in the pages of the Black press. In 1944, in his influential book *An American Dilemma: The Negro Problem and American Democracy,* the Swedish economist Gunnar Myrdal estimated that from 4 to 6 percent of persons of African ancestry—some 750,000 people at the time—had passed at some time in their lives.[88]

The various political alternatives in Black life, despite their profound differences, had one thing in common: They all shared the overriding imperative of somehow getting out from under the boot of white supremacy, and they all seemed unlikely to succeed. Merger or partition, revolution or accommodation, integration or separation—they were all means to an elusive goal. Racial amalgamation and racial separation would seem to be in diametrical opposition, but not everyone saw it so. W. T. Forham, in a 1938 a letter quoted in the *Pittsburgh Courier,* offered that it was his "humble opinion that our avenues of escape are two—the race must fuse with the whites and lose its identity or do as the people in Chicago, Illinois: pray for a 49th state, where a black man will have the chance to be a man in the full sense of the word."[89] In 1940, Merah Steven Stuart, a Black insurance executive in Memphis, wrote: "The Negro must be either an American citizen with all the rights and opportunities that others enjoy; or he must be separate, with all of the opportunities and advantages that will arise from the combined power of his members. The role of an economic chameleon, first separate and then unseparate, to suit the convenience of exploitation, brings the race ever nearer to the exhaustion of its economic resources."[90] The *Pittsburgh Courier* editorialized in 1937: "There is as much diversity of opinion in the Negro group as any other group. We have our chauvinists, it is true, but we also have our integrationists, who are working against group isolation, while between the two groups we have the great mass of watchfully waiting Negroes which refuses to blindly follow either side."[91] What united Black Americans in the 1930s were bitter memories of the past and fragile hopes for a better future. What divided them was their uncertainty on how to achieve this.

Amid the welter of alternatives, many Blacks, such as Karl Downs, believed that integration held out the best way forward, a way to simultaneously assert their shared Americanness with other Americans and their shared Blackness with other Black people. And it meant fighting against Black subordination as the price of "reunion" of Northern and Southern whites. This became a crucial issue for Downs in the late 1930s as a minister in the Methodist Episcopal Church, a predominantly white denomination with about 7 million members at the time, of whom about 300,000 (or about 4 percent) were Black. No predominately white Protestant denomination had as many African Americans, either as a percentage of their membership or in absolute numbers, though the vast majority of Black members were in separate Black congregations like the Scott United Methodist Church in Pasadena. (This accounting does not include the separate and overwhelmingly Black Methodist denominations: the African Methodist Episcopal Church, the African Methodist Episcopal Zion Church, and the Colored [subsequently the Christian] Methodist Episcopal Church.)[92]

The Methodist Episcopal Church was largely a Northern denomination, having lost its Southern component in 1844 as the battle over slavery intensified. By the 1930s, considerable sentiment motivated both halves of the Methodist Church to seek a remarriage, but the Southern Methodists did not want to treat Black Methodists as equals and wanted them segregated into an all-Black "Central Jurisdiction." For most Northern Methodists, the "romance of reconciliation" overwhelmed the objections of Black Methodists, and the plan of union, with its Central Jurisdiction, was approved in May 1936 at a general conference of the Methodist Episcopal Church by a vote of 470 to 83. Of the 47 Black delegates, only 11 voted for the merger. When, at the end of the meeting, the delegates rose to sing "Marching to Zion," most Black attendees stayed in their seats. If the decision had been made, considerable dissention remained. A few months later, at a meeting of the National Council of Methodist Youth—Downs was one of the few Black ministers on its executive council—at Berea College in Kentucky, Downs helped lead a meeting that overwhelmingly (466 to 16) rejected the consolidation plan as "anti-social, anti-ethical and anti-Christian." Downs's objections and those of the National Council of Methodist Youth were ignored, and plans for the merger continued. They were finalized in 1939. The Central Jurisdiction endured until 1968.[93]

In February 1938, the Methodist Episcopal Church held its annual general council in Chicago as the details of the merger were still being worked out. Downs had come from Pasadena to deliver a major address on behalf of Methodist youth, and, as he proudly noted, not just Black Methodist youth. His topic: "What we expect of our church?"[94] (Another speaker at the convention was the fervent lay Methodist and general manager of the St. Louis Cardinals, Branch Rickey.)[95] Whatever Downs' expectations were of his church, they were not met.

When Downs arrived at the Stevens Hotel in Chicago, he discovered that he and the other three hundred African American delegates (of the four thousand Methodists attending the conference) would not be accommodated at the hotel, despite a previous church ruling that no church meeting would be held in a segregated setting. Downs raised a fuss and a commotion ensued. Methodist officials told Downs that he was out of line. This angered him more than the initial refusal by the hotel, as he was "bowed with disgust and shame and seething with the human accompaniment of mental anguish," fighting back "the deep passion of hatred and despair which involuntarily boiled within me." What to do? He thought of leaving the conference but decided against it. He could "blast the thing wide open" in his speech, but Jim Crow wasn't what he intended to speak about, and doing so would just reinforce the perception among whites that "every speaker of a minority group is expected to 'harp' upon injustice," as if they could speak on nothing else, and it was the only subject whites thought them capable of addressing.[96]

Downs gave his speech as planned, but then he wrote a blistering article about his experiences in a prominent Methodist journal, arguing that "the timidity of namby-pamby leaders who cannot 'see the forest for the trees' makes the dream of a united Methodism questionable," and if this was what white Methodists in the North would do to accommodate Southern segregationists, then "it is obvious that, if this is what unification must tolerate, we Negroes have been forsaken."[97] Reminding the Methodists that there were alternatives to the church, Downs suggested that if this had been a meeting of the Communist Party–affiliated American Youth Congress, this would not have happened. He also quoted the final, defiant words of James Weldon Johnson's *Negro Americans, What Now?,* which had become a sort of credo for integration: "I will not allow one prejudiced person or one million or one hundred million to blight my life. I would not allow prejudice or any of its attendant humiliations bear me down to spiritual defeat."[98] When Downs returned to Pasadena, he no doubt told his congregation all about his Chicago experience and how he had to control the passionate emotions that "boiled within" him in order to combat white prejudice in the most effective manner possible. When Branch Rickey, in his famous initial meeting with Jackie Robinson in August 1945, tried to impart a similar message, it was a lesson Robinson had already learned from Karl Downs.

In 1943, Downs left Pasadena and took a new job as president of his alma mater, Samuel Huston College in Austin, Texas. Barely thirty years old, he was hailed as the youngest college president in the country. In short order, he turned the largely moribund institution around, tripling the enrollment from around 220 to 660 students, improving the quality of the faculty, and bringing in speakers such as Langston Hughes and W. E. B. Du Bois.[99]

In the same year, Downs published his only book, *Meet the Negro,* a collection of sixty short profiles of prominent Black Americans in a variety of fields, from Paul Robeson to Mary McLeod Bethune.[100] Langston Hughes, among others, praised the book.[101] Unlike some earlier efforts in the venerable genre of Black collective biography, sometimes called "contributionism," *Meet the Negro* wasn't a humble plea for admittance.[102] It was a ready-or-not-here-we-come announcement of arrival. It opened with the statement: "America is deeply concerned about the 'Negro Problem.'" However, the country was pitifully blind to the "Negro possibility"; subsequent paragraphs argued that "to be born black is more than to be persecuted, it is to be privileged" and that "it is a blessing and not a curse to be born black!" Downs wrote that his life really began when "he discovered that God never intended that he should hang his head apologetically because of the color of his skin." "Fourteen million Black Americans," stated Downs, "stand before the judgment seat of America, pleading for cooperation and understanding, not pity and sympathy. . . . They want their inalienable chance to help fashion a better country and a better world, just the color that they are."[103] If there was any sentiment that united Black America in the 1930s and 1940s, regardless of various political stances, it was a fight against the disabling consequences of white pity. "If a man feels sorry for you," the African American religious thinker Howard Thurman wrote, "he can very easily absolve himself from dealing with you in any sense as an equal."[104] In July 1943, a review of *Meet the Negro* stated that a copy should be "on the shelf of every Negro and [it is] a document to be memorized by every white."[105]

Meet the Negro was a distillation of integration as an ideal and as a demand. However, it contains one overwhelming irony. In its sixty short profiles of African American men and women of attainment, a catalog of strivers, and overachievers, Downs did not include the young man he knew better than any other person he profiled. Based on his collegiate athletic accomplishments, he'd already more than cleared the bar of admittance. He would, more than anyone else profiled in the book, fulfill Downs's ideals.

We do not know if Robinson read *Meet the Negro* when it was published—service in the Army probably did not leave much spare time for reading—but he probably did. Certainly, the two men continued their friendship. When Robinson was stationed during the war at Fort Hood in Texas, he frequently made the ninety-minute trip to visit Downs in Austin.[106] When, in the summer of 1944, Robinson was brought before a court-martial for refusing to sit in the presumed colored section of a bus, one of the first persons he spoke to was Downs, who likely came to Fort Hood to counsel Robinson.[107] When he was discharged from the Army later that year and needing a job, Robinson spent a few months working for Downs as Samuel Huston College's athletic director and basketball coach.[108] And in February 1946, when Jackie Robinson married Rachel Isum, Downs returned to Pasadena to officiate at the wedding.[109]

Downs remained active as a lecturer and writer. In early 1947 he again spoke of Black patriotism and what that entailed: "Whenever America stands as the symbol of freedom and as the torchbearer of democracy, the Negro is lifted up. Without the Negro, America would not be the strong nation that it is today. Without America, the Negro would not be strong race that it is becoming." In answer to the perennial issue concerning "What the Negro wants," Downs offered a long list of particulars: "Paved streets, street lights, parks, swimming pools, nine-month schools, school busses, symphony concerts, recreational opportunities, suffrage, inviting residential sections, adequate hospitalization, and protection of Law." Either "stop lip service to something so sacred as the American Creed" and take down the whites-only signs, "or else change that creed to one of the super-races."[110] In a 1947 commencement address at Bennett College, an HBCU in Greensboro, North Carolina, he told the graduates to "remember, right or wrong, this is your America. You have three choices to make; are you going to let being colored sink, sour, or stimulate you."[111]

When *Meet the Negro* appeared, a reviewer urged readers to buy it "because you can say in days to come that you bought Karl Downs's first book when he was just starting out."[112] Alas, he would write no more books. In the fall of 1947, Downs went to Brooklyn and celebrated the triumphs of his protégé on "Jackie Robinson Day" at Ebbets Field.[113] While in Brooklyn, he suddenly took ill and, against the Robinsons' advice, returned to Texas rather than have his intestinal ailment treated in Brooklyn. He died a few months later after a botched operation by a white surgeon in a segregated hospital. Robinson believed that Downs died "a victim of racism," because after the operation, when postoperative complications set in, rather than "being rushed to the emergency room in the white wing," he was left largely unsupervised in the Negro ward of the hospital.[114] Downs was only thirty-five years old. Robinson wrote in his autobiography that "in ability and dedication," he ranked with "Roy Wilkins, Whitney Young, and Dr. Martin Luther King, Jr," and that had he lived he could well have had a similar career.[115] This seems entirely plausible. One of his eulogists described him with words that would have been at least as fitting for his protégé: He "thrilled at the game of life and accepted its challenges. He played it hard, he played it clean, and he played it fair."[116]

Downs was a great admirer of the influential African American minister and religious thinker Howard Thurman.[117] In 1944, Thurman had left his position as Dean of Chapel at Howard University to become a co-pastor at one of the first congregations in the United States consciously organized as an interracial church. In January 1948, as one his last legacies, Downs invited Thurman to deliver a lecture series at Samuel Huston College.[118] Downs died the following month, so he did not live to hear Thurman's lectures, delivered that April, which were published as *Jesus and the Disinherited* in 1949.[119]

This book became required reading during the civil rights era. In it, Thurman argued that a defining context for the ministry of Jesus was that Jesus and his followers were not Roman citizens, and arbitrary, lawless assaults were always a reality and possibility. "If a Roman soldier pushed Jesus into a ditch, he could not appeal to Caesar; he would just be another Jew in the ditch." A life of such "stark insecurity" bred "complete civil and moral nihilism and psychic anarchy." Only those who have lived "day by day without a sense of security" can understand this. Without being able to rely on the legal system, those without citizenship were always afraid of confrontations with authority, with the ever-present dangers of escalation. Their "values are interpreted in terms of their bearing upon the one major concern of all activity—not being killed. . . . *Not to be killed* becomes the great end, and morality takes its meaning from that center."[120] To thwart this, Jesus dedicated himself to combating what Thurman called the hounds of hell. In Thurman's words, "Whenever [Jesus's] spirit appears, the oppressed gather fresh courage; for he announced the good news that fear, hypocrisy, and hatred, the three hounds of hell that track the trail of the disinherited, need have no dominion over them."[121] And if the disinherited can overcome the hounds of hell, they can face their former oppressors as equals. For Thurman, the "religion of Jesus"—which he carefully distinguished from conventional Christianity—answered how any "underprivileged, disinherited, despised, and disorganized minority" needed to respond to the assaults of the "ruthless majority." The religion of Jesus "started as a technique of survival for the underprivileged," and its message and method taught "you must love without cowardice or fear; you must be wary without hypocrisy and you must be full of peace without contentment."[122] This was a creed for integration and illustrates why—for Thurman, for Downs, and for Jackie Robinson—integration was a necessity. Only citizens can count on protection from that sort of soul-destroying insecurity. But the goal of being a citizen was not merely to avoid a random, anonymous death. It was to triumph over arbitrariness of all kinds. Howard Thurman defined freedom as having "a sense of alternatives," challenging the "impersonal forces that don't even know that as an individual I am here." With more options, wrote Thurman, "standing in my place . . . I can so act as to influence, order, alter, or change the future."[123] This was the goal of integration: to triumph over forces either indifferent or hostile and to be able to choose one's destiny and to make one's future. For African Americans, this was, unavoidably, both a personal and collective task.[124]

One of the first readers of *Jesus and the Disinherited* was Martin Luther King Jr. A few months after its publication, King, then a second-year student at Crozier Seminary, quoted it in one of his student papers. It became one of his favorite books, his dogeared copy accompanying him on many of his travels.[125] Both Howard Thurman and Martin Luther King Jr. were baseball fans and fans of Jackie Robinson. In the academic year 1953–54, Thurman became Boston University's first African American dean of chapel, while King, having completed his coursework, was living in Boston while working on his dissertation. During that year, their paths crossed fairly frequently. In October, Thurman invited King over to his apartment to watch the World Series, which for the third time in five years pitted the Brooklyn Dodgers against the still lily-white New York Yankees. Presumably both men were passionately rooting for Jackie Robinson, Roy Campanella, and the Dodgers, though the Yankees again defeated the Dodgers in the series, four games to two. (It was the last World Series won by an all-white team.)[126]

For Thurman, for King, for Downs, one of the main goals of religion was the liberation from fear and fear's accomplices, deception, and hate.[127] Black Americans must strive to overcome these powerful, negative emotions and replace them with self-pride and a bold but cautious kind of love and the spiritual discipline required to make integration a reality. No doubt Robinson, Downs, King, and Thurman would have agreed with James Baldwin's definition of integration: "If the word *integration means* anything [it is] that we with love shall force our brothers to see themselves as they are, to cease fleeing from reality and begin to change it. For this is your home, my friend, do not be driven from it; great men have done great things here, and will again, and we can make America what America must become."[128] Integration could make America great, again. This was Karl Downs's radical idea.

THREE

Integration Controversies

THE MILITARY AND THE NEGRO LEAGUES

IN EARLY 1942, JACKIE ROBINSON, like most men in the United States of draft age, faced two questions: What would his life be like in the military? And then, after putting his life on hold for a few years, what would his life be like when he was again a civilian? To serve in the military was to face a contraction of one's basic freedoms, to lose the ability to determine what to do and when and where to do it. Come the postwar, there should be recompense: enhanced freedoms and more life choices. Everyone in the country was aware of this contradiction, soldier and civilian, but none more so than Black Americans, who especially held out the hope that wartime sacrifices would bring peacetime benefits. By the time the United States formally entered the war after 7 December 1941, the plans for a better postwar world were well underway.

The treatment of Black soldiers during the war provides an essential context for understanding the signing of Jackie Robinson.[1] The war intensified the question of employment discrimination and discrimination in general and interrogated the meaning of American democracy. It had a profound impact on the way baseball was played during the war years. It raised the unanswerable question that demonstrators against baseball's color line asked in 1945: "If we can stop bullets, why not balls?"[2]

The war was fought with a Jim Crow military. The use of Black soldiers in World War I had given Black Americans a hopeful glimpse of what their citizenship might become, before the bitter disappointments endured during the interwar era. Howard Thurman noted that World War II had a contradictory impact on Black Americans. There was something exciting about the wartime spirit of democratic inclusion, a sense of being part of an enterprise that touched every part of everyday life, and that government both welcomed and commanded participation by Black Americans in a common effort. But many white Americans found even this very modest recognition frightening. As Thurman also wrote, after Pearl Harbor, Japan's "'daring' to attack a white race" gave many whites an excuse to release "the expression of the prejudices against nonwhite peoples just under the surface of the American consciousness." Thurman ventriloquized white America: "Negroes do not know what to do with their new sense of significance. They are flippant, arrogant, bigoted, overbearing. Therefore, they must be curbed, held in check," leading to, on the part of white Americans, "increasing bitterness, intolerance, and hatred," and often on the part of Black Americans, "reactions in kind."[3] In early 1942, the *Pittsburgh Courier* started its famous "Double V" camp—victory for democracy at home and abroad—though it was hardly clear at war's end whether it had ameliorated or exacerbated racial tensions. (Probably both.) But Black Americans were determined that World War II would be the last war they would fight as second-class citizens.[4]

By 1945, there were over 12 million men and women serving in the US armed forces, of whom over a million were African American. Ten years earlier, the total number of persons in the military had only numbered about 250,000, and at the time there were only several thousand Black soldiers serving in the US Army, all in segregated regiments. Of the five Black commissioned officers, three were chaplains. The only position open to Black sailors in the Navy was that of mess mate. There were no African Americans whatsoever in the Marines or the Army Air Corps. The US military accepted Black service personnel only in subservient roles. In 1934, Charles H. Houston, dean of the Howard University School of Law, wrote a letter to Douglas MacArthur, chief of staff of the US Army, complaining of the continued segregation in the military. Black soldiers had not forgotten the broken promises made to them during the last war. They were, on the whole, "bitter and disillusioned." Houston wrote of a time when "Negroes used to take pride in their patriotism." No more. MacArthur tried to assuage Houston: "There has been and will be no discrimination against the colored race." Houston did not put much faith in MacArthur's assurances: "The army cannot expect to slight and neglect colored men in time of peace, and then suddenly imbue them with patriotism by waving the flag in times of war." In a sign of the growing use of the term "integration" in a racial context, the *Pittsburgh Courier* quoted Houston as saying, "What the Negro wants is 'integration into the armed forces in times of peace with equal opportunities in all arms according to merit.' We want nothing more, we shall accept nothing less."[5]

In 1934, the state of the US military was not, for many, an urgent concern.[6] By the late 1930s and early 1940s, the notion of war was becoming, almost daily, less abstract. The situation of African Americans in the military remained unchanged, and there were increasing calls for the full integration of the military.[7] But integration meant different things to different people. Did it mean that Black units would be treated equally in terms of assignments and not relegated to labor details? Or did it mean no Black units? The *Pittsburgh Courier* wrote in 1940 that "the fight for complete integration into the army forces of this country was advanced several steps when the United States War Department announced that it would organize several new Negro regiments."[8] Gordon Blaine Hancock, a prominent and influential Black moderate, wrote in 1938: "Although we may reject segregation in theory . . . and God have mercy upon the Negro who does not . . . we sometimes accept it in practice as a means of lifting ourselves economically and socially. . . . The Negro's military voice will be louder and more insistent if there is a Negro division. . . . A separate Negro division will not be a stumbling block but a stepping stone. It is the unsatisfactory means to a desirable end."[9] Others, such as W. J. Hale, president of Tennessee State College, thought that more segregated units would be a mistake, and "further separation might be dangerous."[10]

Charles Houston, representing the position of the NAACP, argued that Black units would be acceptable "only as a starter" and "if it is made clear the race stands for complete integration into all the branches of the service."[11] In December 1940, William Hastie, a civilian advisor on racial matters to the secretary of war, said that "the fight for a square deal for Negroes in the Army would be far [more] easily won if it were not for the Uncle Tom Negroes who go around asking for segregation."[12] At the same time, the *Pittsburgh Courier,* which a few years earlier had been willing to accept all-Black regiments as a necessary concession to reality, editorialized that "since the Civil War we have had an increasingly vocal class of Negroes who have accepted segregation and urged their people to accept it as better than nothing. They have thought they could beat the ill effects of segregation by accepting and enlarging and glorifying it, and they have been mistaken." They were mistaken because "the more segregation there is, the more we condone and glorify it, the more used to it grow both whites and Negroes, and the less willing is either group to advocate and strive for something better."[13]

No matter where Black writers stood on the issue, the military never wavered from its commitment to segregation in the armed forces, despite unprecedented pressure. Secretary of War Henry Stimson wrote in his diary in October 1940 that "there is a tremendous drive going on by the Negroes, taking advantage of the last weeks of the campaign [for president] in order to force the Army and Navy into doing things for their race which would not otherwise be done and are not in the interest of sound national defense."[14]

The following year, pressure—especially the threat by labor leader A. Philip Randolph to lead a march on Washington to protest discrimination in the defense industry—led President Roosevelt to issue Executive Order 8802, which prohibited racial discrimination by defense contractors and established the Fair Employment Practices Committee (FEPC) to enforce it. It certainly was the strongest federal antidiscrimination ordinance since Reconstruction and a striking example of the growth of African American political power. But this did not directly affect segregation in the military. As Army chief of staff Gen. George C. Marshall said on 8 December 1941, a war was no time to undertake a "sociological experiment," and the coming of war hardened the determination of those running the military to maintain the status quo.[15] Yet while Jim Crow remained the basic rule throughout the war, African American and liberal organizations nibbled at the edges, especially as the war continued.[16] Rather than being limited to menial service tasks, there were Black combat units, Black airmen, and more Black commissioned officers. Henry Stimson and George Marshall to the contrary, the war was a sociological experiment on the grandest possible scale, one that inevitably upended supposedly inviolate racial traditions.

One participant in this experiment was Jackie Robinson. He had no particular interest in joining the military. He tried to obtain a hardship deferment, claiming he was an essential provider for his mother. But the attack on Pearl Harbor ended any question of a deferment, and in April 1942, Robinson was drafted. He was "willing to do his part" and applied for Officer Candidate School (OCS). He passed all the necessary tests but was not allowed to participate. This was Robinson's "first lesson about the fate of a black man in a Jim Crow army." However, due to pressure by the Black press for more Black officers for Black units, the Army's OCS was more fully opened to Black candidates to preserve the façade of segregation. In November 1942, after a good word and assist from boxer Joe Louis, Robinson entered the first integrated OCS class in American history.[17]

He certainly was a natural candidate for a commission. He was college-educated and comfortable interacting with whites. A nagging ankle injury from his football days aside, he had the physical skills of a superb athlete and quickly added expert marksmanship to his array of physical talents. After another assist from Joe Louis, in January 1943 Robinson was commissioned a second lieutenant, assigned as morale officer to his company in Fort Riley, Kansas. The position involved a lot of careful pleading to higher-ups on behalf of his men. There certainly was a surfeit of low morale that needed boosting. Complaints included the myriad injustices of Jim Crow on the base: unequal facilities, the continuous background noise of racial slurs, and the decision to turn Robinson's cavalry unit into a service unit. Rachel Robinson later speculated that he was made morale officer because otherwise he would have been a troublemaker.[18]

Indeed, Robinson's own morale needed a boost. He was not allowed to join the camp's baseball team and was told to join the (nonexistent) Negro team instead. A future Dodgers teammate, Pete Reiser, remembered seeing a Black lieutenant, whose name he did not know, on being told this: He "didn't speak. He stood there for a while, watched us work out, and walked away."[19] He did join the football team, but after he was cut from the squad when it played an exhibition game against the University of Missouri, he quit the team.[20]

In April 1944, Robinson was transferred, along with a dozen other Black officers, to Fort Hood, in Texas. (Opened in 1942, it had been named after the Confederate general John Bell Hood, an example of the uniquely American custom of naming military instillations after traitors who took up arms against the United States in defense of slavery.)[21] Again, after a good word from Joe Louis, he was attached to the 761st Tank Battalion, and he moved from the segregated Midwest to an extended stay in the Jim Crow South for the first time since infancy. The conditions on the base were miserable. Sixty thousand soldiers trained in a stultifying heat amid scorpions, tarantulas, and strict segregation in the bathrooms, officers' clubs, and barracks—where, needless to say, Black soldiers had the least desirable accommodations. One suspects the atmosphere at Fort Hood was not much better than that at Fort Jackson, Mississippi, where, in 1942, one Black soldier complained that "we are treated like wild animals here, like we are unhuman."[22]

There was no relief upon leaving the base. The surrounding area was even more fiercely segregated. On 6 July 1944, Robinson had to take a bus to visit a hospital in a nearby city, and he obeyed the local ordinances about sitting in the back. But he also knew that a month previously, in response to numerous incidents (including the murder of a Black soldier by a white bus driver), the army had proscribed segregation on its bases. Although the move was widely publicized, it seems that many whites had yet to read the memorandum or refused to accept it. When he got back on base, Robinson sat next to a light-skinned Black woman of his acquaintance, whom the bus driver thought was white. The bus driver and Robinson started to argue when the driver claimed that Robinson was breaking the base's segregation ordinances. Robinson retorted that he was sitting next to a Black woman, so he was not breaking the ordinance, and even if he *had* been sitting next to a white woman, there no longer was any ordinance to violate. The argument grew heated. Several MPs were called, and the commander of Fort Hood's military police announced that Robinson was under arrest. He was handcuffed and clapped in leg irons. Charges were subsequently pressed against him for exhibiting disrespect and disobedience to superior officers.[23]

The news of Robinson's arrest made a splash in the Black press. The *Chicago Defender* wrote: "Lt. Jack Robinson, Camp Hood—You're learning what some of us know, a colored man can't win in the South, truth, honor, or anything else notwithstanding." If cashiered for the "move-to-the-back-in-the-bus business" you will have "more friends than then you have now."[24] The court-martial was held on 2 August 1944. There was some talk of the NAACP appointing a lawyer, but this did not happen, and Robinson somewhat reluctantly relied on the services of a white Southern lawyer, who defended him ably.

Much of the trial centered on the question of Robinson's anger. He acknowledged that he had used some mild profanity, but denied, accurately, having told a complaining white woman to "quit fuckin' with me." He also acknowledged that he put a finger in the bus driver's face after being called "a nigger." When asked during the trial, "Do you know what a nigger is?" he replied that his grandmother, born into slavery, had told him this insult was used for "a low, uncouth person" and that he was not such a person.[25] The trial continued to focus on the question of Robinson's supposed easily provoked anger, an accusation that lingered long after the court-martial. In general, in this incident he had followed his personal code of behavior, and his understanding of integration: show no fear to whites, display no undue deference, speak frankly but without hostility (or not much hostility). If white observers interpreted his fearlessness as aggression, that was their problem.

The court-martial took only four hours. Robinson was acquitted on all charges; the case against him had been weak. Given that a conviction would have certainly made headlines in the Black press, by the summer of 1944, the Army was happy to bury the incident. His commanding officer, in a transcript of a telephone conversation before the court-martial, stated: "This is a very serious case and it is full of dynamite. It requires very delicate handling."[26] Robinson knew he had been lucky, perhaps luckier than he at first realized. Without an acquittal, and without an honorable discharge, his subsequent baseball career in the major leagues would have been much more difficult, if not impossible. At the same time, if he had not been brought up on charges, he likely would have gone overseas with his battalion and wouldn't have spent the next spring and summer playing baseball—meaning he wouldn't have been able to become Branch Rickey's choice to break major league baseball's color bar.[27]

After his acquittal, Jackie Robinson, "pretty much fed up with the service," wanted out of the Army.[28] He wrote a letter, violating the chain of command (and hoping to be reprimanded for it), to the adjutant-general asking, because of a nagging ankle injury, to be relieved from active duty. Robinson wrote in his autobiography that "he was hoping that the top brass would view me as a troublemaker who would be better off in civilian life."[29] Whether this gambit had anything to do with it, he got his wish. He was transferred to Camp Breckinridge in Kentucky (another army base named after a Confederate traitor) from where, in November 1944, he was released from military service.[30]

Jackie Robinson believed he had served dutifully and patriotically in World War II, but because he had asserted his rights as a Black citizen of the United States, he had been brought up on charges before a court-martial. World War II was the event that thrust the question of the status of Black Americans into a central place in American political discourse—a place that it has yet to relinquish. There are debates among historians over the extent to which the war fostered the civil rights movement.[31] But one thing is clear: Because of the war and its immediate aftermath, it became difficult, and then impossible, for white America to ignore or pretend not to see or hear the angry voices of Black America.

In October 1944, Jackie Robinson, like millions of other ex-GIs and soon-to-be ex-GIs, was unemployed and in need of a job. Rachel Robinson, at the time his fiancée, perhaps knew his state of mind better than anyone when she later wrote that on leaving the Army, he was "a man without a college degree and without marketable skills. He was desperate to get a job, to help support Mallie, and to marry me," a man "grabbing at a lifeline."[32] The first offer that came his way was from his old pastor, Karl Downs, at Samuel Huston College in Austin, Texas, who wanted an athletic director and basketball coach. Robinson accepted. The team was not very good, but Robinson earned their respect as a patient teacher and as someone who wanted them to dress well and study hard. Robinson did his best to put on a show, playing in warm-ups and exhibition games against nearby military teams. He enjoyed coaching—encouraging his team, arguing with refs—and he might well have returned for a second season (and perhaps some added football coaching duties), but his plans changed when he signed with the Dodgers. All the players on his team knew that he was a better basketball player than any of them or any player on an opposing team. He was, as one of his players noted, restless on the sidelines. Rather than guide others, "he really wanted to play."[33]

Nonetheless, this might well have been Robinson's career path, coaching at historically Black colleges, a path followed by many college-educated Black athletes with thwarted ambitions of a future in professional sports. Only twenty-five years old in 1944, Robinson did not think his athletic career was finished. He supplemented his income from Samuel Huston by playing semipro football as a halfback for the Los Angeles Bulldogs in the Pacific Coast Professional Football League, passing and running for touchdowns in a league which, the *Pittsburgh Courier* noted, practiced "democracy" and "non-discrimination, on the field and in traveling."[34] Probably the most obvious next step for Robinson's athletic career would have been to join his UCLA backfield mates Kenny Washington and Woody Strode and help break the NFL's color line, which they did in 1946 by joining the Los Angeles Rams.[35]

Instead, he decided to play the least heralded of his four collegiate sports, probably because it offered the most regular employment. At Camp Breckinridge in Kentucky he had met Ted Alexander, who in civilian life had been a pitcher for the Kansas City Monarchs. Alexander told him that there might be wartime openings on the club, which was one of the best-known and most storied teams in the Negro Leagues. Robinson wrote to the president of the club, telling him of his interest in playing for the Monarchs. He was invited to join the team in Houston the following March and offered $300 a month. Robinson asked for $400 and evidently received it, which he considered a "financial bonanza."[36] When he reported, he found that "spring training" just meant playing the first games of the season; Robinson came to the Monarchs with low expectations, and even these low expectations were not met. Although the Monarchs were the cream of the Negro Leagues, renowned for their esprit de corps, Robinson found the team and Black baseball in general "a pretty miserable way to make a buck."[37] He disliked the extensive traveling and nights spent sleeping on the team bus and the relatively sparse crowds.

There was something else. As his teammate Othello "Gangster" Renfroe remembered, “He had a different baseball background from most of us . . . because he played under white coaches.” As the *Baltimore Afro-American* reassured its readers after his signing by the Dodgers, “He has had a complete lifetime experience of being ‘integrated’ with whites in mixed schools. He has been a star performer on white teams in competition with other white teams.”[38] But what was a possible advantage in breaking in with the Dodgers was perhaps a problem in playing for the Monarchs.

Robinson had played on highly disciplined teams in well-ordered conferences, before large crowds, with none of the slackness of the Negro Leagues and, of course, without its constant reminders of the submission of Black people to the realities of Jim Crow. Renfroe continued: “We never had any doubts about Jackie’s ability, but we wondered if he could take the stuff that he took in the majors. We never thought he could take it. A couple of times we would pull up to service stations in Mississippi where drinking fountains said white and colored and we would have to leave without our change. Jackie’d get so mad. . . . We had a lot of players we thought were better ball players—but they picked Jackie for his intelligence.”[39] Pasadena was hardly a racial paradise, but he had never really lived or played in a Jim Crow state, his recent time in the Army excepted, and he had no interest in returning to Southern segregation. After two months, he later told *Time* magazine, he was ready to leave the Monarchs, a job with “no future.”[40]

Opinions differed on Robinson’s season with the Monarchs. He had not played high-level baseball since the 1940 season at UCLA, when he hit a mere .097.[41] In 1945, his baseball skills were somewhat rusty, and he probably could have used a real spring training. Some teammates and others in the league expressed reservations about his fielding and throwing, though he soon became the regular shortstop. There were questions about his hitting as well, though he ended the season with a .345 batting average. Even the white press noticed: the *New York Times* in June 1945 touted him as one of “Negro baseball’s leading shortstops.”[42]

Future Hall of Fame first baseman Buck Leonard, who played winter ball with him in Venezuela in 1945–46, later stated that “Robinson didn’t look so good because he hadn’t been playing as long as some of us. He was a hustler, but other than that he wasn’t a top shortstop.”[43] At the same time, the Black press, before his signing with the Dodgers, showered praise on him as "California's gift to the sportsworld," doing "a grand job at shortstopping."[44] Some of the criticism he received after the signing reflected the reality that although he was clearly a very good ballplayer, if there had to be just one person to break the major-league color barrier, Robinson wasn't the obvious choice. The most renowned player in the Negro Leagues, the Hall of Fame pitcher Satchel Paige, put his jealousy aside and said, gallantly and probably not quite believing his own words, that "they didn't make a mistake by hiring Robinson. They couldn't have picked a better man." He spoke in part to counter ignorant and racist comments, such as the suggestion by *New York Daily News* columnist Jimmy Powers that Robinson had a "1000-to-1" chance of making it in the majors, or the opinion of Cleveland Indians pitcher Bob Feller that if Robinson "were a white man I doubt they would even consider him as big-league material."[45] But in October 1945, Jackie Robinson put the Negro Leagues behind him. He did not look back.

The signing of Jackie Robinson by Branch Rickey to the Brooklyn Dodgers in October 1945 meant that white baseball and Black baseball, long operating on separate, parallel (but definitely unequal) tracks would finally collide. The major leagues and the white minor leagues survived the collision. The Negro Leagues did not. Negro League baseball became the first major casualty of integration. From its origins in early nineteenth-century America, from the mists of rounders, town-ball, and one-wicket cricket, there were Black baseball players. They played with whites; they played on their own teams. The question of when white ball players first started to refuse to play with their Black counterparts also dates back almost as far as we have records.

The emergence of professional baseball after the Civil War coincided with the slow and steady retreat of white America from any ideal of racial equality. Still, at least sixty Black ballplayers were in the minor leagues through the 1890s, and three played in the major leagues. William Edward White played one game for the Providence Grays in 1879, becoming the first African American to play in the National League and the only formerly enslaved person to play in the major leagues, though he was probably passing as white. Two brothers, Moses Fleetwood Walker and Weldy Walker, played for the Toledo Blue Stockings of the American Association, then considered a major league, in the summer of 1884.[46] But occasions for white and Black ballplayers to play professional ball together diminished, and the exceptions and anomalies became fewer and fewer until they ceased. When, in 1887, the major-league St. Louis Browns refused to play a scheduled exhibition game against the best professional African American baseball team, the New York Cuban Giants, the *New York Times* claimed, incorrectly, that the incident marked "the first time in the history of baseball that the color line had been drawn."[47]

Organized on Long Island in 1885, the New York Cuban Giants, a team without Cubans, is considered the first fully professional Black baseball team. For many years, unlike in organized white baseball, Black baseball was more a matter of teams than leagues. Most teams had an irregular, barnstorming schedule, primarily but not exclusively playing other Black teams. Segregation in baseball, as in so many other areas of life, did not eliminate contact between Black and white players but reordered the context of their interactions and often reinforced existing racial hierarchies. It also promoted the creation of independent Black counter-institutions. "In no other profession," Black baseball's first historian, Sol White, wrote in 1907, "has the color line been drawn more rigidly than in base ball." It was maintained and enforced with unwavering and unbending rigidity from the 1880s until Robinson signed with the Dodgers in 1945.[48]

The refounding of the Negro National League in 1933 (which originally operated from 1920 to 1931) and the creation of the Negro American League in 1937 gave Black baseball new solidity in its structures and more publicity for its players. Attendance was up, in part because these leagues, largely based in northern cites, had an ever-larger potential fan base with continued Black migration from the South. They often played their games in major-league ballparks, rented for the occasion, providing considerable revenue to the owners of the major-league teams. The war years and into 1946 were the best of times for Negro League baseball and a teasing prelude for the worst of times that soon followed.[49] One of the crushing ironies of the history of Negro League baseball is that its very success, and the achievements of its stars, only strengthened the case for the integration of white baseball. Its achievements fostered its destruction.

As a business, Black baseball suffered from problems endemic to all Black businesses, starting with the hard fact that 90 percent of the American market was not very interested in what they had to sell, and the 10 percent who were tended not to have a lot of money.[50] The league structures were weaker. Teams appeared and disappeared. Without a reserve clause, binding players to their current employer, it was easier for them to jump from team to team. The difference between official games and exhibitions was often not clear; umpiring was often suspect; statistical records were maintained haphazardly. The Negro Leaguers toiled to the near complete indifference of white America. Through the end of 1945, Babe Ruth had been mentioned in the *New York Times* 6,103 times. By comparison, among the most prominent Negro League players, the *Times* had mentioned Satchel Paige 46 times, Josh Gibson 12 times, Oscar Charleston once, and nary a mention of James "Cool Papa" Bell.

But if white baseball fans did not know or care about Black baseball, the reverse was not true. Black ball fans avidly followed the major leagues, in part because some teams playing near centers of Black population, such as the New York Yankees under Jacob Ruppert, actively cultivated African American visits to their stadiums.[51] That said, American culture in the 1930s and 1940s had profound asymmetries. Mainstream culture was overwhelmingly white and, with only a few exceptions, was either ignorant of or patronizing toward Black culture. A constant lament of Black sportswriters was that Black sports fans paid far too much attention to the major leagues and not enough to the Negro Leagues. In 1938, the *Chicago Defender* wrote of a group of Black men whooping it up listening to a game on the radio between the Detroit Tigers and Cleveland Indians, only to be chastised by a Chinese man who said that as long as there were no Chinese players in the major leagues, it would be humiliating to be a fan of the sport.[52] The following year, an April 1939 editorial in the *New York Amsterdam News* decrying "Naziism [*sic*] in Baseball" complained that another baseball season was opening "without a single Negro player," lamenting the fact that "thousands of Negroes will be in the stands on opening day in every ball park in the country. They are among the most rabid fans in the country."[53] As sportswriter Art Rust Jr., who grew up in Harlem in the 1930s as a fervent baseball fan, once put it, "the toughest thing" for him was the necessity of "rooting for a bunch of cracker ballplayers."[54]

In 1940, Violet Moton Foster made what she called a "Plea for More Segregation" in the pages of the *Chicago Defender.* It was very similar to W. E. B. Du Bois's call for segregation in *The Crisis* six years earlier. Black Americans needed to develop a stronger collective economic base and reject the "pseudo-freedom that insidiously weakens our common resolve to do something about our poor [situation] as American Negroes" and cease "the foolish idea that we should be grateful because America treats us no worse than she does." African Americans had traded their "Blackness, lost [their] tight-kinked hair" in exchange for empty promises. Instead, Foster argued, "in segregation lies the only hope of economic freedom and, in rapid sequence—social, political, and intellectual equality." It was time to stop "dissipating our precious energies on such relatively unimportant issues as being able to eat in a white man's restaurant, or sleep in a white man's hotel."[55]

But unlike Du Bois, Foster was a baseball fan. She argued that when "the light of reason breaks through the red haze of emotionalism," Black Americans should "give up such childish projects as trying to get one or two Negro ballplayers in the 'big leagues.'" Instead, African Americans should "voluntarily segregate ourselves into our own ball parks where Negro teams are playing against each other and against the mighty drawbacks of lack of proper training facilities, lack of regulated diets, and (worst of all) lack of support from members of their own race." Foster did not see this as a complete avoidance of white America but the only way to compete against it as equals. She predicted that if Black baseball followed her suggestions, "we will see the day when nine stalwart brown boys face nine ace white players on a diamond where winners of a world series is being decided," a world series between the Negro Leagues and the White Leagues. To her, "Self-segregation will prove a quicker and less painful way of race integration than either segregation forced upon us by the white man or quasi-acceptance which now keeps us from the full recognition of our deplorable position in the United States."[56]

Among Black journalists and sportswriters, Foster's position was not popular. The first concerted push to open organized baseball beyond the occasional column in the Black press had begun in the early 1930s. The *New York Daily News,* not known for its embrace of liberal or progressive causes, argued in a 1933 editorial entitled "What's Wrong with Baseball" that one of the things that needed changing was the color line.[57] A few weeks later, the liberal sportswriter Heywood Broun, speaking to a convention of baseball writers, called for Black players to be admitted to the major leagues. Baseball officials, among them Branch Rickey, were generally noncommittal but "open" to the proposition.[58] The same year, a writer for the *Pittsburgh Courier* predicted that "along about 1935 some major league team in the doldrums will gain nationwide publicity by signing a Negro player. There will be a mighty thunder of pros and cons. There will be the little matter of segregation at the hotels on the road, and there will be threats of boycotts by fans. Nevertheless, gate receipts will increase sharply, whether from the impetus of curiosity, appreciation, or desire to heckle."[59] This prediction was about a decade premature, but the results it forecast would happen.

The push to end the color line in baseball revived, with greater force, in the late 1930s. It reflected a greater interest on the part of the Black press to promote integration with a steady migration of baseball's color line "from the sports pages to the front pages."[60] It also reflected the growing influence of the CIO (Congress of Industrial Organizations) and organized labor in general. At the same time, the Communist Party, in its Popular Front mode, wanted to expand its agitation to include something as "American" (and only abstractly related to the means of production) as baseball, which was why the sports column in the *Daily Worker* pressed for the end of segregation in the sport.[61] But so did many mainstream publications, from liberal newspapers like the *New York Post*[62] to Catholic newspapers[63] to more conservative newspapers, including the *New York Daily News*[64] and *New York Daily Mirror*,[65] both maintaining bitterly anticommunist editorial positions. Black ball players also received more attention, often in the form of testimonials from major-league stars, whether major-league Hall of Fame pitchers Dizzy Dean praising Satchel Paige or Walter Johnson stating in 1939 that Josh Gibson was the best catcher in baseball, bar none.[66] A steady drip of "if only it were possible" statements about Black ballplayers by white players, managers, owners, and even the occasional league president deftly buck-passed the responsibility to some other part of white baseball. In many cases, inaction was attributed to the likely opposition by the fans.

For his part, *Pittsburgh Courier* sportswriter Wendell Smith complained in May 1940 that President Roosevelt, who spoke frequently about democracy and the need for racial harmony, hadn't seen fit to address the question of employment discrimination and segregation in baseball. Smith acknowledged that, in the grander scheme of things, baseball was not that important, "but it provides us an excellent opportunity to prove beyond a reasonable doubt that Negroes have ability, are fair, and willing to fight. Baseball is only a game. But it can do so much to inform the public of what we are capable of doing."[67] This is precisely the role that Jackie Robinson would play, and Wendell Smith would become a close friend, the ghostwriter of Robinson's first autobiography, and a key figure in his signing by the Dodgers.

The question of whether Black baseball would be better served by separate Black institutions or in combination with white organized baseball ran parallel to the argument about separate Black units in the US Army. Opponents offered myriad reasons for keeping Black baseball and white baseball separate, but most observers thought the argument for uniting them were stronger. In 1942, Joe Bostic, a Black sportswriter, sportscaster, and radio personality in New York City, weighed in on the "proposition of Negroes playing in the so-called major leagues." By the early years of World War II, "the war situation and its democracy theme [had become] a springboard for many 'beefs,' [and] this question has taken on the status of a 'cause.'" Bostic was somewhat skeptical. He was convinced that "the entry of even one player on a league team would serve to monopolize the attention of the Negro and white present followers of Negro baseball to the great injury of the Negro baseball exchequer" and would likely "kill it." Bostic suggested that one alternative would be the admission of an entirely Black team into the major leagues, but he recognized that this was unlikely to happen. In short, "From the idealist and democratic point of view we say 'yes' to Negroes in the other two leagues. From the standpoint of practicality [and] commerce 'no.'"[68]

Bostic was widely pilloried for his stance, called a "spineless twentieth century uncle tom" in the *New York Post* and a fascist and reactionary elsewhere.[69] He soon recanted. Bostic now argued (and he was hardly alone in this) that rather than destroying the Negro Leagues, "maybe the entry of Negroes into the majors will wake the boys up and they'll mend their ways." He noted that as long as the Negro Leagues had a monopoly on African American talent, they would feel little pressure to fix their own houses.[70] Whatever his rationale, two years after opposing integration, in March 1945, Bostic would take two Negro League players to the spring training camp of the Brooklyn Dodgers and demand that Branch Rickey give them a tryout.

Bostic's ambivalence was perhaps extreme but not unusual among the Black press and fans of the Negro Leagues. They wanted the Negro Leagues to thrive. At the same time, they wanted Black players in the major leagues. The most consistent criticism in the Black press of the owners of Negro League clubs—not all of whom were African American—was that, as Lucius Harper argued in the *Chicago Defender* in March 1938, "the owners of colored ball clubs do not look with favor upon the big leagues admitting black players. They believe it will do harm to the interest of their clubs." A few weeks later, Cum Posey and Gus Greenlee, co-owners of the Pittsburgh Homestead Grays, said it wasn't so. The goal of Black baseball was the "entrance of [the] Negro Leagues into White Organized Baseball and entrance of Negro League Players into the Major Leagues."[71] In 1942, J. B. Martin, president of the Negro American League, stated: "I am against discrimination in any form, regardless of financial considerations, I want them to make the grade."[72] Most sportswriters did not really believe Greenlee, Posey, or Martin.

Negro League owners could, by the early 1940s, scarcely say otherwise in public, but their situation was inherently ambiguous. In 1943, Lem Graves Jr., a sportswriter for the *Norfolk Journal and Guide,* complained that the "principal enthusiasm" for breaking the color line in baseball was the preserve of "Negro sportswriters and a few white sportswriters," while "the issues of democracy, justice, job opportunities, fair play seldom occur to Negro ball players [and] Negro club owners."[73] By the late 1930s and early 1940s, the Negro Leagues were coming in for more criticism on the general slackness of their operations. There was also concern that some of the owners had made their fortunes in the numbers game and illegal gambling.[74]

To some extent, this critical approach to the Negro Leagues was a product of more skeptical attitudes toward Black institutions generally among

Black intellectuals and the Black press in the late 1930s and early 1940s. They believed that many Black institutions had as their primary justification mere self-perpetuation, with their leaders concerned with self-glorification while isolating their followers from the broader society. When the owner of a Negro League club told *New York Amsterdam News* columnist Dan Burley that "if there was no segregation, we wouldn't have colored ball clubs; we wouldn't make money, and we'd all probably be out of business," Burley berated him and others for their selfishness in hindering Black athletic progress as well as for their lack of business insight. He argued that "they'd make far more money developing and selling colored players to the big leagues than they'll ever make playing barnstorming games and exhibitions in Jim Crow parks."[75] Burley might have been right about their self-interest, but the club owners understood the precariousness of their businesses much better than he did.

In 1943, Lem Graves of the *Norfolk Journal and Guide* interviewed Cum Posey, owner of the Negro National League Homestead Grays, who posed Graves a question: Would the owner of his newspaper sell its best talent to the *Norfolk Virginian-Pilot* "simply for the novel experience of seeing a Negro" on the staff of a white newspaper? Graves admitted it was a tough question. He replied by asking, "Is it not sound long range reasoning that this expediency [segregation], mothered by necessity, must eventually give way to a broad integration of all Americans into the general pattern of this way of life?" If so, wouldn't Black businesspeople who "capitalized so successfully within the small sphere permitted them in discriminatory America find broader pastures for their talents in the vaster market which is the whole United States?"[76] Yet the Cum Poseys of the world had no illusions about how easy it would be to translate their entrepreneurial skills to the wider white world. In 1950, a study of Black businesses noted that the dropping of "anti-Negro barriers in professional baseball" posed the choice between racial solidarity and racial advancement, a puzzle without a satisfactory answer.[77]

As for the Black players themselves, sportswriter Sam Lacy reported in 1939 that Negro Leaguers were "indifferent about entering [the] major leagues." The general sentiment among the players was that rather than worrying overmuch about the major leagues and a day that might never come (and if it did, it was likely to be for a younger crop of Black ballplayers), the Negro Leagues needed to fix and strengthen their own house.[78] It was one thing to call for baseball to be integrated. It was another to be tasked with doing the integrating. Most players were "none too anxious to face the miserable inconveniences of traveling with white teams and meeting discrimination on a daily basis."[79] There was a deep concern that integration would only snatch a few of the best Negro League stars for the major leagues, leaving the Negro Leagues and the players to fend for themselves. And even those most likely to be signed to major-league contracts, such as Satchel Paige, wanted the comradery the Negro Leagues provided. "You might as well be honest about it. There would be plenty of problems, not only in the South, where the colored boys wouldn't be able to stay or travel with the teams. . . . All the nice statements in the world from both sides aren't going to knock out Jim Crow."[80]

Black sportswriters told Paige to stick to pitching and avoid politics, but players in the Negro Leagues felt an inherent ambivalence toward their teams and leagues. On one hand, as Cool Papa Bell told an interviewer, playing in the major leagues was a possibility "so removed, we never thought of that." He never played in the major leagues but nonetheless told an interviewer that his greatest thrill in baseball occurred when "they opened the door to the Negro. When they said we couldn't play and we proved that we could, that was the biggest thrill to me."[81] Hall of Famer Buck Leonard, forty years old in 1947, said much the same: "I don't think anybody really felt sorry for himself until after Jackie Robinson integrated with the Brooklyn Dodgers. Then everybody started thinking 'maybe we should have been there all along.' It was a shocking thought. Some of us weren't prepared for it."[82] An important aspect of the push for integration was simply the desire to be widely acknowledged and recognized for one's achievements. "Many a time I said it didn't matter," said Negro League and New York Giants Hall of Famer Monte Irvin, "but it really did. You wanted to be known for what you did best."[83]

Many players and sportswriters refused the either/or of the Negro Leagues or the major leagues. They wanted both. Some suggested the inclusion of a Negro League team in the majors or the incorporation of the Negro Leagues within the structures of minor-league baseball. Lucius Jones, writing in the *Atlanta Daily World* in August 1942, argued that the agitation for Black players in the major leagues was having a positive impact on the Negro Leagues by forcing needed reforms. [84] A writer in the *Norfolk Journal and Guide* suggested in late 1945 that if Jackie Robinson could play in major leagues, then white athletes could play in the Negro Leagues: "Negro fans, who are becoming increasingly progressive, would welcome such an idea because they can see that integration must work in both ways to be reasonable and acceptable."[85] (Unfortunately, integration has rarely worked both ways. White Americans have never had much interest in joining Black organizations or institutions, going to Black churches or colleges.)

By the war years, some of the loudest defenders of the Negro Leagues became the staunchest defenders of maintaining segregation, such as *The Sporting News,* the so-called "bible of baseball," which stated in a 1942 editorial: "The country has a great Negro major league, which draws heavy support from the colored folk. If its ranks were raided by the American and National Leagues, with their tremendous resources, it would have fewer stars and the caliber of ball which has made it an attraction would be so lowered that the Negro loop, of necessity, would sink to the status of an inferior minor circuit, with subsequent decline in enthusiasm by fans and prestige of performers."[86] Sometimes your enemies can see your situation with more clarity than your friends.

One of those interested in having it both ways, preserving the Negro Leagues while supporting the entrance of African Americans into the majors—was Robinson himself. He felt little loyalty to the Negro Leagues, and he had not particularly liked his time there. Indeed, Rachel Robinson wrote that "Jack quickly came to hate life in the Negro Leagues."[87] Robinson offered this critique in a 1948 article in *Ebony* titled "What's Wrong with the Negro Leagues." In the article, Robinson recognized that some of the problems with the Negro Leagues were the problems of being Black in America, marginalized in almost every possible way. Still, he stated that he left the Negro Leagues to improve them: "I was convinced that my leaving Negro baseball would stimulate interest in the colored leagues." And Robinson hoped that this new attention would be a catalyst for reform and "improve the status of all Negro ballplayers and place Negro baseball on a par with the rest of organized baseball."[88]

The Black press offered unanimous praise for Robinson signing with the Dodgers. "Democracy has finally invaded baseball, our great national pastime," wrote Fay Young of the *Chicago Defender.*[89] Yet one question that the Black press could not avoid—which the white press usually ignored—was what effect Robinson's signing would have on the Negro Leagues. The issue was joined when the Dodgers refused to compensate the Monarchs for Robinson's services. The owners of the Monarchs complained to the new baseball commissioner, Albert "Happy" Chandler, about this but received no satisfaction. (Subsequently, there was compensation to Negro League owners by major-league clubs for most other player signings.)[90]

However, in short order, Black sportswriters who had spent years haranguing the Negro Leagues for their limitations and hostility to integration, became Black baseball's biggest boosters. By 1948, they were urging, with increasing desperation, that "Negro League Baseball Must Survive," at a time when Jackie Robinson was getting as much press coverage in the Black press as all of the Negro Leagues combined.[91] But overall, the Black press itself was focusing increasing attention on the handful of African American ballplayers in the major leagues rather than the hundreds of players in the Negro Leagues.[92] Although the speed of the demise of the Negro Leagues surprised most observers, it was a lost cause. By 1949, the Negro Leagues were no longer playing on a major-league level.[93] (Even in its death throes, it produced extraordinary ballplayers: Henry "Hank" Aaron played for the Indianapolis Clowns in 1951; Ernie Banks for the Kansas City Monarchs in 1953.) But most of its ballplayers were out of luck. About 311 men were on the rosters of the twelve Negro League teams in 1947; by the end of the 1953 season, only 35 former Negro leaguers had played in the major leagues. The number increased to around 50 if we include players like Aaron, who joined the Negro Leagues subsequent to 1947.[94] Many more played in the minors, often unfairly languishing there due to the informal quota of three Black players on a team that persisted through the 1950s and most of the 1960s.[95] As a consequence, the decline of the Negro Leagues meant that by the 1950s, there were fewer African Americans playing ball at the highest level than any time before or since, a very regrettable consequence of integration.

Yet the Negro Leagues not only employed ballplayers. There were Black coaches, managers, publicists, front-office personnel, and club owners (some of whom were white), and ancillary professionals such as sportswriters. They too were out of work, and there was no room for them in white organized baseball. After its demise, the Negro Leagues became more honored in death than in life. It is now universally considered to have been, at its peak, a legitimate major league, equal in talent to white major-league baseball. Statistics from the major leagues and the Negro Leagues are no longer separated from those of the National and American Leagues. Some observers have seen the end of the Negro Leagues as an almost wanton act of self-destruction on the part of African Americans, furthering the agenda of white America to strangle successful Black institutions. Poet and activist Amiri Baraka held Robinson personally responsible for the death of Negro League baseball. Baraka, who grew up as a fan of the Negro League Newark Eagles, saw Robinson as a "synthetic colored guy" fashioned "out of the California laboratories of USC [*sic*]," who proceeded to "rip off" what Black players had in the Negro Leagues "in the name of what you ain't never gonna get," forcing Black fans who wanted to go to a baseball game to "sit next to drunken racist [expletive]."[96] Many others, less immoderately, have expressed similar sentiments.[97] But as historian Jules Tygiel has written, "Few in the 1940s posited [the Negro Leagues] as a preferable alternative to major league integration."[98] Sam Lacy, the pioneering sportswriter for the *Baltimore Afro-American* said that after Robinson joined the Dodgers, "the Negro Leagues was a symbol I couldn't live with anymore."[99] What had once been essential had become a burden.

Tygiel asserted that Black baseball, unlike the Black church, music, or historically Black colleges and universities "lacked any legitimacy outside of a segregationist context."[100] This echoes what Ralph Bunche, a leading skeptic of separate Black institutions, said in 1935 when he wrote that "Negro businesses are almost entirely the product of segregation" and can be characterized as "defensive enterprises."[101] These comments seem unfair. Sol White, historian of Black baseball, may have been a bit biased when, in 1930, he called the Negro Leagues "one of the great institutions of the race," but he was not alone in these sentiments.[102] In the end, the Negro Leagues died not because they weren't loved but because they couldn't make a profit. Black baseball, like all separate and segregated Black institutions, inspired mingled emotions among participants and patrons: anger at being excluded from vast stretches of white America; frustration at the limitations of Black institutions; and a deep, justifiable pride in what Black people had been able to create under the most difficult conditions. At the same time, as much as Sol White prized Black baseball, he did not want Black players excluded from the major leagues and exhorted that baseball "should be taken seriously by the colored player, as honest effort with great ability will open an avenue in the near future wherein he may walk hand-in-hand with the opposite race in the greatest of all American games—baseball."[103]

Surely the Negro Leagues had a cultural function that the integration of major-league baseball could not replace. In the summer of 1945, New York City Mayor Fiorello La Guardia established a Committee on Baseball. (This is discussed in greater detail in chapters 4 and 5.) In its confidential report for the mayor, the committee acknowledged: "It has been pointed out that organized Negro baseball would not have been necessary had it been integrated into the system the same way as other minority groups." So would the end of segregation mean the Negro Leagues had lost their reason for continued existence? The report said no. "Yet, many familiar with Negro baseball feel that Negro teams meet a need among Negroes which would not be met by their integration into the profession. The Negro baseball game is much more a gala community affair in which there is a considerable amount of visiting, much more of a holiday spirit, and a release that comes from participating in an all-Negro affair which would not have been possible otherwise."[104] What Negro League baseball celebrated, in a way that Blacks on major league teams could not, was freedom from white domination. The report suggested, as did many observers of baseball at the time, preservation of some Negro League teams within the existing structure of major- and minor-league baseball, perhaps on the AAA level, the highest level of play in the minor leagues. This was probably the preferred outcome of ending baseball's color line for most African American observers. But it did not happen for several reasons. The Negro Leagues held no sentimental value for major-league executives. They did have a certain economic value. Some teams, such as the New York Yankees, earned as much as $100,000 a season in stadium rental fees from Negro League teams, a major consideration behind Yankee president Larry MacPhail's adamant opposition to ending segregation in baseball. But once the signing of Negro League talent commenced and the quality of play declined, attendance slackened and there was no need for major-league executives to preserve the Negro Leagues.

Some scholars of the fight to integrate baseball have called the African American demands to the end the color line in organized baseball while strengthening the Negro Leagues "paradoxical."[105] But there was nothing paradoxical about it. Black Americans wanted both. Why should Black people do all the sacrificing to realize integration? Most understood that the entrance of Blacks into the major leagues would radically change, and probably in some way diminish, the Negro Leagues. At the same time, most people also felt that in some fashion Negro baseball could and should be preserved. If the major leagues and the Negro Leagues had been able to negotiate as equals, no doubt the future of the Negro Leagues would have been quite different. But major league executives, like Branch Rickey, were only interested in Black ballplayers, not in preserving the Negro Leagues. Perhaps there could have been a different outcome to this history, but this is the history we have. Whether the demise of the Negro Leagues was an instance of integration's success or of integration's failure will long be debated.

FOUR

Integration's Test Case

NEW YORK CITY

IN MOST RETELLINGS OF the "great experiment" that ended segregation in major-league baseball, especially as the narrative is etched in popular memory, it is a tale of just two men: Branch Rickey, the president of the Brooklyn Dodgers, and Jackie Robinson, the great experiment's test case. But that is only part of the story. It is also a tale of a city. New York City not only provides the story's setting but is a major protagonist in its own right. The city had a liberal mayor and powerful progressive politics, along with a rising crescendo of Black and white activists, journalists, and union leaders demanding an end to baseball's color line. New York City was the largest city in a state that was the first in the nation to pass an antidiscrimination ordinance modeled on that of the federal Fair Employment Practices Committee. This also required the catalyst of the right historical moment—that brief historical blip while the passion for postwar democratic reform was still urgent, though before the Cold War divided, diminished, and shredded the progressive left. Keith Crook, perhaps our finest chronicler of the complicated events that led to the signing of Jackie Robinson, has called it a "Goldilocks moment," when so many things had to be "just right."[1] The signing of a Jackie Robinson might have happened in another major-league city in a different time, but it is no accident that it took place in New York City in the fall of 1945.

Branch Rickey was a man of many aphorisms. The best-known, coined decades before he came to Brooklyn, was "luck is the residue of design."[2] In planning the signing of a Black player for the Dodgers, Rickey—meticulous, cautious, and thorough—left nothing to chance. So much so that in his telling, no one but he and Jackie Robinson played much of a role, an "argument from design," in which he assumed the role of the prime mover. But it was luck that brought Rickey to New York City in the fall of 1942, when the efforts to break baseball's color barrier were already well advanced. Rickey had a complex relationship with the forces clamoring for the end of segregation in baseball, but he was (as was Jackie Robinson) a beneficiary of their efforts. In New York City's great victorious year of 1945, the most important domestic triumph was the city's victory over baseball's color line.

When Jackie Robinson and Nate Moreland had a tryout with the Chicago White Sox in Pasadena in March 1942, the Sox's manager, Jimmy Dykes, told the *Pittsburgh Courier* that the lack of Black ball players in the major leagues was the result of "an unwritten law. The issue is out of our hands as us managers. We are powerless to act and it's strictly up to the club owners and Judge Landis to get the ball a-rolling."[3] The commissioner of baseball, Judge Kenesaw Mountain Landis, was not pleased by Dykes's comments, and he was even less pleased when Dodgers manager Leo Durocher made similar comments a few months later, saying he wouldn't "hesitate a minute to sign up some of those good colored players if I got the okay"; but he added that there was a "grapevine understanding or subterranean rule" standing in the way.[4] Importantly, this time, these comments were made in Brooklyn rather than faraway Pasadena, and they made their way into the *Daily Worker,* the newspaper of the Communist Party. Landis held a meeting with Durocher, who made the common excuse of claiming that he'd been misquoted. And on 15 July 1942, Landis went on the record to state that, the opinion of some managers notwithstanding, there was "no rule, formal or informal, or any understanding—unwritten, subterranean, or sub-anything—against the hiring of Negro players by the teams of Organized Baseball."[5] He said that if any team wanted to hire a Black player, it would be "all right with me. That is the business of the managers and the club owners."[6] Some observers saw this, incorrectly, as a change in policy, but it was not; it was just reiterating the standard position that baseball executives had, from time to time, made.[7] As Dan Parker, a sportswriter for the *New York Daily Mirror,* wrote, "Negroes were not barred but not admitted either."[8]

But if Landis's comment wasn't a change of policy, it did bring new attention to segregation in baseball. An unwritten law is, of course, not a law; it is a pact, a pledge that only works so long as all participants obey it. As Red Barber, the radio sportscaster for the Dodgers, once stated: "All the men in baseball understood the code. A code is harder to break than an actual law. A law is impersonal. Often a man breaks a law, is clever enough to get away with it, and people think he is a smart fellow. But when you break an unwritten law, the code of omerta, you are damned, castigated, banished from the club so to speak. You are a renegade, a scoundrel, an ingrate, a pariah."[9] Or, as the civil rights activist Paul Robeson, very generously, told the assembled owners of the sixteen major-league baseball clubs in December 1943: "I never presumed that there was any agreement among you gentlemen to bar Negro ball players, but merely that you hate to initiate a policy that has not been initiated before."[10]

But to say that there is no *unwritten* law generally means that there *is* an unwritten law, and claiming it doesn't exist weakens it. Unwritten laws work best if they remain unspoken, a taboo so powerful it is assumed as a first principle. Baseball's unwritten law was not merely the injunction not to hire Black ballplayers but also the assumption that segregation was the natural order of things. It did not need to be justified. It was not the responsibility of major-league baseball to defend its practices. It was the task of those who would challenge segregation to prove, beyond any possible doubt to every possible objection, that Black players belonged in the major leagues.

Whether Landis was the major impediment to the signing of a Black player by a major-league club or whether he was merely carrying out the wishes of the club owners has fostered much discussion. The correct answer is surely both: Baseball owners and Landis had designed a system to diffuse and deflect ultimate responsibility from any of the principal actors. The owners hired Landis and gave him enough authority to give the impression to the public that he was a "czar," but no one is a czar to their employers. If no one has final authority, no one can make a final decision.

After Landis's statement there were rumors, which did not pan out, of tryouts of Black players in the big leagues and the Pacific Coast League.[11] Also in response, in late July 1942, State Assemblyman William T. Andrews of Harlem announced the formation of the Citizens' Committee to End Discrimination in Baseball and was made its chair. The announcement was made at a midtown Manhattan gathering with support from the CIO unions; Black leaders, including Walter White and Adam Clayton Powell Jr.; members of the Communist Party USA as well as liberal Republicans and Democrats; and Effa Manley, the owner of the Negro League Newark Eagles.[12] That October, Andrews and the committee planned to press the issue at white organized baseball's winter meetings and exhort the war-depleted clubs to immediately sign Black players.[13]

The owners did not agree to hear Andrews and his committee, but a year later, in December 1943, during the annual baseball meetings, Landis did agree to let a group of Black newspaper publishers address baseball executives, who made the case for setting up a system whereby Black ballplayers would be admitted into major- and minor-league baseball at the level appropriate for their talent and that the owners issue a statement to this effect. Landis reiterated his statement about no unwritten law, no agreement, "subterranean or sub-anything," about the hiring of Black athletes for the major leagues. At the same meeting, Landis also invited Paul Robeson—onetime All-American football player at Rutgers, singer, actor, and stalwart of the left, who was then starring on Broadway in the title role of *Othello,* acting alongside a white Desdemona—to address the owners. Landis must have given Robeson some assurances that his pleas would be answered, since Robeson wrote shortly afterwards that there was "every reason to believe that before the next season starts, Negro players will be in the Major Leagues."[14] Most New York sportswriters viewed this unprecedented meeting as a matter of minor interest, and owners did their part to keep things inconsequential by issuing no statements and asking no questions of their invited guests. According to a reporter from the *New York Post,* many owners were aggrieved, privately resenting "that their business has been made the focal point for the elimination of racial prejudice," and they wanted to know why "the problem is not solved first in more important fields such as medicine and education." And if "the Army and the Navy and industry are not meeting the issue squarely, why should baseball?" These were good questions but amounted to nothing but more buck-passing and led to more endless waiting for someone else to make the first move while secretly hoping that no one would.[15]

Contrary to Robeson's expectations, there were no Black players in the major or minor leagues for the 1944 season. There is no reason to think that Landis had reconsidered his position on Black athletes in major-league baseball before his sudden, unexpected death in November 1944. This left the protection of the unwritten law in the hands of the owners, and it soon became clear that nothing had changed. A few weeks after Landis's death, major league's elder statesman, the venerable and venerated Connie Mack, owner and manager of the Philadelphia Athletics since 1900, spoke to the *Pittsburgh Courier.* While he acknowledged that, with the end of the war in sight, the times were a-changing, he added that the "integration of Negroes into the ranks of organized baseball will come by mutual consent of league club owners rather than a move by any single team owner." This would not happen, however, until "everything would be satisfactory to everybody." Or, as the headline for the article stated, "Connie Mack Vague on When Negroes Will Crash Majors."[16]

Mack was specifically asked about "Example A," Jackie Robinson, recently discharged from the Army and a "shortstop deluxe." Mack said that he had heard of him and that he was presumably a good ballplayer. Yet Mack divulged his true feelings about Robinson to Larry MacPhail, president of the New York Yankees, four days after his signing: "It was a great disappointment to me to see that Branch Rickey has signed a negro for his Montreal Baseball Club."[17] A few months after Rickey signed Robinson, the owners took a secret vote to decide the question of whether it was advisable to sign Black players. The vote, said Rickey, was fifteen against to one in favor.[18] Still, without Landis, the underpinning of organized white baseball's opposition to signing Black players had been weakened. And this occurred precisely when the forces arrayed against color lines, in baseball and in every area of social and political life, were under challenge as never before. Black Americans shared a hope, often more intensely than other Americans, that the war's end would bring, in the words of David Levering Lewis, a "redemptive peace."[19] World War II, a war for democracy abroad while maintaining antidemocratic institutions at home, fueled as much rage as hope. These two contradictory but complementary emotions fed the demand for integration to take advantage of the possibilities the war opened. Nowhere in the United States had the sentiment for Black citizenship amassed as much political capital as in New York City.

In 1943, Roi Ottley, a native New Yorker, a reporter for the *New York Amsterdam News,* and an editor for the Federal Writers' Project of the Works Progress Administration (WPA), published, to considerable acclaim, a survey of Harlem and contemporary Black America. *New World A-Coming* presents its thesis in its title.[20] (The book's title became a popular catchphrase and inspired Duke Ellington to compose, in the same year, a short jazz piano concerto of the same name.) What did Ottley find? A proud, confident, and determined Black America. "The black man knows what he wants," wrote Ottley, and "today his problems cannot be swept under the rug." Although "Negroes may quarrel among themselves about minor issues," he wrote, "on the question of their *rights*—moral, economic, and political—which to them mean the right to integration in American life, they form a solid bloc, each member of it being fiercely group-conscious."[21]

In *New World A-Coming,* Ottley wrote that white politicians' scramble for Black votes in Northern cities had engendered a new sense among Black voters of their political importance, in some ways resembling the situation Black voters "enjoyed during the early Reconstruction era."[22] Someone who was determined to give this second Reconstruction a happier outcome than its predecessor was Harlem politician Adam Clayton Powell Jr. A new type of Black politician, Powell's base of power was his ministry at Harlem's Abyssinian Baptist Church, which made him largely unbeholden to existing political machines. He had gained political influence as a protestor and agitator for Black equality and employment in Harlem's white-owned department stores, on the city's buses and subways, and at the 1939–40 World's Fair, among other places.[23] To use a term that was briefly popular in the 1930s but unfortunately never really caught on, Powell was not just an activist, he was a "vociferant."[24] From the mid-1930s on, he was a charismatic and noisily opinionated gadfly.

In August 1943, a major riot shook Harlem. (Although there was looting, it often was nothing more than groceries.) In all, seven hundred people were injured, six hundred were arrested, and six persons, all African Americans, were killed—all but one by police fire.[25] The episode in Harlem was part of a wave of racial disturbances and uprisings in the summer of 1943 that saw 240 cities, towns, and military bases experience racial violence.[26] Powell blamed the violence on the "blind, smoldering and unorganized resentment against the Jim Crow treatment of Negro men in the armed forces and the unusual high rents and cost of living forced upon Negroes in Harlem."[27]

A few months later, Powell declared his candidacy for Congress and spent most of 1944 campaigning for a seat, running in a newly created House district that, after decades of gerrymandering, would finally give Black New Yorkers a congressional voice. Powell would be elected that fall, the third African American elected to Congress in the twentieth century and the first Black member of Congress ever elected from New York State. Throughout the ups and downs of his long political career, there was one constant: He would tell whites what he thought Black people wanted or needed, and he did not terribly care about hurt feelings. In April 1944, while campaigning for his congressional seat, Powell created a stir when he asserted that, if elected, "I will represent the Negro people first. I will represent after that all the other American people."[28] He would, after being criticized, find more diplomatic ways of saying the same thing, but this would remain his opinion throughout his career.

Despite his "Black first" ideology, in the 1940s there was no cause more important to Powell than integration. To be sure, his understanding was distinctive. He said in 1940 that he wanted "Negroes to be Americans by becoming so integrated in American life that the white race couldn't hurt a Negro without hurting the white race," a keep-your-friends-close-and-enemies-closer model of integration.[29] Early in 1945, Powell published his first book, *Marching Blacks,* in which he proudly proclaimed himself to be a radical and stated that "the Negro has always been a revolutionary, not because he is black, but because he is a man." Powell stated that "Civil War II" began on 7 December 1941—a war between the "irresistible force" of "the awakened and united new Negro" and their white allies versus the "immovable object" of "intolerant, anti-democratic, fascist prejudice concentrated in the South but spreading rapidly, especially during the war period, into every section of America."[30] And perhaps one war would not be enough for Black America to declare victory. When interviewed in 1948 as to whether he'd thought there ever would be Black players in the major leagues, he replied: "No I did not. Not in my lifetime. I was afraid it might take another war before it could happen."[31]

According to Powell, avoiding this new civil war meant reconciling what politically active Black Americans wanted and what sensitive whites must concede: "Today there is not a handful of Negroes in America who believe in any other way to solve the problem than by way of integration." After making clear that integration was not the same as assimilation, or fobbing off Black people with vague promises, toothless legislation, or token gestures—favorite nostrums of the "case-study crack pots," "social-work mercenaries," and "swivel-chair liberals"—he stated: "The Negro masses almost to a man today insists on integration." This would mean a full inclusion of Black Americans in every aspect of American life, an integration that will "out of the rubble of present day democracy" and the "rotten decaying political life in America" build an "edifice that include[s] all race, all creeds and all classes."[32] For Powell, there was no more militant path for Black America than integration.

The rise of Adam Clayton Powell Jr. to political prominence highlights the distinctiveness of New York City politics. In 1945, the city was neither a Democratic nor a Republican stronghold. It was a progressive city that had a five-party system. The mayor, Fiorello La Guardia, was completing his third term. La Guardia had backed Roosevelt in 1944 and was truly a Republican in name only. He wasn't running for a fourth term in part because neither the Republicans nor the Democrats would back him. But in addition to the Democrats and Republicans, three minor parties tilted the city's politics leftward. No city in the United States had a stronger Communist Party than New York. Still vibrant in 1945, the party held two seats on the city council: Benjamin Davis and Peter Cacchione. Both were outspoken supporters of ending white baseball's discriminatory policies. The American Labor Party, founded in 1936 as a vehicle to allow New Yorkers to vote for Roosevelt without providing aid and comfort to Tammany Democrats, had ties to the Communist Party. This led, in 1944, to a split and the formation of the Liberal Party, who were non-communist, and in some ways anti-communist, but were still strong social democrats and quite left of center.[33] This proliferation of political parties persisted because of the possibility of cross endorsements, one candidate running on multiple party lines. A supreme example of cross-endorsement flexibility in New York City politics in 1945 was Benjamin Davis Jr., the Communist councilman from Harlem who was endorsed for reelection by both Democrats and Republicans.[34]

All political parties in the city were paying increasing attention to Black voters. During these years, New York, like all Northern cities, was undergoing a rapid surge in its Black population—from 327,706 in 1930, to 458,888 in 1940, to 747,608 in 1950. And in a state whose politics was perpetually poised between downstate Democrats and upstate Republicans, it was clear to all that courting the "Negro vote," then migrating from the Republicans to the Democrats but still up for grabs by any party, was a political necessity.[35] Beyond the numbers, New York City was also home and headquarters to most of the nation's leading civil rights organizations: the NAACP, the National Urban League, and, during the war, A. Philip Randolph's shorter-lived March on Washington movement. Since the mid-1930s, Black activists and their white allies had been protesting discrimination in employment, housing, and public accommodations, first in Harlem, then citywide.[36] Black politicians both fought city hall and sought to influence it and shape its policies, with some success.

None of this should leave the impression that the city didn't experience myriad racial problems and tensions. The city was run by white men. During the war years, New York was not quite segregated but was certainly not integrated, either. And the sort of integration that did exist often didn't find favor with those in power. A few months before the Harlem riot in August 1943, the most famous dancehall in Harlem, the Savoy Ballroom, was closed by order of the New York Police Department, acting on the behest of the US Army, which charged that the Savoy was a den of "vice." The real reason for the closing was worries that too many white soldiers and sailors in the wartime city were dancing with Black women. (In the aftermath of the riot, as a sop to Harlem leaders, the Savoy was authorized to reopen.)[37] Housing discrimination was rampant in a city where restrictive covenants were still legal. New housing developments, such as Metropolitan Life's massive

Stuyvesant Town complex on the East Side, could, with Robert Moses and (less obstreperously) La Guardia's political support, refuse to rent to Black tenants. (This policy engendered massive but unsuccessful protests.)[38] The Black press hailed modest breakthroughs, such as a blood bank that was more concerned with Type A and Type O rather than Type Black and Type White; a hospital that allowed Black physicians and nurses to take care of white patients; and the first 5th Avenue department store that hired Black salesclerks to serve white customers.[39] Black travelers could not stay in many downtown Manhattan hotels or branches of the YMCA. Prospective Black lodgers were often told to take the A train and try their luck uptown. Until 1945, the ferry taking passengers to the Statue of Liberty had white and colored restrooms.[40] Broadway theaters and movie houses were largely nonsegregated, but if African Americans wished to have a bite before a show, they often had few choices besides putting their nickels into the slots at the Automat.[41] Many unions and schools if not formally segregated might as well have been.[42] The New York Public Library system largely kept Black librarians out of libraries in white neighborhoods, including the main branch at 42nd Street.[43] Many civil service positions, especially in the uniformed services, remained largely white. Police brutality remained a burning issue of concern.[44]

With a strong labor movement and active civil rights and labor rights movements, some of these problems were addressed.[45] However, during the war, with its economy directed toward the production of war materiel, nothing was more paramount than trying to ensure that Black workers received a fair share of the new economic bounty. A. Philip Randolph, Harlem's militant labor leader, wanted to do something about Jim Crow in the military and among defense contractors. Using a tactic that had become standard in New York City, he promised to hold a massive demonstration in Washington in July 1941 to call attention to the cause. Roosevelt and his aides wanted, at all costs, to make this demonstration go away. After first trying to avoid the issue, they met with Randolph and other labor leaders. Then Roosevelt blinked and issued Executive Order 8802, establishing the Fair Employment Practices Committee, which was tasked with investigating and banning discriminatory practices in the defense industry. It was the first federal government action against discrimination since

Reconstruction.[46] Its limitations were plentiful: It lacked enforcement powers. The members of the committee were often integration-skeptical white Southerners. Congressional enemies mounted determined efforts to circumscribe and limit its work. Yet by 1945—both by investigation and exhortation—it had accomplished much.[47] Between 1943 and 1945, African Americans employed in the defense industry increased from 3 to 8 percent, and the number of Black Americans working for the federal government tripled.[48] And at times, the FEPC could make even more dramatic interventions, such as its role in August 1944 in helping to crush the so-called hate strike by white Philadelphia transit workers opposed to the hiring of Black motormen and conductors.[49]

However, the FEPC operated only with the power of an executive order, not with the authority of law, so it could be curtailed, weakened, and ultimately ended by congressional action, as happened in 1946. As an alternative, states could pass their own version. In March 1945, New York became the first state to do so, ratifying an FEPC-like law, the Ives-Quinn Act.[50] This was a dramatic turnabout. New York was a liberal state and had passed a liberal state constitution in 1938, including civil rights provisions, but one of the most careful students of the subject, Tod Ottman, has written that in 1939, "beyond the Black community, the broader public, Republican and Democrat alike, exhibited a near total lack of concern for race issues."[51] But the coming of the war changed this. In March 1941, Gov. Herbert Lehman created the Governor's Commission on Employment Discrimination; he followed this shortly by pushing through the Mahoney Act, which made it a misdemeanor for a defense contractor to refuse to hire anyone on account of their race, creed, or religion. In 1942, the Governor's Commission issued a pamphlet, *How Management Can Integrate Negroes in War Industries,* written by the Black political scientist, civil rights activist, and Lincoln University (of Pennsylvania) professor John A. Davis, who emphasized that management must never seem "timid, apologetic, or uncertain" about their position, and nothing was more important than the "careful selection of the first colored worker," someone with the technical and personal skills to be comfortable as a trailblazer, neither too aggressive nor too submissive.[52] Someone, in every profession, like Jackie Robinson.

When Thomas Dewey became governor in 1943, he considered letting the Governor's Committee on Discrimination in Employment expire.[53] The rebellion in Harlem in August of that year changed his mind, and he tasked the legislature to draft new antidiscrimination legislation.[54] The resulting bill, known as the Wicks Bill after its chief sponsor, State Senator Arthur W. Wicks, a Republican, would have banned discrimination in employment, education, and housing, with a maximum fine of $5,000, one year imprisonment, or both.[55] However, in March 1944, Dewey killed the Wicks Bill, thinking of his presidential ambitions.[56] This provoked howls of outrage from liberal and Black organizations, and Dewey did reauthorize a special committee for the next session, in early 1945—by which time he would either be in the White House or not have to worry about currying favor with Southern Republicans, at least until 1948. He chose Irving Ives, a fairly liberal Republican assemblyman, to head the committee. Ives and Elmer F. Quinn, a state senator and Tammany Democrat, produced the bill that became known as the Ives-Quinn Act. It was considerably less expansive than the Wicks Bill (fines were reduced from $5,000 to $500), and its scope was limited to employment discrimination. There was massive lobbying in support of the legislation from ninety organizations, among them African American, Jewish, and Catholic organizations; both AFL and CIO unions; and the left and liberal political parties.[57]

At the same time, equally massive lobbying efforts were deployed against it, including influential organizations such as the Bronx, Brooklyn, Queens, and Buffalo chambers of commerce; the New York Board of Trade; the Real Estate Board of New York; and the New York State Bar Association.[58] Their main objection was that government bodies had no right to tell private businesses whom they could and could not employ. The *New York Times* agreed, editorializing that the bill, if passed, would lead to numerous "'nuisance suits' and other racketeering" by civil rights groups, and that employers "will feel compelled to employ, or retain in their employment, obviously inefficient workers."[59]

Although, as Mason Williams writes, "La Guardia never really felt comfortable with the idea of government regulation of private employment practices," the mayor realized the necessity of the new law.[60] He had also been a supporter of the FEPC and was generally supportive of efforts to improve the lot and lives of Black New Yorkers.[61] In his defense of the bill,

La Guardia tried to answer its critics: "As I read the bill it does not give preference to anyone because of race, creed, color, or religion. It does not compel an employer to employ quotas or to employ less efficient persons because of race, creed, color, religion, but it specifically prohibits discrimination solely on these grounds, as intended in the constitutional provision."[62] La Guardia went on to note, correctly, that those opposed to the bill would cloak themselves in abstract opposition to the evils the bill was addressing: "I venture to predict that everyone who appears before this committee in opposition to the bill will qualify, will preface, will commence his remarks by a statement that all are in favor of equal protection by the law and are all against discrimination but. And right there let me say it is the 'but' that very often hinders necessary reform. All this bill does is to translate into law that which everyone all over the state has been talking about for the past ten years."[63]

La Guardia was correct. Most of those opposing the bill in public had their "buts." The *New York Times* editorial that condemned the Ives-Quinn bill, for instance, stated that racial discrimination was a real problem and was "evil" and "un-American."[64] If La Guardia supported Ives-Quinn, many of his close associates did not. Robert Moses, La Guardia's powerful parks and recreation commissioner, acknowledged that he was "fully aware of the fact that discrimination has been practiced by many employers, often without rhyme or reason. Everyone knows that Negroes had been outrageously discriminated against in the past." However, he thought the situation was improving and that employment discrimination should be addressed with "carrots of education, moral suasion, conference, and reason, and not the sticks of potential fines and jail sentences." In contrast, the passage of the bill "will set the clock back."[65] He also wondered whether the bill would lead to the establishment of "Hitlerian" quotas of the sort that had been used in Germany, in higher education in the United States, and elsewhere, to discriminate against Jews and others.[66]

Another close La Guardia ally was C. C. Burlingham. The so-called first citizen of New York, this famed civic reformer and opponent of municipal corruption organized a collective letter published in the *New York Times*. The letter opened by stating that its writers were "strongly opposed to discrimination because of race, creed, color, or national origin." As for the proposed legislation, however, "the remedy is worse than the disease." The letter compared the bill to the Volstead Act, the enabling legislation for the amendment prohibiting the sale of alcohol. (Comparisons of integration legislation to Prohibition were very common.) However, "It is as impossible to destroy prejudice and discrimination by law as it is to control opinions or morals."[67] Burlingham couldn't find a prominent African American to sign the letter and prevailed on Oswald Garrison Villard, a cofounder of the NAACP and the longtime editor of *The Nation,* to add his name. In brute and crude language, Burlingham wrote that Villard's signature was worth "a thousand niggers."[68] (One suspects Villard's grandfather, the abolitionist William Lloyd Garrison, wouldn't have been pleased by his signing the letter. We can debate whether the need to cloak racist sentiments in a disavowal of racist intent was a step forward or backward.)

Some accounts give Governor Dewey far too much credit for the passage of the Ives-Quinn Act.[69] However, after much agonized fence-sitting, he decided to back the bill because he became convinced that the issue of discrimination, "fanned into flames by zealous advocates," was not going away; therefore, to diminish this issue, "it may well be that the Party's interests will be well served by the adoption of this legislation in some form, followed by a real, genuine interest in making it work."[70] If political expediency in 1944 dictated Dewey kill a civil rights bill, political expediency in 1945 dictated the opposite. Almost all opposition to the bill was by Republicans, and many Republicans who backed the bill did so under duress.[71] Thus, Ives-Quinn became law, establishing the State Commission Against Discrimination (SCAD). Whatever Dewey thought in private, he did make a spectacle of the signing ceremony, handing out two dozen ceremonial signing pens and committing himself and his administration to the cause of desegregating businesses.

The passage of Ives-Quinn led many in the progressive and Black press to think the bill would be the lever that would pry open major-league baseball's locked doors. Nat Low, in the *Daily Worker,* wrote after the passage of Ives-Quinn that it "heralds the end of Jimcrow in baseball—not only in New York State, to which the bill applies—but in all the states and in all the baseball leagues," in part because of the "heavy fines that the bill entails."[72] He expected that the next step "will be taken by Negro ballplayers themselves who will undoubtedly apply formally for jobs with the three New York major league teams." And he predicted, whether on a major or league level, "they will be signed to contracts for the 1945 season."[73] Low underestimated how difficult it was for a potential employee to apply for a job the employer said did not exist. Perhaps the *Daily Worker* was placing too much faith in the liberality of capitalist institutions.

Meanwhile, the Communist Party councilman from Harlem, Benjamin Davis Jr., called for an investigation of the three major-league franchises in the city under the new law and made it an issue in his reelection campaign.[74] So did Brooklyn Democratic assemblyman Philip Schupler, who in July called on the Dodgers to demonstrate that they would follow the "letter and spirit of the Ives-Quinn Law."[75] The Black press also was enthusiastic. Bob Williams, in the *Cleveland Call and Post,* suggested that the law might be applied not only to the three New York City teams but also to the other thirteen major-league teams that visited the city to play. Of baseball franchise owners, he wrote: "They are not so certain that the New York law with teeth like a bear trap will not snap its jaws of retribution upon any team playing in New York which discriminates against Negroes!" But Williams, like everyone else, was uncertain how much "farther open the door will be shoved" by the new law.[76] The *Pittsburgh Courier* strongly advised baseball's owners not to wait and see how the law would be applied and to obviate the need for its punitive provisions by voluntarily signing Black players. It further fretted that if the law was applied, it would only "antagonize managers, players, and fans, and subject the Negro players to terrific pressure and to all sorts of harm" and open the door to "whatever extremists [that is, the Communists] may do in their effort to break down the color barrier."[77]

La Guardia said of the Ives-Quinn bill that it translated "into law that which everyone all over the state has been talking about for the past ten years"[78] For many New Yorkers, such a bill had been a dream, and it represented the best and highest ideals of the New Deal and the Roosevelt and La Giardia administrations. But by the time Ives-Quinn became effective in July, there was a new president in the White House, and there soon would be a new mayor in Gracie Mansion. La Guardia was not seeking reelection. He had badly wanted to see a major-league team in New York City sign an

African American ballplayer. He had done much to help bring it about. By all rights, the October 1945 announcement of the signing of Jackie Robinson should have been a final feather in his cap, a worthy last hurrah. For the most part, it wasn't. And this was because as a fervent anticommunist, a conservative Republican who disliked Roosevelt, Rickey saw to it that he, and no one else, would receive the lion's share of the credit for signing Jackie Robinson.

“International Day” at the Brookside Plunge, Pasadena’s municipal swimming pool, in 1933, during the three hours a week—Wednesday from 2 to 5 p.m.—when non-whites were permitted in the pool. (Courtesy of the Pasadena Public Library, Pasadena, California)

Jackie Robinson as a UCLA basketball player. (NoirTech Research, Inc.)

Rev. Karl E. Downs, 1936. (Image courtesy of the General Commission on Archives and History of the United Methodist Church, Madison, New Jersey)

Jackie Robinson, Samuel Huston College basketball coach and athletic director, winter of 1944–45, with, from right, Rev. and Samuel Huston College President Karl E. Downs, Jackie Robinson, Dr. Everett H. Givens, and Kenneth Lamkin. (Austin History Center, Austin Public Library)

Members of the United Warehouse and Wholesale Workers Union (CIO) protest to end segregation in baseball, New York City, ca. 1942. (NoirTech Research, Inc.)

Jackie Robinson as a Kansas City Monarch, 1945. (NoirTech Research, Inc.)

New York State Gov. Thomas E. Dewey signing the Ives-Quinn Act, banning discrimination in employment and education, 12 March 1945, as co-sponsors Assemblyman Irving M. Ives, left, and Senator Elmer F. Quinn look on. (Library of Congress, Prints and Photographs Division)

Jackie Robinson signing a Dodgers contract, with Branch Rickey, 1948. (NoirTech Research, Inc.)

Jackie Robinson at Ebbets Field. (NoirTech Research, Inc.)

Jackie Robinson at bat. (NoirTech Research, Inc.)

Jackie Robinson critiques the Negro Leagues in *Ebony* magazine, June 1948. (NoirTech Research, Inc.)

Jackie Robinson testifies before the House Committee on Un-American Activities, July 1949. (NoirTech Research, Inc.)

Jackie Robinson Jr.'s third birthday, with his proud parents and others, St. Albans, Queens, November 1949. Birthday boy in front of cake, and David Campanella, son of Roy Campanella, to his immediate right. (Courtesy Rucker Archives, Society for American Baseball Research)

Jackie Robinson, vice president for personnel, Chock full o'Nuts Corporation, early 1960s. (Courtesy Rucker Archives, Society for American Baseball Research)

Jackie Robinson and Malcolm X and other members of the Nation of Islam in a friendly get-together in a Harlem coffeeshop, 1960. (NoirTech Research, Inc.)

Jackie Robinson and New York State Governor Nelson Rockefeller, 8 February 1966. (Courtesy New York State Archives)

Jackie Robinson, Rachel Robinson, and son David Robinson at March on Washington, 28 August 1963. (NoirTech Research, Inc.)

FIVE

Branch Rickey and Integration

IN EARLY NOVEMBER 1942, New York Lieutenant Governor Charles Poletti (soon to be, albeit briefly, the governor) spoke to the *People's Voice,* a newspaper that had been created earlier that year largely to provide a Harlem mouthpiece for Adam Clayton Powell Jr. Poletti, a member of the board of the NAACP and a former treasurer of the Urban League who was longstanding in his commitment to Black New Yorkers, told the reporter that "the treatment we give the Negro is the test of our belief in democracy," promising the "integration of the Negro into every department of the state civil service," an end to discriminatory practices by labor unions, and support for the civil rights of every New Yorker. He also promised that the New York state government would do whatever it could to see to the "elimination of discrimination in major league baseball."[1] A few days earlier, on 30 October, the Brooklyn Dodgers had announced that Branch Rickey had been hired as club's new president.[2]

Branch Rickey did not want to move to New York City. He was a lifelong Midwesterner and had no interest living elsewhere. His roots in Missouri were deep, both in his chosen profession and in his social and political activities. But he came to the city for the same reason that millions of others have: He was looking for work. Before joining the Dodgers, Rickey had been a baseball executive in St. Louis since 1913, first with the St. Louis Browns and since 1917 with the St. Louis Cardinals. In his job with the Cardinals, he largely created the modern position of the general manager. He was a key reason the Cardinals were the most successful National League team through the interwar years, winning six World Series and nine pennants between 1926 and 1942.

Rickey pioneered several innovations, among them the mechanical pitching machine, the sliding pit, and the hitting tee. But his best-remembered innovation was the modern farm system, the tentacular octopus whereby major-league clubs squeezed the financial and organizational independence from minor-league teams, which then became wholly controlled feeder clubs for major-league franchises. Though at the top of his profession, Rickey left because the Cardinal's owner, Sam Breadon, wanted him out. It was not an amicable parting. In a November 1942 letter, Rickey wrote of being consumed by "bitterness" and said that Breadon was the "most despicable cheap man I have ever known." (The accusation was more often directed at Rickey than by him.) He took the Brooklyn job to place as much distance between himself and St. Louis as possible, but he was not looking forward to starting "a new life, a hard job, and in a place so far removed from the familiar habitat I had come to love so deeply."[3] His previous experience in New York City had been largely limited to an unhappy stint in 1907 as a player with the New York Highlanders (not yet the Yankees) as a below-replacement-level sore-armed catcher, where he contributed to a still-standing record of thirteen stolen bases allowed in a single game.

He would strive to make a better impression during his second stay in the city. After arriving in Brooklyn, he promised to "make Brooklyn the baseball capital of the world, by Judas Priest."[4] ("Judas Priest" was one of Rickey's favorite euphemistic expletives, along with "Balzac.")[5] And this is more or less what he accomplished, New York City's other outer borough team notwithstanding. There is little doubt that Rickey laid the foundation for the triumphs of the "Boys of Summer" years, even though Walter O'Malley forced him out of Brooklyn after the 1950 season. Between 1947 and 1956, the Brooklyn Dodgers won six National League pennants (and save a play at the plate in 1950 and a Bobby Thomson home run in 1951, was one out away from winning two others.) In 1955, the Brooklyn Dodgers won their one and only World Series. During this span, Dodgers players won five National League MVP awards and four Rookie of the Year awards. It was not an accident that all the Dodgers' awards went to African Americans.

Rickey was a man with strong opinions and a stronger personality. Born Wesley Branch Rickey in Stockdale, Ohio, in 1881, he was a devout and serious Methodist. His very public faith was mentioned in almost every article about him, often in uncomplimentary ways. He was also a shrewd businessman who drove hard bargains; a keen buyer and seller of baseball flesh, he usually came out ahead in his transactions. Rickey was a teetotaler and a Sabbatarian who never attended ball games on Sunday. Rickey's Methodism was moralistic rather than evangelizing, the calm and sober Methodism of the Chautauqua circuit rather than the hothouse fury of the revival meeting, a faith that was less concerned with saving souls than in seeing society securely anchored on firm ethical and religious principles. Rickey was also a Republican who never forgot that the Republican Party was the victor in the Civil War, a believer in what historian Barbara Gannon has called the "won cause."[6] Racial politics were not at the center of his political agenda, but he never accepted lynching or extrajudicial violence against Black Americans. By 1908, he was campaigning for Republicans, and he became a significant figure in Missouri's Republican politics by the 1930s. He was urged by Missouri friends to consider tossing his hat into the ring to run, variously, for governor, for senator in 1940 (against Harry S. Truman), and even to consider a run for president in that same year.[7] He knew and was admired by the era's most prominent Republicans, among them Herbert Hoover, Wendell Wilkie, and Thomas Dewey.[8]

Rickey has often been called a conservative Republican, which is not inaccurate, but it is imprecise. He was a moderate Republican progressive, deeply concerned about what was called the "social crisis," but wary of governmental interventions to solve it. In the years around 1908, as administrative secretary of the local YMCA in Delaware, Ohio, he helped arrange speakers with progressive inclinations such as Jane Addams, Jacob Riis, Walter Rauschenbusch, and, to address the "Negro question," Booker T. Washington.[9] However, like many old-school Republican progressives, by the 1930s he was fiercely opposed to FDR and the New Deal, complaining in 1937 that Roosevelt governed by "usurpations of legislative" prerogatives.[10] However, by 1940, without losing his deep disdain for FDR, he supported the interventionist Wendell Wilkie and backed FDR's Lend-Lease program of assistance to Britain in 1941.[11] In late 1943, Rickey thought Wilkie deserved renomination and wrote a friend that the Republicans had to nominate someone who "cannot be properly charged with the kind of reactionary conservatism, or whatever you care to call it, that puts the party into an isolationist position."[12] Wilkie, by 1943, was well into what his biographer David Levering Lewis has called his "civil rights pivot," endorsing the Fair Employment Practices Committee (as did the platform at the 1944 Republican Party convention) and the *Pittsburgh Courier*'s Double V for Victory campaign. He worked with the leaders of the NAACP and the National Urban League and spoke at the NAACP's national convention—something FDR would never do.[13]

As a prominent Methodist layperson, Rickey was familiar with and presumably approved of the work of the Federal Council of Churches, which issued several strikingly strong statements about the evils and perils of racism in the United States and its impact on the global war effort.[14] In 1944, the General Conference of the Methodist Church declared, "We believe that all men are children of God and brothers one of another. No group is inherently superior or inferior to any other. . . . We look to the ultimate elimination of racial discrimination within the Methodist Church."[15] The statement referred to the all-Black Central Jurisdiction of Methodist churches that Karl Downs had railed against, which was created in 1938 to separate Black Methodist congregations from white ones. (It was not discontinued until 1968.) Rickey facilitated a meeting between Robinson and his friend Edward D. Soper, president of Rickey's alma mater, Ohio Wesleyan University, and the author of *Racism, A World Issue.* In *The American Diamond,* Rickey quotes Soper: "Of all the ills to which humanity finds itself heir today, there is none more virulent and none which has so many facets as race."[16] Another sentence captures Soper's (and doubtless Rickey's) view on how to address it: "The Christian Church has failed at the point of race relations as any other institution, if not more; yet it is the only hope of the world today."[17]

Certainly by baseball standards, Rickey was a high-brow intellectual, a thoughtful reader of serious books, someone who cared deeply about the burning issues of the day. During the war, Black Americans were pushing the question of their citizenship to the center of American politics. It is hardly a surprise that Rickey's beau ideal of a politician was Abraham Lincoln. If Rickey at times sounded like the Great Emancipator, it wasn't accidental. He amassed a sizable collection of Lincolniana in which he underlined choice passages, and this practice evidently became more intense during his Brooklyn years.[18] A 1940 article about Rickey claimed, "He reads everything he can get his hands on about Abraham Lincoln. Not just because he happens to be a good Republican, but because the 'study of Lincoln was the study of politics.'"[19] Rickey was often compared to Lincoln after the 23 October announcement in Montreal. The *Montreal Star* published an admiring cartoon of Rickey being fitted for a stovepipe hat, Emancipation Proclamation in hand. When Robinson played his first minor-league game in Jersey City, it was hailed in the same paper as "another Emancipation Day for the Negro race. A day Abraham Lincoln would like."[20]

On the other hand, his critics, such as *Daily News* sportswriter Jimmy Powers, wrote in early 1946 of detesting "Branch Rickey's pompous statements that he is another Lincoln and that he has a heart as big as a watermelon and loves all mankind."[21] There is some debate regarding how much Rickey encouraged the comparison. Whatever one makes of it, both Lincoln and Rickey were Midwest Republicans who were, and are, celebrated for their involvements in the cause of the rights of Black Americans and criticized by those who thought their approach to racial politics was too slow and self-serving. Whatever Rickey's private views, if his career had ended in 1942, before the move to Brooklyn, he would not be remembered today as a champion of civil rights. There is little evidence of any involvement in the fight for Black equality or close association with Black leaders while he was in Missouri.

Branch Rickey was fully of his time, place, class, race, and background. On 22 August 1941, Rickey was staying at the Greenbrier, the exclusive resort in White Sulphur Springs, West Virginia, that had been built in the mid-nineteenth century with slave labor and certainly did not allow any Black guests. Rickey, before and during his arrival in Brooklyn, often ate, took meetings, or stayed in such places. Perhaps inspired by his antebellum surroundings, he wrote a letter to Larry MacPhail, a protégé and the president of the Brooklyn Dodgers, about a baseball matter, concluding with a very unfunny joke about an old Black woman being afraid of the devil.[22]

> Did you ever hear the story of the fat, old colored woman who was in a high state of agitation listening to the parson's sermon on the subject of the devil? In the great climax the parson said, "The debbil am a big, black man with long horns and a forked tail," and just then the old colored lady let out a big poop. The parson immediately squinted one eye and pointed his finger. "Yes, and sister Johnson, sittin' way back dah in the corner, if you f . . . when you hear me describe the debbil you sure will s . . . when you see him."

The anecdote reveals the casual and thoughtless racism of a privileged white man writing to someone of his own class who may have appreciated Rickey's pathetic attempt at humor. But their paths would soon diverge. A year after sending the letter, Rickey would replace MacPhail as president of the Dodgers. By 1945, MacPhail was president of the New York Yankees, and these two formerly close friends would have an acrimonious falling out. MacPhail emerged as the most prominent and vehement public opponent of ending the major-league color line; he did everything in his power to preserve it. Branch Rickey would sign Jackie Robinson. Could the Rickey who wrote this letter have signed Robinson? Perhaps. But by 1945 he was living in New York City. And living there pushed him and changed him more than he would ever acknowledge.

Rickey would often tell the story of Charlie Thomas, his teammate on the Ohio Wesleyan baseball team, who was reduced to tears when he was not allowed to stay with his white teammates in a hotel. One purpose of relating the story is give the impression that his views on civil rights had been set decades before the Dodgers. There is some evidence that Rickey chafed at the persistence of segregation at Sportsman's Park in St. Louis, the last major-league park to be desegregated (in 1944, after Rickey left the city). He likely discussed his qualms with his family and close friends. But he didn't go public with his objections. Perhaps, good Methodist that he was, he witnessed or heard about what happened when, in December 1937, the African American minister Howard Thurman addressed a large conference sponsored by the National Methodist Student Conference in

St. Louis. Despite promises to the contrary, Thurman was denied service in the hotel's dining room. Thurman considered not giving his address but decided that he would, after telling the audience what happened: "The time will come when you are in the same position as the men who made this commitment on your behalf. When that time comes I want you to remember this experience." After the talk, Thurman answered a few questions. One person asked, "How can we put moral approval on that which we know to be immoral?" Thurman answered, "I do not know how we do it, I only know we do," adding that "we often hold our moral judgment in suspense, and say now, 'Well, I will do this. I will go through the motions; but I am not going to put my imprimatur on it.' The trouble is, I am what I do, including my reservations."[23] As Rickey knew, you earn no credit, as a person or as a Christian, for tolerating evil while nursing a guilty conscience.

Why did Branch Rickey sign Jackie Robinson? And what does this tell us, if anything, about the struggle for civil rights and integration as a whole? Their first meeting on Montague Street on 28 August 1945, when stripped of its other significances, was a job interview. And as in most job interviews, the interviewer asks most of the questions, and the interviewee—nervous, and in this case uncertain of what job he is actually interviewing for—tries to respond as best as he can. But as job coaches recommend, often the best strategy for a potential hire is to "interview the interviewer." And as Branch Rickey was fully aware, he was being interviewed and tested not only by Jackie Robinson but also, in a broader sense, by the tens of thousands of people not in the room determined to end baseball's color line. Only he began the conversation knowing what was at stake, what he wanted to achieve, and the likely consequences of its failure. If he did not come to an agreement with Robinson, the question of who would be the first African American player on the Dodgers might well be taken from his hands.

Rickey's intentions in signing Robinson are difficult to determine, because his motivations were genuinely complex, a mix of Christian idealism and capitalist self-interest. Rickey, with his habitual garrulity, was a master deflector of his real intentions, possessing a knack for making even his simplest decisions seem very complex. His most enduring Brooklyn nickname was the "Mahatma," so dubbed by a local sportswriter citing a passage from John Gunther's *Inside Asia,* which described Mohandas K. "Mahatma" Gandhi as an "incredible combination of Jesus Christ, Tammany Hall, and your father."[24] Rickey could use his gift of gab to either enlighten or befog.

There are two basic explanations for Rickey's signing of Robinson. Rickey generally insisted that the decision was the culmination of a carefully considered multiyear master plan, unfurled with an Olympian disregard for the politics of the moment. When he came to Brooklyn, he was no doubt a man with a plan. Things might be possible in New York City that were impossible in St. Louis. The other explanation is that Rickey's actions display as much improvisation as pre-preparation. No doubt, by the summer of 1945 he was beset upon and harried. Arthur Mann, Rickey's usually obliging amanuensis, wrote an unpublished article that was originally intended to accompany the announcement of the Robinson signing. He wrote that after Rickey arrived in Brooklyn, "without warning or apparent reason, he was besieged with telephone calls, telegrams and letters of petition on behalf of black ball players. They were from Negro clubs, churches, the clergy and recognized communist groups." It was, in Mann's telling, this "staggering pile of missives" that convinced him that "the Dodgers had been chosen as a kind of guinea pig."[25] Rickey no doubt came to Brooklyn to explore the possibility of signing a Black player. But how concrete and how determined his intention was is unclear. In any event, his plan was adjusted and amended as events unfolded. However, the more pressure applied on Rickey to act, the more important it became for him to deny that pressure played any role in his decision making. Rickey was ungenerous with sharing credit for the signing of Robinson, in part because, as Mann acknowledged, many of his petitioners were on the left. This conservative, anti–New Deal, and fiercely anticommunist Republican knew that Robinson's signing would be most loudly applauded by the New Deal liberals and communists, while many of those closest to him personally or politically would look askance or glumly assent to his decision. He undertook the single most courageous political act of his life even as he often denied that it had anything to do with courage or politics.

In Rickey's telling, he had a six-step plan for signing a Black player. First, speak to the owners of the team; second, speak to the stockholders and get their approval. Step three involved scouting for the right player, and, when the time was right, proceeding to step four: getting the press and the public behind the scheme. Step five involved drumming up the right sort of Black support, and step six required acceptance of the player by his teammates.[26] Rickey stated that "the very first thing I did when I came to Brooklyn in late 1942 was to investigate the approval of ownership for a Negro player. There was a timeliness about the notion, the Negro in America was legally but not morally free. I thought the right man with control of himself could be found."[27] In January 1943, he met with the imperious George V. McLaughlin, president of the Brooklyn Trust Company—his nickname was George the Fifth—who controlled the interests of the heirs of Dodgers owner Chales Ebbets. Rickey told McLaughlin that "we are going to beat the bushes, and that might include a Negro player or two."[28] Arthur Mann, who wrote biographies of both Rickey and Robinson, provides two different accounts of McLaughlin's response to Rickey's plan in his respective books. It was either, "I don't see why not. You might come up with something. If you find the man who is better than the others." Or, "My God, Rickey, you've got to know you're doing this not to solve a sociological problem."[29]

Rickey tried to convince all who would listen, and perhaps himself, that his motivations, his real reasons for signing a Black player were entirely mercenary.[30] It is certainly true that Rickey felt the way to sell the signing of Robinson (or someone like him) to the wider public was not by asking what the Dodgers could do for Black America but what Black America could do for the Dodgers. Or, as Rickey told Harold Parrott, the traveling secretary of the Dodgers, probably in late 1945 or early 1946: "Son, the greatest untapped reservoir of raw material in the history of our game is the black race. The Negroes will make us winners for years to come. And for that, I will happily bear being called a bleeding heart, and a do-gooder and all that humanitarian rot."[31]

The next step was to convince the Dodgers stockholders, all of whom, in the tightly held corporation, could sit around a table, in this case a table at the New York Athletic Club (NYAC). It was an odd place for a meeting of this sort, since even in the 1940s, the NYAC was notorious for its exclusion of Blacks and Jews.[32] This irony aside, the meeting at the NYAC went well. Those present were pledged to absolute secrecy, not to divulge Rickey's plan to anyone, even their wives. It was a wartime Manhattan Project for the Brooklyn Dodgers.[33]

But the next step, in many ways the most important, was to find the "right player." Here the real questions begin. He did not sign a Black player for the Dodgers for the 1943, 1944, or 1945 seasons. Perhaps Rickey was cautious, or overcautious, because the stakes were so high, and he was afraid that any misstep might cause a fatal setback. Or perhaps the search, though serious, lacked a certain sense of urgency. During the war years, complaints about white baseball's segregation intensified. As well as being an affront to democracy, it was a practical matter: The war-depleted ranks of major-league franchises made a seemingly irresistible case for hiring Negro League stars, at least as a "Rosie-the-Riveter" sort of wartime exigency. Instead, general managers acquired the services of players in their baseball nonage or dotage, too young or old to be drafted or otherwise unqualified for military service, like one-armed outfielders. In 1944, during spring training, Rickey reported that the Dodgers had only eighteen players, mostly those classified 4-F, that he could count on for the entire season and proposed pooling minor-league talent with other clubs.[34] Nothing came of this, but in 1945 he signed Babe Herman, a former Dodgers great who hadn't played in the major leagues since 1937. He also persuaded Dodgers scout Clyde Sukeforth, a forty-three-year-old former Dodgers catcher who last appeared on a major-league roster in 1934, to play for eighteen games before letting Sukeforth retire again and claim his bit of baseball immortality later in the season by being the scout who invited Robinson to come to Brooklyn.[35] Many complained, as did Brooklyn state assemblyman Philip J. Schupler, that rather than rounding up players from "various homes for the aged," Rickey might consider the "many talented and able colored ball players available."[36]

Rickey was definitely in 1943 and 1944 scouting players of African descent, primarily in Mexico and the Caribbean, and claims to have spent $25,000 in all on his scouting efforts.[37] In 1943, Rickey made two attempts to sign Silvio Garcia, a dark-skinned Cuban shortstop, but the efforts concluded when Garcia was drafted into the Cuban army.[38] In 1943, in response to a request, the Dodgers invited Japanese American teenagers held in internment centers to participate in a nationwide series of Dodgers tryout camps. "The fact that these boys are American boys is good enough for the Brooklyn team," exclaimed his son, Branch Rickey Jr., head of the Dodgers farm system. (How the internees would make their way to the tryouts was left unexplained.) The *Pittsburgh Courier* commented in September 1943 that while "this shows a laudable liberalism on the part of the Dodgers, . . . we could be much more enthusiastic about it if Negro youths were not being barred."[39]

Wartime emergency or not, Rickey signed no Black players during the war. And by the time he did sign Robinson, many observers, like Horace Stoneham, owner of the New York Giants, tentatively acknowledged that the signing was "a fine way to start the program," before adding "but we have hundreds of returning servicemen and only if they fail to make the grade will we have room for new players."[40]

But 1945 would prove to be different. For one thing, Judge Kenesaw Mountain Landis was no longer commissioner of baseball, although to replace him, team owners continued the practice of hiring a politician with no baseball background to rule over them. Albert B. "Happy" Chandler was a former (and future) governor of Kentucky and one of the state's sitting US senators. He did not have the accumulated power and gravitas hoarded and exercised by Landis.[41] It was not until early 1945 that Rickey began to tell those close to him—his family, Dodgers team officials, and Dodgers broadcaster Red Barber—of his plans.[42]

Rickey, who had contentious run-ins with Landis dating back to his Cardinals years, was no doubt happy to see Landis go. By the end of 1943, Rickey clearly was frustrated by Landis's hypocritical claim that there was no color bar in baseball. In a transcript of a conversation between them from December 1943 that has been preserved, Rickey complained of being "beset with a great many petitions and a great many visitations [about the color line]. That they become embarrassing is not the point; they become time-taking, and, from a publicity standpoint, they become important." Wouldn't it make more sense, Rickey suggested, rather than denying a ban on Black players existed, just to acknowledge that this was official policy? (And thereby force Landis and the owners to acknowledge that the ban existed.) But this was precisely what Landis and the owners did not want to do, because saying the ban existed would have been terrible politics. "I don't think that would be good. I think that would be indefensible" because it might lead to "a foot-race run by sixteen Major League managers to sign up Negro ball players."[43] (And this gives lie to another facet of an unwritten law. Rather than simply banning Black ballplayers outright, alternative explanations were necessary, most of which implied that they weren't ready or good enough for the major leagues. In some ways, this could be more hurtful than simply banning Black ballplayers for their skin color. In any event it was a subterfuge that Landis evidently did not really believe.)

Another difference in 1945 was that by spring training, the Ives-Quinn Act had become law. Jimmy Breslin has asserted that Rickey pushed his friend Thomas Dewey to support the bill and then went to Albany to lobby for it, but as Breslin provides no sources for this and no one else reports it, it seems unlikely.[44] It seems more plausible that his attitude to the bill, and to civil rights legislation in general, was deeply ambivalent. In a speech given on civil rights to the Brooklyn Rotary Club in 1944, he mentioned that the Eighteenth Amendment had set back his favorite political cause of prohibition, one he still deeply believed in, by imposing an unpopular policy on an unwilling public.[45] "Very possibly the introduction of a Negro into baseball, even without force, might similarly throw back their cause of racial equality a quarter century or more," making the case that "forcing" Black players on major league teams would be a mistake.[46] He voiced further concerns the following year, in July 1945, after the Ives-Quinn Act had gone into effect. While he was making a final decision to contact Jackie Robinson, he philosophized that "advancement in racial problems has doubtless seemed too slow to contemporaries in all ages. It has been difficult to understand why progress from slavery to full equality of opportunity has seemed beset by delay and opposition." Again using the example of prohibition, he argued that legislation cannot be allowed to get too far ahead or fall too far behind public opinion. "Revolutions," he said, "are evidence of impatience with evolution." He cautioned that "in our effort to be progressive—and to secure for ourselves and our posterity the blessings of liberty—we must indeed give consideration to the possibility of untimeliness, the sheer inopportunism, the sad cost of an overreaching experiment. Let us not attempt what cannot be held if gained."[47] At the same time, and unlike many others, his belief in a philosophy of moving slowly on civil rights was not an excuse for doing nothing at all. But it was an effort to depoliticize, as much as possible, the end of baseball's color line and ensure that the white guardians of America's white institutions, and not those excluded, would control the pace of integration.

After Robinson's signing was made public, Rickey was at great pains to state that his signing had nothing to do with Black protests or civil rights demands: "I have not been pushed into this. I signed Robinson in spite of the pressure groups who are only exploiting the Negroes instead of advancing their cause."[48] In a slightly more nuanced statement, referring to the Ives-Quinn Act, he told he told the *World-Telegraph* that "while the time is fast approaching when every professional baseball club in state of New York will be forced to sign Negro players," he, however, had "signed Robinson in no contemplation of legal penalties for failure to give Negro players a fair chance."[49]

Rickey wanted Black Americans to play their part in his scheme by behaving as if the hiring of Robinson was not the harbinger of more important changes to come. They needed to avoid extravagant rooting for Robinson. In early 1947, he told a group of about thirty Black professionals in Bedford-Stuyvesant, who were pledged to secrecy, that "if Jackie Robinson does come to the Dodgers [i.e., if promoted from the Montreal Royals], the biggest threat to his success—the one enemy most likely to ruin that success—is the Negro people themselves." This was of course totally untrue and put the entire burden on Black Americans to satisfy white anxieties. His statement was premised on a deep class bias, too: namely Rickey's worry that the Black hoi polloi would "strut" and "go out and form parades," "fight," and "get arrested." He needed the Black middle-class businessmen before him to keep them in line. "Let me tell you this," said Rickey, punctuating his statement by a smash of a fist on a tabletop, "if any individual, group, or segment of Negro society uses the advancement of Jackie Robinson in baseball as a triumph of race over race, I will regret the day I ever signed him to a contract, and I will personally see that baseball is never so abused and misrepresented again."[50]

Supposedly, Rickey's speech was received by his Brooklyn audience with "deafening applause." Although many, I suspect, were applauding Rickey's signing of Robinson and not his threats. To be sure, one should not discount the power of what has been called the Black middle-class "politics of respectability."[51] Sportswriter Lucius C. Harper, writing in the *Chicago Defender,* noted that "one loudmouth uncouth Negro" could undo ten years of accumulated goodwill in ten minutes, and that unless the "crude and nauseating mannerisms" of "this type of Negro [were] not suppressed, he will soon turn the North into the South."[52] In May 1947, Fay Young, also in the *Chicago Defender,* wrote that "there shouldn't be the necessity of devoting this column to the unwarranted actions of Negro baseball fans as a whole, yet we cannot avoid warning our fans that they are *more* on trial than is Robinson." Young warned his readers to forebear "whiskey drinking, profane language and boisterous conduct" and confine their urination to appropriate locations: "Telephone booths are not men's washrooms."[53]

These concerns accepted the view of most whites; that in cases of integration into formerly all-white institutions, it was Black behavior, and not white behavior, that was on trial. Or that somehow any Black fan watching the Dodgers on the road would care more about whether the Pittsburgh Pirates or the Cincinnati Reds won a particular baseball game rather than root for the success of Jackie Robinson. But Rickey underestimated the intelligence and savvy of Black baseball fans. Perhaps the admonitions from the Black press and ministers helped, but they had learned, through their life experiences, when and how to respond forcefully to slurs and when discretion was the better part of racial valor—eyes on the prize. In his autobiography, Robinson praised "all those black people sitting in the stands [keeping] from overreacting when they sensed a racial slur or unjust decision. They could have blown the whole bit to hell by acting belligerently and touching off a race riot."[54] These certainly were Rickey's anxieties, along with a perhaps warranted fear that interracial violence in the stands would mar Robinson's debut.

What Rickey and other baseball executives were also afraid of, on some level, was that attending games would come to be perceived as a "Black experience" and would discourage white attendance. An August 1946 report by baseball executives, prepared for the commissioner's office, stated that the greatest danger of Black players in the major leagues was that any increase in the number of Black fans "in parks such as the Yankee Stadium, the Polo Grounds [the upper Manhattan home of the New York Giants], and [Chicago's] Comiskey Park [that is, ballparks in or near large African American neighborhoods] could conceivably threaten the value of the major league franchises owned by these clubs."[55] Integration and inclusion of some Black players into a previously all-white institution was fair and fine, as was encouraging Black fans to attend ballgames. But transforming major-league baseball into something else, something Blacker, was another matter. The question of "tipping points" would haunt the advocates of integration as inclusion throughout the civil rights era.

Rickey in his later years would become a frequent speaker at meetings of the NAACP and other Black organizations, but perhaps he never fully overcame some ambivalence about civil rights legislation. As late as 1950, he could state that "legislative force can delay rather than accelerate the problem" of racial progress.[56] In 1956, before a middle-class Black Atlanta audience, he said that he wasn't sure if "legislators ought to drive against a prominent and very antagonistic" white majority with too much political or legal force "too fast [and] too far. I'm not sure that the 18th Amendment might repeat itself," and would only hinder "a problem that is now in my judgment fast being solved."[57]

Rickey wanted to set an example, not a precedent, legal or otherwise. Rickey did not want to be compelled to sign a Black player, and he did not want the other team owners to be compelled to sign Black players. Instead, he thought that if he could demonstrate the utility of having talented Black players on the Dodgers, other teams would eventually feel obliged to follow his example just to keep up—and this is just what happened. Rickey might have wanted the process to unfold more quickly (it took a dozen years for the last all-white team, the Boston Red Sox, to follow the Dodgers example), but all deliberate speed was preferable to an outside mandate that would have forced owners to do so. But this is not how the main thrust of the civil rights movement unfolded, propelled by executive orders, court decisions, and legislation, all of which were more concerned with classes of persons rather than individuals. One reason for the signing of Jackie Robinson was that Branch Rickey wished to forestall and prevent the passage of further civil rights legislation.

But whatever Rickey's ambivalence about the Ives-Quinn Act, that didn't mean that he couldn't use the new law to his advantage. According to his widow, Jane Rickey, her husband told her over the breakfast table in March 1945: "It says in the paper, Mother, that Governor Dewey has just signed the Ives-Quinn Law. They can't stop me now."[58] Unlike many, from the outset he understood that the greatest impact of the new law would probably be less in its punitive provisions than in encouraging businesses to hire Black workers. Rickey, it would seem, like many other Republican (and some Democratic) politicians in the state, was a philosophical opponent yet political supporter of Ives-Quinn.

As the 1945 season got underway, many others also saw Ives-Quinn as the tool that could and would finally pry open baseball's locked doors. In March 1945, Rickey found himself in Bear Mountain, New York, about fifty miles north of New York City, where the Dodgers had their wartime spring training facilities. On 6 April, Joe Bostic, the sports editor for the left-wing *People's Voice,* showed up, unannounced, with two Negro League players, pitcher Terris McDuffie of the Newark Eagles and first baseman Dave "Showboat" Thomas of the New York Cubans, along with a reporter from the *Daily Worker.* Bostic asked Rickey to give them a tryout.[59] In his columns, Bostic had frequently lambasted Rickey as the epitome of the pious hypocrite, often with an accompanying drawing of a Black man giving a white man a swift kick in the rear end.[60] Rickey, predictably, was furious at being put on the spot and at the very left-wing auspices of the surprise visitors, but after a discussion he agreed to give the two players a tryout the following day.[61]

The tryout went reasonably well, but Bostic later claimed Rickey merely "went through the motions," or as an *Atlanta Daily World* headline put it, "Negro Stars Don't Impress Bums Boss."[62] Questions were raised in the Black press about whether the two players promoted by Bostic were the most appropriate choices, since both were in their middle to late thirties, but Bostic had encountered difficulties finding willing Negro Leaguers for what seemed like a quixotic undertaking.[63] It seems likely that Bostic was interested in providing an early test for the Ives-Quinn Act, though it would not go into effect until July. The *Baltimore Afro-American* wrote that the Bear Mountain episode "marked the first gunshot in the campaign to envelop major league baseball as a result of passage of the state FEPC law . . . which makes it compulsory for private enterprise to hire qualified job applicants as a result of race."[64] Rickey supposedly told one friend after the workout, "Now more than ever I must start my search for the right colored man to enter organized baseball."[65] If the unsuccessful Bear Mountain tryout did indeed deliver a metaphorical kick to Rickey's rear end on the matter of signing a Black ballplayer, Bostic's visit more than accomplished its purpose.[66]

Ten days later, at Fenway Park in Boston, came the only other tryout of Negro League players by a major-league club that spring. This time, the invocation of state power was explicit, and the tryout was at the team's invitation. Isadore Muchnick, a Democratic member of the Boston City Council, had threatened not to renew the annual exemption that the Red Sox and the Braves received to play ball on Sunday unless they held a tryout for Black ballplayers. Both teams agreed, though in the end, only the Red Sox participated. Muchnick, who had forced the issue, contacted *Pittsburgh Courier* sportswriter Wendell Smith, who suggested that Jackie Robinson, of the Kansas City Monarchs, would be a good candidate, along with Sam Jethroe of the Cleveland Buckeyes and Marvin Smith of the Philadelphia Stars.[67]

Robinson and the two others came to Boston, and Robinson, with his fielding and hitting, banging a few balls off the high left-field wall, particularly impressed the assembled Red Sox observers.[68] Predictably, there was no follow-up. Robinson was annoyed that he'd angered his manager with a request for time off and then trekked from Kansas City to Boston for a tryout that could not have been more perfunctory. The three Negro League players were not provided uniforms; they faced high school pitchers throwing batting practice; and after a while, a high-ranking Red Sox official in the largely empty stadium—figuring the charade had gone on long enough—shouted, "Get those n—s off the field."[69] Robinson told off Wendell Smith: "This is why I hesitated to come. It burns me up to come 1,500 miles to have them give me the runaround."[70] But sometimes cynical runarounds can have silver linings. Rickey had previously asked Smith to keep an eye out for Negro League talent, and when he called Rickey after the tryout, touting Robinson, Rickey asked the sportswriter to stop in Brooklyn on his way back from Boston. When they met, according to Smith, Rickey raised his bushy eyebrows and said that he'd heard of Robinson as a collegiate football and basketball star but didn't know about him as a baseball player. And so, in mid-April 1945, Rickey first heard of Jackie Robinson the baseball player and liked what he heard about him as an athlete and as a person.[71] Soon hints of something afoot made their way into the sports columns of the Black press, such as this item in the *Pittsburgh Courier* in late April: "There is no doubt whatsoever that Branch Rickey, boss of the Dodgers, is in some vague way interested in the Negro ballplayer and Negro baseball."[72]

But many thought that Rickey was more interested in reinforcing the color line rather than shattering it. Rickey's first public statements in 1945 on race and baseball seemed to favor continued segregation. In May he announced his support and financial assistance to create a third Negro League, the United States Negro League (USBL). The Brooklyn Brown Dodgers, which would have a brief and inglorious history, would play in the league. Everything about the United States Negro League is murky. Was Rickey's goal the appropriation of the Negro Leagues? Or, alternatively, did he want to incorporate the existing Negro Leagues as a sort of "super AAA" league within white baseball? Or was Rickey just trying to make it easier to scout Negro Leaguers? In announcing his support for the new league, he "would not discuss from any angle the question of Negro players in the white major league baseball." Maybe he was simply hedging his bets.[73] Perhaps Rickey was toying with many options, unsure which would be most viable.[74] The USBL was not well received by the Black press. Fay Young in the *Chicago Defender* fumed that "Rickey is no Abraham Lincoln or Franklin D. Roosevelt, and we won't accept him as a dictator of Negro baseball!"[75] After the announcement, a sportswriter for the *New York Age* asked, "Did you ever hear such double talk from such a big pompous ass in your life? I predict it will be a cold day in hell when that windbag puts a Negro in a Dodgers uniform."[76]

Whatever Rickey's motivation, the Brooklyn Brown Dodgers (which did play a few games in 1945 and 1946) provided a cover for him to scout the Negro Leagues. Rickey sent three scouts on separate occasions to observe Robinson with the Monarchs, not telling them about the other two. Wid Matthews reported that he was an expert protector of the strike zone. Tom Greenwade called him the best bunter in baseball. George Sisler said that every aspect of his game was superb, though he had some doubts about his throwing arm. In the end, after making some personal inquiries about

Robinson and his years at UCLA, Rickey decided that Robinson was the one; he was "the ideal Negro star," Rickey later said, "to lead the invasion of organized baseball."[77]

At the end of August, after observing Robinson from afar, it was time for the Dodgers to speak to him directly, and Rickey sent Clyde Sukeforth to make the connection.[78] On 24 August, Sukeforth introduced himself to Robinson, who was out of the lineup with a sore arm, and watched the Monarchs play the Lincoln Giants in Comiskey Park in Chicago. Robinson was appropriately skeptical when Sukeforth approached him after the game. But Robinson, disenchanted with his time with the Monarchs, was willing to hear Sukeforth out. After the game, the two men met in his hotel room. Sukeforth had to bribe the operator to let Robinson use the passenger elevator. (During the war years, prominent hotels in Northern cities were frontiers in the fight against segregation.)[79] Sukeforth invited Robinson to come to Brooklyn to meet with Rickey, though he thought he was probably scouting Robinson for the Brooklyn Brown Dodgers. They met again in Toledo (where Sukeforth had to convince a railroad clerk that yes, he wanted to share a Pullman suite with a Black man), and then the pair traveled on to New York.[80]

Robinson spent the night at the Theresa Hotel in Harlem and the next day attended the Dodgers offices on Montague Street in Brooklyn Heights for the famous meeting. Rickey and Robinson spent a while just staring at each other before they started talking, perhaps with Rickey wanting to size up the very dark-skinned man sitting in front of him or perhaps calming himself before proceeding to the momentous conversation about to unfold. And then Rickey, who often peppered prospective hires with a barrage of personal questions ("Do you believe in God?") opened the meeting.[81] The first question was whether Robinson had a girl. Robinson, understandably offended, thought it was a "hell of a question," the sort of question that those in positions of authority can ask subordinates but not the reverse, a question that Robinson might have seen as a typical example of the intrusive, prurient white fascination with Black sex lives. But Rickey's intentions were probably less to pry than to get a sense of Robinson's emotional solidity and support system. When Robinson said he had a girl, without mentioning that he and Rachel Isum were currently going through a bit of a rough patch, Rickey was delighted. When Rickey told Robinson that "a man needs a wife and a good home, especially when he has a man's work to do," he was telling Robinson, in the language of the day, that he would likely find few people he could completely trust in the journey that awaited him: not his teammates, not his bosses, not the throng of naysayers and yeasayers that would surround him, perhaps not even Rickey himself. He needed one person to be an utterly honest and reliable point of reference besides himself. And if he asked the God question, Rickey was no doubt delighted to learn that not only was Robinson a churchgoer, but they both were abstemious and belonged to the same denomination. Satisfied with Robinson's answers, Rickey then revealed the purpose of the meeting. He did not want Robinson to play for the Brooklyn Brown Dodgers, but for the Brooklyn Dodgers. Robinson remembers that his "reactions seemed like some kind of weird mixture churning in a blender. I was thrilled, scared, and excited. I was incredulous. Most of all I was speechless."[82]

Then came the best-remembered part of the conversation. Rickey asked Robinson if he had the guts to make it as a major leaguer. Robinson, with "the heat coming up into my cheeks," knew how to respond to insinuations of cowardice. Guts Robinson had aplenty, and he told Rickey as much. Backing down from a fight was not in his nature. Rickey told him that this was not the sort of courage he was looking for. He was "looking for a ball player with guts enough not to fight back." Rickey then proceeded to outline to Robinson the challenges he would face, spraying a long list of racist epithets and expletives and outlining the situations he was likely to encounter both on the field (brutal bench jockeying, head-hunting pitches, malicious high spiking) and off (the array of invidious treatments meted out to Black Americans who had the presumption to travel or associate with whites in hotels, trains, and restaurants).

Rickey was asking questions of Robinson to which he already knew the answer. One of the main reasons Rickey wanted to sign Robinson was precisely that he had spent most of his athletic career playing with white teammates and for white coaches against white opponents and before white crowds, all of whom knew and sometimes used anti-Black slurs. Robinson already knew how to maintain his self-respect, how to choose his spots, and when to fight back and when not to. Nothing Robinson would face with the

Dodgers, none of the epithets, none of the on-field confrontations, could or would have the potential adverse consequences of what he had already endured less than a year earlier, having to defend himself in a court-martial.

Rickey then pulled out a copy of Giovanni Papini's *Life of Christ*, first published in 1921 and translated into English two years later.[83] Rickey was an admirer of the book, and he read an excerpt to Robinson on turning the other cheek. Papini explains this means "not receiving the second blow. It means cutting the chain of the inevitable wrongs at the first link. Your adversary who expected resistance is humiliated before you and before himself. He was ready for anything but this. He is thrown into confusion, a confusion which is almost shame. . . . Every man has an obscure respect for courage in others, especially if it is moral courage, the rarest and most difficult kind of bravery. . . . Quietness, when it is not stupidity, gentleness, when it is not cowardice, astound common souls as do all marvelous things."[84]

Yet this Brooklyn "Mahatma" was no Gandhian, and neither was Robinson: turning the other cheek had never been one of his favorite scriptures. Some sixteen years later, one of his syndicated columns was titled "Negroes Tired of Turning the Other Cheek."[85] He'd been tired of it in 1945. He wrote in his autobiography that he "would not have made a good soldier in Martin's [MLK's] army. My reflexes aren't conditioned to accept nonviolence"; his instinct, when attacked, was "instant defense and total retaliation."[86]

In many ways Rickey's advice to Robinson was the opposite of Gandhian nonviolence. It was a tactic, not a strategy. Papini's Christ turned the other cheek as a gambit, an effort to confound and startle his opponents. Gandhi's pacifism was no secret, and there was no surprise involved, having broadcast his intended actions to his adversaries well in advance. In essence, Rickey told Robinson to avoid confrontations at all costs. Gandhian nonviolence is all about confrontation. Rickey wanted to depoliticize what both men knew was an intensely political act. For Gandhi, perhaps the original practitioner of the maxim "the personal is political," everything was political. Rickey tried as hard as he could to make the signing of Robinson about one person's athletic capabilities. Gandhi saw the entire point of nonviolence as collective; if one person is felled, another is ready to take their place. One person cannot challenge an army or challenge the state.

A mass of people dedicated to nonviolent action perhaps can. Rickey did everything he could to discourage the interpretation of Jackie Robinson's signing as anything other than a smart business decision for the Dodgers, rather than seeing Robinson, as he surely was, as a stand-in for the hopes and aspirations of millions of Black Americans for full citizenship. And by 1945, while there was gathering strength—"a great, conscious movement of Negroes," one "not unlike the great Indian movement with which Gandhi and Nehru are associated"—neither Rickey nor Robinson could imagine that radical nonviolence would become central in the struggle for Black citizenship.[87]

But if Rickey was a Papinian rather than a Gandhian, and despite the differences between these thinkers' philosophies, there was at least one deep affinity. Both perspectives were essentially religious and placed great emphasis on spiritual discipline. What Rickey really wanted was someone with enough spiritual discipline to control his more aggressive impulses, and someone who had enough innate aggression to use it as a tool. Without temptation, professions to saintliness ring hollow.[88] Integration, too, was a spiritual discipline, and for Jackie Robinson, it was a viscerally physical discipline as well. What Rickey sensed, if only implicitly, was that the discipline of sublimation was a key to integration. There is no stronger emotion than intense anger or hate. Rickey wanted someone who knew how to hate but who also knew how to bottle it up, control it, and transform it. For the Jackie Robinsons of the world, the stronger the hatred of white racism and racists, the stronger the impetus for integration. The goal was to hate oppression more than any particular or specific oppressor. And even if Robinson was temperamentally ill-suited to practicing radical nonviolence, he could, from his own experience, appreciate what that degree of self-control involved. And this he admired. When the sit-in protests began in 1960, Robinson praised the protesters for using the "Gandhian method by which Negroes in the South are forging a new chapter in the struggle against human indignity."[89]

In Robinson's rookie season with the Dodgers, the notorious bench jockeying he experienced when the Dodgers first played the Philadelphia Phillies—orchestrated by the vilely racist and antisemitic Ben Chapman—was perhaps the key episode in his entire major-league career. He wrote in his autobiography that "this day, of all the unpleasant days of my life, brought me closer to cracking up than I ever had been. . . . What was I doing here turning the other cheek as though I wasn't a man?" And then, "For one wild and rage-crazed minute I thought . . . what a glorious, cleansing thing it would be to let go. To hell with the image of the patient black freak I was supposed to create. I could throw down my bat, stride over to the Phillies dugout, grab one of those white sons of bitches and smash his teeth in with my despised black fist." Although his major-league career might have come to an abrupt and early end, he could tell his son "what his daddy could have been if he hadn't been too much of a man."[90]

Masculinity, and its performative demonstration, was always important to Robinson, and this included "physical challenge and response . . . [to] attempts to intimidate."[91] At this, Jackie Robinson was a master, a man, who, during a game, said his Kansas City Monarchs teammate Othello Renfroe, was hotter "than a burner" and who had a " truly copious, ever-available supply of nouns, verbs, and adjectives that went awfully well with that temper."[92] This was the code, in and out of baseball, in 1940s and 1950s America, conflating courage with masculine aggression. And this identification perhaps resonated even more deeply with Black males, so afraid that calmness would be interpreted as weakness, amiability as docility. Rickey wanted a militant fighter for racial justice who could hold back his militancy so that Rickey could say that his signing of a Black player had nothing to do with racial militancy. Robinson would not be easy-going or complacent. He would always have, and constantly hone, his "edge." He would become the most celebrated Brooklyn Dodger of them all, but nobody ever called him a bum. Rickey admired Robinson, he would write in 1952, because he was "very aggressive" but had "enough control of himself not to let anything impair his competitive ability."[93]

In August 1945, after two hours, the fateful meeting was over. Robinson left with a contract for $600 a month, a $3,500 signing bonus, and an obligation to return to the Kansas City Monarchs, whose management was very annoyed that he had taken a breather from his shortstop duties to make an unexplained visit to New York City. However, he soon left the Monarchs and returned to Pasadena. Although Rickey had pledged Robinson to silence, news of the meeting soon began circulating. Rickey called Wendell Smith of the *Pittsburgh Courier* to acknowledge that there had been a meeting but told him it was entirely about Robinson's place in the new Negro League Rickey was promoting and had nothing to do with a position with the Dodgers.[94] For his part, Robinson dismissed the reports as "just rumors."[95] Dan Burley, in the *New York Amsterdam News,* speculated that Robinson had been told to "hold himself in readiness to make a jump if the pressure got too hot on Brother Rickey." Burley was convinced, rightly, that "the 'Great Day Is A Comin' mighty soon."[96]

His conviction lay in a sense of ferment in the cause of ending organized white baseball's color line. After Ives-Quinn provided impetus to the agitation, many activists in the spring and summer of 1945 became involved in the cause. In 1945, what evidently was the first picket for integration at a major-league ballpark happened when a small group of some twenty or so protesters, led by Hubert Jullian, a one-time Garveyite, and James Pemberton, a state assemblyman from Harlem, picketed Yankee Stadium.[97] The group called for Black spectators not to attend the game, evidently with some success.[98]

The most concerted effort to attack Jim Crow in organized baseball came from the progressive left. In April 1945, East Harlem congressman Vito Marcantonio introduced a resolution calling on the federal government to investigate baseball's color line.[99] In June, the Metropolitan Interfaith and Interracial Coordinating Committee held a large public meeting on Jim Crow in baseball that featured fiery speeches by Michael Quill, the left-wing labor leader and member of the New York City Council, Nat Low of the *Daily Worker,* Joe Bostic of the *People's Voice,* and Edward Larson, regional director of the FEPC. Most speakers called for court action.[100] Out of this meeting was formed the Committee to End Jim Crow in Baseball, which was chaired by Benjamin Goldstein, a member of both the Metropolitan Interfaith Committee and the American Jewish Congress.[101]

The Committee to End Jim Crow in Baseball would have a brief, crucial, and rather glorious role in the struggle to end baseball's color line. It was formed in part because the Ives-Quinn Act gave the committee's demands a credible legal threat. However, that threat remained somewhat speculative; no one knew quite how, when, or in what way the State Commission

Against Discrimination, formed by the act, would investigate or intervene with the city's three major-league clubs. The strategy of the Committee to End Jim Crow in Baseball was less hypothetical. It was planning two rallies for 18 August, to be held at Ebbets Field and the Polo Grounds, to protest baseball's color line. The Communist Party endorsed the rallies, and Benjamin Davis was announced as one of the speakers. But the committee was endorsed across the political spectrum and drew support from far-left activists like Paul Robeson to liberal Democrats such as Eleanor Roosevelt to Tammany Democrats like William O'Dwyer (who would be elected mayor of New York City that fall) to his Republican-Liberal Party challenger Jonah Goldstein, and from O' Dwyer's eventual successor, Vincent Impellitteri.[102]

Despite the organization's mainstream support, its intentions were quite militant, and there were plans for the demonstrators to continue their protests during the games, inside the stadiums.[103] Rickey asked Dan W. Dodson, professor of sociology at New York University, to ask Mayor La Guardia to call off the demonstrations, but La Guardia probably didn't need Rickey's or Dodson's promptings to worry that the possible disturbances at the rallies might be harmful to the cause. He put pressure on the committee and its sponsors to cancel the demonstrations, and they did.[104]

One reason La Guardia could prevail on the committee to curtail their planned demonstrations was that on 11 August he had formed to the Mayor's Committee on Baseball to investigate segregation in the sport. It was a subcommittee of the Mayor's Committee on Unity, which had been formed in the aftermath of the Harlem uprising of August 1943.[105] That committee, with its classic, midcentury New York City ethnic composition—four Catholics, four Jews, four Black Americans, a representative of the AFL and of the CIO, and four others—investigated incidents of racial and religious intolerance. La Guardia thought it a model of how to address racial tensions, and he hoped groups such as this committee could help avoid the sort of murderous riots that occurred after World War I.[106] Dodson was appointed as the executive secretary.[107] The emphasis was on conciliation rather than confrontation. La Guardia told the committee not to be a "headline group," not to hold hearings in which accusations were traded; instead, it should use amelioration and conciliation to achieve its goals. Dodson believed that prejudice was largely situational and that "you don't worry about the prejudices people possess too much. You create situations which bring them together for common purposes and allow them to work out their relations to each other in the best climate you can."[108]

The subcommittee on baseball had ten members, including Rickey and Larry MacPhail, Dan Dodson, and a number of other civic leaders, of whom the best known was the famous tap dancer Bill "Bojangles" Robinson, one of its two Black members, who served alongside the Rev. John H. Johnson, who was a Harlem minister, a La Guardia supporter, and, in 1948, president of the Negro National League. The response to its formation was unenthusiastic. The *New York Amsterdam News* wondered what more needed to be studied, "since all the facts of the matter have been common knowledge" for decades. White baseball would not let Black athletes play in their games. One more committee was merely "beclouding" the issue.[109] Dodson later wrote that "the appointment of a committee is a standard technique for delaying action," and he was not surprised that many observers thought this was just what La Guardia was doing.[110]

The committee had been Branch Rickey's idea. Dodson, in 1954, wrote that Rickey asked him to come to Montague Street for a meeting and divulged his plan to sign a Black player. But he didn't want to give the Committee to End Jim Crow in Baseball any credit. So he asked Dodson to establish a committee under La Guardia's auspices that would sideline the Committee to End Jim Crow in Baseball. But Dodson's dilemma, when Rickey proposed the formation of the Mayor's Committee on Baseball, was that he didn't know if he could trust Rickey. As Dodson later wrote, "The major purpose I could see for the committee was that it was a stall for time. You could not tell its members this. Yet had Rickey not delivered—had he been bluffing, as so many contended—I would have been totally discredited."[111] After attending a meeting of the larger Committee on Unity, Rickey never attended a meeting of the smaller baseball committee.[112] (As for MacPhail, in September he made public what he had long said in private, denouncing the "pressure campaign" being fomented by "groups of political and social-minded drumbeaters" pushing for a Black player in the major leagues. As for his part, speaking of Negro League players with signed contracts, he had "no hesitancy in saying that the Yankees have no intention of signing Negro players.")[113]

On 1 July 1945, the Ives-Quinn law went into effect, and in August a member of SCAD, Elmer Carter, who was African American, met with the three owners of the New York baseball clubs. When Carter met with Rickey, the latter told him, according to his recollection, that for many years he "had planned to sign a Negro player and had been scouting Negro players for about two years and had found one infielder of great promise" and might sign him in the near future, so there was no need for Carter to intervene.[114]

If Dodson was just going through the motions with the La Guardia committee on baseball, he worked hard to prepare a serious report, the "Tentative Proposal for Report of the Mayor's Committee on Baseball," which stated that "there was never a more propitious moment than the present, when we are concluding a terrible world war to put our house in order. . . . Organized baseball owes the same responsibility to the community as does every other sport, business, or industry to make sure that this vicious poison of race segregation is eliminated."[115] La Guardia was planning to announce the results of the baseball subcommittee's investigations on his regular Sunday afternoon broadcast, on 21 October. Rickey, through Dodson, asked him to hold off for a week. The mayor's committee had undermined the Committee to End Jim Crow in Baseball, and now he would undermine the mayor's committee.

Then, on 23 October 1945, came the big reveal. Rickey—probably in an additional attempt to distance himself from the implications of the event and also perhaps to place it outside the context of the Ives-Quinn Act and the forthcoming New York City mayoral election—decided to stage the announcement in Montreal, out of the United States altogether. He was not present. The announcement revealed the signing of a Black player to a minor-league contract, an attempt to give the revolutionary news a matter-of-fact air. No one, of course, saw the announcement as routine.

If Rickey denied that politics had anything to do with the signing of Robinson, many observers argued that politics, and particularly Ives-Quinn, had everything to do with it. On 25 October, the *Daily Worker* claimed that almost all credit for the signing of Robinson went to Ives-Quinn and the massed righteous indignation about baseball's color line—Rickey was simply its passive instrument.[116] The *New York Amsterdam News* said much the same thing, arguing that "Dewey's FEPC brought an open door" and that "it is commonly agreed that without the State Commission Against Discrimination, the fight to get Negroes into the Big Leagues would only be a word-of-mouth hope, and only that."[117]

The same article quoted C. B. Powell, editor of the *New York Amsterdam News,* in praise of Ives-Quinn: "What it has done for baseball, I am sure it will do in other fields of employment. . . . It is certain that other organizations will soon follow suit."[118] This was the hope of its supporters—and the fear of its opponents. But both sides exaggerated its potential efficacy and primarily paid attention to its punitive provisions. The many who saw it as the New York State version of the FEPC imagined it as a re-creation of the FEPC at its most forceful, which directly challenged workplace discrimination. That was not quite how Irving Ives understood his eponymous law. Saying in May 1945 that the bill was intended to work primarily through "conference, conciliation, and persuasion," he expected that minority groups would approach the new law with an "attitude of helpfulness." That is, they would not make immoderate demands. He speculated that if the penalties in the new law were too frequently applied, it would be an indication that "something is fundamentally wrong" with the law.[119] And, in practice, this is how Ives-Quinn worked: by moral suasion rather than threats. Between 1945 and 1961, SCAD heard 6,616 cases. A probable cause for complaint was found in only 20 percent of them. Of these 1,365 cases, only five respondents were brought to public hearings, and two were settled before the hearings.[120] Compliance was easy. All that firms accused of workplace discrimination had to do to avoid a judgement was to post, in a prominent place where workers could see it, a poster listing the regulations of SCAD and promise to mend their ways. By 1956, former fierce critics of Ives-Quinn, such as Robert Moses, could allow that SCAD had "worked reasonably well," but only because the "left-wingers" had been kept in check.[121]

By January 1946, the law was already encountering widespread criticism and was being dismissed as a "joke" or a "dead letter" by progressive groups.[122] In defense of the law, Elmer Carter said that "this is no law you can cram down the throats of American businesses, because the whole social setup in America is based on discrimination."[123] The fact that the punitive provisions of the law were so rarely invoked was proof, Ives said in

1947, that "today the amount of discrimination in the State of New York is almost at the vanishing point."[124] The Ives-Quinn Act did not end employment discrimination in New York State. Nor did it end the color line for New York City's other two major-league teams, the Giants and the Yankees, which fielded their first Black players in 1949 and 1955, respectively. But by early 1946, its supporters could claim that "much credit for the signing of Jackie Robinson by the Brooklyn Dodgers should go to the commission [SCAD]."[125]

Despite Rickey's ambivalence about Ives-Quinn, it's clear that during the war he was increasingly concerned about the growing political salience of the "Negro Problem."[126] When it came to wartime accounts, the essential text was undoubtedly that of Swedish sociologist Gunnar Myrdal and his corps of associates: *An American Dilemma: The Negro Problem and American Democracy* which took 1,483 pages to explore its every dimension.[127] The book received a great deal of attention in the mainstream press, and Branch Rickey read it (or, more probably, at least skimmed it).[128] Like no book before it, *An American Dilemma* detailed the pervasiveness and the consequences of racial discrimination in extensive and exhaustive detail.

An American Dilemma contains multitudes. But the book was less a call for Black political activism than an extended effort to arouse and prod the white conscience. Despite its subtitle, *An American Dilemma* argued that the "Negro problem" was basically a white problem. "Although the Negro problem is a moral issue both to Negroes and to whites in America," Myrdal announced in the introduction, the book would give "*primary* attention to what goes on in the minds of white Americans" because it is "the white majority group that naturally determines the Negro's 'place.'"[129] Myrdal argued that what he famously called the "American creed"—the belief in freedom, equality, and fairness—was implicitly believed by most white Americans. They simply had to understand that, to be meaningful, this political and moral undergirding of the American experiment had to be extended to all Americans. This was Rickey's understanding. He was part of a movement, but it wasn't a political movement; rather it was a gathering of awakened white consciences responding to injustice and iniquity. He said shortly after signing Robinson that "this is a movement that cannot be stopped by anyone." Its opponents may delay it, but its victory was inevitable. He determined to sign Robinson because "I could not turn him down because he was a Negro. My conscience wouldn't let me. I knew I was right, and when a man is right, he can do no wrong."[130] The Myrdal report was generally skeptical of Black organizations and Black institutional life, arguing that on the whole, Black culture "is a distorted development, or a pathological condition, of the general American culture."[131] *An American Dilemma* has almost nothing to say about baseball, but there is little doubt that this is how Rickey viewed the Negro Leagues: as an essentially pathological caricature of major-league baseball, a racket. [132] Instead of supporting Black institutions or Black cultural values, Rickey envisioned an integration of Black individuals into America's mainstream white institutions.

Moreover, Myrdal was skeptical of interracial working-class alliances because he thought that working-class whites were highly prejudiced and likely to see Black workers as potential competition. Therefore, "the Negro's friend—or the one who is least unfriendly—is still rather the upper class of white people, the people with economic and social security who are truly a 'noncompeting group.'"[133] Rickey's strategy for getting the Dodgers to accept Robinson was premised more on white pity than interracial solidarity. When challenged by loyal Rickey associate Arthur Mann regarding his order to Robinson not to fight back, Rickey quoted from Alexander Pope's *Essay on Man:* "Yet seen too oft, familiar with her face / We first endure, then pity, then embrace." The Dodgers will first "endure Robinson, then pity him, then embrace him."[134] Something like this happened. Many of his teammates first tolerated him; then, as they saw him being name-called, beanballed, and high-spiked, and as he, following Rickey's orders, said nothing and did nothing, they felt bad for him, pitied him, and embraced him as one of their own, at least for purposes of winning ballgames.

But pity is an emotion of condescension, an emotion usually extended from a superior to an inferior. If there was one sentiment that Robinson and his fellow seekers for full citizenship abhorred, it was white pity. Integration was a fight against pity, against being viewed as objects of charity. Pity and racism were the good and bad cops of white racial attitudes, both hindering Black advancement. As Robinson's mentor, the Rev. Karl Downs wrote, what African Americans wanted from white allies was "cooperation and understanding," not their pity.[135] Pity is the opposite of solidarity. Rickey never fully overcame a vision of civil rights premised on helping hands from above rather than on agitation from below.

This meant that progress on integration would be, or should be, necessarily slow and orderly, without jerks or sudden surprises. In 1955, Rickey was the subject of an extended article in *Sports Illustrated*.[136] He told the reporter that his decision to hire Robinson had nothing to do with "liberalism": "Hell's fire! [Me] the Sunday school mollycoddle, the bluenose, the prohibitionist has been a *liberal!* No, no, no—this has nothing to do with Jackie Robinson, I contend there was no element of liberalism there."[137] But as evidence for this, he reached for his dog-eared copy of Frank Tannenbaum's *Citizen and Slave: The Negro in the Americas* (1947).[138] He read the book's final paragraph to the reporter:

> Physical proximity, slow cultural intertwining, the growth of a middle group that stands in experience and equipment between the lower and upper class; and the slow process of moral identification work their way against all seemingly absolute systems of values and prejudices. Society is essentially dynamic, and while the mills of God grind slowly, they grind exceedingly sure. Time will draw a veil over white and black in this hemisphere, and future generations will look back at the history of strife as it stands revealed in the history of the people of this New World of ours with wonder and incredulity. They will not understand the issues that the quarrel was about.

Now, Rickey might not have been a liberal, but Frank Tannenbaum, a Columbia University sociologist and historian, surely was. Some thirty years earlier, he had spent a year in prison for his support of the Industrial Workers of the World. He was still a supporter of the New Deal and a man of the liberal left.[139] The book Rickey read from initiated the "Tannenbaum thesis," which held that slavery in Latin America was less harsh than the institution in North America because in Latin American colonies and countries, enslaved persons were included as members of society. Later scholarship challenged much of this work, noting that it underplayed the realities of race and racial caste in Latin and South America, especially for persons of African descent. But Americans who read the book in the 1940s believed it offered hope that the quest for racial equality was not a fantasy and that there was a place where it actually worked.[140]

Rickey came to spring training in 1947 with a copy of Tannenbaum's book, filling it with notes. It did not work at first. As Leo Durocher, manager of the Dodgers, remembered, "Mr. Rickey had some kind of a pipedream that as soon as the [Dodgers] players recognized how much Jackie could help us, they were going to demand that he be brought up" [promoted from the Montreal Royals to the Dodgers]. What happened was the exact opposite: a petition to keep Robinson off the Dodgers was signed by five veterans. At this point Durocher offered his famous version of the Tannenbaum thesis in quashing the revolt: "I don't care if the guy is yellow or black, or has stripes like a fucking zebra, I'm the manager of this team and I say he plays. What's more, I say he can make us all rich, and if any of you cannot use the money, I will see that you are all traded."[141]

The most important implication of the Tannenbaum thesis, Rickey saw, was that full inclusion of racial minorities could, in time, smooth away and eventually erode the sharp edges of racial hostility. Segregation denied American society of the full benefits of the abilities of Black Americans, and the goal of integration was to let society benefit from everyone's talents—like major-league teams benefiting from Black ballplayers. Rickey and Tannenbaum became friends. In 1956, Rickey wrote Tannenbaum, urging him to issue an updated edition of *Slave and Citizen.* "There is no problem facing us nationally or internationally comparable to the Negro problem."[142] When Rickey discovered Tannenbaum it was a eureka moment. "This is it," he wrote, sure that time could replace force as the prime mover of racial progress.[143]

Rickey understood Tannenbaum to mean that because integration could work through the machinery and friction of social forces, there was no (or little) reason to artificially hasten things through legislation and many reasons not to. Rickey thought that reading Tannenbaum would benefit more militant advocates of integration, those who sought to act with "quick ardor in whetting" their "knive[s] for forceful surgery."[144] To him, increasing proximity between the races, their "cultural entwining," was proceeding apace, and legislation could likely hinder its progress. Yet this separation of culture and social practice from the law was a misreading of Tannenbaum and in some ways a reversal of his argument, which maintained that society was, as much as anything else, a product of its laws.

By the late 1950s, Rickey was addressing conventions of the NAACP, telling them that "it is not fair to expect one-tenth of the population to carry the burden of a great national problem, which properly belongs to the other 155,000,000." While he still advised Black Americans to use "discretion" and "patience," they also needed to "use every method short of violence" in the "struggle for civil rights."[145] However, he still believed that "you cannot make people good by making laws," but he now argued that "the right legislation creates the climate which encourages people to be good."[146] It should be noted that while Robinson did believe that change "overnight" was impossible and impractical, like many civil rights advocates, he regularly railed against counsels of "patience."[147]

In 1964, both Rickey and Robinson wanted the liberal Republican governor of New York State, Nelson Rockefeller, to be the next president of the United States. (Robinson was working for Rockefeller's campaign.) However, Sen. Barry Goldwater (R-AZ), an opponent of that year's Civil Rights Act, won the Republican nomination. In the fall, Robinson became a prominent supporter for the election of Lyndon Johnson. Rickey, more quietly, supported Goldwater and contributed to his campaign in what would be his last presidential vote. (He died the following year.)[148] Charitably, one might say Rickey found it impossible to break the voting habits of a lifetime. The civil rights revolution would lead to a searching and critical transformation of every institution in American life, not least the Democratic and Republican parties. Jackie Robinson understood this. It is not clear that Branch Rickey did, even when the Republican Party betrayed the legacy of his beloved Abraham Lincoln.

Branch Rickey had a framed sign in his office in Brooklyn. "He that will not reason is a bigot; He that cannot reason is a fool; He that dares not reason is a slave."[149] Over the course of the last half century, the word "racism" has largely supplanted "bigotry" as a term to describe the negative treatment of African Americans. "Racism" was a term Rickey rarely used. It was just coming into mainstream use in the 1940s and was more likely to be used in reference to German antisemitism than anti-Black attitudes at home.[150] (It does not appear as an index term in Myrdal's *An American Dilemma.*) As Daryl Michael Scott has noted, "Prior to the war, the terms 'integration' and 'racism' were hardly a part of the vocabulary of race relations."[151] Both were global, totalizing concepts. Racism was the disease. Integration was the cure. Bigotry, on the other hand was usually seen as something personal, subjective, irrational, and unnecessary. Racism was collective, something imbedded and inherent in the social structure. Bigotry is not an "ism." Branch Rickey, courageously, opposed the irrationality of racial bigotry. Jackie Robinson opposed the almost diabolical rationality of white supremacy.

The signing of Jackie Robinson changed not only the reality of integration but also its meanings and how it would be understood in the future. There were two models: Integration as inclusion emphasized a voluntary, top-down effort spurred by awakened consciences, the American creed, and Christian beneficence. Integration as Black citizenship was integration as a mass movement, forever pushing and pushing against white resistance, requiring something more forceful than white goodwill to enforce change, knowing that racial proximity was as least as likely to breed contempt as familiarity.

From the outset, Jackie Robinson and Branch Rickey had different understandings of the significance of what they had accomplished together. Rickey, interviewed in the *Pittsburgh Courier,* with a Black readership in mind, said in early November 1945 that "people who agree with me must be careful not to boast or brag about it. It must be a natural thing, if possible. They must not antagonize those who oppose the move." As for Ives-Quinn: "Some writers have implied that I did this because of the new anti-discrimination bill that we have in New York," which he adamantly denied, adding that he had been searching for a Black player for three years. He wished other owners would voluntarily follow his lead, adding, "I hope they won't be forced into it by legislation because that is always undesirable."[152]

Speaking to the *Baltimore Afro-American,* Robinson also remarked on the impact of the weight of public opinion on Rickey's decision: "I know that my position was obtained only through the constant pressure of my people and their press. . . . I owe it to the colored people who helped make it possible and I hope I shall always have their goodwill."[153] The constant pressure he spoke of had, among other things, contributed to the passage of the Ives-Quinn Act. If Branch Rickey had tried, as much as possible, to make the signing about a single individual, Robinson knew—and this is one of his earliest datable political statements—that his signing was not about him but about all Black America.

SIX

At Bat During the Cold War

On 10 February 1946, the Rev. Karl Downs returned to Pasadena and officiated the wedding of Jackie Robinson and Rachel Isum. Soon afterward, the newlyweds had to embark for Daytona Beach, Florida, for Robinson's first spring training with the Dodgers. They had a harrowing trip from Los Angeles. Because they were African American, they were bumped from flights and had to ride from Pensacola, Florida, to Daytona in the back of a Jim Crow bus. Arriving exhausted in Daytona, they were not allowed to stay with the other Dodgers. On 5 March, they were forced to leave the house where they were staying in Sanford, Florida, because of a threatened a riot.

But as important as the success of the "great experiment" was to Branch Rickey, he was not in Florida. On 6 March, Rickey was in Fulton, Missouri, at Westminster College—where he was a trustee—to listen to President Truman introduce the main speaker, former British Prime Minister Winston Churchill. The latter told the assembled audience that "from Stettin in the Baltic to Trieste in the Adriatic an iron curtain has descended across the Continent."[1] The beginning of Jackie Robinson's career with the Dodgers coincided with the "Iron Curtain" speech and the real beginning of the Cold War.

Two days after the Robinsons were married, on 12 February, Sgt. Isaac Woodard, a decorated veteran just discharged from the Army, was returning home to North Carolina from a base in Augusta, Georgia. The bus driver evidently didn't like something Woodard said when requesting a rest stop. He was taken off the bus at the next stop, arrested, and savagely beaten. By morning, he had been permanently blinded. The incident caused a national furor, and it enraged Truman, not previously known for his commitment to Black causes. Within a few months, he'd established the President's Committee on Civil Rights, and this marks the real beginning of his commitment to civil rights. In December 1947, the committee's report, "To Secure These Rights," called for a vigorous governmental civil rights agenda. In July 1948, Truman issued an executive order desegregating the military. In June 1947, the United Negro and Allied Veterans of America (UNAVA) awarded its initial set of "Freedom Awards." Jackie Robinson was one recipient. Isaac Woodard was another, honored for "his refusal to submit to the vicious deeply rooted southern policy of intimidation."[2]

We do not have a very good sense of Jackie Robinson's politics before his signing with the Dodgers, in part because outside of his immediate circle of friends and family, few bothered to record his opinions. (His politics, like Karl Downs, were presumably liberal and probably leaned Democratic.) After his signing, everybody cared about his politics, and every other every aspect of his life. In late 1945, he said: "I feel that if I flop, or conduct myself badly—on or off the field—then I'll set this advancement back a hundred years."[3] He had to play good baseball; he also knew that his behavior, as ballplayer and otherwise, would be subject to the strictest scrutiny, and he knew that this extended to his politics. And he knew that, like it or not, he had become a spokesperson for Black America.

After Robinson's sterling 1946 season with the Montreal Royals, the big question was whether he would make his major-league debut with the Dodgers the following spring. This was the topic of discussion in a thousand Black barbershops, including the one where the distinguished Black sociologist Horace Cayton went for a haircut. He later wrote about his conversation with his barber. His barber asked what would be key to Robinson's elevation to the Dodgers. His play during spring training? The attitudes of his white teammates? Branch Rickey? Happy Chandler? None of those, the barber said. "It all depends on Joe." "Joe who?" asked Cayton. "Joe Stalin." The barber explained: "It's very simple, friend. As long as Russia is a threat to the United States, these white people are not going to push us around too bad. I suspect they might give us a few breaks, like letting us play in the big leagues. But if Russia is not a threat, then the United States will revert to being the racist country it always has been." In his own voice, Cayton concluded: "I'm not trying to say that the Russians will be the saviors of the Negro race, or that Communism is good or bad. . . . But I think it is important to realize how the Negro is conceiving of his struggle in terms of this global struggle, and how my barber has grasped some of their implications for himself, the Negro people in general—and let's not leave this out—for Jackie Robinson."[4]

Cayton's barber was correct. Joe Stalin would play an important role in Jackie Robinson's baseball career. During World War II, the embarrassment of Jim Crow made a mockery of America's professions that it was fighting a war for democracy. There was concern about the "Negro Problem" and a new militancy among African Americans. Would a confrontation with the Soviet Union enhance this process? Or would African Americans be blamed, as usual, for all the country's ills, foreign and domestic? Jackie Robinson's career with the Dodgers began with the intensification of both the Cold War and the struggle for civil rights.[5]

Robinson was called up to the Dodgers. On 15 April 1947, amid a torrent of publicity, Robinson made his major-league debut at Ebbets Field. One article on the game quoted an anonymous Dodgers player as saying it felt strange having a Black teammate, but he wasn't opposed to it: "I'm for him if he could win games. That's the only test I ask." The reporter added, "That seems to be the general opinion."[6] That summer, Langston Hughes expressed the feelings of millions African Americans: "Maybe if the Dodgers win the pennant, a hundred years from now history will still be grinning." The Dodgers won the pennant. Robinson was named Rookie of the Year by the *Sporting News,* diehard defenders of segregated baseball. Having no alternative, the magazine acknowledged that things had changed and announced that the "sociological experiment" had nothing to do with the magazine's decision; Robinson had been "rated and examine solely . . . on the basis of his hitting, his running, his defensive play."[7]

Let us fast-forward. If the goal was to see Jackie Robinson as a line in a box score, it worked, up to a point. His teammates, upset by his treatment at the hands of his racist tormentors and buoyed by his on-field prowess, accepted him as one of theirs. The famous story of Dodgers shortstop Pee Wee Reese putting his arm around Robinson as a gesture of solidarity against taunting from the stands in a game in Cincinnati appears to be apocryphal, but there seems little doubt that Robinson was accepted as a teammate by most players, if not as a social equal.[8] Racial tension in the Dodgers locker room abated, but never ended. Neither did racist "bench-jockeying."[9] Nor did slights from hotels, restaurants, and other public accommodations. This was very painful for Robinson, but he tried to rise above it and generally did not want to give his tormentors the satisfaction of seeing his pain. In 1949, he was voted the National League's Most Valuable Player and probably should have won it again in 1951. Each year from 1949 through 1953, he finished either first or second in the National League in the then-nonexistent statistic of Wins Above Replacement. By 1949, the Robinson rules were relaxed by Rickey, and Robinson became more aggressive in defending himself against taunts and challenging miscarriages of umpiring. Robinson soon developed a reputation as an aggressive umpire castigator, always ready to spout off on behalf his teammates. He was variously called by sportswriters "combative," "emotional," a "showboat," along with aspersions that were more political—an "agitator," a "rabble rouser" on a "soap box," someone who "should be a player, not a crusader."[10] But even when Robinson's crusades were ostensively confined to on-field matters, he was seen as both an agitator and someone who—following a well-known stereotype—was just another hot-headed Black man who couldn't control his emotions.

Jackie Robinson's main occupation was that of ballplayer, and like many other ballplayers, he could have merely stuck to his craft, saying little, doing the baseball equivalent of what a Fox News host infamously told basketball great LeBron James to do: "Shut up and dribble."[11] But this was not Jackie Robinson's way. He would not remain quiet, either on matters directly relating to baseball or those that did not. And he had no hesitation in calling out Black teammates, notably Roy Campanella, or other Black stars, such as Willie Mays, whom he felt did not display sufficient outrage at the treatment of Black Americans.[12] Robinson was an example of how white America wanted Black Americans to act: humbly grateful for opportunities offered to them, prime examples of what Blacks could achieve in white America if they played by the rules. At the same time, he was an example of what white America feared Black Americans were really like: outspoken and angry. Let us examine two instances of his anger and outspokenness, in reverse order.

On 2 June 1954, Jackie Robinson played one of the 1,382 games he would play for the Brooklyn Dodgers between 1947 and 1956. For Robinson, it was a day—and a game—to forget. Nonetheless, 2 June 1954 was important to Robinson, less because of its uniqueness but for its representativeness, another slog, and another day in which his actions and their motivations were scrutinized to exhaustion by the pop psychologists of the press box. It was another day on which he was a screen onto which white fears were projected. On that day, the Dodgers were pitted against the Milwaukee Braves. It was only the second year since the Braves had moved from Boston, but Milwaukee, as Robinson would write in 1955, was the National League city in which he received his "worst booings."[13]

In the top of the fifth inning the score was Braves 5, Dodgers 2, in Milwaukee County Stadium. It had been raining on and off since the beginning of the game, so few on either side thought the game would go the regulation nine innings. Indeed, the two teams probably shouldn't have bothered to play the game on that soggy night in Milwaukee. In the bottom of the fourth inning, a Milwaukee batter took first base on what the Dodgers, and most observers, agreed was only ball three, not ball four. This loaded the bases, and the Dodgers, in high dudgeon in the dugout, threw towels onto the field in a futile protest. Their anger increased when the next batter, Eddie Matthews, hit a grand slam home run.[14]

The Dodgers and Robinson were still angry when Robinson was first at bat in the fifth inning, and he told the umpire that he was responsible for "the worst call I ever saw." The umpire, Lee Ballafant, told Robinson to "get in there and hit or I'll throw you out." To which Robinson replied, "You might as well throw me out, for you've messed up everything, anyway."[15] Whether or not the reported word "messed" was a euphemism for something stronger, the umpire obliged Robinson, and he was tossed. At this point, he flipped his bat in the general direction of the visitors' dugout, but because of the wet conditions, the bat slipped from his hands, slid across the top of the dugout, and grazed an usher before hitting two fans, Mr. and Mrs. Peter Wolinsky. The bat gave Mrs. Wolinsky a serious bump on the head. Robinson gestured in apology to the victims of his errant bat immediately afterward and apologized to the lady when interviewed later. The Dodgers, perhaps inspired by Robinson's ejection, rallied for five runs in the top of the fifth, all unearned, winning the rain-shortened game, 7–6. According to reports, fans sitting in the stands near where Robinson's bat hit the Wolinskys "were incensed and many of them made threatening gestures" and "broke for the steps in the direction of the field." Authorities were sufficiently worried that a phalanx of police officers accompanied Robinson and the other Dodgers to their bus.[16] There are no indications in the press reports, or in later accounts by Robinson and others, of any overt racial hostilities in the episode or that the angry fans yelled racial slurs, but there clearly were fears that Robinson was being singled out for violent retribution.[17]

Robinson called Mrs. Wolinsky the following morning, but the Wolinskys were unappeased, claiming the incident had caused "severe nervous shock." They sued Robinson for $40,000, an amount roughly equal to his 1954 salary. The suit was dismissed when it was established that Robinson had already settled with the Wolinskys for $300 apiece, though Robinson later stated, "No one sued me, though it was threatened."[18] "I'm sure everyone would agree—except my enemies—that the bat throwing was an accident."[19] However, Robinson regretted that the incident "has made enemies for me."[20] He was also fined $50 by the National League.[21] All in all, for Jackie Robinson, 2 June 1954 was a day to forget.[22]

Most observers agreed that Robinson had not deliberately thrown the bat into the stands, but many thought that it was no accident that Robinson's recklessness and lack of emotional control had once again sparked a regrettable on-field incident. For famed *New York Herald-Tribune* sportswriter Red Smith, Robinson had been "unseemly," put on "a shabby show," and had made "a travesty of the sport." He accused National League officials of "temporizing" in their mild punishment of Robinson.[23] The Black press, with a mix of admiration and condemnation, reported on what they described as Robinson's "fit of rage," remarking that Brooklyn's "fiery star" was "embroiled again" in the sort of controversy that continually dogged him, on and off the diamond.[24] It's hard not to agree with the sportswriter for the *Norfolk Journal and Guide,* who wrote that this was a case of Robinson "being criticized no matter what direction he took in trying to work out the issues involved" in this and other controversies.[25] Some articles on the errant bat incident mentioned earlier incidents of Robinson's umpire baiting, notably a running battle with umpire Frank Dascoli. In separate incidents in 1951 and 1952, Dascoli said Robinson had called him a "dago" and a "wop."[26] Robinson denied the accusations, and his teammates backed him up, but the impression continued that Robinson was a hair-trigger taker of umbrage. For his part, he did tend to harbor the suspicion that the umpires, all of whom of course were white, allowed their biases to manipulate baseball's rules to his detriment.[27] Some sportswriters remembered another controversy: In the winter of 1952, Robinson had answered in the affirmative when asked if the Yankees, still an all-white club, were prejudiced against Blacks and Black ballplayers, thereby creating a minor furor. (George Weiss, general manager of the Yankees, professed to be "shocked," by Robinson's comments, adding that "when a Negro comes along who can play good enough ball to win a place on the Yankees we will be glad to have him," but the organization would not hire a Black ballplayer "just for exploitation." Note: the Yankees had passed on signing Willie Mays.)[28] The commissioner of baseball, Ford Frick, asked Robinson to avoid the issue in the future.[29]

No one was more critical of Robinson than Bill Keefe, sportswriter for the *New Orleans Times-Picayune,* who said out loud what others had only implied: that Robinson had been "pampered and humored by the officials of organized baseball."[30] Later, Keefe blamed Robinson's civil rights militancy for the passage of a new Louisiana bill that banned interracial sports in that state (a ban that Keefe had approved of). Keefe said of Robinson that he was a "persistently insolent and antagonistic trouble-making Negro" and—like other self-appointed Southern white guardians of African American interests—deemed Robinson an "enemy of his race."[31] In response, Robinson wrote him a letter in which he rejected the charge of being insolent, but he acknowledged he hadn't been subservient and wondered if Keefe would call white ballplayers like Ted Williams, notorious for his tangles with the press, insolent, or was it that he was "insolent for a Negro (who has the courage enough to speak against injustices such as yours and people like you)." Closing the letter, Robinson wrote, "I am happy for you, that you were born white. It would have been extremely difficult for you had it been otherwise."[32]

The case of Jackie Robinson's errant bat was, in the end, a one-week story, a minor baseball rhubarb. Sportswriters were soon opining on more current and pressing matters. And in any event, on and around 2 June 1954, if you turned from the sports pages to the front pages of your newspaper, there was much more important news to read about than a bat flung in Milwaukee. And Jackie Robinson was as interested in the front pages as the sports pages.

In early June 1954, the most talked-about person in the country was US Senator Joseph McCarthy (R-WI), who was then at the apex of his pernicious influence. In early June, his hearings into alleged communist subversion in the US Army reached their fevered climax. On 2 June, the twenty-fifth day of the Army-McCarthy hearings, McCarthy alleged communist infiltration of the CIA and of the military's nuclear weapon facilities. The lead story in the *New York Times* on the morning of 2 June was that the Atomic Energy Commission had announced its decision to strip the nuclear scientist J. Robert Oppenheimer of his security clearance. During its first year and half, Eisenhower's Department of Justice had added numerous organizations to its list of subversive groups and had initiated deportation proceedings against communist-affiliated noncitizens. A 2 June press release closed by promising the American people that the "constant surveillance of Communists in this country is a twenty-four-hour, seven-days-a-week, fifty-two-weeks-a- year job" and assuring them that the Eisenhower administration was up to the task.[33]

But Eisenhower wished to pursue his anti-communism without the constant irritant of McCarthy. On 9 June 1954, lawyer Joseph Welch decried McCarthy by exclaiming: "You have done enough. Have you no sense of decency?" The incident provided McCarthy's critics with an opening.[34] These hearings marked the effective end of his political dominance as America's self-appointed anti-communist inquisitor. It began his precipitous tumble, which soon reduced him to a self-pitying drunkard. He died disgraced at the age of forty-eight. But if McCarthy soon exited from prominence, his insidious eponym, McCarthyism, would outlive him, and hard-edged anti-communism would remain a preoccupation of American political life for years to come.

June 1954 also saw an intensification of the United States' undeclared war against the Soviet Union and communism abroad. On 3 June 1954, the *New York Times* reported on the early stages of a coup d'etat against the progressive Guatemalan government of Jacobo Árbenz. It was a poorly kept secret that the coup was engineered by the CIA. It would be successful. For decades afterward, Guatemalans would suffer from its consequences, paying the toll of repression and genocide.[35] Early June was also several weeks after the climactic defeat of French forces in Vietnam at the battle of Dien Bien Phu on 7 May. As France was preparing to withdraw its army, the *New York Times* noted on 3 June that American military advisors would probably in the near future begin training the local, non-communist military forces. "Responsible United States observers here feel," the *Times* reported, "that Indochina is by no means lost, but that haste must be made to build up the Vietnamese National Army. They hold this is a vital necessity."[36]

If the McCarthy hearings were the biggest national story in the spring and early summer of 1954, two weeks and two days before 2 June, on 17 May 1954, McCarthy was temporarily toppled from the lead story by the epochal decision of the US Supreme Court in the case of *Brown v. Board of Education of Topeka, Kansas,* in which the court ruled unanimously that school segregation was unconstitutional. Alongside Vietnam, the role of the federal government in advancing the rights of Black Americans would dominate American politics for the next two decades. If the *Brown/Briggs* decision did nothing else, it moved the question of Black citizenship to the center of American politics. The decision was certainly still a live issue on 2 June 1954. The *Times* quoted an Arkansas state representative as saying, "I am wondering if the Supreme Court Justices are not communist-infiltrated and maybe Senator Joseph R. McCarthy should investigate the Supreme Court."[37] The governor of South Carolina, James Byrnes, himself a former US Supreme Court justice, announced that he would withstand the "threats" of the NAACP, and, if forced, he would recommend closing the state's public schools rather than open all-white schools to Black children.[38]

Another event in May and June 1954, this one involving the Dodgers, illustrated some of the integration challenges ahead. Until that season, when playing in St. Louis, the white Dodgers would stay at the Chase Hotel, while the Black players stayed at the Adams Hotel. However, in 1954, the Chase offered to house the Black players, though they would remain barred from the dining room and other hotel services. Of the six African Americans on the Dodgers team, including Roy Campanella, Don Newcombe, and Joe Black, only Robinson opted to stay at the Chase, the others preferring the Adams. Campanella stated, "They [the Chase] didn't want us for seven years. So, as far as I am concerned, they can make it forever." Robinson believed that even if the conditions at the Chase were humiliating, only by staying at white hotels like the Chase could Black Americans effect future change. The dispute, writes Neil Lanctot, "destroyed whatever little remained" of the friendship between Robinson and Campanella; both men resented being played against one another. "The antis still hate Robinson because he refuses to 'stay in his place,'" wrote Joe Bostic in the *Amsterdam News*. "And the complement to this is the exaggerated fawning over Roy Campanella as the fellow everyone loves." The Black press took sides in a situation in which complete consistency was very difficult. Some wrote that Robinson had "gotten awful swell headed lately." Others noted that Robinson's role leading the vanguard challenging segregation was "difficult, thankless." Personal animosities aside, the Chase Hotel episode raised serious questions about the nature and pace of integration and about how the recent US Supreme Court decision would unfold.[39]

What did Robinson think of the events of June 1954? Carl Prince has written that "Robinson was anticommunist and he did not like [CBS television broadcaster Edward R.] Murrow's television denunciation of McCarthy," but Prince provides no evidence and undermines this claim with an anecdote that in 1952, despite the discomfiture of other Dodgers, Robinson welcomed Murrow to the Dodgers' clubhouse. [40] Robinson believed that McCarthy's demagoguery had made it all too easy to label civil rights activists as communists, a label he had vociferously protested. In 1952, he was one of many celebrities who recorded a brief "This I Believe" segment for Murrow's radio show, telling Murrow's audience about the complexities of his patriotism and adding that the United States was, for all its imperfections, a genuinely "free society." Implicit was the Cold War comparison to the unfree Soviet Union.[41]

But if Robinson thought McCarthyism went too far, he probably came to think that the *Brown/Briggs* decision didn't go far enough or fast enough. He wasn't expecting miracles. A few months before the decision was handed down, Robinson had been queried about the case. He told the *Los Angeles Times* in February 1954 that "anything done overnight is dangerous, but if you do it slowly, seeing all along what is happening, that is the type of foundation that lasts." While he allowed that "integration in schools in the South must be taken a step at a time," he also added that "there should be a goal which makes 1956 better than 1954 and 1958 better than 1956. Then, maybe in 1960 the schools would be fully integrated."[42] But by 1960 he would be incensed at white officials calling for African Americans to, again, exhibit more patience.

On both issues, anti-communism and integration, Robinson's position was sophisticated and nuanced. But in the end, the incident of the thrown bat on 2 June 1954 represented just one more day on the field when Jackie Robinson, America's racial oracle, had his every action analyzed and scrutinized as an augury for America's racial future. What did Jackie Robinson's anger portend for America's racial future? Or, more simply, "What do they want?"

By the end of his career, Robinson was widely seen in the sports press as someone suffering from "foot-in-mouth disease," someone who might be "one of baseball's finest competitors, but would never rank as one of baseball's outstanding diplomats," an "outspoken man who finds it congenitally impossible not to speak his mind." He found *too much* to be outspoken about, in the words of *New York Times* sportswriter Arthur Daley.[43] Frankie Frisch, a baseball Hall of Famer who was also famed for his flashes of on-field temper during his playing days, was asked, after Robinson's retirement, about his chances of joining him in Cooperstown. With kindred superciliousness, Frisch stated that while he "thought that Robinson always popped off a bit too much," he allowed that this shouldn't bar him from the Hall. Robinson wrote in his autobiography that "as long as I appeared to ignore insult and injury, I was a martyred hero," but the "minute I started to sound off—I became a swellhead, a wise guy, an 'uppity nigger.'"[44]

Perhaps the most basic contradiction in our understanding of Jackie Robinson is that he's remembered both as a man who kept silent and a man who couldn't shut up. The image of Robinson as the suffering servant of integration began almost immediately with his signing by Rickey, and it's this image that introduced him to the American public. It's the image that has endured—a man who had enough guts not to fight back. In September of his rookie season, he was the subject of a cover story in *Time* magazine, where he was praised for following Joe Louis's admonition "not to get cocky" and for mastering the art of "turning the other cheek."[45] This became the dominant image of Robinson: By having enough guts not to fight back, not to protest, he won his fight. Half a century later, in 1997, a group of third-graders in a class in Brooklyn, no doubt repeating what they had been taught, told a reporter for the *New York Times* that Robinson's greatest achievement was that "when others fought back, he held his temper." Or, as another student put it, "Jackie Robinson was very determined not to talk back." In this regard, the student promised to try to do better to avoid getting into fights with his little brother.[46] This is, no doubt, good advice for third-graders, but less so as a strategy for confronting systemic racial inequalities. Robinson was both an example of how white America wanted Black Americans to act (humbly grateful for opportunities offered to them) and an example of what white America feared Black Americans were really like, even if (or perhaps especially if) they projected a veneer of politeness.

However Robinson managed his anger, he always did so in the context of what it meant to be an American—which meant, in the 1950s, navigating the two main issues of the day: the Cold War and the civil rights movement, which for Robinson were always connected.[47] Was Robinson getting angry at incompetent umpiring or the systematic subordination of an entire race of people? Was he standing up for his rights, like any proud American, or was he challenging the American way of life, like an ungrateful malcontent? But if on 2 June 1954, the broader political implications of umpire bating were implicit, on 18 July 1949, they'd been front and center.

There is little indication that during World War II and its immediate aftermath, Jackie Robinson had any particular animus toward communism or organizations with communist ties. He no doubt learned much of his politics from his mentor, Karl Downs. *Meet the Negro,* Downs's 1943 book, certainly included persons on the progressive left, some of whom were close to the Communist Party, such as Hugh Mulzac, Adam Clayton Powell Jr., and Paul Robeson (the latter hailed by Downs as "the People's Champion"), and some who'd broken with the communists, such as A. Philip Randolph and Richard Wright, alongside many entertainers and celebrities who were not known for their political involvements.[48] The book neither celebrated nor denigrated the communist left. One lesson Robinson undoubtedly learned from Downs was political sophistication. If he chose to acknowledge or work with communists or organizations close to the Communist Party, he did so knowingly, not blindly or naively.

After signing with the Dodgers, Robinson had numerous connections with left-of-center persons or organizations close to the Communist Party. Several weeks thereafter, according to Benjamin Davis—member of the New York City Council, prominent Communist Party member, and an ardent advocate for ending baseball's color line—there was a reception for Robinson. In his autobiography, Davis notes that he had attended the reception, and so had Robeson. Robinson "commended [Robeson] for his contributions to the struggle." Robinson also spoke "a few kind words [about Davis's] city council resolution, [which] he had heard about on the West Coast."

In November 1946, the International Workers Order, a fraternal and cultural organization close to the Communist Party, announced the opening of an interracial Solidarity Center in Harlem, with Robinson listed as a member of the advisory board.[49] The same month, American Youth For Democracy, another organization close to the Communist Party, announced awards to be given to, among others, former Vice President Henry Wallace and to Robinson.[50] Robinson was also, from 1946 through at least February 1948, on the advisory board of the United Negro and Allied Veterans of America (UNAVA), a sort of left-progressive alternative to the American Legion.[51] He praised the organization in 1946, saying that it was addressing "the burning problem of housing, discrimination in employment, education, and on the job training facing Negro veterans [who] demand an immediate solution."[52] UNAVA was placed on the list of subversive organizations by the US attorney general in December 1947.[53] UNAVA had often sponsored concerts by Paul Robeson and had defended him against red-baiting accusations.[54]

Jackie Robinson and Paul Robeson had often observed one another's remarkable careers. They had much in common, starting with the athletic skills that had first brought them to national attention—both had starred in college football at predominantly white universities. Robeson, 6 feet, 2 inches tall and of a striking athletic build, was in 1919 an All-American tight end at Rutgers University. In 1941, the *Pittsburgh Courier* published an "all-time, All-American Colored Stars from white universities" list. Both men, their names following one another in alphabetical order, made the first team; Robeson was named tight end and Robinson was the team's quarterback.[55] If Robinson was perhaps twentieth-century America's most versatile athlete, Robeson was perhaps twentieth-century America's most versatile American, period. Both men are better known for their achievements off the gridiron. For Robinson it was baseball. Robeson possessed a commanding physical presence and a magnificent bass-baritone speaking and singing voice and made his mark as a singer and an actor. They also felt that their talents as athletes or entertainers were not an end in themselves but gave them a platform to speak about the pressing political issues of the day. In the words of Bill Mardo, a sportswriter for the *Daily Worker,* "both men—from the git-go—couldn't tolerate second-class citizenship."[56] If there was one model for Robinson's eventual chosen path as an athlete and former athlete using his celebrity as a platform for outspoken activism, it was probably Paul Robeson.

By the late 1930s, Robeson became identified with the culture and politics of the Popular Front. He celebrated not only African American culture—there has been no finer singer of the concert versions of classic Negro spirituals—but also celebrated music and folk songs from around the world. He then lent his good name to a plethora of good causes, including the integration of baseball.[57] Robeson was never a member of the Communist Party, but there is no question that he was close to many party members and often supported its positions.

Robeson was at the peak of his popularity in the early 1940s. He was starring on Broadway in the title role of *Othello.* His concert repertoire included the patriotic cantata "Ballad for Americans," of Popular Front origins, which was admired across the political spectrum. He also recorded songs opposing war during the period between the Hitler-Stalin pact and the Nazi invasion of the Soviet Union. Afterward, he sang songs supporting the Soviet war effort, including a rousing rendition of the Soviet national anthem—singing, in sonorous tones, in praise of Stalin, while remaining outspoken in his support of civil rights.[58] But when Commissioner Landis invited him to speak to baseball executives in December 1943, some in the Black press wondered if Landis had asked Robeson to speak precisely because of his communist ties—that is, did Landis seek to tar the cause of desegregating baseball by associating it with Robeson—though there is no evidence of this.[59] Rickey, too, wondered why Landis had invited someone with communist ties to address the meeting.[60]

As for Rickey, he had always been fiercely anti-communist. Although there was a general "honeymoon" toward the Soviet Union in the United States when both countries found themselves in all-out war against the Nazis, by no means was everyone happy with this alliance, especially conservative Republicans. Rickey recognized its necessity, but no more. Branch Rickey was a regular subscriber to anti-communist magazines like *Counterattack,* the sort of bottom-feeding journal that peddled lists of supposed communists, sympathizers, and "fellow travelers" with the intention of blacklisting them and making their lives difficult. Rickey was perhaps especially sensitive on this question, because, unlike most fervent anti-communists, he had done something that the Communist Party approved of and had strongly supported.[61] In early 1948, he told a crowd at Wilberforce University, an HCBU, "There is a Communistic effort to get credit for 'forcing' us to sign Robinson. But I warn you against it."[62]

In 1945, Paul Robeson was at the apex of his fame and popularity. On 18 October 1945, he was awarded the NAACP's Spingarn Medal, seen as the most prestigious honor for a Black American. A week later, on 23 October 1945, Robeson was in Montreal, appearing in a sold-out concert the same day the Montreal Royals held their press conference announcing the signing of Jackie Robinson. After his Montreal concert, a bevy of reporters clustered backstage to get Robeson's opinion of the news. Robeson declared that "a bridgehead has been made." He was convinced, based on the many conversations he'd held with Americans over the years, that they would welcome this step. "This is wonderful news. I am happy that at least one team has had the courage to break down an anti-democratic notion."[63]

By 1949, things were very different. The center-left coalition of communists and non-communists that had successfully pushed for the end of baseball's color line and had supported Robinson was in tatters. The 1948 presidential campaign of former Vice President Henry Wallace on the Progressive Party ticket delivered the coup de grace. The Progressive Party opposed the growing intensity of the Cold War, and this forced left-liberal progressives to choose between Wallace and Truman. The Democratic Party under Truman's leadership, compared to FDR's, was both more stridently anti-communist and more forthcoming on Black civil rights, having committed itself to an expansive civil rights program and desegregated the military. In the aftermath of the Wallace campaign, several of the CIO unions that had advocated for ending baseball's color line would be expelled from the CIO for their communist ties. As for Benjamin Davis, a few days after Robinson and the Dodgers played in the 1949 World Series, he and several other national leaders of the Communist Party were convicted for violating the Smith Act for their supposed crime of advocating for the violent overthrow of the government. Appeals proved fruitless, and Davis would eventually spend over four years in federal prison.

Paul Robeson's career and reputation were in a bad way, as well. In early 1949, Robeson undertook a concert tour of Europe in lieu of eighty-five canceled concert dates in the United States.[64] (In 1950, to prevent Robeson from finding friendlier venues for his talents [and making him an example for other leftists], the State Department revoked his passport. It was not restored for eight years.)

In April 1949, Robeson, was in Paris for a meeting of the Soviet-sponsored World Committee for the Partisans of Peace. In his address, he said that the wealth of America had been built "on the backs of white workers from Europe . . . and on the backs of millions of blacks. . . . And we will not put up with any hysterical raving that urges us to make war on anyone. We shall not make war on the Soviet Union."[65] However, an AP story about the event recast his remarks, and its version became the text that was the basis of the subsequent controversy: "We denounce the policy of the United

States government, which is similar to that of Hitler and Goebbels. . . . It is unthinkable that American Negroes would go to war on behalf of those who have oppressed us for generations against a country that in one generation has raised our people to the full dignity of mankind."[66] Robeson was widely denounced for the AP's incendiary version of his speech. Former friends and associates turned on him: Adam Clayton Powell Jr., who now repented his onetime close association with the Communist Party; Mary McLeod Bethune; and Oscar Hammerstein II, who suggested that Robeson was no longer an appropriate singer for Hammerstein's lyrics to "Ol' Man River."[67] Connecticut officials wanted to ban Robeson from returning to the state where he had his home.[68]

The House Un-American Activities Committees (HUAC) sent a letter (less than a subpoena, more than a suggestion) to Jackie Robinson on 9 July 1949 asking him, as one of a number of African American notables, to testify before the committee and condemn Robeson. Branch Rickey very much wanted Robinson to testify. Apparently, HUAC had been interested in having Robinson speak since 1947.[69] There was uneasiness among the Dodgers staff as to whether it was a good idea for Robinson to appear, but Rickey and Arthur Mann were strongly in favor, and their views prevailed.[70]

Robinson at first seems to have been ambivalent about testifying. Perhaps he worried that he would be subpoenaed if he declined, and if he didn't testify, he would be labeled a communist sympathizer. As he acknowledged in his testimony, many people, many of whom were not associated with the communist left, had urged him not to testify, but he felt obliged to do so anyway, out of a "sense of responsibility."[71] Why did he testify? He probably thought, as did many others, that the cause of Black citizenship, circa 1949, was enough of an uphill struggle without being further weighted down by an association with communism. Or perhaps it was sheer cussedness. He felt pressured not to testify by the NAACP—an organization not known for its pro-communist sympathies. "That made me decide to go ahead and do it."[72] And though Rickey no doubt really wanted him to testify, if Robinson had strongly objected, Rickey probably would have let it pass. In the end, though, it was Robinson's decision.

A draft version of his testimony, prepared by Harold Roettger of the

Dodgers staff, offers evidence that he wasn't just doing Rickey's bidding. Robinson, for good reason, rejected Roettger's draft. It didn't say what Robinson wanted to say, and it spent too much time making unwarranted claims about Black progress since 1865: "Today my people cannot be horsewhipped. They cannot be victimized by cruel and unusual punishment. Nor can I be deprived of life, liberty, or property without due process of law." It reduced current racial problems to a breezy, "well, nobody's perfect" exculpation: "Of course we still have some provincialism, a flash of sectionalism now and then, a lynching party or two."[73] Instead, Robinson prepared his testimony with Lester Granger, the executive director of the National Urban League.[74]

The week before Robinson's testimony, there had been a parade of witnesses before the HUAC attacking Robeson. Some statements were unhinged, accusing him of betraying his race, of wanting to be the "Black Stalin" with delusions of grandeur, the front man for "a deliberate Communist conspiracy to inflame religious and racial minorities" as a prelude to an attempt at a Leninist-Stalinist revolution. Some, like Lester Granger himself, testified less hysterically, telling the committee that the "the prescription" for blocking communism was "less worry about Robeson and more concern for democracy."[75]

Robinson's testimony on 18 July was similar to Granger's. Unlike the speech provided him by the Dodgers, Robinson did not make great claims about the speed of Black progress and instead spoke of its slowness. He remarked that two years after his debut, only seven Black athletes played in the major leagues, clustered on three teams. He wanted to make it clear that "every Negro worth his salt is going to reject any kind of slurs and discrimination, and is going to use every bit of intelligence . . . to stop it. This has absolutely nothing to do with what the Communists may or may not be trying to do." He told the committee that "white people must realize that the more a Negro hates Communism because it opposes democracy, the more he is going to hate the other influences that kill off democracy in this country—and that goes for racial discrimination in the Army, segregation on trains and buses, and job discrimination."[76] He also insisted that condemning communism did not mean he was also condemning legitimate agitation for African American civil rights, telling the committee that if a communist "denounces injustice in the courts, police brutality, and lynching," it is no less true because a communist says it.[77]

Robinson did not mention Robeson until the eighteenth paragraph of his statement; he called Robeson's statements in Paris "silly"—which, as invective goes, is a lot milder than "subversive" or "traitorous." He didn't really denounce Robeson, didn't call him a communist, didn't hyperventilate on communist conspiracies. He said Robeson had the right to his opinion. He mentioned that there were, of course, Black pacifists, who—like all pacifists—would not take up arms for their country. He even challenged the premise of the hearings when he said that to ask whether Black Americans were loyal to America was to make this a question for debate, whatever the answer. He stated that his testimony wasn't "said as any defense of the Negro's loyalty, because any loyalty that needs defense can't amount to much in the long run."[78]

Robinson's statement before HUAC was widely praised in the white press. The *New York Times,* mixing its baseball metaphors, editorialized the next day that Robinson had pitched a shutout and had made "four hits and no errors."[79] He was the recipient of awards, including from the Catholic War Veterans at a Dodgers game, though he insisted on receiving the award under the stands.[80] His appearance before the committee received more mixed reviews in the Black press. Some hailed his statement as reaching "the heights of moral grandeur."[81] The *Baltimore Afro-American* editorialized that what Robeson was really saying in Paris was that white America cannot demand Black loyalty when there are "millions of colored people in the South who can't vote, who are terrorized by mobs at the least provocation, and cannot get a decent job or a decent education."[82] Robeson himself, not needing another enemy, said that Robinson "had done more for his race than any colored man of modern times," but added that any African American who voluntarily testified before HUAC was choosing the wrong venue. He hoped the two of them would soon have the opportunity to meet and talk.[83] W. E. B. Du Bois was less charitable, grumbling in August 1949 that "when we want to study race relations in our own borders we summon a baseball player."[84]

The atmosphere of the Cold War did not appreciate nuance. Most of the media was not interested in Robinson's views on civil rights, only in the question of whether he attacked Paul Robeson, which he did. And whatever one makes of Robeson's views on the Soviet Union, Robinson was attacking a great champion of Black civil rights; he did so when Robeson was being subjected to governmental persecution; and he spoke before a committee that was notorious for its reactionary anti-communism and racism. Roy Campanella's son claimed that his father was also called to testify but turned down the committee. Whether this happened is unclear, but if it did, Robinson would have been well-advised to have done the same.[85]

The year 1949 was open season on Paul Robeson, a reality highlighted on 27 August, when he was the center of attention at a riot instigated by assorted anti-communists and Klansmen in Peekskill, New York, which prevented him from keeping a singing engagement in that town that was a fund raiser for left-wing causes, an event that was widely called the "Robeson riot."[86] According to sportswriter Bill Mardo in an account in the *Daily Worker,* he went up to Robinson the next day and showed him an account of the Peekskill incident. Robinson was angry, and he was quoted as stating "Paul Robeson should have the right to sing, speak, or do anything he wants to," that "in America you're allowed to be anything you want," and since being a communist was not outlawed, "if Mr. Robeson wants to believe in Communism, that's his right. I prefer not to."[87] Despite his appearance before HUAC, Robinson continued to patronize locations identified with left-wing causes. Several days after his testimony, the Jackie Robinson Fund, a charity trying to raise money for polio care, held a fundraiser at Cafe Society, a famed nightclub in Greenwich Village, one of the first nightclubs in New York City with an interracial seating policy. It is best remembered as the club where Billie Holiday introduced the antilynching classic "Strange Fruit" in 1939. By 1949, red-baiting had led to bad publicity and diminished attendance, and Cafe Society would soon close its doors permanently. Jackie Robinson presumably had allowed his name to be used and had agreed to the venue. That fall, the Jackie Robinson Fund held another fundraiser—Jackie and Rachel Robinson were in attendance, along with Billie Holiday and many other celebrities—at Rockland Palace in Harlem. A few months earlier, a rally and fundraiser for Paul Robeson on his return from Europe had been held in the same place.[88]

At the same time, Robinson was not through denouncing communists. Later in 1949, the Young Progressives of America sent a telegram to National League President Ford Frick claiming that umpire Bill Stewart, who threw Robinson out of a game that season—his first such tossing, but not his last—was racially motivated. Robinson told the *Baltimore Afro-American* that the telegram "made me mad as hell. The moment I read it, I realized they were trying to read something racial into the incident, or that they were trying to make Stewart prejudiced. I tore up the telegram. I recognized the Communistic touch. I'd much prefer if they let me handle my own affairs."[89] Robinson's angry response might have been somewhat more believable if he hadn't been so indignant when thrown out of the game—and the thought that the umpire was biased no doubt had crossed his mind.[90] That fall, the Freedoms Foundation at Valley Forge, in Valley Forge, Pennsylvania, gave Robinson one of its highest awards—and $1,500—in a tribute to his HUAC testimony and his upholding of "the American way of life." He shared the award with federal Judge Harold L. Medina, honored for his handling of the recent trial of twelve leaders of the Communist Party USA (among them Benjamin Davis), applauding the harsh sentences he meted out after their conviction.[91]

Robeson suggested in 1956 that "if Jackie Robinson had the opportunity, he would probably change his testimony. He has perhaps rejected many of the things he said."[92] Perhaps not, at least publicly. The following year, reviewing his baseball career in *Look* magazine, he stated that he did not regret "any part of these last ten years" and singled out his opportunity to "speak on behalf of Negro Americans before the House Un-American Activities Committee" and "rebuke Paul Robeson."[93] But this might have been his stubbornness talking. Later in life, speaking to the novelist (and prominent former communist) Howard Fast in 1970, he abdicated responsibility, saying that "if Mr. Rickey had told me to jump headfirst over the Brooklyn Bridge, I would have done it."[94] This was something of a cop-out and blames Rickey for what was ultimately his decision. More honestly, in his final autobiography, he wrote that he had grown "wiser and closer to painful truths about America's destructiveness" and that he had gained "increased respect" for Robeson, while saying that he had "never regretted" his appearance though implying that he could have handled it differently.[95]

In his closing remarks before HUAC, Robinson said, "We can win our fight without the Communists, and we don't need their help."[96] This was both so and not so. It is certainly true that the great victories of the civil rights movement in the 1960s occurred after the Communist Party had been reduced to impotence, and the NAACP and leaders of the legal fight against segregation, such as Thurgood Marshall, always kept the Communist Party at arm's length. But it's equally true that the Communist Party played a crucial role in pushing forward a civil rights agenda in the 1940s and 1950s, not least in ending the color line in baseball.[97] It is impossible to know how the civil rights movement would have unfolded without the anti-communist purges of the late 1940s and early 1950s, though undoubtedly it would have been different. McCarthyism left personal and organizational wreckage in its wake. Robeson never really recovered.[98] Still, it's striking how many members of the "old left" continued to play important roles in civil rights after the demise of the Communist Party. Those activists could now use their radicalism and organizing savvy to attack the excesses of the Cold War without having to defend what was indefensible: Soviet totalitarianism.[99] One of the best things the Communist Party produced was ex-communists. But given the pervasiveness of anti-communism in the United States in the early 1950s, it's easy to see why non-communists like Jackie Robinson strove to separate themselves from those close to the Communist Party. However, it would be a mistake, as several recent historians have argued, to assume that the non-communists lacked either the motivation or the skill to organize effectively for civil rights efforts and to challenge Western imperialism in Africa and Asia.[100] And perhaps the saddest aspect of this is how anti-communism made enemies of former allies over an issue, the Soviet Union, which in the end had little do to with the civil rights struggle. Robinson's testimony was not forgotten. Malcolm X, who was engaged in a long-running feud with Robinson, said in 1963 that back in 1949, the "white man" was "searching for a colored person dumb enough" to be used, and "you [Robinson] let them sic you on Paul Robeson." Robinson wrote that he would not "dignify" Malcolm X's attempted slur and said only that "if called upon to defend my country today, I would gladly do so."[101] Jackie Robinson did not like to back down from a perceived slight. Rachel Robinson perceptively wrote of her husband: "I think Jack was rightly proud and protective of his integrity—I have never known a more honest person—but his manhood and his integrity were so closely linked that any innuendo struck at his essence, making him extremely sensitive to challenges. . . . Later when the civil rights movement as we know began to surface, he was ready, a spirited, practiced proponent of civil liberties."[102] If Robinson and Robeson had ever had the long talk that Robeson had suggested, one suspects there would have been far more agreement than argument. Both men knew by bitter experience what it meant to grow up Black in the United States. And both men were proud patriots, nonetheless. The ultimate tragedy of his testimony is that Robinson felt he had to attack Robeson even though he knew that his cause, the quest for integration and Black citizenship, had few more eloquent defenders.

SEVEN

White Brooklyn, Black Brooklyn

EXITS AND ENTRANCES

THE DODGERS, OF COURSE, played their home games at Ebbets Field, which was located in New York City. Yet the Dodgers, as everyone knew, might be "in" New York City, but they were "of" Brooklyn. In urban folklore, the connection between the Dodgers and Brooklyn was deep, as thick as the borough's fabled patois, with a structural bond between borough and team that was, or so everyone thought at the time, well-nigh unbreakable. Few Brooklynites would have disagreed with Leo Durocher, who said in early 1958 that if he had been asked which was more likely to leave New York City, the Brooklyn Dodgers or the Brooklyn Bridge, he would have bet on the bridge.[1]

In 1942, 20th Century Fox released a very forgettable movie, *It Happened in Flatbush*.[2] It was based, very loosely, on the Dodgers pennant-winning 1941 season, the team's first National League title in two decades, which was followed, however, by a World Series loss to their inevitable opponent, the New York Yankees. The series is best remembered in baseball lore for Dodgers catcher Mickey Owen dropping a third strike that cost the Dodgers a game, and perhaps the series. The film concerns a former ballplayer, nicknamed "Butterfingers" because of an error he made at a crucial time, who is subsequently hired to manage the Brooklyn team (not called the Dodgers). At first, his players dislike him for his martinet style of managing, but everything turns out all right in the end. The film includes footage taken during real games at Ebbets Field.

Most interesting for our purposes is that the film is saturated in what might be called the midcentury Brooklyn mythos, in which the borough was seen as an isolated and self-contained world apart, a world of working-class white Americans and European immigrants, a world in which rooting for the Dodgers was the central tenet of its civil religion. This was the point of *It Happened in Flatbush,* and the film presumes a wide familiarity with the Brooklyn mythos, as if all of America identified Brooklyn as the national home for lovable eccentricity.

Before any dialogue, right after the opening credits, the film explained its premise:

> This is fictional
> But anything might happen
> And usually does—
> On a strange island just off the eastern coast of the United States—
> Its people are friendly
> Could even be taken for Americans—
> But they have a language, customs, and a tradition all their own
> The name of this island is—
> BROOKLYN!

Brooklyn, in the mythos, is an island unto itself, culturally not part of New York City, nor even geographically on Long Island, but existing in splendid isolation and indifference to the rest of the world. Brooklyn, of course, has a long history of a diverse population, including indigenous Lenape bands such as the Canarsie, a shameful history of high levels of slavery, and a proud free Black history. But in the film's mythos of Brooklyn, its inhabitants were exclusively white. And until 1947, so were the Dodgers.

The origins of the Brooklyn mythos are difficult to trace, but a reasonable starting date is 1898, when the nation's third-most populous city suddenly became New York City's second-most important borough. Although invidious comparisons between it and the other borough across the East River were hardly new, after 1898 they became even more inescapable, ubiquitous, and generally unflattering. As James Agee, author of an acerbic 1939 profile of Brooklyn, argued, Manhattan with its "mad magnetic energy" renders all around it a provincial afterthought, making Brooklyn by comparison "featureless," a flat world without end, "an immeasurable proliferation of house on house, street by street," a place "so little known, and to many so laughable."[3]

It was the houses, row on row, that struck observers such as Agee. As the 1938 *WPA Guide to New York City* stated: "Brooklyn is best known . . . as a residential quarter."[4] In the first half of the twentieth century, the population of Brooklyn surged, from 1,167,000 in 1900 to 2,698,000 in 1940, catching up to and considerably surpassing the population of Manhattan. This population explosion required the rapid building of tract after tract of new housing of the sort that Agee disparaged. Although Brooklyn had an industrial base—one that, alas, was in decline by the time Jackie Robinson joined the Dodgers—it had always prided itself, preeminently, as a place to come home to. For Agee, in an elegantly overwritten putdown, Brooklyn was "an exorbitant pulsing mass of scarcely discriminable cellular jellies and tissues; a place where people merely 'live.'"[5] But Brooklyn was not an undifferentiated protoplasmic blob. It had recognized parts, divisions, and sections. These were called neighborhoods. And Brooklyn was not merely a borough of homes. It was a borough of neighborhoods.

The neighborhood is an elusive geographic idea, at once rooted and unfixed. Often a neighborhood is just a center with vague and debatable boundaries. Because they usually are not political jurisdictions, they are mutable and are a product of social changes. They can grow or diminish, suddenly emerge or slowly vanish. But "the neighborhood" was the malleable building block of twentieth-century Brooklyn. Many of the neighborhood designations in Brooklyn had formerly been legally distinct villages, towns, or even separate cities, which lost their independent status with the City of Brooklyn's expansion over the course of the nineteenth century. It was only in 1894 that the town of Flatbush became incorporated into the City of Brooklyn, and only in 1896 that the City of Brooklyn finally became coextensive with Kings County. (When Ebbets Field opened in 1913, much of Flatbush was still farmland.) But by the 1940s, this complex history had been largely forgotten, and Brooklyn was now simply a borough in which its myriad internal political jurisdictions had been downgraded to mere "neighborhoods."

The growth of Brooklyn over the first half of the twentieth century was largely due to European immigration: the dominant ethnic groups were Irish, Italian, and Jewish, and they lived alongside Poles, Scandinavians, and others. In 1930, there were 868,770 Brooklynites not born in the United States, or 34 percent of its population. If we add their children, immigrants and first-generation Americans comprised about half of the borough's population. The Brooklyn mythos presumed a broad ethnic harmony. (In *It Happened in Flatbush* an Irish family serves kosher corned beef to a guest.) While there certainly was no lack of racial tension in Brooklyn during these years—marked by numerous incidents of anti-Semitism, anti-Catholicism, and evidence of other ethnic divisions—most white Brooklynites ignored these undercurrents. They would have argued that although there might have been the occasional tiff or spat, there were no serious crises, and there was a harmony deeper than any surface inharmoniousness.[6]

But this was a defensive harmony, always alert to the possibilities of contamination and penetration from the wider world—what Carl Prince has called "Brooklyn's ethnic isolation."[7] Brooklyn's neighborhoods were sites of pride and turfs to defend, especially if attacked by outsiders. Some inhabitants were stifled by its insularity. The writer Alfred Kazin, a native of the Brooklyn neighborhood of Brownsville, wrote that he and his peers "measured success by our skill in getting away from it."[8] Barbra Streisand, Brooklyn-born in 1942, Broadway-bound in 1963, said that growing up in Brooklyn for her only meant "baseball, boredom, and bad breath."[9] The notorious and stigmatizing maps of the Home Owners' Loan Corporation (HOLC) of the late 1930s, which introduced the term "redlining" to the language, gave weight to the charges of Kazin and Streisand. Real estate evaluators were unimpressed by Brooklyn and assigned its highest, A rating to only one neighborhood, while relegating the other forty-eight neighborhoods to the scarlet letters of C and D. (The Ds included the Dodgers' home neighborhood of Flatbush.)[10] It's worth keeping in mind that with few exceptions the low grades cannot be explained as examples of anti-Black racism. Most of these neighborhoods, if ethnic, were overwhelming white. But like James Agee and Alfred Kazin, the mapmakers at HOLC saw Brooklyn as a dull and drab backwater, sleepy, shoddy, and provincial beyond all description.

The characteristic and endlessly caricatured working-class New York City accent, once called the Bowery dialect, by the 1920s had moved across the East River to be redubbed "Brooklynese."[11] In 1929, the *Brooklyn Eagle* began to give lessons on Brooklynese: "Thursday" as "tozday," and the Dodgers' Babe Herman as "hoi-man."[12] In 1935, the *New Yorker* published Thomas Wolfe's famous short story in Brooklynese "Only the Dead Know Brooklyn," on the borough's unnavigability. During this period, Brooklyn became the butt of thousands of unfunny jokes. A doctor asks a recruit where he is from. "Brooklyn." The doctor cracks wise: "Any other defects?" A passenger asks a cabbie where they are. "Nowhere," says the cabbie. "This is Brooklyn."[13] Such derision led to the formation of the Society for the Prevention of Disparaging Remarks Against Brooklyn, whose members—250,000 strong, according to the highly unlikely claims of the organization's president—had by 1946 tallied three thousand Brooklyn slurs.[14] But arguably, the Brooklyn anti-defamation society didn't get the joke. These tales were primarily told by Brooklynites to try to keep the outside world at bay, proud of their isolation and difference, fearful of seduction by everything Brooklyn was not. As for being nowhere, the cabbie, if he had read his Sir Thomas Moore, could have told his passenger that another word for nowhere is "utopia."

In this developing Brooklyn mythos, the Dodgers played a central role. The decentralized nature of Brooklyn, a borough of neighborhoods, gave the Dodgers a unique role as a borough unifier; the team was exhibit A of the gentle self-deprecation that was actually an assertion of deep pride. This started with the team's name, one of the few team nicknames that poked fun at itself by adopting a name reserved for shirkers, layabouts, and (during World War I) draft evaders. A "trolley dodger" was a pedestrian, hapless perhaps, but possessed of enough mother-wit to avoid dangerous collisions. The nickname, shortened, became the team's official name only in 1932. It perfectly fit the interwar Dodgers, the team where players fielded fly balls with their heads and ran into triple plays with three men on third base. They were "daffy" and lovable losers. They were the "Bums," unshaven chewers on cheap cigar butts rescued from the gutter, proudly plebian. Their home turf was a working-class borough, but its working class both worked hard and loved to play, and its strongest political impulse was anti-elitist and anti-cosmopolitan. As someone says in *It Happened in Flatbush:* "New Yorkers, dem foreigners; Brooklyn is my homeland." And any true Brooklyn patriot, like William Bendix in Alfred Hitchcock's *Lifeboat* (1944), would, in his final delirium, babble of Ebbets Field.[15]

Branch Rickey was, of course, never a real Brooklynite, in part because a real Brooklynite had to be a native (as opposed to the many Manhattanites, born and raised anywhere else on the planet, who were proud, "real New Yorkers" by choice). Rickey knew that as president of the Dodgers, he had his part to play in upholding and maintaining the Brooklyn mythos. Speaking to the *New York Times* shortly after his arrival in Brooklyn, and extending an unexpected olive branch to the borough's beer drinkers—"this is the town where you get your onions and your suds"—he opined that "baseball has deep roots here, which undoubtedly explains the fanaticism of the fans. Some ungovernable effusions have given color to the opinion that all Brooklyn is daffy. When you have devotion, however, you'll have effervescence because it has to flow over." Rickey went on to suggest that working-class Brooklyn was judged, unfairly, by a different standard than the overly rambunctious goalpost-demolishing fans at elite colleges.[16] But it certainly was true, Rickey argued, that there was something unique about Dodgers fans. "I find that baseball is stimulated here to a far greater extent than anywhere else. I find [it] in my mail and on the phone and in the man I meet on the street. The Brooklyn fan is far different from the one in St. Louis or elsewhere. Why?" Rickey asked. "Ask a Manhattanite where he lives and he'll tell you 'New York.' A Brooklynite, however, will tell you at least 'Brooklyn' but is more likely to answer 'Greenpoint,' or 'Columbia Heights,' or whichever one of the twenty-one distinct communities in which he lives. . . . When anything comes along that is distinctly Brooklyn, they rally behind it, because it is an expression of themselves, even an entity as lowly as a baseball team both part and not a part of New York City."[17]

Into the Brooklyn mythos, in 1947, stepped Jackie Robinson, who helped bring it to its "boys of summer" apotheosis, an epitome of democracy and the practical realization of the American creed, and served as a harbinger of the reality that the days of white Brooklyn were numbered. Many stories are told of white Brooklynites who identified with Robinson's struggle for acceptance in a way that transcended mere politics; they admired his determination to triumph over his adversaries by his demonstration of inner strength. People who felt ostracized or demeaned by a physical disability, or ostracized for something beyond their control, identified with Robinson, aided by his frequent appearances at the borough's churches, synagogues, Ys, boys and girls clubs, and schools. The Dodgers provided common ground; Brooklynites of all ethnic backgrounds went to the games, and their devotion in the 1940s and 1950s was "classless and polyglot, like the borough itself."[18]

But once Jackie Robinson joined the team, the Dodgers could never be entirely above or outside politics and race. To root for the Dodgers was to root for the success of the "great experiment." Ira Glasser, the longtime executive director of the American Civil Liberties Union (ACLU), grew up in a Jewish neighborhood in Brooklyn in which Black people were out of sight and out of mind. But as a young boy he was a passionate Dodgers and Robinson fan, and when asked what most influenced him in his career as a civil liberties attorney, the answer, without hesitation, was Jackie Robinson. He later found that many like-minded persons of his age and background, perhaps especially Jews, also used Robinson as a catalyst for a career in social justice.[19] At the same time, there were others, such as the man who told journalist Peter Golenbock that "when Robinson came up, there were a lot of adults who dropped their allegiance to the Dodgers. . . . It was a lot of union guys saying 'sure, first they get into baseball, and then they'll be taking my job.'"[20]

Jackie Robinson's joining the Dodgers is remembered as one of the most celebrated of "famous firsts." But as historian Craig Wilder has noted, the Brooklyn of Robinson's era, the 1940s and 1950s, was more of a place of famous lasts and unwanted endings than hopeful beginnings. In 1947, one of the borough's two daily newspapers, the *Brooklyn Citizen,* published its last issue. The better-known daily, the *Brooklyn Eagle,* ceased publication in 1955. Brooklyn's major industries—the Brooklyn Navy Yard in Fort Greene, the waterfront in Red Hook, the sugar refineries in Williamsburg—were all increasingly moribund. In 1956, the last Brooklyn trolley had its final run.[21] And, of course, one year later, with no more trolleys to dodge, there was the most famous last exit from Brooklyn. And with the decamping of the Dodgers for points west, the borough itself changed. The unfunny genre of the Brooklyn joke faded.

However, the borough's most significant ending in the 1950s had nothing to do with the end of the Brooklyn Dodgers. It was the beginning of the end of white Brooklyn. In 1940, Brooklyn's population was 96 percent white, which was roughly in line with the percentages in the other "outer boroughs," but the real contrast, and the only one that mattered, was to Manhattan, where 16 percent of its residents were Black and nonwhite. However, if much of the first wave of the Great Migration of Black Southerners to New York City primarily landed in Manhattan and Harlem, the Black population of Brooklyn also was growing exponentially. From 1900 to 1940, it increased more than five-fold, from about 20,000 to 110,000 (out of a total population in 1940 of almost 2.7 million people). Bedford-Stuyvesant was beginning to attract mainstream attention as "Brooklyn's Harlem," but for most white Brooklynites, Black Brooklyn was barely discernible. Yet it was beginning to be noticed.[22] If Brooklyn prided itself as a borough of neighborhoods, it was no longer solely a borough of white neighborhoods.

How do you get to Ebbets Field? Practice, practice, practice. But even then, you might have to ask a Brooklynite. On 11 April 1947, Robinson would play there for the first time, in an exhibition game against the Yankees. He didn't quite know the way. As Robert Gruber, a freshman at Erasmus Hall High School was walking to school, "a black man in a late model car stopped, and in a distinctive voice asked me, 'Excuse me, fella, which way to Ebbets Field?'" Gruber told him, the driver thanked him, and Gruber realized he had been talking to Jackie Robinson. "When I told the story in the school lunchroom that day, a few black kids came over and shook my hand."[23] And so concluded Jackie Robinson's epochal journey—many years in the making—to Ebbets Field, with the assistance and good wishes of Brooklynites, white and Black.

Jackie Robinson made many white Brooklynites take notice and to think about race not as something far away, in the news, but on their neighborhood streets. Lester Rodney, the sportswriter for the *Daily Worker* (who played an important role in ending baseball's color line), wrote that during the mid-1920s, "I was in a high school with ten thousand students and I don't remember a single black kid there. We're talking about Bensonhurst and Boro Park. Later on there were a few black kids, usually the kids of parents working as servants or laborers or chauffeurs and lived in some pretty poor homes near there. Blacks were an abstraction to us."[24] A Dodgers fan, Bill Reddy, told an interviewer that when he grew up in central Brooklyn, "there was very little prejudice against blacks because we didn't come into contact with them much." If he ever wondered why there weren't Black players in baseball, "it never occurred to me that a guy wasn't playing because he was a different color than the other guys[.] I thought they weren't playing because the guys who were playing were better."[25]

We can take these statements with a large grain of salt. If these fans were unacquainted with Black Americans, it seems unlikely that they were entirely unfamiliar with the usual range of ethnic and racial slurs and stereotypes that were part of the street education of everyone growing up in New York City in the 1940s and 1950s. Black Brooklynites regularly reported incidents of racial exclusion, and it seems likely that as the Black population of Bedford-Stuyvesant increased in the first half of the twentieth century, so did conscious efforts at excluding them from neighborhoods, schools, and other local institutions.[26]

And if Robinson opened minds for some Brooklynites, his presence was an invitation for others to ever more firmly shut theirs. Black Americans remained outside of their world, lacking the ties of neighborhood kinship, and they wanted to keep it that way. But the little universes of their neighborhoods were changing—and getting smaller.

If the first wave of the Great Migration was a steady stream, the second phase, after the war, was more like a mighty river. Brooklyn was now a primary destination. The population flow was not just from the American South but from Puerto Rico, Haiti, and the Anglophone islands in the Caribbean. If Brooklyn's population was 4 percent nonwhite in 1940, by 1950, the ratio had risen to 8 percent; 15 percent by 1960; 27 percent by 1970; and 44 percent in 1980.

In 1975, writing about how Brooklyn had changed in recent decades, journalist Jimmy Breslin traced the changes back to "the late 1940s [when] they started to come, men with cotton-bailing hooks in their pockets, and sad-faced women with arms leaden from hours spent jiggling small children in busses and railroad coach cars from Greenville in South Carolina and Waycross in Georgia." Some prospective Brooklynites came by air, touching down "at old Idlewild Airport," which "became filled with the poor arriving on cheap flights from Puerto Rico."[27] One of the first consequences of this darker and blacker Brooklyn is that it made Dodgers owner Walter O'Malley worry that white fans were not and would not be as willing to travel to Flatbush, and he began to explore other venues for the franchise.[28]

If there's a basic difference between Southern racism and Northern racism, it's that Southern racism always flourished amid the presence of large numbers of Black Americans, while Northern racism—certainly the toxic versions that flourished after World War II—erupted when new Black neighbors entered the Northerners' political horizon as disrupters. Racism in the South was, to many whites, a source of stability, a reinforcement of the hierarchy of the races. In the North, racism was often a reaction to instability, to a perceived challenge to the standing social order and white status. The reaction to Black migration was both similar and dissimilar to previous concerns over immigration streams (e.g., the Irish, the Jews, the Italians). The moral panic was certainly present: the fears that this new wave of migration, often tellingly called an "invasion," would turn things upside down and make things worse. But the subsequent absorption and acceptance of the new population did not follow the old script. No neighborhood was capacious enough to be shared. White Brooklynites, for the most part, tried to keep Black Americans out of their neighborhoods, and when this failed, they left their neighborhoods, and often Brooklyn, entirely. Historians debate whether suburbanization was a cause or effect of the "urban crisis," but the reality was that after World War II, large numbers of working-class families could afford to leave New York City for the suburbs, and it generally was far easier for white families to do so than Black ones.[29]

In the early postwar years, Jackie Robinson was perhaps the most famous and lauded of Brooklynites, the epitome of Black Brooklyn. He was a man bursting with pride, and in this way, he was a model for Brooklyn's new arrivals. The Dodgers were now upwardly mobile, a national symbol of the ability of white and Black Americans to work together, to play together, and to win together. But the Dodgers did not live together; for the most part, white Dodgers lived in white neighborhoods, and Black Dodgers lived in Black neighborhoods. The presence of larger numbers of racial minorities would challenge and redefine Brooklyn's self-image as a borough of harmonious neighborhoods. Branch Rickey had provided Jackie Robinson with a place to work. When it came to a place to live, he was largely on his own. When he arrived in New York in 1947, he, Rachel, and infant Jackie Robinson Jr. first lived in the Hotel McAlpin, on Herald Square on 34th and Broadway. When the hotel opened in 1912, it was supposedly the largest in the world. It was only toward the end of World War II that major downtown hotels in large cities in the North permitted Black guests to register in any significant numbers.

In 1945, Black guests were not allowed to stay in many downtown hotels in Manhattan, and as late as 1948, the *New York Amsterdam News* was publishing lists of hotels that were accepting Black guests.[30] When Black Americans were allowed to register at big downtown hotels, they often met with restrictions of some sort: Eating at the hotel might be limited to room service, they might be barred from the pool, or a white person of authority might be required to vouch for them prior to registration. It seems likely that the Robinsons' stay at the McAlpin came about through prearrangement with the Dodgers.[31]

After two weeks, they left the hotel for a range of accommodations in Brooklyn and Queens. A woman visited them and offered to share her apartment in Bedford-Stuyvesant, at 526 MacDonough Street, with the family, but this proved to be a tenement infested with roaches, an all-too-common reality in the neighborhood. In 1948, they moved to Tilden Avenue and 53rd Street in Flatbush, close to Ebbets Field, and they occupied the top floor of a two-family house. This neighborhood was white and heavily Jewish, but Rachel Robinson remembered discrimination "even in this predominantly Jewish neighborhood. We heard rumors of a petition being circulated to prevent our black landlady from purchasing the house we were to live in. By this time we were happy to have our lives under our control at last."[32] But when they moved in, they made some close friends. The Robinsons, who had little contact with Jews in California, found their exposure to Jews and Jewish culture fascinating, and for the remainder of his life, Jackie would have many Jewish friends and associates, support Jewish causes, and be vigilant against anti-Semitism. As early as 1949, he identified with Jewish and Zionist causes and became a leader and frequent speaker for Brotherhood Week, sponsored by the National Conference of Christians and Jews. He was also a spokesman for the B'nai B'rith's Anti-Defamation League.[33]

The Robinsons, wanting a house and backyard of their own for their growing family, then moved in 1949 to St. Albans, in southeastern Queens. St. Albans, adjacent to Jamaica and South Jamaica, was an area of middle- and even upper-middle-class housing and since the 1920s had the largest cluster of privately owned Black homes in New York City.[34] Jamaica was also the center, in the 1920s, of Ku Klux Klan activity in New York City. In the late 1940s, as more Black families moved into St. Albans, some found notices on their doors posted by the "Ku Klux District of St. Albans."[35]

In February 1947, a few months before Robinson joined the Dodgers, J. H. Richardson, a supreme court judge in Queens—in the New York state legal system, the supreme court is, confusingly, a lower-level appellate court—had ruled that a restrictive covenant on a property lot in Addisleigh Park, in St. Albans (which limited its sale to "Caucasians") remained in force. The decision was unanimously upheld by a higher state appellate court. Then, in a deus ex machina from Washington, in May 1948, the US Supreme Court ruled that restrictive covenants were legally unenforceable, and the land sale went through. But from the perspective of white segregationists in Addisleigh Park, trying to enforce restrictive covenants was a belated closing of the barn door. By May 1948, of the 325 homes in Addisleigh Park, 48 were owned by Black families.[36] Like his teammate, Roy Campanella, the Robinsons moved to Addisleigh Park.

At first, Robinson sounded like the typical (or stereotypical) happy but chores-laden suburban homeowner, telling the *Brooklyn Eagle* and the *Washington Post* in August 1949, "We moved into another house on a quiet, tree-lined section. We've got furniture to move, walls to paint, floors to scrape. It's on a nice, big, plot, about 100 feet by 110 feet square. There's lot of green for Jackie Jr. to run around on. It's in a friendly section of New York's Queens County. White families live on both sides of me. I get along fine with them." (Although one of the neighbors had been president of a block association formed a few years earlier with the express purpose of keeping Black families out of the neighborhood. He later apologized to Robinson.)[37]

St. Albans had developed a reputation as one of New York City's most celebrity-studded neighborhoods for the Black bourgeoisie. Such well-known entertainment figures as Count Basie, Lena Horne, and Ella Fitzgerald called it home, as well as the Robinsons and the Campanellas.[38] St. Albans remained a "mixed" neighborhood, but like many such neighborhoods in the 1950s, it was undergoing a rapid racial transition.[39] On one hand, the Robinsons found St. Albans to be too white. The Black families near the Robinsons had few school-age children, and most of the Robinsons' childrens' friends were white. Rachel Robinson even said they were not living in "a strongly black environment."[40] When in November 1949 a photo of Jackie Robinson Jr.'s third birthday party appeared in the *New York Daily News,* there was some criticism raised about the abundance of white faces and the paucity of Black ones.[41]

On the other hand, St. Albans was suffering from the unequal treatment common to Black and perceived Black neighborhoods in New York City. The Robinsons were worried about this. St. Albans's public schools were not of the highest quality, with aging and inadequate physical plants.[42] The schools were becoming overcrowded and had resorted to double sessions. As Robinson wrote in 1960, "There was one development that concerned us. As the community grew in Negro population we saw that young families with several children were replacing older families with few or no children, with the result that not only was the school becoming overcrowded, but it was becoming virtually an all-Negro school."[43] He then elaborated: "Many people may ask 'what's wrong with an all-Negro school?' We would say 'nothing' if these Negro youngsters lived in an all-Negro world, but we were unwilling to ignore the fact that our kids were growing up in a predominantly white country in a world populated by a great variety of people."[44]

So the Robinsons decided to move to a house with extensive grounds in a community with better schools. Rachel Robinson spent her Sundays pouring over the real estate section of the *New York Times.* "We wanted," she wrote, "to be in a racially integrated neighborhood where we would have space, clean air, good schools, friends for our children, and a strong sense of community. . . . I spent a year in vain searching from Long Island to Connecticut for such a place, and in the process encountered a whole array of discriminatory practices used to exclude blacks on one pretext or other."[45] But if no racially integrated upper-middle-class neighborhood existed, the Robinsons sought the alternative, an upper-middle-class neighborhood that was white. Pining for a big suburban dream house—their new home in North Stamford, Connecticut, was sometimes described as a "mansion"—was perhaps the archetypal 1950s housing dream, but it was complicated for the Robinsons. As one commentator noted, "Jackie is not too poor to buy a house, he is too dark."[46] Robinson's income in 1954—$40,000 from the Dodgers and more on the side—placed his family in the top 1 percent income bracket.[47] The property he purchased in Connecticut reflected this. The eight-acre wooded site had a private lake, and the new house built on it cost a reported $65,000 in 1953. Translating this into 2026 dollars—about $760,000—no doubt severely underestimates what such an estate would cost today.[48]

It had not been easy for the Robinson family to move to North Stamford. Rachel Robinson encountered numerous difficulties. Some homeowners, learning of her race, refused to show her their homes. On another occasion, she bid for a house at the asking price, only to have the owner pull it from the market. Realtors tried to steer her away from the tonier and more exclusive neighborhoods.[49] The difficulties the Robinsons encountered in trying to purchase a house became a news story, and coverage in the *Bridgeport Herald* brought attention to their plight. This prompted some residents in Stamford to assist the Robinsons in finding a sympathetic realtor and a suitable location for their new house, to be built from the ground up. After a few snubs, they found bankers willing to give them a mortgage.[50] The owner of the site the Robinsons purchased, a home builder, had to be convinced that selling to a Black family would not result in a loss of future work in the area. "I thought a long time before making the sale" but felt "that the majority of the people here would have no objection to a man of Jackie Robinson's character."[51] When the Robinsons' intention to move in was announced, several families on the block sold their houses.[52] Not all the Robinson's new neighbors welcomed their arrival. A dentist whose house was directly across the road from them did not want them living close by because he was "concerned with the value of his property."[53]

Many white homeowners in Connecticut felt the same way about middle-class Black neighbors. A 1957 survey conducted by the Connecticut Commission on Human Rights of residents of predominantly white but racially mixed private residential neighborhoods, such as North Stamford, found much concern from white homeowners worried about plummeting home values that might be caused by nearby African American families. The survey revealed that 75 percent of the Black families who used white realtors found the experience unpleasant, and half of the white families reported hearing talk of "doing something" when the news broke of an African American family moving in. In practice, this ranged from insulting remarks, trying to buy back the property, and breaking windows to poisoning the family cat. Overall, 90 percent of African Americans surveyed approved of having white neighbors, compared to only a third of white respondents who approved of Black families in their neighborhoods.[54]

At the same time, some members of the Black press questioned whether Robinson was "trying to escape his own race" by moving to an exclusive, all-white suburban subdivision.[55] This accusation he and Rachel vociferously rejected.[56] In late 1954, Rachel Robinson denied that her family "came up here because we didn't want to live with Negroes." They moved because of what was best for their children, and given their interest in extensive acreage, "tell me where you can find that in a Negro neighborhood?"[57] Moreover, the *Philadelphia Tribune* (a Black newspaper) reported that she said that "she and her famous husband have no interest in racial intermarriage. . . . We are proud of our race. We do feel, however, that Negroes and whites and other people should learn to live together in friendship."[58] She would say the same many decades later. "Contrary to the prevailing propaganda that black middle class families move out of black neighborhoods and attempt to put the struggle for equality behind them, we took the struggle with us consciously and with purpose with each of our moves, we enlarged our capacities to do more for those who needed help."[59]

By all accounts, the Robinsons loved their new home and developed close friendships with several of their white neighbors. In 1960, Robinson said that he and Rachel "wanted our children to have these intangible advantages—not to mention many tangible advantages—of living and working in an integrated community and school. . . . We also felt that someone had to lead the way in this struggle for integrated housing, and that if we lacked the courage to do it then we had no right to ask others to bemoan our fate."[60] This was the essential dilemma of integration understood as racial mixing, the often impossible choice between racial solidarity and racial advancement.[61] The Robinsons were wealthy enough to avoid the most common pitfall that befell racial pioneers: moving to a previously white neighborhood that because of their very presence, all too soon became entirely, or almost entirely, Black. However, they were unable to avoid the other horn of the dilemma, moving to a white neighborhood where few Black families followed.

In 1972, in his autobiography, Robinson was less sanguine about living in a predominantly white neighborhood. The community had become only slightly more racially mixed in the almost two decades he lived there. "We now realize how much being 'the only black' can hurt. In talks with us as they grew up, our children made us realize what a heavy burden had been placed on them. . . . [They] went through a loss of identity" through various slights, taunts, and exclusions.[62] Integration for Robinson was an imperative, but as he knew from his years with the Dodgers, it created problems as well as solving them. Race mixing was a byproduct of integration, but for Robinson it was never its goal. Integration was the promise of more vibrant communities, better schools, a superior quality of life. But for all-Black neighborhoods to achieve this, African Americans had to be able to live in previously all-white areas. The goal of integration, of effective Black citizenship, was the right and ability not to be excluded from living anywhere and not to be excluded from doing anything Black Americans wanted and were capable of pursuing. Jackie Robinson believed that by moving to Connecticut, he was helping to expand the scope of Black possibility.

If anything, the challenges the Robinsons faced in moving to a tony, exclusive enclave in the suburbs redoubled Jackie Robinson's commitment to fighting for open access to housing for all African Americans. In 1952, while still living in Queens, he became involved in desegregating Levittown, the massive housing development for lower-middle-class families that rose on the potato fields of Hempstead, Long Island. Its developer,

William Levitt, did not want "to take a chance on admitting Negroes and then not being able to sell his houses."[63] Robinson supported the Committee to End Discrimination in Levittown and said, "This man Levitt . . . cannot be a real American to have such policies."[64] (When Levitt, a few years later, opened another segregated Levittown outside of Philadelphia, Robinson again actively protested and gave support to a brave, beleaguered Black family who nonetheless moved in. William Myers received three hundred letters of support, but of them all, "Jackie's letter really touched me.")[65] In 1957, as head of the Committee For Fair Housing, he supported passage of New York City's Sharkey-Isaacs-Brown bill, which would have prohibited discrimination in apartments and multiple unit dwellings and most private homes in the city. The committee promised "protest action on an extended scale" unless the bill was passed, which it was that fall, the first law of this sort ratified in the United States.[66] Robinson also called on the state legislature to pass similar legislation "protecting everybody's right to freedom of choice in finding a place to live."[67] (Facing stiff opposition from realtors who claimed the bill would "Sovietize housing," the Metcalf-Baker Fair Housing Law was finally passed in 1961.)[68] In 1958, Robinson received an award from the New York Committee for Desegregation in Housing for his commitment to ending housing discrimination.[69] In the 1960s, he wrote against California Proposition 14, an unfortunately successful attempt to override California's fair housing laws, and he sharply criticized the halting congressional efforts to pass an open housing bill.[70] (The federal Fair Housing Act was signed on 11 April 1968, its passage only finally prodded by the assassination of Martin Luther King Jr.)

The new laws were laudable, but they were weakly enforced and did little to stem the increased segregation of New York City, though the laws did make it somewhat easier for middle-class Blacks to find appropriate housing. As Wendell Pritchett, one of the best students of this subject has written, by the 1960s, "fair housing was winning the ideological battle while losing the integration war." It was important not to be barred from living in a neighborhood that had been previously all white or predominantly white. But it was equally important to have good quality housing available for families of modest income in Black neighborhoods. Wealthy Black families, middle-class Black families, and poor Black families each had shared yet distinct problems in finding adequate housing. Their problems stemmed from a common cause: their second-class citizenship. And this remained the true whether they lived in North Stamford, Connecticut, St. Albans, Queens, or back in Brooklyn.

By the mid-1950s, Flatbush, and by extension all of Brooklyn, was sometimes called "Jackie Robinson Land."[71] Perhaps the presence of Black athletes on the Dodgers was just the most visible sign of Brooklyn's rapid transformation. In 1954, the *Brooklyn Eagle* ran a fifteen-part series on the growth of Black Brooklyn. The series, meant to allay white fears, on the whole tried to accentuate the positive, but it was not mealy-mouthed in identifying the problems Black Brooklynites faced. The article stated that Black Americans wanted "a place to live—not survive"; and they wanted "to make Brooklyn a better place to live."[72] The series identified housing as the "single greatest problem facing the Negroes in Brooklyn." The Rev. Milton Galamison, near the beginning of a long and controversial career as an advocate for Black New Yorkers, told the *Eagle* that "as long as there is an iron band of segregation around us, the same situation will be reflected in our schools, our churches and other institutions. A new home just isn't available to the Negro; second hand homes, second hand churches—that has been our history."[73] Another article in the series stated that:

> A Negro, for all practical purposes, still can't purchase a new house in Blyn.
> A Negro still has no access to the free private housing market in Blyn.
> A Negro can purchase a "hand me down" house—but only at the risk of being hog-tied by an avaricious speculator.
> A Negro can rent in limited areas—but only at the cost of enormous rentals, crowded conditions or poor service.[74]

The series gave examples of the difficulties middle-class Black residents encountered when they tried to buy homes in Flatbush, "in the shadow of Ebbets Field."[75] One of the Black homeowners told the *Eagle* that "I love my people dearly. But in order to advance, we must spread out." Integration was necessary and integration was possible, and the series detailed efforts to establish interracial community organizations. It acknowledged that projects built by the NYC Housing Authority were housing Black families out of proportion to their population numbers, "but there just aren't enough of the new buildings to go around."[76] The final article in the series invoked the shades of Walt Whitman and Henry Ward Beecher, and the current example of Jackie Robinson, to make the case that "Brooklyn, With its Climate of Freedom [is a] Haven to Negroes." In retrospect, the series in the *Eagle* overestimated the ability of white Brooklynites to adapt to the borough's changing racial demographics. If the series was blunt in pointing out the potential flashpoints of racial tension in Brooklyn in 1954, it failed to anticipate that, over the next decade, racial attitudes would harden and grow increasingly brittle. The coming urban crisis would dispel any illusion that integration's path would ever be smooth and untroubled.

Branch Rickey's embrace of Frank Tannenbaum's theories of race (discussed in chapter 5) spoke to his deeply held belief that familiarity breeds respect, that actual contact with the racial other can dispel and erode illusions and fears, and that disparate people can discover that working together is a more effective way to reach goals than working against each other. It's the creed of integration as inclusion. On a baseball team, where self-interest prompts collective goals, it often works. For housing, it often does not. Proximity can breed competition and contempt, a fear of being displaced or replaced. Black Brooklyn felt excluded. White Brooklyn felt threatened. This failure has many explanations. The main cause, surely, was white racism and its accompanying stereotypes and prejudices. Many whites did not want Black or other "nonwhite" ethnicities as neighbors or living in any sort of proximity. As a Brooklyn matron told James Agee in 1939, she lived in a "*dreadful* neighborhood; dreadful. Negroes on Myrtle Avenue. Syrians within two blocks of us, nudging us. *I do wish they'd clear them away.*"[77] But rather than Black families leaving, for the most part it was the white families that relocated. Explanations for the white exodus from Brooklyn include the availability of inexpensive housing in the suburbs, the declining industrial base and slow evaporation of blue-collar jobs, and rising levels of crime. White Brooklynites blamed Black newcomers for the problems. Black Brooklynites blamed long-time residents for their hostility and pointed to the seeming police indifference to crime in Black neighborhoods and claims of police brutality. But perhaps beyond everything else was the determination of Black Brooklynites to live as full citizens and the fears this engendered. To reiterate the *Brooklyn Eagle*'s plaintive words, they wanted "a place to live—not survive" and "to make Brooklyn a better place to live."[78]

Let us quickly look at two Brooklyn neighborhoods. Canarsie, on the eastern edge of Brooklyn, near Queens, until the 1940s was sparsely populated, underbuilt, and in the words of the 1939 WPA guide "a dispiriting flatlands" with "a perpetual reek" from a nearby garbage dump. Or, in another account, it was a neighborhood of "mud, mortgages, and malaria."[79] James Agee, in 1939, biblically called it the "abomination of desolation," a neighborhood at "the end of the world," the sort of neighborhood that even other Brooklynites mocked for its out-of-the-way cluelessness; or, looked at in another way, for its unadulterated Brooklynness.[80] If Brooklyn in the 1940s was defined as being far from the action, there was no part of Brooklyn further away than Canarsie. Which made it, very importantly, a haven of white Brooklyn. Its population increased from about 30,000 in 1950 to 50,000 in 1960, to 80,000 in 1970.[81]

As Black Americans and Puerto Ricans moved into other neighborhoods, they largely stayed out of Canarsie. And the residents of Canarsie were determined to keep it that way. They saw the worst in Black Brooklyn: the crime, the poverty, and the supposed low moral standards of its residents.[82] This was fueled by "memories of white Brooklyn," memories that were invariably idealized, of a borough that was "one big happy family."[83] In Canarsie, Jews and Italians learned to put aside older enmities to unite against a common foe. It was a neighborhood that imagined itself besieged and would defend itself by any means necessary. This meant keeping Black Americans out of its schools (in Canarsie, as in so many Brooklyn neighborhoods in the 1960s and 1970s, a flashpoint), its housing, and often, its streets and stores, and doing so through political organizations, respectable and less so.

Canarsie was the home of the semilegendary Society for the Prevention of Negroes [or an alternative word] from Getting Everything, or SPONGE. They saw themselves as defenders of a Brooklynese turf to be protected by fists, fights, and, on some occasions, firebombing in reaction to the occasional Black family that had the courage or temerity to move to Canarsie.

None of this is to suggest that white Canarsie residents did not have legitimate grievances—high crime rates were not just the product of racist imaginings, and neither was the sense that the city, its economy, and its social services were declining. But no neighborhood, regardless of how fiercely its residents defend its turf, is an island, and there was no way for white Brooklynites to win a war against a Brooklyn that was increasingly and irreversibly nonwhite.

The second neighborhood, Brownsville, about a mile away from Canarsie, became an overwhelmingly, paradigmatically working-class Jewish neighborhood in the early decades of the twentieth century, proudly inward looking. In 1940, Brownsville was 6 percent African American in the poorer parts of the neighborhood.[84] Whites from Brownsville, as in Brooklyn as a whole, had a great ability to ignore and dismiss thoughts about potential Black neighbors. "We didn't think about them. They were the people three or four blocks away you passed coming home on the subway."[85] The late 1940s and early 1950s were, in the words of Brownsville's premier chronicler, Wendell Pritchett, the "optimistic years." But the optimism decayed when interracial initiatives foundered. More white families moved away—46,000 between 1950 and 1958—and more nonwhite families moved in. By 1962, the neighborhood was more than half Black and Puerto Rican. By 1970, Brownsville was 77 percent Black, 19 percent Puerto Rican, and 4 percent white.[86]

Still, for many, integration remained an achievable dream in the Brooklyn (and New York City) of the late 1950s and early 1960s. It was clear that housing was becoming increasingly divided by race, with every neighborhood seen as either "white" or "Black and nonwhite." But there was still hope that the schools, by busing, by careful attention to catchment areas, could preserve an element of racial mixture, often less for the mixing itself than for the other benefits of integration: treating all students with the respect and attention they deserve, conveying to Black students that they weren't an afterthought.

At the same time, a sense of urgency was fueled by the perception that any chance for integration in the public schools was slipping away. Many observers had already declared it a lost cause. The distinguished sociologist

Nathan Glazer asked in 1962, "Is 'Integration' Possible in New York Schools?" He answered the question with a negative: "Much of the professional integrationist 'reasoning' is based on the fallacious assumption that learning aptitude is somehow improved by racing mixing per se."[87] But those advocating for integration had far broader agenda than simply race mixing. In 1954, at the beginning of the integration controversy in New York City schools, integration activist Kenneth Clark, in the aftermath of *Brown/Briggs,* said that segregated schools in New York City were not just about "gerrymandering" to create all-Black schools but also about denying students in all-Black schools the facilities and pedagogical excellence equivalent to those available to whites. Integration meant improvement of the educational outcome for all Black students, regardless of the racial mix of their school.[88] A decade later, Charles Silberman, an educational reformer in the Kenneth Clark mode, wrote at the height of the integration debates in New York City: "Integration is a moral imperative, the greatest moral imperative of our time. But integration should not be confused with the mere mixing of Negroes and whites in the same classroom, or the same school, or the same neighborhood."[89]

This was Jackie Robinson's understanding of school integration as well. In early 1964, he wrote: "I am in favor of bussing of children [to achieve greater balance], which seems to be an unholy idea, as far as many people are concerned. I want to caution, however, that we must not lose sight of the necessity for the Board of Education to do much to improve schools that are still segregated," such as sending the best and most experienced teachers to such neighborhoods as Harlem and Bedford-Stuyvesant.[90] Racial balance was one way to achieve integration. But racial balance in itself was less important than the insistence that no schools in the city should be able to exclude Black students. Raising the level of educational opportunity for all schools, including those that were primarily or exclusively African American, was another. These methods of obtaining integration were reinforcing.

Busing was the flashpoint in integration controversies in New York City. The practice almost always involved busing Black students into predominantly white schools (almost never the reverse.) The Board of Education's response to the calls for busing was at best halting. When, in late 1963, the incoming president of New York City's Board of Education, Bernard Donovan, said the city had "a board of education, not a board of integration," Robinson was one of many Black leaders who insisted "Donovan Must Go!"[91]

Donovan stayed, but statements such as his helped spur the most concerted citywide push for integration in the city's history. Its leader was the Rev. Milton Galamison, pastor of the Siloam Baptist Church in Bedford-Stuyvesant. Working closely with the NAACP and interracial groups, he decried the board of education's tacit acceptance of segregated schools. When the board balked at implementing the committee's plans for moving toward a more integrated school system, Galamison called for a one-day strike for integration for 3 February 1964. Around 464,000 of the city's public-school students (about 45 percent) did not attend school that day. The walkout has been called the single largest protest during the civil rights era, and it brought together a remarkable and never to be reassembled spectrum of support, ranging from Norman Podhoretz, editor of *Commentary,* to Malcolm X.[92] Unsurprisingly, Robinson was a strong supporter of the boycott, seeing it as a "magnificent display of unity and purpose and non-violent militancy," paying tribute to the students who participated and their parents, as well as Galamison and the other organizers of the protest.[93]

But Galamison's movement soon fizzled. Support for integration was a mile wide and an inch deep. When the board of education did little to address the issue, calls sounded for more militant tactics. When Galamison called for further boycotts and more militant tactics to force integration—such as a "stall-in" to block highways on the opening day of the 1964 World's Fair in Flushing Meadows, Queens—Robinson did not agree. He wasn't opposed to confrontation. The previous summer, he'd participated in a demonstration organized by CORE (Congress of Racial Equality) to hire more African American workers at the construction site for a new hospital in Brooklyn. Robinson walked the picket line wearing a placard reading "Jobs for everyone, if not jobs, jail."[94] But he thought such tactics as the stall-in would lose critical white support, which is what happened.[95]

Robinson thought white liberal support was crucial because he knew how much hate the civil rights movement was generating among white Americans. What many called (and still call), somewhat euphemistically, the "white backlash," Robinson always called by its proper name, the white "counterrevolution," which was not centered in the South but the North.

And this would be met by a Black counter-counterrevolution. Hoping he didn't sound too alarmist, in early 1964 he wrote that unless there was some sort of interracial accommodation, "there will be bloodshed and violence in northern and eastern communities that will make the Birmingham incidents seem like a Sunday school picnic."[96] If alarmist, he was also prescient, predicting the long hot summers of the mid-1960s. While he condemned the Black "lunatic fringe" that in his opinion was making this confrontation more likely—he had Malcolm X in mind—his real worry was the gathering forces of the white counterrevolution. He supported integration and would work with liberal white politicians such as Nelson Rockefeller to ward off the alternative, a race war in which Black lives and progress on civil rights would be the main victims.[97] Black and white cooperation was essential to prevent this. But if the alliance failed, and push came to shove, he knew which side he was on.

In neighborhoods like Canarsie and eastern Queens, the counterrevolution had arrived. The "neighborhood," that building block of white Brooklyn, and the neighborhood school became the citadels of the counterrevolution. Parents and Taxpayers was an organization created in the early 1960s to insulate white local schools from the presence of Black students. Subsequently, the idea of the "neighborhood" or "community" school became a catchphrase for those trying to turn away Black (and other nonwhite) students.[98]

But if Black students were to be excluded from white schools, they soon demanded community schools of their own. And they, too, were wary of outsiders and had good reason to fear that outsiders would interfere with their plans. In the fall of 1968, Brownsville stood at the epicenter of what was the bitterest fight over education and race in the city's history. When the Ocean Hill–Brownsville Community School Board locked horns with the United Federation of Teachers (with Black control over local schools challenging the union and its heavily Jewish membership), it precipitated a citywide strike that shut down schools for almost two months, in what amounted to a fierce parting of the ways between liberals and leftists, Jews and African Americans.[99]

When this happened, Robinson, the supporter of Jewish causes and lifelong supporter of integration, took the side of the Black nationalist–

inspired school decentralizers. During the boycott for integration in 1964, Robinson had praised Bayard Rustin, saying he "exhibited the same mark of genius" he had displayed in organizing the March on Washington.[100] By 1968, he and Rustin were on different sides, despite their broadly similar centrist and anti-communist civil rights politics. In the 1968 strike, Rustin was an ally of the United Federation of Teachers and its combative leader, Albert Shanker. Robinson accused Rustin of being "one of the few race leaders who gave aid and comfort to the activities of Albert Shanker in the recent school strike—a strike directed against the good and welfare of the Black community." He also accused Rustin of trying to "curry favor with white folks" and of raising "the dirty flag of Black antisemitism." He noted that if there was any increase in Black antisemitism, the fault lies "with Shanker and those who approved his tactics," stopping just short, said the author of the article, of calling Rustin an Uncle Tom.[101] Untangling the claims and counterclaims of the school strike goes beyond the scope of this book. Robinson saw no inconsistency in supporting the fight for integrated schools in 1964 and supporting community control in 1968. The thread connecting them was the quest for Black citizenship.

The fight over decentralization in Ocean Hill–Brownsville in 1968 was one indication of the emergence of a new Black Brooklyn. Another was Bedford-Stuyvesant's election that year of Shirley Chisholm, the first Black woman elected to the House of Representatives. There have been profound changes in the borough in the half century since Jackie Robinson's passing. It is a new Brooklyn. Nostalgia for the Lost Cause of the Brooklyn Dodgers has faded as the team slowly slips from living memory. (By 2031 the Dodgers will have played in Los Angeles for as many years as they played in Brooklyn.) There will never be a statue of Walter O'Malley in Brooklyn, but the rage that led many to compare him to Hitler and Stalin has abated.[102] Truth is, Brooklyn has done just fine without the Dodgers. Brooklyn no longer needs a baseball team to center its identity. Within a few years of the Dodgers leaving, the beginning of the "rise of brownstone Brooklyn" in the 1960s saw new life, new money, new energy and ideas in neighborhoods such as Park Slope and Carroll Gardens.[103] Brooklyn is as vibrantly ethnic as it was during the Dodgers' heyday; it's now populated by African

Americans, West Indians, Latinos, Asians, and a hundred different ethnicities. And Brooklyn is a borough that has lost its inferiority complex. A backwater no more, it's cosmopolitan, a borough of hipsters, rappers, and gentrifiers. Starting with Shirley Chisholm, it has become an incubator for powerful Black politicians, such as Al Sharpton, Eric Adams, and Hakeem Jeffries. Brooklyn is now a place to move to, rather than away from.

But if the Dodgers have really left Brooklyn, Jackie Robinson has not. He is buried in Cypress Hills Cemetery, close to where Ebbets Field once stood. Since 1997, the former Interboro Parkway, snaking its way between Brooklyn and Queens, has been called the Jackie Robinson Parkway. But more significantly, Brooklyn has become a model of how integration as full and effective citizenship can work—not just Black citizenship but full citizenship for all ethnic minorities, proud of their backgrounds, proud to be Americans. Integration, as always, is fraught, but it is still tried and it still works.[104] Brooklyn still has many problems, of course. Affordable housing is a key issue, as is the juxtaposition of great wealth and great poverty. Ethnic citizenship is flourishing in Brooklyn. Integration has, and always will have, its opponents. But the roots of contemporary Brooklyn can be seen in Jackie Robinson's career on and off the field.

EIGHT

After the Dodgers

INTEGRATIONS SOUGHT AND DENIED

AFTER HIS RETIREMENT, JACKIE ROBINSON was one of the most visible spokespersons, provocateurs, and propagandists for civil rights and integration, lending his celebrity and unflagging energies to the cause. As one biographer wrote, from 1956 to 1960, he "arguably was the nation's most prominent civil rights advocate."[1] Perhaps, but there is no question that 1956 was a pivotal year both for him and for the civil rights movement. That year, as Robinson prepared for what proved to be his final season in professional baseball, Martin Luther King Jr.—who came to epitomize the cause of integration—first came to national attention. In February 1956, a few months after the Montgomery bus boycott began in December 1955, King was featured in his first substantial write-up in the *New York Times*. He was quoted as saying, "Integration is the great issue of our age, the great issue of our community. . . . We are in the midst of a great struggle, the consequences of which will be world-shaking."[2] The following month, the *Times* ran a feature on King, quoting him again: "I am for immediate integration. Segregation is evil and as a minister I cannot condone evil."[3]

Dr. King emerged as a national figure even as mass protests in the Deep South marked the most intense period of the long, postbellum struggle for civil rights for Black Americans. That struggle would culminate in the eradication of legal segregation in the South, and it would challenge formal and informal segregation in the North. In 1956, King and his supporters understood integration to mean ending racial exclusion and racial humiliation. Black Americans insisted on full citizenship and demanded being treated with the respect, privileges, and responsibilities of that citizenship. Transportation policies weren't the key purpose of the Montgomery bus boycott. Rather, "We Negroes have replaced self-pity with self-respect and self-deprecation with dignity."[4]

By the mid-1950s, the language of integration was changing. There was a growing sense that integration's goal had become tantalizing, more urgent, but somehow more distant: Every step forward made clearer the great distance to the final goal. King could call for "immediate integration," but activists now saw integration less as a concrete political demand that could be quickly satisfied than an ideal that gleamed on a distant horizon—something to be approached but perhaps never fully realized, democracy's asymptote.

An alternative vocabulary developed that described intermediate steps. A new word became popular in the early 1950s: "desegregation." To give a definition from 1952: "*Desegregation*—i.e., the mere admission of Negro students to existing institutions for white people—does not constitute *integration*."[5] As the distinguished psychologist and civil rights and integration activist Kenneth B. Clark stated: "Integration is a matter of the human heart; desegregation is matter of practical organization." He differentiated between warm-hearted acceptance and (often grudging) tolerance.[6] If desegregation was largely positive, even if slow, a more pejorative term arose that described a similar phenomenon. "Tokenism" came into wide use only around 1960. If the idea was familiar, the term was new. In that year, civil rights leader A. Philip Randolph decried tokenism as a "thin veneer of acceptance masquerading as democracy,"[7] or fobbing off African American aspirations for equality with superficial, cosmetic changes. Other observers saw tokenism as an "insidious sedative," the "opiate" of the movement for integration. When New York City's mayor Robert F. Wagner pointed to two African American appointees in his administration, Congressman Adam Clayton Powell scoffed: "Two out of two million persons of color was tokenism in its highest form."[8] Perhaps the term became popular because so many halting efforts at integration ended either in cul-de-sacs or by awarding African Americans impressive titles without the commensurate authority.

But if neither tokenism nor desegregation amounted to integration, then what *was* integration? By the early 1960s, both Martin Luther King and Jackie Robinson were decrying tokenism and white invocations of civil rights "patience." They thought that desegregation, even when "one hundred percent complete," would not amount to integration. Desegregation merely signaled the absence of segregation. King believed integration was positive, the "welcomed participation of Negroes into the total range of human activities"—that is, full citizenship and perhaps an even fuller "recognition of the sacredness of the human personality."[9] He regarded desegregation as a short-term legal fix to the problem of racism. Integration, to him and to Robinson, was a lasting, spiritual solution, the basis of the "beloved community."[10] And the key to the beloved community was pluralism, a lack of coercion, a maximizing of choice, including addressing historic inequalities and injustices.

The meaning of integration was changing in other ways as well. The original dichotomy, integration versus segregation, was largely seen in terms of legal segregation in the South, though African Americans and their supporters knew that there were many forms of discrimination and segregation beyond those legally mandated, and these forms of segregation existed and persisted outside of the states of the old Confederacy. When the *Brown/Briggs* decision came down in 1954, Kenneth B. Clark claimed that the New York City schools were segregated and becoming more so—something the Robinsons experienced in their years in St. Albans. This claim was vociferously denied by city officials, who argued that since no laws required all-Black or all-white schools, segregation didn't exist in the city's schools.[11] Civil rights activists countered that an all-Black school in New York City, with overcrowded classes taught by less senior teachers in an inferior physical plant, was a segregated school. Within a few years, a new term came into wide use. Promoted by the NAACP and the National Urban League, "de facto segregation" stood opposed to "de jure segregation."[12] If the term was a little misleading—for instance, the board of education's zoning policies and decisions about where and when to build new schools certainly contributed to school segregation in New York City, as the

Robinson's discovered in St. Albans—it stood for a higher principle. There is no neutrality. If you are not actively fighting for integration (and this includes governments, civic organizations, and private individuals), you are aiding and abetting segregation.

This was the dilemma of integration in the mid-1950s. Could the goal of integration be reached slowly, by piling increment upon increment, until its collective force became irresistible? Or would integration's success require something more drastic to break the back of segregation, something more convulsive, something more revolutionary? Langston Hughes, in one of his columns about his fictional Harlem everyman, Simple, recounted this conversation in 1955: "We are being rapidly integrated into every phase of American life, from the army and navy to schools, industry, advancing, advancing," said Hughes. To which Simple replied, "I have not advanced one step. Still the same old job, same old salary, same old kitchenette, same old Harlem, and the same old color." Simple suggested that things wouldn't really change without another civil war against white supremacy, but if Black people wanted to win this civil war, they had best arm themselves with nuclear weapons.[13]

This was the reality of integration that Jackie Robinson faced. He believed in the importance and necessity of steady progress. But he also wanted weapons. Massive protests and boycotts were one weapon. Convincing powerful politicians to implement sweeping reforms was another. He would organize on the streets and would work with both mainstream Democrats and Republicans. He deeply believed in both Black self-reliance and interracial cooperation because he thought that the cause of Black citizenship could only be won by Black advocacy, and though African Americans had to do by themselves and for themselves, integration would also require outside assistance.

In 1960, the Baltimore *Afro-American* observed that Robinson, after retiring from sports, still "seem[ed] to thrive on controversy."[14] This was true for both Robinson the athlete and Robinson the civil rights advocate. Perhaps more than before or since, the quest for Black unity was central to Black politics. This in turn placed potential disunity at the center of Black politics. No civil rights organization was more important to Robinson than the NAACP. But he had no problem publicly calling it out. In 1962, the NAACP's executive director, Roy Wilkins, complained, somewhat petulantly, that the NAACP was doing almost all the work while Martin Luther King was getting all the credit. Robinson wrote, in rebuke, "It is dangerously foolish for our leaders to divide our ranks when we need our greatest unity."[15] But he also wrote in the same year that the demand for Black unity could be a trap. "I have been pleading for Negro unity for years. But if sticking together means you continue to endorse a man simply because he is black—or green—or white—when you truly feel he has been wrong, you can have that kind of sticking together."[16]

The civil rights era was also a time for righteous indignation, and civil rights leaders were often judged by the degree and sharpness of their anger. There was an outpouring of Black anger at the nature of American society; a similar flood of white anger at the temerity of Black anger; and Black anger at white anger. Black anger was also directed at Black Americans who were judged to be insufficiently angry. Those so judged to be lacking in outrage, however, were often very angry, both at their accusers and at white Americans. "Uncle Tom" was a favorite epithet and was probably used too freely and casually. Jackie Robinson was often accused of being one, though he sometimes flung the accusation back at others. In 1968, after one of many such attacks by Black militants, he stated, "I intend to Tom for no one, black or white."[17] The decade of the 1960s gave rise to yet another new term: "generation gap." And the representatives of an older generation were often suspect. As the African American religious thinker Howard Thurman, a man in his seventies, wrote: "As the older generation . . . we have been angered by their anger, even though secretly we marvel at the courage of their anger. . . . They turn and rend us because we have sought to nourish them with our sense of our failure."[18]

Jackie Robinson shared these sentiments, always willing to criticize those he basically agreed with, like Roy Wilkins, even as he tried to understand those with whom he was often in vehement disagreement, such as the members of the Nation of Islam. Robinson appreciated civil rights moderates for their practicality and liked the radicals for their lack of moderation. He understood the need for both. As the *New York Amsterdam News* noted in 1962, he was the embodiment of the famous statement, usually (though incorrectly) attributed to Voltaire: "I disapprove of what you say, but I will defend to the death your right to say it."[19] Perhaps the main quality that helped Robinson navigate the rapid currents of Black politics in the 1960s and early 1970s was a radical honesty, a commitment to be true to himself. He best expressed this quality to Roy Wilkins, this time in private correspondence: "I am sorry that you cannot accept honest criticism. . . . When I speak it's because I know what I am doing. I am sorry the truth hurts so much."[20]

On 8 December 1956, Jackie Robinson was awarded the prestigious NAACP's Spingarn Medal, the first athlete to receive the award. It was, he said afterwards, the high point of his career, if not of his life: "To be honored in this way by the NAACP means more to me than anything that has happened to me before."[21] During the ceremony, he said that the award was a vindication for the way he had conducted himself in the athletic spotlight. He had been encouraged "not to speak up every time I thought there was an injustice," told "that I should just let things work themselves out without involving myself in them."[22] Yet he had not done that. Robinson saw it as an award for his outspokenness. But what few knew at the Spingarn ceremony was that Robinson had already decided that he had played his last professional baseball game.

Among those left in the dark about his decision were the Brooklyn Dodgers, who, on 12 December traded him to the rival New York Giants. Robinson was insulted by the trade. He announced his retirement and refused to report to the Giants. This unleashed a torrent of commentary, most of it negative. But if Robinson was spared from having to play for the Giants or the Dodgers in 1957, that worst of all possible years for National League baseball in New York City, he had to find gainful employment. Even a Hall of Fame career like Robinson's in no way left a player financially set for life. "We could afford very few family vacations," Rachel Robinson wrote, in explaining why the Robinsons often accepted the invitation extended to Robinson and other star athletes to stay for free in Grossinger's, the Borscht Belt resort.[23] They still had to earn a living, preferably one that would support them in the way to which they had become accustomed.

Major-league baseball showed limited interest in employing Robinson in some capacity, and he wondered why that was—whether because of his race, his temper, or the widespread belief that whites would not take orders from African Americans. There had yet to be any Black coaches or managers at any level in major- or minor-league baseball. In any event, he was reluctant to leave his family and the New York metropolitan area to coach or manage in a distant city. Like many men who grew up fatherless, he was determined not to be an absent parent to his children. After the 1956 season, he asked a friend, Martin Stone, to hunt out appropriate business opportunities. The day he was informed of his trade to the Giants, he signed a contract with Chock full o'Nuts, a New York City chain of coffee shops and luncheonettes, as vice president in charge of personnel relations, for $30,000 a year.[24] The salary was generous, in 1957 dollars, and the position enabled him to live at home with his young family.

Of course, nothing concerning Jackie Robinson lacked a racial context or dimension. And he again was a racial pathbreaker, perhaps as much or more so than in baseball. His position as a vice president marked the entry of Black Americans into white corporate America.[25] Although Robinson was not quite the first African American to enter the upper echelons of white corporate hierarchy, he was probably the most prominent Black middle manager to date, and likely the first African American executive to have his photograph in the business section of the *New York Times*.[26]

Yet the biggest difference between his stints with Dodgers and Chock full o'Nuts was that his hiring in 1957 was not a turning point and did not really open the gates of corporate America to African Americans. His employment became less a precedent than an exception to the pervading rule of "whites only." Black executives with any degree of real authority were rare and would remain so at least into the 1960s.[27] It was an example of "tokenism" in a way that his joining the Dodgers was not.

But in many ways, Chock full o'Nuts presented a bigger challenge than the Dodgers. His athletic ability was never seriously doubted, not by himself or others, and he soon confounded the racists and skeptics who thought otherwise. But Robinson had little to no relevant business experience, and business acumen is less quantifiable than athletic prowess. White Americans, overall, were more willing to watch Black athletes perform than welcome them to the sanctums in which real money could be made. Robinson wrote in his autobiography, "In the business world I always strove to learn as much as I could so I would not be just a figurehead."[28] But as Robinson knew well, there was probably no Black man in America more likely to be hired as a figurehead than himself.

The alternative to positions of questionable influence in white-run corporations was the venerable path of working within the Black business world. This was a much smaller universe, largely limited to serving the African American market, which represented about 10 percent of potential American consumers, and not a particularly wealthy slice. In large part because of an informal embargo from white-owned financial institutions, Black businesses were often built on shaky financial foundations. However, Black businesses held out the promise of control, ownership, and real authority in ways that were impossible in white businesses. Black businesses also had the more elusive promise, beyond economics, of building and strengthening the social and political realities within Black communities. Jackie Robinson would work in both the white and Black business worlds, but in reverse order from his baseball career. He would work for Chock full o'Nuts, a white-owned company, until 1964. After 1964 and for the rest of his life, he would work in the entrepreneurial equivalent of the Negro Leagues.

Chock full o'Nuts was an unusual sort of white-owned business, which was why its founder and owner, William Black, was interested in hiring Jackie Robinson. Black felt he needed an African American to oversee personnel matters. Black, né Schwartz, was born in eastern Europe around 1902, although he was raised in Brooklyn and was one of the many Jewish entrepreneurs Robinson would work with. After receiving an engineering degree from Columbia University, Black found that antisemitism limited the market for Jewish engineers, so he went into the retail nut business. By 1932, he owned a chain of eighteen nut shops in the city. Black kept the name but not the product as he converted his stores into quality, low-cost luncheonettes and coffee shops.[29] By 1960, Chock full o'Nuts was selling 100,000 cups of coffee a day and had annual revenues of $30 million.[30]

In part because of his early experiences with antisemitism, Black was committed to opening stores in African American neighborhoods and to hiring African Americans to work in his shops.[31] The Chock full o'Nuts on 125th Street became a Harlem institution.[32] In 1958, there were reports that among Chock full o'Nuts's 1,000 employees, 80 percent were African Americans.[33] In 1963, according to Robinson, the company had thirty-three lunch counters in the city, with 1,200 employees, of whom all but 50 or 60 were African American. .[34] In 1969, the *New York Times* unfunnily and unfairly, with a hefty dose of racial malice, printed a letter that defined "Black Power" as "the all-pervasive climate in any Chock full o'Nuts restaurant when one sits at a counter and waits for service; and waits and waits."[35]

Robinson was hired to provide a Black face, and a very famous one, in the company's upper management as a liaison with its Black workers. By all accounts, he was diligent and hardworking and did a fine job. But it is also clear that he was hired, in part, to prevent the unionization of the company's work staff. Black later said, tellingly, "I hired Jackie because a majority of the people who work for me are colored—and I figured they would worship him."[36]

Black was a generous employer who paid his workers well and extended to them several benefits, including health insurance, pensions, and an annual bonus.[37] But one of the goals of his "welfare capitalism" was to dissuade workers from choosing to unionize, and Robinson was a key player in this effort. In 1958, Local 262 of the Retail, Wholesale and Department Store Union lost a vote, 22 to 44, at a Chock full o'Nuts plant in Harrison, New Jersey, where the coffee was roasted and food was prepared. The National Labor Relations Board ruled the election fair, even though it found Robinson and another vice president had engaged in "appeals to racial prejudice." According to the allegations by the union, Robinson told the Black workers in the plant that the unionization effort had been spurred "because white workers were jealous of his position," and should the union win, "all Negroes would be fired." A Black worker with ten years' seniority was told by Robinson that he could vote in the union election as he chose, "but he shouldn't stick his neck out," and if he was active in the union, "he couldn't help him in any way."[38] In a later unionization effort in 1963, six employees involved in the union effort were fired, and Robinson defended the decision to terminate the workers, albeit reluctantly. He had been on vacation and had not been consulted.[39]

For the rest of his life, Robinson would occasionally be dogged by accusations that he was opposed to unions. His friends, such as onetime Manhattan borough president Percy Sutton, argued that at Chock full o'Nuts, Robinson he was just doing his job by opposing unionization—it was not an ideological crusade.[40] These accusations certainly contributed to his decision to quit the company in 1964, telling the press that he did not want to "want to work in any job where I would be a figurehead."[41] Robinson felt he had been made "the scapegoat in the union situation," and he didn't like it.[42] He also didn't like it when company executives asked him to make clear that his statements on civil rights were his own and did not reflect the position of the company.[43] Robinson left his position with the company, his major effort to work as an executive in a white business, with some bitterness, feeling that he had been used and that his racial identity and celebrity had been exploited. He also felt that to some extent he had been forced to choose between his job and civil rights advocacy.

Starting in 1957, being a civil rights advocate would become an ever more important aspect of how Jackie Robinson understood his public role. In the early 1950s, he had often been a featured speaker for the National Conference of Christians and Jews (NCCJ), and in 1954, he became chair of its Commission on Community Organizing. But the NCCJ understood its work as more educational than political, and in its southern affiliates, its commitments did not always extend to an active opposition to segregation.[44] But after winning the Spingarn Medal, Robinson became one of the NAACP's leading advocates. One of the first things he did after his retirement from baseball was to embark on an eleven-city tour for the NAACP Freedom Fund, with the goal of raising $1 million for the organization. He told his audiences that "ninety-four years is long enough to wait for full citizenship rights, and unless Negroes push hard now," the opportunity might well be lost.[45] By the summer of 1958, he was elected to the NAACP's board of directors and became cochair of its life membership campaign.[46] He openly criticized the critics of the NAACP and in 1960 wrote Martin Luther King that he was "quite disturbed because of reports I have been receiving that people who claim to represent the Southern Christian Leadership Conference are saying the NAACP has outlived its usefulness."[47]

For the rest of his life, he was both an ardent supporter of the NAACP and its sometime critic, prodding it to more militancy. It was a complex organization with many moving parts. Militant local branches existed alongside less militant branches, and the national office was generally unenthusiastic about large-scale public protests. Robinson's temperament was ill-suited to an organization that sometimes placed caution above boldness. Lecturing on behalf of the NAACP in Atlanta in 1957, he told his audience, "Negroes should do everything short of violence to achieve what is rightly ours under the constitution." At an NAACP convention in 1958, he said that "colored people have failed miserably in not taking the initiative in the civil rights struggle" and argued that if African Americans do not fight for their rights, whites certainly will not. The NAACP needed "a more aggressive stand" and needed to "get on the street and sell the importance of the NAACP to the little man."[48]

An early example of Robinson "getting on the street" took place a few months later, in the fall of 1958. That October, Robinson was a leader of a little-remembered march on Washington: "10,000 in Youth March Say Integrate," ran the headline in the *Baltimore Afro-American.* Like the more famous march on Washington five years later, it used the organizational talents of A. Philip Randolph, had backing from several labor unions and civil rights organizations, and featured speakers including Robinson, Harry Belafonte, and Coretta Scott King. The NAACP, skeptical of the efficacy of demonstrations, did not back the Washington march, and when the head of the New York chapter, no doubt reflecting the opinion of Roy Wilkins, said it had been a waste of time and money, Robinson bitterly refuted the accusation, stating that people were losing interest in the NAACP because of just those sorts of attitudes.[49]

In 1960, he enthusiastically welcomed the beginning of the protests on luncheon counters. He promised to lead the "largest picket line in the history of New York City" against the Harlem branches of Woolworths and Grants, the national chains of five- and ten-cent stores that were segregated in their Southern affiliates.[50] Shortly thereafter, in Cleveland, he joined a picket line against a chain store, telling the crowd, "We are going to cause trouble until we get our equal opportunities. What has happened in South Korea [a recent student-led revolution that toppled dictator Syngman Rhee] can happen in south Alabama or on the south shore of Lake Erie."[51] He told crowds that one of his least favorite words in the English language was "patience." He'd heard it from YMCA officials in Pasadena who were trying to explain why Blacks couldn't use their swimming pool and from sportswriters who told him, "Jackie, you can't push this thing. It will come of itself. You're only endangering your career."[52] But he told students that real patience, a refusal to be dissuaded from one's objectives, was the basis of true protests. He related an incident that happened in one of his very last professional baseball games, during an exhibition tour of Japan by the Dodgers after the 1956 season. A crowd of forty thousand came to see the Dodgers play, but the game was interrupted by a torrential rainstorm and was cancelled. Japanese officials told the Dodgers that "every one of the 40,000 assembled would sit in the stands through the downpour through tomorrow morning, to protest the curtailed game." The Dodgers played the game in the rain.[53] Sit-ins can work.

But if his heart was with the sit-in protesters at luncheon counters, his head was with the NAACP. What was most important for Black Americans was to speak in as unified a voice as possible. If he at times thought the NAACP was a lumbering behemoth, its size mattered more than its gait. What the NAACP sometimes lacked in dynamism, it made up for in stature, voice, and accumulated political heft. Robinson, despite his occasional public remonstrances, continued to speak on behalf of and tout the work of the NAACP. In terms of large, politically active Black organizations in the late 1950s, the NAACP was past its glory days, but in some ways, it remained the only game in town. The old Black left was moribund, while the new Black left was waiting to be born. Other civil rights organizations, like CORE and the National Urban League were relatively minor players. The sit-in protesters and Martin Luther King had charisma aplenty but were backed by weak organizations. The NAACP was building on its legal and political victories, such as the *Brown/Briggs* decision and the Civil Rights Act of 1957, the first comprehensive civil rights legislation passed since Reconstruction. The NAACP was both avowedly anticommunist and vigorous in its fight for the rights of Africans against imperialism and apartheid.[54] It was committed to integration and saw enhancing Black citizenship as a way of furthering the rights of all Americans. Robinson told a Chicago audience in 1957 that "in our struggle for civil rights we must not be motivated by color but by our love of God and for freedom. I would resign as head of the campaign [for the Freedom Fund] if I thought the NAACP was fighting for the rights for Negroes alone."[55]

In fighting for universal human rights through the particularity of one's own ethnic group, Robinson had a model and example in mind: the Jews. Jackie Robinson as a Dodgers player became one of the country's most prominent philosemites. Through coming to Brooklyn, a borough whose population was almost half Jewish, he found that Jews were among his most supportive fans and sportswriters, his family's most welcoming neighbors both in Brooklyn and in Connecticut. Jewish people were his business partners, his hosts for numerous after-dinner addresses, and his political allies. For many years the Robinson family's favorite vacation spot was Grossinger's, the famous resort in the heart of the Jewish Catskills.[56] He appreciated the ways Jews fought against antisemitism—a fight Robinson fully embraced—and linked prejudice against Jewish people with prejudice against Black Americans.

Yet he was also aware of the differences between the two groups. By the 1950s, Jewish people had entered the mainstream of American life in ways African Americans had not. At Chock full o'Nuts, he worked for a man who had come to the United States as a penniless Lithuanian immigrant, and other examples of Jewish entrepreneurial success were all around him. In politics, in the recent history of New York and Connecticut, the two states in which he had residences, there had been Jewish governors, US senators, state attorneys general and comptrollers, while there had not been an African American elected to a statewide office, in any state, since Reconstruction. If hardly eradicated, antisemitism in the United States had been pushed beyond the margins of respectability, reduced to a "low ambient hum," while anti-Black racism certainly had not.[57] And Jews had accomplished this not by emphasizing their particularity but by demanding equal rights and citizenship for all, as in the overwhelming, organized Jewish support for the Ives-Quinn Act.[58]

Yet Robinson's admiration for Jews did not always avoid stereotypes, as in this Baltimore speech in 1957: "I'm not going to talk about how much money the Jewish people have (we know that they control the money), but I believe that we have at least four times as many colored people as there are Jewish people. I can understand that we don't have the capital [that

Jews have]. But nevertheless with four times as many people if we can just try to make everyone understand the importance of working together. The Jewish people, when they want to do something, they start going out [to do it]."[59]

That said, in early 1960, in a column about antisemitism in Europe and the specter of the "revival of Hitlerism," Robinson penned as eloquent a statement of civil rights universalism as one could imagine: "Since every last one of us is a member of some vulnerable minority—whether it be by race, religion, national origin, political party, education, occupation or other differences—none of us is safe once group-hate is unleashed against any other."[60] Robinson always anathemized antisemitism and praised the Black-Jewish alliance. Even as the alliance was fraying. In August 1968, he wrote, "I think very frankly that the Jew has been our [Black folks'] greatest ally. We go back even before the Negro started pressure in civil rights, and the Jew was there working with their organizations." The literature on (or exposing the myth of) this supposed golden age of Black-Jewish political harmony is voluminous.[61] To the extent this era existed, Jackie Robinson was perhaps its avatar.[62]

In his work with the NAACP, King and the Southern Christian Leadership Conference, the SNCC, and other civil rights organizations, he did not seek a political career or office for himself—perhaps a natural step for one of his immense celebrity. He stuck to his pledge of 1959: "I have no plans whatsoever of running for public office. I feel I can be of better service by remaining outside of politics."[63] Possibly this was because, for most of his post-baseball career, there was no obvious position for him to seek, perhaps other than the seat occupied by Harlem congressman Adam Clayton Powell, and if he had run against Powell as a Republican, he undoubtedly would have lost. He sometimes stated that the income that a political career (at least an honest political career) could provide was not the financial return he sought. As he said in 1960: "Many of my friends have asked me about politics from time to time, and I have always answered I couldn't afford to be a politician."[64] Or perhaps, given his unique access to powerful politicians and his media presence, political office struck him as superfluous. After all, his endorsements carried substantial political weight.[65] Robinson had many platforms to make himself heard. In 1959, WMCA, a

New York City radio station, began to broadcast *The Jackie Robinson Show,* which featured such guests as Eleanor Roosevelt and New York City mayor Robert Wagner.[66] That same year, in April, the *New York Post,* at the time the liberal stronghold among the city's dailies, gave Robinson a thrice-a-week column; in it, alongside his thoughts about various sporting matters, he opined freely on the political issues of the day. Made available to other newspapers through syndication, it was probably the first widely published column by an African American that appeared in white newspapers.[67] It was discontinued in the fall of 1960 after he announced his support for Richard Nixon in the presidential race, and did not resume.[68] This was unfortunate and speaks to certain narrowness of vision on the part of the *Post*'s editors. Although he would, for most of the 1960s, have a syndicated column in the Black press, it's a minor tragedy that he was cut off from a wider white readership thereafter. However, whatever the medium and whatever challenges he encountered, Jackie Robinson made himself heard on the issues of the day.[69]

Robinson usually claimed to be as "independent as I can be."[70] He wrote in 1962: "The Negro will continue to be held down so long as he continues to let Democrats—or Republicans—feel their vote is in their pocket. The Negro . . . should keep the parties guessing. He should vote for the man and the issues rather than as a bloc for either party."[71] Several years later, he stated that "a phalanx of Republicans and Democrats are able to forget party lines when it comes to standing up for good old white supremacy. . . . The Negro people—forgetting party lines—should rise up in massive retaliation against the[se] hypocrites." Quoting and approving the comment of an unnamed young man he had met in Brooklyn, he wrote: "Partisan politics is a luxury only the white man can afford."[72] That said, he was a Republican-leaning independent, supporting a Democratic nominee only if there was no suitable Republican alternative, although this was happening, over the course of the 1960s and early 1970s, with increasing (and for Robinson, distressing) regularity.

A historian of the Republican Party has written that "a scenario in which the conservative faction would take over the entire party and force all Republicans to dance to their tune would have strained credibility in 1960."[73] By 1972, this scenario was certainly seen as possible but not inevitable.

Jackie Robinson spent his political life waging war against this happening, and as he expressed in 1964, "I would love to be a Republican."[74] But the problem was, as he'd written the year before: "You would think that, just once in a while, the Republicans would forget and do something right on the race issue."[75] As late as 1971, he wrote President Nixon he "felt strongly that is not good policy for any minority to put all of their eggs in one political basket." But with the "anti-black" Spiro Agnew as his vice-president and 1972 running mate, he told Nixon that supporting him was impossible.[76]

In hindsight, it appears that Robinson was railing against an unstoppable historical tide, trying to hold back the sea. That is not how he, and many others, viewed it at the time. Certainly Robinson, unlike many others, recognized the underlying problem. If the Democrats became the party of Black America, the Republicans would eventually become the party of non-Black and anti-Black America. And this is what happened. The consequences have been even worse than Robinson could have imagined, and a straight line can be drawn from the Republican Party courting segregationists such as Strom Thurmond to the dark, racist, antidemocratic rage of Donald Trump. But Jackie Robinson believed enough in American democracy, and worried enough about white racism, to envision two political parties sympathetic to Black needs. The country was just beginning to recover from the long night of the racism of the Democratic Party. He did not want a repeat. We are all the poorer, and worse off, because Jackie Robinson and other moderate Republicans lost their battle for the soul of the Republican Party.

That said, one did not need to be especially clairvoyant to perceive the direction toward which the Republican Party was slouching by 1960. In 1959, Robinson wrote that many Republicans had formed "an unholy alliance with southern Democrats."[77] By the late 1950s and early 1960s, while the Democrats were still the party of the segregationist South, many Republicans *aspired* to be the party of the segregationist South.[78]

Robinson enjoyed participation in national politics. He was gratified by the attention he received from some of the most influential politicians in the country, and he thought that his voice needed to be heard at a time when African Americans were still a rarity in the highest echelons of power. In 1952, he supported the Democratic candidate for president, Adlai Stevenson, despite his lackluster platform on civil rights.[79] Perhaps that reflects an early identification as a New Deal Democrat. But in the 1950s, he soon became an admirer of President Eisenhower. In November 1953, at the fortieth anniversary dinner of the Anti-Defamation League, President Eisenhower went out of his way to shake Robinson's hand, crossing the dais to do so. Robinson was elated and wrote Eisenhower to tell him so.[80] Although he supported Eisenhower in 1956, he soon became disenchanted with his turtle's pace toward racial equality. In May 1957, Robinson said, "Negroes have every right to believe that Eisenhower has forgotten them." Several months later, after the desegregation crisis at Central High in Little Rock, Arkansas, musician Louis Armstrong said of Eisenhower that "the government can go to hell," and Robinson heartly concurred.[81] His final verdict on Eisenhower's civil rights inaction was damning.[82]

In 1960, Robinson became deeply involved in presidential politics. Despite his Republican leanings, the first presidential candidate he campaigned for was Sen. Hubert Humphrey (D-MN), a strong supporter of civil rights, in the 1960 Democratic primary in Wisconsin.[83] But Humphrey lost to the eventual nominee, John F. Kennedy, and Robinson did not trust JFK or his brother Robert. After Kennedy captured the nomination, Robinson complained that "the Democrats have considerably less appeal to Negro voters this year than any time since the death of Franklin D. Roosevelt."[84] Robinson's great fear was that Northern Democrats, to govern effectively, would sacrifice civil rights to seek comity with Southern Democrats, or, as he wrote in 1959: "A weak Democrat as president with Southerners heading up the top committees would be far worse than a Republican *president* who would at least be willing to express himself on this matter of civil rights."[85] (If by 1960 the formerly "solid South" was increasingly up for grabs, Kennedy did better than his predecessor, Stevenson, recapturing Louisiana and Texas for the Democrats.)

This left him to support the Republican nominee, Richard Nixon, and Robinson was an enthusiastic campaigner for him in the fall. He hoped that in the course of the campaign, Nixon would "disengage himself from the restraint of supporting Eisenhower policies with which he may not have been in full accord."[86] Nixon, both a star-struck fan and a consummate politician, played Robinson like a fiddle, writing him obsequiously: "While you disclaimed any pretensions toward being a political expert, it seems to me that you handled this subject with the same agility which you always show on the baseball diamond."[87] Robinson's decision to write favorably about Nixon and actively campaign for him evoked a good deal of incredulity. (Among those who disagreed with him on this was Rachel Robinson.) He received "an avalanche of mail" with "many wondering how I could ever consider supporting 'Tricky Dicky.'"[88]

Robinson probably supported Nixon in part because he thought that such a determined and implacable anti-communist would take Cold War pledges to fight segregation seriously. In the fall of 1960, invoking the potential threats to American power of Fidel Castro, Nikita Khruschev, and Gamal Abdel Nasser, Robinson quoted Nixon as saying, "Every act of discrimination is like handing a gun to the Communists."[89] Nixon lost the election, in part because, despite Robinson's personal pleading, Nixon refused to call Georgia authorities to urge the release of Martin Luther King from prison. (Robert Kennedy made the call.) Robinson was beside himself, but despite this and other dissatisfactions with the campaign, he stuck with Nixon to the end. By the next year, he complained that by the end of the campaign, Nixon had "given up on the Negro vote," and as a result the "Negro vote beat Nixon."[90] Nonetheless, in 1962, he gave Nixon a second chance. In an interview given to the *New York Times* in April, his interviewer reported that Robinson was "impressed, and continues to be impressed, with Nixon's position on civil rights." Robinson said that "he was straight on the issues that were important to me. But Kennedy is a very much better man than I anticipated."[91]

But by 1963, Nixon's growing accommodation to the segregationist South infuriated Robinson. "I fought for you," Robinson would write in "An Open Letter to Dick Nixon," "because I believed you to be sincere on the racial question and I believed Senator Kennedy to be insincere."[92] In this, he declared he had been mistaken, but nonetheless, he continued to run hot and cold about the Kennedys. Robinson continued to criticize Kennedy in the early years of his presidency, though after Kennedy's major address on civil rights in June 1963, Robinson said that he had won his vote for 1964.[93] In that fall he strongly supported Kennedy's successor, Lyndon Johnson, though he just as strongly opposed Robert Kennedy's New York

State senatorial bid that year and was no more enthusiastic about his 1968 presidential run.[94]

In the early 1960s, Robinson saw the main culprit on the Republican Party's road to ruin in Sen. Barry Goldwater (R-AZ), who he thought was trying to fashion "some sort of white man's party out of the GOP." He wondered why so many Republicans were not sufficiently concerned about the threat.[95] Goldwater's assiduous courting of the white South and his opposition to the Civil Rights Act of 1964 were to Robinson a declaration of war against Black Republicans and Black Americans in general. Just before the tumultuous Republican convention in San Francisco in 1964, he stated that Goldwater was "a bigot, an advocate of white supremacy and more dangerous than Governor Wallace. If Senator Goldwater announced a change in his views I would not believe him."[96] At the convention in San Francisco, liberals were hooted and hollered at and sometimes physically attacked. "I believe I now know," he wrote in the convention's aftermath, "how it felt to be a Jew in Hitler's Germany."[97] Robinson would later describe the convention as a "nightmare" that "disgraced and vilified every decent thing that had ever been Republican." It was the party's "greatest disaster," he said, and he accused Goldwater supporter Richard Nixon of having "ravaged and raped" the best traditions of the Republican Party.[98]

Still, Robinson persevered in trying to save the party from itself. For much of the last years of his life, his hopes for the Republicans and the nation centered around the enigmatic and slippery figure of Nelson Rockefeller. The New York governor had considerable political gifts, but the tragedy of his life, as he saw it, was that with all his money, fame, and talent, he couldn't buy, or perhaps a bit more fairly, couldn't win, the presidency. And arguably the tragedy of Jackie Robinson's political life was that, until almost the very end, he believed that a Nelson Rockefeller presidency was essential for the future of the country.

Rockefeller was elected governor of New York State in 1958 and was reelected three times, serving until 1973. He also sought, unsuccessfully, the Republican nomination for president in 1960, 1964, and 1968. In December 1974, President Gerald Ford appointed him vice president of the United States. He became the titular figure for an entire political ideology, the "Rockefeller Republican."[99] In the spring of 1964, when Robinson left

Chock full o'Nuts, it was to become a member of Rockefeller's campaign staff. From 1966 to 1968, he was a member of Rockefeller's state administration as the Special Assistant for Community Affairs and avowed on multiple occasions that "I am a Rockefeller Republican."[100]

One characteristic of the Rockefeller Republican, and no doubt this was most important to Robinson, was a strong commitment to civil rights. In 1960, when Rockefeller made his first somewhat tentative bid for national office, he made this a core of his campaign. He gave a speech in Chicago to the NAACP that was hailed in the *Amsterdam News* as the "strongest, most forthright, ever made by a major political candidate on the rights and equality of the Negro," a veritable "Magna Carta of civil rights." Rockefeller advocated for legislation addressing voting rights, employment, and discrimination in contracts, and called for the Justice Department to use all its powers to enforce school desegregation, to end housing discrimination, and to create job training programs. He called for these words to be included in the platform of the upcoming Republican convention, while insisting that it wasn't words but actions that mattered.[101]

Jackie Robinson was among those impressed, and he campaigned with him for Nixon that year, after Rockefeller failed to win the nomination. In 1962, he campaigned with Rockefeller during his gubernatorial reelection bid. In 1963, he touted his presidential candidacy for 1964 in the *Amsterdam News,* saying that it was "imperative that the Republican Party line up behind the banner of Nelson Rockefeller."[102] Another columnist in the *Amsterdam News* said much the same: "In many of the crises we have faced in the Deep South, Nelson Rockefeller's voice is the first to be heard," and "I am convinced that Nelson Rockefeller has a real grasp and understanding of what the Negro revolution is about and is committed to its goals."[103] This columnist's name? Martin Luther King Jr.

But Rockefeller's genuine civil rights idealism was tempered by his overweening ambitions and Republican realities. In 1960, he praised the civil rights commitment of the Republican assembly leader Joseph Carlino, who a few years before had baldly stated that "the problem of discrimination does not exist in New York State" and who continued to leave some of the strongest provisions of proposed civil rights legislation on the cutting-room floor.[104] In at least two cases, in 1959 and 1961, over the objections of Jackie Robinson and other civil rights leaders, Rockefeller allowed the extradition of Black escapees to Southern states (Florida and South Carolina) in cases in which there was serious doubts about their guilt and deep worries about how they would be treated after their rendition.[105] In 1964, Rockefeller vetoed several pieces of legislation that would have strengthened New York City's anti-bias regulations.[106]

Robinson perhaps rationalized some of these anti–civil rights decisions by Rockefeller as forced concessions to political necessity, but there were lines that Rockefeller crossed that Robinson never could. After his valiant campaign against Goldwater in 1964, and after getting booed and hissed at the Republican convention, in the end Rockefeller endorsed the Republican nominee. This endorsement prompted Robinson to write Rockefeller that, evidently, he now saw Goldwater as "a man of courage and integrity." Accusing Rockefeller of rejecting "the ideals and principles" for which he had always stood, his endorsement of Goldwater was to Robinson "one of the most disappointing things that has ever happened to me."[107] But he overcame his disappointment and subsequently joined his gubernatorial staff. He understood the limits of his influence. When, in 1966, Rockefeller refused to support the creation of a Civilian Complaint Review Board, Robinson did not directly attack Rockefeller, but instead praised its backers, the two Senators from New York State, Jacob Javits and Robert Kennedy.[108]

In 1968, Robinson again promoted the idea of a presidential run, though Rockefeller did not pursue his candidacy for long. Robinson left Rockefeller's staff in 1968 to campaign for Hubert Humphrey. Had he lived, in 1972 he probably, reluctantly, would have voted for George McGovern. He would not have voted for Nixon.[109]

Over the next few years, Rockefeller moved sharply to the right on welfare and crime and in his opposition to busing. In May 1972, and only a few months before his own death, Robinson wrote Rockefeller, stating that he had lost faith and confidence in him and accusing the governor of having lost the "sensitivity and understanding" that he once possessed: "Getting ahead politically is more important to you than what is right." Robinson avoided specifics, but there can be little doubt that he was primarily concerned with racial matters. He closed the letter, "I am just confused and discouraged and feel a good friend has let me down."[110]

Rockefeller responded quickly. He too was saddened at the exchange but wrote that "times have changed, Jackie," and that he had learned that "liberalism ceases to work at some point if not controlled by realism."[111] For Robinson this was the liberalism and realism of fools. Rockefeller, after Robinson's death, would move farther to the right, reconciling with segregationists such as Strom Thurmond and George Wallace.[112] As Marsha Barrett has written, despite his early commitment to civil rights, by the end of his career Rockefeller had "squandered one of the Republican Party's most high-profile opportunities to create a multicultural, cross-class consistency and delegitimated the GOP tradition of providing an active government attuned to the changing needs of Americans."[113] Robinson was perhaps writing of Rockefeller when, in the closing pages of his 1972 autobiography, he wrote "I believed in following principle even if the man didn't seem to offer outstanding possibilities. I never believed in backing out just because things weren't the best that they could be."[114] Jackie Robinson spent his political life searching for the powerful white politician who would share his commitment and passion for integration. None of Robinson's forays into presidential politics had particularly happy endings.

Robinson no doubt felt that he had no choice. In 1962, explaining why he now preferred golf to baseball, he said, "I like to participate. I'm not a spectator, and never have been."[115] Watching from the sidelines never appealed to him. The point of political protest was to gain political power. He was equally opposed to tests of political purity and to weak compromises that conceded too much without adequate return. The year before, in 1961, President Kennedy wanted to nominate a Black man to a significant position in his administration but felt the country wasn't quite ready for a Black cabinet member. However, he appointed the distinguished African American urbanist Robert C. Weaver to head the Housing and Home Finance Agency. By early 1962, Kennedy had not kept his promise to issue an executive order on open housing, and his civil rights initiatives were widely seen by Black leaders, including Robinson, as dilatory and inadequate.[116] What should Robert Weaver do? Robinson wrote, in perhaps an implied criticism of Weaver: "If the President of the United States thinks he can satisfy the Negro because he has made some nice appointments . . . he is sadly mistaken."[117] A prominent Black journalist suggested that Weaver, in not openly criticizing Kennedy while running an agency that was notorious in its discriminatory policies (which he'd been unable to really change), had sullied his reputation and was honor-bound to resign. Robinson disagreed and thought it a cheap shot. He wrote: "We are not impressed when someone important quits a club in New York or Washington because of the sudden realization that the club does not admit Negroes. If these same people wished to make a real contribution they would remain in such organizations to change discriminatory policies." The very fact that a Black person has been hired to run "an agency which has practiced—and still practices—discrimination is an indication that this kind of discrimination is doomed." Robinson concluded, "Once you quit, your voice is lost."[118]

Robinson was often torn between the desire to wield the influence of an insider and wishing for the unencumbered outspokenness of an outsider. What was most important was having the choice. Albert Hirschman raised this dilemma in his classic book *Exit, Voice, and Loyalty*.[119] Loyalty was a key virtue for Robinson, but he saw it as reciprocal, not a one-sided virtue. "We have never let our country down," he said in 1961. "We have answered the call to arms and we have contributed to its welfare in many different ways. And we'll keep reminding them of all of our rights until we get them."[120] He was born into a country in which African Americans were granted neither voice nor exit; they were neither listened to nor able to freely chart their own destinies. He demanded both. He rejected hypocritical calls for patience, but he knew that the goal of integration required both tenacity and persistence. He learned the limits of trying to influence powerful national politicians but never gave up trying. He knew how to exit an impossible situation, but he was not a quitter. And from umpires to presidents, everyone knew that Jackie Robinson never, ever, lost his voice.

NINE

The Business of Integration

JACKIE ROBINSON'S JOB AT Chock full o'Nuts was only one of the many ways he earned an income after his retirement from baseball. His business ventures were extremely varied. If he was not quite, if you'll pardon the expression, a jack of all trades, he was a jack of many. Among other things he was a banker, an insurance executive, a housing and resort developer, a haberdasher, a sports broadcaster and promoter, a public relations flack, a human resources administrator, an actor, a fast-food franchiser, a television salesman, and the head of a construction company.[1]

No doubt he was hired for many of these ventures because he was Jackie Robinson. During his Dodgers years, like many star athletes, he was a serial product endorser. Early in his career, he endorsed a board game called the Jackie Robinson Official Baseball Game, Chesterfield cigarettes (he wasn't a smoker), Bond Bread—"always on his home plate"—as well as lines of caps, jackets, shirts, and pants. He signed various deals with magazines and book publishers and played himself, fairly credibly, in the 1950 film *The Jackie Robinson Story.*[2] In 1952, he opened a menswear store in Harlem, but his name was not enough to overcome the relatively high prices of its merchandise, and he sold his share in 1958, having made very little money.[3] During his baseball career, he participated in and organized a number of barnstorming tours. In 1965, he was the color commentator for weekly baseball games broadcast on the ABC network, and the following year he was the general manager of a long-forgotten Brooklyn Dodgers professional football team.[4]

Robinson had his share of business successes and failures. But he always remained acutely aware that whatever he did, he would remain a symbol and exemplar to millions of Black Americans. He wanted to show that business ownership was an honorable and necessary a way for African Americans to move toward full citizenship. In 1965, Robinson paraphrased a well-known statement by Malcolm X, saying it was favored by "demagogues" and opponents of sit-in demonstrations at lunch counters: "I don't want to beg the white man to serve me a cup of coffee in his restaurant. I want to own the restaurant. I want to own the land it stands on."[5] To which Robinson replied, "Well and good." He agreed that "if the Negro is to mature into the role he deserves to enact in this society—it will have to be done, not only through protest, but also through production."[6]

What Robinson called "job integration," being hired as an employee, was not enough. He called for Black "involvement in the world of business from the standpoint of becoming a producer, a manufacturer, a developer and creator of business, a producer of jobs. . . . I am tired of being just a consumer."[7] Much talk in recent years has focused on the reality of structural racism, which means in part that formal, legal equality is relatively meaningless without real economic equality. It is a proposition that no prominent African American leader, from Booker T. Washington on, has ever seriously doubted.

In 1963, noting the sight of more Black faces in national advertisements by large companies as a "by-product of the Negro Revolution," he argued that "the buck and the ballot are our most potent weapons with which we can punish our enemies and reward our friends."[8] After 1966, when the term became popular, Robinson was apt to say that Black enterprises were "the kind of black power that I advocate, the wise use of our dollar."[9] But unlike Malcolm X, he believed that building a strong Black economy was a step toward integration, not racial separation. It is one of the paradoxes, or essential principles, of Jackie Robinson's understanding of integration: Interracial cooperation was the best way to build vibrant Black institutions. If this did not happen in baseball, he held out hope it would work in other areas of American business practice.

His business ventures often directly addressed situations of discrimination. "I had a dream," he wrote in 1967. He wanted to develop a Black-built, first-class golf club, constructed and owned by Black Americans but open to everyone. Robinson was an avid golfer and had been rejected for membership in the High Ridge Country Club, an all-white country club in Stamford, Connecticut.[10] He was often invited, as a celebrity, to play a round at exclusive all-white clubs, knowing that others wouldn't receive similar invitations. So Robinson and some Black investors looked for a suitable property. One prospective deal fell through in 1966 when the owners of a club that had fallen on hard times discovered that the potential buyers were African Americans. A few months later, Robinson headed a group of investors who attempted to purchase a 216-acre plot in Lewisboro, New York, in Westchester County. Residents of Lewisboro raised any number of objections, and the conditions for building the club became so onerous that investors withdrew from the project. Not for the first or the last time, Robinson's model for effective collective Black action was based on a precedent set by Jewish Americans: When denied membership in gentile country clubs, "the Jew responded by pooling his resources and buying his own club." But as his fellow Black investors withdrew, he was "disgusted" by their "defeatism" and their willingness to settle for "patronizing invitations" from white country clubs.[11] This particular dream did not become a reality.

Another dream almost did. Life insurance is one of the most venerable of Black-owned businesses; many of the largest Black-owned businesses at midcentury were life insurance companies, whose customers sought some sort of hedge against life's myriad cruelties and uncertainties. The large, white-owned companies had treated Black customers, wrote Robinson, with "scorn, contempt, and injustice."[12] In 1964, Robinson and a group of Black investors founded the Gibraltar Life Insurance Company, but Robinson and his co-investors had difficulties in arranging the initial stock offering. In 1966, Hamilton Life Insurance Company, with $500 million in policies underwritten, purchased Gibraltar and made Robinson cochair. This was, for Robinson, "a dream come true."[13] Robinson did agree that perhaps Philip J. Goldberg, the owner of Hamilton Life, had hired him primarily because of his name, and it was a "grandstand play," though "motivation wasn't important. . . . As long as Negroes are brought into the mainstream of American business, and young Negroes are encouraged by my career, that's all that counts."[14] Alas, it was a grandstand play and little else. By early 1968, the Securities and Exchange Commission had suspended trading in the company, New York State prohibited it from issuing new policies, and Jackie Robinson was out the $25,000 he had invested, much to the ire of his family.[15]

In 1965, Robinson praised a Harlem resident who'd purchased a local franchise of the Chicken Delight chain, a popular food franchise of the 1960s.[16] One of the dominant business trends in the late 1960s and early 1970s was the development of franchising, in which the individual stores are owned by their proprietors while remaining part of a larger chain that standardizes the product and handles regional and national advertising. From a mere handful of franchised companies in the immediate postwar years, by 1969 there were 150, and by 1971 there were 100 additional franchise companies vying for business. Soon franchises, especially fast-food restaurants, were ubiquitous.[17] There was both optimism that owning a franchise outlet was a relatively easy way for persons of moderate wealth to find success in business and worries that many franchise agreements were disadvantageous to the franchisee, especially minority franchisees.

Both issues were discussed at a 1970 hearing of the Senate Small Business Committee, at which Jackie Robinson testified. He told the senators that "a black man would have a better chance of success with a franchise than he would in starting out in business in other ways." He added that creating a large Black middle class was more important than making a handful of Black millionaires. Robinson saw this as another way to integrate: Black-owned businesses serving Black neighborhoods while backed by the financial clout of large corporations. Robinson told the Senate that this was true "Black capitalism" as opposed to the version of Black capitalism then being touted by Richard Nixon, economic development as an alternative to civil rights protests.[18] Robinson was testifying because he had become a promoter of Sea Host, a fast-food chain promoting inexpensive seafood. His position there was a considerable come-down from his role at Chock full o'Nuts; rather than being an executive, he was just a front man, a shill, trying to promote franchise purchases to Black investors.[19] Sea Host declared bankruptcy a few months after Robinson's testimony and is deservedly forgotten.

Perhaps Robinson's most lasting area of entrepreneurship was in housing. As we have seen, support for suitable, affordable housing for Black Americans was one of his most urgent concerns. As early as 1951, there was talk of building the Jackie Robinson Gardens in Bedford-Stuyvesant, a five-hundred-unit development, of which he would have been the public face for a group of investors "We feel there is a need for more and better housing in Brooklyn. This will be our contribution to keeping kids off the streets by providing comfortable homes and a place for planned, supervised, recreation."[20] This came to naught, but he was convinced that "housing is the first thing." Without good housing, nothing else matters.[21] In 1963, Robinson and boxer Floyd Patterson announced plans to build an integrated community in Wurtsboro, New York, about eighty miles north of the city, but this plan fizzled out.[22] Other unrealized plans involved building low-income housing in Puerto Rico and on the island of Jamaica.[23] But in 1971, he established the Jackie Robinson Construction Corporation, with ambitious plans, including a $9 million development in Yonkers and a $14 million development of six-story apartment buildings in Brooklyn, with the Urban Development Corporation providing most of the mortgages.[24] The Jackie Robinson Construction Corporation was probably his favorite post-baseball entrepreneurial involvement. Rachel Robinson wrote of it, "In the last years of his life Jack finally found the business opportunity he had been searching for a decade earlier."[25]

Reviewing this mix of business successes and failures, it seems fair to ask: What sort of businessman was Jackie Robinson? One of his associates in his construction ventures in his later years strenuously rejected the notion that he didn't have business acumen. "You could explain something to Jack and he would remember it"; though "he was not one to command the absolute small details . . . he mastered the implications, he had an understanding of the financial impact." He was "plenty smart" in business matters but sometimes too "trusting of people he happened to like."[26] That seems like a fair assessment of Robinson's strengths and weaknesses as an entrepreneur. He made some good decisions and some not-so-good decisions. Sea Host was not the only company that trafficked in Jackie Robinson's reputation and harmed it in the process. If his celebrity brought him recognition and access in the world of politics and civil rights, it perhaps was a liability in the business world, where Jackie Robinson the icon was often more important than Jackie Robinson the executive. And the world of start-ups in which he spent most of the last decade of his life is a world in which risk, and the occasional failure, is just part of the price of doing business. And Black business start-ups were riskier still. One prime reason for this was the lack of Black capital and the reluctance of whites to invest in Black enterprises.

Robinson's involvement with the Freedom National Bank was in some ways his greatest success and his greatest failure as a businessman. Harlem had long lacked adequate banking services, as was true for Black communities in general. A 1967 survey of four thousand commercial banks indicated that less than one-twentieth of one percent of their assets were invested in Black neighborhoods. There were no large Black-owned banks in Harlem before World War II. Harlem's banking needs were served by white banks, which took their profits downtown while often refusing to make loans to locals. This scenario was all too common for would-be African American borrowers. The practice of redlining, codified by the FHA in the 1930s, declared some neighborhoods unsuitable for business or home loans. Redlined maps were used by banks and insurance companies to systematically starve neighborhoods like Harlem of new housing stock and ensured the deterioration of existing housing.[27]

In his autobiography, Robinson quoted a white bank president from Connecticut who said "he had never known a Negro in whom he had confidence for more than a $300 loan."[28] In the mid-1960s, the only significant Black-owned bank in Harlem was Carver Federal Savings and Loan (later Carver Federal Savings), which at the time was largely limited to home mortgages. After an initial hesitation—"after all, what did I know about banking?"—Robinson was persuaded by Harlem businessman Dunbar McLaurin to become chairman of the board of a new bank, the Freedom National Bank. It opened with much fanfare on 4 January 1965, with good wishes from Vice President–Elect Hubert Humphrey and many others.[29] In many ways the bank was a success. Articles praised its "tremendous growth" (or perhaps, more realistically, its "steady growth") in 1970, when the bank had almost $40 million in deposits, 25,000 depositors, and a good record of helping Black businesses of all kinds.[30]

The ribbon-cutter on the bank's opening day was Alex Quaison-Sackey, the Ghanian president of the General Assembly of the United Nations, the first African in that position. He told the crowd that he hoped Black economic projects such as this would lead to a birth of "a non-racial society in years to come when all men will discontinue the practice of referring to men by color."[31] This is what Jackie Robinson said as well, hailing the opening of a "bank that is color blind." It was "interracially owned and operated": its board members and executives included a number of Anglo-American and Jewish businesspeople who had been active in Harlem for many years, "though [it was] controlled mainly by Negroes," which Robinson acknowledged was a difficult balance to achieve. It would be a bank where the "Negroes in the picture are not simply 'fronts' for whites—which sadly, is often the case."[32]

"Color blind" is a widely misunderstood term—it became popular when almost all existing racial references in law and social custom were biased against African Americans. Color-blindness required recognizing the historic injustices that had held back African Americans and African American businesses. As Robinson wrote of the bank's founding, "It is symbolic of the determination of the Negro to become an integral part of mainstream of our American economy."[33] Integration happens when African Americans can create their own strong businesses.

But for all the apparent success of Freedom National Bank, it was troubled from the outset. Dunbar McLaurin, the Harlem businessman who was the real initiator of the bank, who'd recruited Robinson to participate, and who was expected to be the bank's first president, was forced off the project, in part because of clashes with Robinson and other directors. McLaurin then angrily complained to the Harlem press, unfairly, that the whites involved in the bank were running the show and that Robinson and the other Black directors were their puppets.[34] Robinson was not amused.

In addition, the sale of common stock, which the bank wanted primarily to raise from Harlem residents to make it a "community" enterprise, went so slowly that the opening had to be twice delayed.[35] The effort to raise money from the Harlem community faced two problems: Not that many people had sufficient free income to invest; and those who did were sometimes skeptical of investing in Black enterprises, preferring safer (and whiter) places to park their money. Robinson bitterly complained about such attitudes. And this was connected to another problem with the bank. Robinson and the other directors absolutely did not want the bank to be seen as some sort of charitable enterprise, a way of helping Black communities through white largess, or, as he put it, "We did not want the white banking community to coddle us because we were a black bank." He decried "this kind of paternalism" because it had been deleterious to the success of Black enterprises. On the other hand, to serve the Black community, the bank "without being loose in policies . . . had to be less rigid than white banks have been under similar circumstances."[36] Robinson wanted neither pity nor scorn for the bank. He wanted it to be treated as any white-owned bank would be treated, and he wanted recognition of the special circumstances that being a Black bank in Harlem entailed.

By the late 1960s, Robinson was growing worried about Freedom National's increasing load of write-offs for bad loans and worried that the bank executives "had a tendency to favor friends on the basis that one can trust one's friends in business—an utterly risky philosophy." In his autobiography, he writes that in 1968, one of the most powerful executives on Wall Street had come to him and said, "If you want to save Freedom National Bank, the only way you are going to be able to do it is to take it over and clean house. You are in serious trouble."[37] Robinson acknowledged that he had been "guilty of a very serious mistake" by not paying sufficient attention to the day-to-day operations of the bank. In 1971, Robinson forced the resignation of William Hudgins, who had been Robinson's good friend and president of the bank since its founding. All of this was very taxing. "The more involved I got with the bank problems, the sicker I became."[38] Whether the bank's woes contributed to his early death, it clearly was a heavy weight he carried in his last years.

In his autobiography, which appeared in the fall of 1972, Robinson writes that he debated whether to speak frankly about the problems at Freedom National. He decided that he needed to tell the story as an object lesson in "the need for maturity and stability for black business." He was confident that the bank had "weathered the storm," but it had not. The bank's history after Robinson's death was a series of ups and downs, and in 1990, it declared bankruptcy and went out of business, to the great consternation of Harlem and Black business executives in New York City.[39] Black banks are never too big to fail.[40]

In the last decade of his life, Robinson was challenged by a new Black politics that was deeply skeptical of the sort of mainstream Black politics he espoused and for whom integration was anathema. His interactions with the new politics were complex, combative, thoughtful, and fruitful. In Harlem in the 1960s, there was one main representative of this new brand of politics—Malcolm X.[41] Robinson knew him well. In 1959, as a follow-up to Mike Wallace's famous program, *The Hate That Hate Produced,* which introduced much of white America to the Nation of Islam, Robinson concurred with Wallace's denouncement of the organization. Within a week, Malcolm X, the leader of the Nation in Harlem, denounced the program.[42] By 1960, they were acquainted. In her tribute volume to her husband, Rachel Robinson published a photograph taken that year of Robinson and Malcolm X, along with members of the Nation of Islam, sitting and chatting amiably at a Harlem lunch counter. She noted, "I would like to know what was said."[43] So would we all. Theirs was a relationship in which their mutual respect was often overshadowed by their mutual antagonism, often delivered in tit-for-tat denunciations in the Black press. If Malcolm saw Robinson as a "paid parrot," Robinson accused the Nation of Islam of being a "hate group" and frequently reiterated his position that "we consider black supremacy as dangerous as white supremacy."[44]

Robinson often complained that Malcolm X's popularity was created by the need for the mainstream press to have a Black bogeyman, and that he was, however tonsorially unlikely, the "fair-haired boy of the white press."[45] The white press, he wrote in 1964, "continues to be his press agent. On the front page they glorify Mr. X whenever he takes a deep breath. On the editorial pages they condemn his extremism."[46] At times, Robinson could wax conspiratorial, in a "just asking questions" mode. In the summer of 1963, he asked, without a shred of evidence, whether "the Muslims are receiving important aid and sponsorship from outside the race?"[47] For Robinson, it was all too convenient: Just as major civil rights legislation was being considered, a Black group emerged that frightened whites with talk of violence and gave plausible evidence that Black Americans, too, hated integration and just wanted to hang out with their own kind. "If Malcolm X and his organization," he wrote in the summer of 1963, "believe in separation, want to form an all-Black community somewhere, just go," but, he added, "I don't see how they can say with a straight face that their theories represent the will of the masses of the Negro people" when "the masses of the Negro people, in cities all over the country, are demonstrating, sometimes at the risk of their lives, [to] give witness that they want integration, the opposite of segregation."[48]

In November 1963, Robinson, in a column in the *Amsterdam News,* accused Malcolm X of fighting his Negro revolution from the relative safety of a Harlem soapbox rather than in the South, where civil rights activists like Medgar Evers were being murdered.[49] Malcolm, as was his wont, responded in a slashing, ad hominem style, accusing Robinson of still being a shifty runner, but now on political basepaths; he was "still trying to win 'The Big Game' for your White Boss, no longer Branch Rickey's boy, but Nelson Rockefeller's or any other rich white man willing to pay enough."[50] In his response, Robinson called out Malcolm's "racist views," his "sick leadership," and said that "Negroes are not fooled by your vicious theories that they are dying for freedom to please the white man." To be attacked by Malcolm X was a "tribute," an honor, and a privilege.[51] The nasty exchanges might well have continued, except that they took place just as Malcolm X was being drummed out of the Nation of Islam and silenced by Elijah Muhammad. Robinson remained a skeptic during Malcolm X's final year, after his break with the Nation, arguing that if he was sincere in his changed views of the civil rights movement, he owed all the civil rights leaders he had attacked (including, no doubt, Robinson himself) a big apology.[52]

But there was another level to their interactions. In 1962, when the HUAC was considering investigating the Nation of Islam, Robinson wrote, "In spite of my differences with the Black Muslims, they have as much right to hate the white man—if it is true that they do—as any white man has the right, legally, to hate the Black man."[53] And as he often pointed out, white racists did not merely hate African Americans; they relegated them to second-class citizenship, even if they didn't engage in violence against them. "As much as we disagree with the Muslims, we do not consider that their organization has done half as much to rate the label of a hate group as the Klan or the Citizen's Councils."[54] If the Nation of Islam was growing, it was in response to the "stupidity and brutality of some aspects of white society." There were occasional public events, as in the fall of 1962, when Robinson and Malcolm X would declare that, for all their differences, they were both fighting for the same goal.[55] In Robinson's worldview, the Nation of Islam of the 1960s replaced the Communist Party of the 1940s and 1950s. Their anger at white racism was legitimate, though their means of addressing it were not; their influence and numbers were exaggerated both by their defenders and by the opponents of civil rights, although for different reasons. After Malcolm X's assassination, in a column titled "Martyr Malcolm," Robinson wrote that despite their substantial differences, "many of the statements he made about the problems faced by Negro people were nothing but the naked truth." In the end, both men prized Black unity as their highest political goal, and to achieve it, they bitterly criticized people who they thought stood in its way.[56] Jackie Robinson accepted that many Black Americans found Malcolm X's defiant and uncompromising rhetoric inspiring. On some level, so did he. He had been telling off white America for years. But there was no alternative, he thought, than to fight for integration, fight for their full rights as American citizens.

But this fight could borrow a tactic from Malcolm's playbook. A few months after Malcolm's assassination, Robinson wrote a column strongly supporting the Deacons for Defense, a group of armed Black civil rights activists, who, in Robinson's words, practiced "an eye for an eye" for those who sought to "scare, hurt, or kill black or white civil rights demonstrators." He supported the Deacons "100 percent," and as much as he respected Martin Luther King's philosophy of nonviolence, the time had come "for the Negro [to] finally say, 'Scuse me, Dr. King,' and stand up and fight back."[57] Jackie Robinson was an integrationist by any means necessary.

Robinson's support of integration often left him entangled with Adam Clayton Powell Jr., an old Harlem congressman who found the new politics of 1960s Black radicalism very congenial. He had written about Jackie Robinson as early as 1939, complaining that "white folks sho' is peculiar," referring to the reluctance of Southern football teams to take the field against UCLA.[58] Powell's newspaper, the *People's Voice,* was an ardent advocate for ending the major-league color line, and Powell's general outspokenness certainly contributed to the pressure on Branch Rickey to sign a Black ballplayer. After his election to Congress in 1944, becoming one of only two Black members of the House, he took his outspokenness to a national stage. In 1961, he became chairman of the powerful House Committee on Education and Labor.

Robinson was angry when in 1963 Powell called for boycotts of the NAACP, CORE, the National Urban League, and the Southern Christian Leadership Conference because of the role whites played in these organizations: "We have to have organizations where Negroes control policy" (though in fact Black Americans had effective control of policy making in each of these organizations).[59] Robinson answered him, defending the NAACP and the role of whites in the organization. He stated that for a long time he'd hesitated to lambast Powell, "because I did not want to give ammunition to those enemies of yours that are enemies of the Negro people."[60]

By the late 1960s, Powell was dogged by accusations of financial impropriety and corruption. In March 1967, by a vote of 307 to 116, the House of Representatives refused to seat him because of his financial corruption. Robinson was outraged that white congressional malefactors, guilty of similar conduct, had not been refused their seats or been expelled. His removal was a sign that "the white power structure is on the warpath, and things are going to get rougher and rougher against the Negro." Democrats and Republicans alike voted to remove Powell, Robinson said, because of his perceived "uppity-ness" and because "the white American, in the main, does not like a Negro who speaks his mind."[61] The New York state Republican Party, including Governor Rockefeller, supported James Meredith, the first African American to attend the University of Mississippi, to run against Powell in a special election that year. Martin Luther King and Roy Wilkins professed neutrality in the race. Not Robinson. He said that Meredith "sold himself for whatever he could get" and argued that "this is not a political issue, but a racial issue," adding that all Black voters needed to support Powell.[62] That is, they needed to support him in the special election because of the circumstances of his exclusion from Congress, not because he was necessarily the best person for the job: "I have always been anti-Powell simply because I believe he could be the greatest influence for Negro progress but so far I don't believe he has lived up to his potential by any means."[63]

By the fall of 1966, the term of the moment was "Black Power," and Powell gave a talk on the subject that Robinson thought was "magnificent," in part because he differentiated his understanding of Black Power from that of Stokely Carmichael, who had popularized the phrase. Powell's understanding of Black Power emphasized faith in God, Black initiative and productivity, and Black people taking collective responsibility for their fate. Robinson disagreed with Powell that Black civil rights efforts over the past five years had been "a magnificent exercise of near futility with our marches, our picketing, and now our rebellion." However, he did agree that "further use of these tactics would resolve in futility."[64]

Meanwhile Robinson's reaction to Stokely Carmichael, the Black radical who had, to some extent, assumed Malcolm X's mantle was similar. While criticizing and excoriating his ideas, he defended his right to his opinions and argued that whites who claimed that it was Black militants who were holding back progress on civil rights needed to look to themselves. In early 1968, he stated, "I'm not for the things" Carmichael stood for, but he still he worried about him and other Black radicals being targeted for possible arrest by the FBI.[65]

Robinson was often sympathetic to Black activists' outspokenness, regardless of whether he agreed with what they said. He admired Muhammad Ali: After Ali won the heavyweight championship in 1964 and announced his membership in the Nation of Islam, Robinson said that Ali had as much right to be a Muslim, or a member of the Nation of Islam, as any American had to choose their own religious affiliations. Although he thought that Black Americans "want to be integrated into the mainstream of American life" and not isolate themselves, he cautioned that if white America continued to refuse to "grant us the same rights as any citizen in this land," the Black Muslims (Robinson's term) would continue to grow in popularity. Moreover, Robinson admired Ali's boastfulness and his catchphrase, "I am the greatest." In 1964, he wrote that African Americans, with their sense of inferiority, perhaps had to claim their superiority simply to feel equal to whites. If Black people “learn to believe in themselves one iota of the way [Ali] does, we'll be in great shape.”[66] In 1967, when Ali refused induction into the military and was stripped of his boxing titles, Robinson again came to his defense: Ali was hated because he was an “outspoken black man.” Standing up for his beliefs made him a hero, a man willing to “act out of his deeply rooted convictions” and take the consequences—although, as for the principle he was fighting for, Robinson “could not agree with it.”[67]

Of course, the political issue behind Muhammad Ali's draft refusal was the era's other dominant political issue, the Vietnam War, and by the late 1960s, the racial dilemma in the United States had become inextricably entwined with the opposition to the war, especially after Martin Luther King denounced the war in April 1967. Robinson, long a supporter of the war, was quick to assert that King “was so utterly on the wrong track in [his] stand on Viet Nam.”[68] He believed that “we must defeat Communism in Vietnam and fascistic bigotry at home,” and that the two causes were one, both ideologically and practically. To break with Johnson over Vietnam was to create a rupture with the president who had done more to advance the status of Black Americans than any president since the Civil War.[69] But as with Ali, he accepted his and King's different positions on Vietnam without rancor. He said of King that despite their differences, “he is still my leader.” He made that clear “because I would not want bigots and those who secretly disagree with him to find comfort in my disagreeing with him.”[70]

In early 1968, he still maintained that “President Johnson should renew his often repeated resolve not to back down on the nation's commitment to Vietnam.”[71] However, when African American singer Eartha Kitt in January 1968 created a furor by bitterly criticizing the war to the face of the First Lady, Lady Bird Johnson, Robinson defended her right to speak her mind and saw some of her critics as being racially motivated.[72]

For Robinson, as for almost everyone else in the United States, 1968 was a year of tragedy and division. After the North Vietnamese Tet offensive in February, his public defense of the war became muted. In April, Robinson's first thoughts after hearing of King's assassination, a man whom he thought was “the greatest American of the twentieth century,” were “shock and disbelief,” and he entertained thoughts of “retaliation.”[73] In his first column in its aftermath, he decried the violence that had broken out in Black neighborhoods. While stating, "I cannot claim to be a deeply religious person," he wrote one of his most searching columns, a heartfelt examination of how evil persists despite the redemptive power of God.[74] In his next column, an account of his attendance at King's funeral at Morehouse College, he found the sense of shared purpose reaffirming. "While many people seemed to be thinking in recent years that the quest for integration was a lost cause," all those who gathered in Atlanta knew that the cause was vitally alive. But he found white America had "swiftly recovered from its sense of guilt" and had "casually and effortlessly returns to business as usual."[75] In the assassination's aftermath, he thought it highly probable that "a well-planned and organized conspiracy" had been behind King's murder.[76]

How had King's murder changed Robinson? In May 1967, he had written of King that "you have called the United States—unfairly I feel—the greatest purveyor of violence on earth."[77] By the following summer, with King lying in a freshly dug grave, he could write: "American society, whose white rulers spend so much time cautioning black people to be non-violent, is one of the most violent 'civilizations' on the map. And the rest of the world knows it." Sounding more like Stokely Carmichael than the erstwhile cold warrior, he added: "Black people are not afraid to die and there are hundreds of thousands of young Black people who would rather make a last-ditch stand for freedom in the ghettoes of their cities than in the jungles of Vietnam."[78]

Like many veterans of the civil rights movement, Robinson listened intently to the anger of young Black radicals, and, without totally agreeing with them, tried to incorporate their ideas into his thinking. In his final years, Robinson still believed in integration. But if in 1947 the way toward integration and citizenship had been to participate in a formerly all-white baseball league, twenty years later, the path to integration required different tactics. Jackie Robinson penned in late 1967 that "maybe we as Negro athletes have 'been around' too long, accepting inequities and indignities and accepting worn-out promises about how things are going to get better. If this is the way youngsters feel, believe me, I can sympathize with their point of view." To this end, he quoted his old sparring partner, Malcolm X, "the late and brilliant leader, [who] once pointed out to me in the course of a debate that: 'Jackie, in days to come, your son and my son will not be willing to settle for things we are willing to settle for.'"[79]

Robinson was writing about his support for the planned boycott by Black athletes of the 1968 Summer Olympic Games in Mexico City. In 1964, the International Olympic Committee had banned South Africa from competition. In 1967, South Africa, promising to field an interracial team (though leaving apartheid untouched) was pushing for reinstatement. In the spring of 1967, Robinson was the principal facilitator of a statement signed by thirty prominent Americans urging the IOC to keep South Africa out of the games.[80] That fall, Harry Edwards, who had founded the Olympic Project For Human Rights, announced a proposed boycott of the Olympics by Black athletes, and a number of prospective participants, including college basketball great Lew Alcindor (later Kareem Abdul-Jabbar) indicated their support of the boycott. When Tommie Smith, one of the boycott's leaders, said that he had trained all his life for the Olympics but would give it all up, and his life if necessary, to change racial conditions in the United States, Robinson said that "he had to honor a young man [with] an attitude like that" and became a strong supporter of the boycott.[81] Twenty years after Robinson gained a national voice by breaking an athletic color barrier, he supported an effort by Black athletes to gain a louder voice by refusing participation in a white-run competition,

A similar complexity can be observed in Robinson's reactions to, and interactions with, other Black radical causes in the late 1960s and early 1970s. When armed Black activists staged an attention-attracting takeover of the student union at Cornell University in April 1969, Robinson contacted its leaders to better understand them.[82] At the same time, he never gave up faith in the mainstream civil rights movement. In 1969, he wondered why Whitney Young shouldn't "be the hero of the Black community rather than Eldridge Cleaver" (the Black Panther Party leader).[83] But he also wanted to listen to what Cleaver had to say. Robinson met with the Black Panthers, and, if not supporting their positions, defended their right to hold them without persecution from the police.[84] Writing in the *Amsterdam News* in April 1969, he noted that a few years earlier, all violent acts in the Black community were being blamed on the Nation of Islam, and this was not true. Yet "today, every criminal act is blamed on the Panthers." Describing an attack in Brooklyn on a group of Panthers who were set upon by a mob that included off-duty police officers, Robinson wondered why none of the attackers had been arrested and what would have happened if two hundred Black men had beaten up thirteen white men.[85]

In his own way, Robinson, if not a Black nationalist, had always seen his racial identity as the core of his political identity, and he saw no contradiction between being a "race man" and a passionate supporter of integration. During the New York City teachers' strike in the fall of 1968, he had an exchange with William F. Buckley Jr., a conservative publisher and columnist. Buckley had accused Robinson of being racist for asserting that he was "Black first, American second" and for saying, "If that is racism so be it. . . . I am proud to be Black. I am also embattled because I am Black."[86] This was not a new position. He'd written in 1964 that while many politicians believed that they were Americans first, and whatever their race or ethnicity second, he was "a Negro first."[87] When, in 1969, Bayard Rustin criticized the interest in creating Black Studies programs in colleges as "stupid," Robinson responded that it was "stupid to characterize the demands of these young people as stupid." Robinson accused Rustin of having "got[ten] so much beyond the struggle and above the battle that he doesn't realize that all people have the right to knowledge of their heritage."[88] Robinson refused to place himself "above the battle": that is, he wouldn't view the African American struggle for citizenship from what he saw as the vantage of a condescending outsider, which was what he believed Rustin was doing. He was not agreeing with Black radicals as much as refusing to disavow them. He agreed with Rustin that most Black Americans still wanted their full rights at citizens. But he disagreed that this required them to embrace their citizenship on the terms set by the dominant culture. It was time for white America to do the adjusting.

But this wasn't happening. In the late 1960s and early 1970s, busing school children to obtain racial balance in New York City and elsewhere had become a critical political issue. It was denounced as "forced busing" by a wide spectrum of politicians, both Democrats and Republicans.[89] This infuriated Robinson and many other civil rights leaders because it felt, rightly, like a death-knell for coordinated governmental efforts to end de facto school segregation. In a March 1972 letter to Richard Nixon, he explained that his vision of integration was not about race mixing but obtaining full citizenship and that busing was a means to this end. "Non-integrated schools, no matter what, are not equal in terms of educational opportunities," Robinson wrote. "The idea that blacks want busing for racial balance is erroneous. This notion springs from white America. While it is important that as a nation we have understanding and racial equality, I could not care less about integration except that it is only way to build a strong country."[90]

A dream deferred shrivels. This shaped Robinson's mood in the last years of his life. As he wrote Nixon: "To go backward in 1972 is certainly no credit to America, and history will show it was not to your credit to urge a nation to go downhill after the promise of a new day."[91] Symbols he'd once embraced as bringing Americans together he now rejected as divisive because they denied Black Americans their distinctiveness. In 1953, he'd told Edward R. Murrow that when he'd played his first World Series game in 1947, standing on the field before the game, he'd "experienced a completely new emotion when the National Anthem was played. This time, it is being played for me as much as for anyone else."[92] By 1971, he told the *New York Times* that he "wouldn't fly the flag on the Fourth of July or any other day. When I see a car with a flag pasted on it, I figure the guy behind the wheel isn't my friend."[93]

In 1972, a quarter century after signing with the Dodgers, major-league baseball and its commissioner, Bowie Kuhn, had to be shamed into inviting Jackie Robinson, in failing health caused by diabetes, to throw out a ceremonial baseball at that year's World Series. Robinson's official contacts with major-league baseball for many years had been few and fleeting. He was reluctant to attend and agreed to do so only after receiving a promise that he could speak his mind. He used his platform to criticize baseball for not yet hiring its first Black manager: "I hope the day will come when I'll be able to look down the third base line and see a Black man in the coaching box as the manager of a major league team."[94] His physical health was failing. Former teammates at the World Series who saw the nearly blind, white-haired man of faltering gait were shocked by his appearance.[95] Less than two weeks later, on 24 October 1972, he died of a heart attack.

He was universally mourned, from the highest echelons of power to the average baseball fan to all Black America. Former enemies abandoned their enmities. President Nixon found the right words to say, as did Berry Shabazz, the widow of Malcolm X, who told the *Amsterdam News* that her late husband had enjoyed a "great respect for Jackie Robinson."[96] No doubt he did. Everybody respected Jackie Robinson. It started with his profound sense of respect for himself. "Respect" was a word that turned up in many of the eulogies and memorial tributes. An editorial in the *New York Times* commented, as did many eulogies, on the paradox of his anger: "His discipline and restraint were as crucial to the larger cause of black advancement in that first season as his aggressive defense of his rights were to black self-respect in his later years."[97] Wendell Smith, the former *Pittsburgh Courier* sportswriter, who would die within the month, said that wherever Robinson went, whatever he did, "he demanded respect."[98] The *Chicago Defender* wrote that "not only are his feats as a ballplayer unimpeachable, but his command for respect for himself, and [for] all Black people will always be remembered."[99]

Respect was a word that Robinson had often used to describe his own career, his own life. In *Baseball Has Done It* (1964), Robinson told the story of an umpire who toward the end of his playing days told him, "I liked you much better when you were less aggressive." How can one respond to this? Robinson retorted: "I'm not concerned with you liking or disliking me. All I ask is that you respect me as a human being."[100] In his autobiography, he returned to the question of his anger. While playing with the Dodgers, he had to deny his "true fighting spirit so that the 'noble experiment' could succeed. When it finally did I could become my own man; many people resented my impatience and honesty. But I never cared about acceptance as much as I cared about respect."[101]

What did respect mean to Black Americans in the late 1960s and early 1970s (besides a genre defining mega-hit for Aretha Franklin in 1967)? The demand for respect was another way of demanding full citizenship, a test for the real meaning of integration. It was a rejection of the need to seek approval from those who would dominate your life or to live by their standards. It was a rejection of the crushing societal hierarchies that presumed to tell Black people (or women, the disabled, gays and lesbians, or any group in American society hobbled by the burden of disrespect) how to live their lives, how to be full American citizens. R-E-S-P-E-C-T. Sometimes it must be spelled out. It's a song that Jackie Robinson helped Aretha, and many, many others, to sing.

EPILOGUE

The Last

IMMEDIATELY AFTER JACKIE ROBINSON'S death, there was a torrent of tributes and eulogies. However, in the quarter century after his passing, if he was not exactly forgotten, his life and achievements received relatively little attention.[1] This began to change around 1997 and the fiftieth anniversary of his debut with the Dodgers. In that year, he became the first (and still the only) player in baseball to have his number, 42, retired by all major-league teams. In 2004, he became the first player in baseball to have an annual celebration, Jackie Robinson Day, held on April 15, the day of his debut with the Dodgers in 1947. In 2009, it was decided that henceforth, on every April 15, the number 42 would be unretired for the day, and every player and all on-field personnel would wear his number. There is no more honored or venerated player in the history of baseball than Jackie Robinson.

Indeed, there are few more venerated persons in all American history. In recent decades, whenever a list of the "greatest one hundred Americans" is compiled, he is invariably included.[2] When the list is ordinally ranked, he usually appears near the top, one of the greatest of the great, listed as high as nineteenth, twenty-second, and thirty-fifth.[3] After Martin Luther King Jr. and sometimes one or two others, he is the highest-ranking Black American. He is usually the highest-ranking athlete. On the left, Peter

Dreier included him in *The 100 Greatest Americans of the Twentieth Century: A Social Justice Hall of Fame,* in which those celebrated are arranged by birthyear, and Robinson is sandwiched between Fannie Lou Hamer and Pete Seeger.[4] On the other side of the political spectrum, in 2020 Donald Trump complained that "angry mobs are trying to tear down statutes of our founders."[5] He proposed the creation of a National Garden of American Heroes. Jackie Robinson was one of the first thirty-one persons named in the original executive order for this sculpture garden, his name appearing alphabetically between Ronald Reagan and Betsy Ross. Since his return to power in 2025, Trump has again been promoting this idea.[6]

Jackie Robinson has certainly earned his exalted ranking among the greatest and most significant and venerated Americans. But there is something slightly odd about his position. He is surrounded by presidents, powerful politicians, captains of industry, and the leaders of great social movements—people who by their actions directly changed millions of lives. This was not Jackie Robinson's accomplishment. He is honored for what he started. The civil rights movement did not begin in 1945, but his joining the Dodgers is for many a convenient starting date, the first real sign of the momentous changes to come. He is also remembered as much for *how* he broke baseball's color line than for the fact of its shattering, doing so while showing such grace under pressure, without succumbing to his fears or his hatreds, with consummate discipline, with the sort of inner reserve we all hope we can draw on if we ever find ourselves in comparable situations. Or perhaps Jackie Robinson has been in recent years celebrated in some quarters because it's an easy way to acknowledge the Black entrance into the mainstream of American life without having to ask messy questions about what the civil rights movement, or Jackie Robinson, really stood for.

Jackie Robinson has come to epitomize the heroic in American life. Heroic greatness is all in a day's work for superb athletes, who often have the label thrust upon them at an early age, and Robinson lived his entire adult life within its aura. Heroic greatness is mythical. It often centers on individuals with remarkable strength and physical agility, someone who demonstrates immense courage in accomplishing a transcendently difficult task—a dragon slayer and giant killer who vanquishes an enemy before whom others quailed or failed, a hero whose internal strength is the source of their outward abilities. This is Jackie Robinson's brand of mythic heroism. He is the sort of hero one finds in children's books, where heroism can flourish without complicating complexities. In one book, written by his daughter Sharon, her father went to the frozen pond in the backyard of their Connecticut home to test whether the ice was thick enough for skating. She and her friends held their collective breaths. The ice did not crack, and his daughter concluded that "my dad is the bravest man alive."[7] In many of these books, outsiders find strength by identifying with his struggles his courage. A deaf man who had dealt with ridicule and contempt all his life identified with Robinson and relied on his hearing son to relay in American Sign Language Red Barber's call of Dodgers games on the radio. Then father and son went to Ebbets Field together to root Robinson on.[8] A young Chinese immigrant in Brooklyn, trying to adjust to a new language and culture, admired Robinson for his perseverance to overcome hostility. Her idolization of Robinson culminated when she got to introduce him at an assembly in her public school.[9] Morgan Jackson, a softball player at Clemson and East Carolina Universities, first read a book about Negro League baseball and Jackie Robinson in third grade. She "became fascinated with the book because they looked like me and played baseball—I was already into softball, but they gave me more inspiration," Johnson recalled. "When I went to Clemson, I decided I wanted to wear No. 42 because of Jackie Robinson, his perseverance and his resilience dealing with everything that's going on during the Civil Rights Movement—and still being able to play the game with passion. I carried that with me because that's what helped push me to be my best and know that when trials do come my way, I can make it through."[10] His very public heroism helped inspire millions of acts of quiet and unrecorded heroism that formed the bedrock of the civil rights movement and forms the substrate of every successful movement for social change.

Jackie Robinson has earned this sort of adulation. But when we turn our heroes into statues and place them on pedestals, they frequently become marmoreal, mute, and, often, uncontroversial, no longer able to challenge those who take their names in vain. "Unhappy the land that needs heroes," wrote Bertolt Brecht.[11]As important as heroism is, Brecht was saying that you can't rely on it to solve your country's problems. Every land is an unhappy land. Everyone wants a piece of Jackie Robinson's heroism. The conservative Jackie Robinson is seen as a self-made man, a capitalist, and (very inaccurately) as someone who accomplished much without the need for government intervention to pave his way.[12] The liberal Jackie Robinson demonstrated the folly of racial exclusion and forced the country, and various Republicans and Democrats, to live up to its highest ideals. The radical Jackie Robinson is uncompromising, a race man who seeks social justice for all, whose greatest worry is that white America's commitment to equal rights for all Americans is shallow and fickle. To some extent he fits all those characterizations. To properly honor Jackie Robinson is to remember and honor his complexities and the inherent complexities of the civil rights movement. Robinson abhorred pigeonholes.

Jackie Robinson is in no danger of being forgotten. But the same cannot be said of integration, the cause at the core of his political identity. There are no statues dedicated to integration; few children's books celebrate it; and no one celebrates Integration Day. The cause of integration languishes. The word "integration" sounds like a relic from the 1960s, like "groovy" or "hippie." It sounds, wrote scholar Sharon Stanley in 2017, "oddly anachronistic," a tired slogan from a long-concluded and half-remembered struggle.[13] Recent prominent accounts of African American history often have little to say about integration, and little of that is positive. In Ibram X. Kendi's award-winning *Stamped from the Beginning*, he praises Georgia freedmen and freedwomen for "rejecting integration" and criticizes Marcus Garvey's "assimilationist opponents" for "constructing Black integration into white spaces as progress."[14] The much-discussed *1619 Project*, a review of African American history over four centuries, has no index entry for integration. It is only a slight exaggeration to say that integration, and the controversies surrounding it, is not treated as a major issue in many recent works on African American history, which relegate it to a matter of relatively little intellectual or historiographic interest.[15] Let me repeat what Rebecca Stiles Taylor wrote in 1941: "If for Shakespeare 'to be or not to be' was the question," now "to integrate or to disintegrate is the question of the hour."[16] Integration is still the question of the hour. As is the question of whether the United States will integrate or disintegrate.

What of the fate of integration since Jackie Robinson's death, since

1972? Let us keep historian Judith Stein's admonition in mind. All too often, "'integration' is either a bloodless construct measured by statistics, which can hide as much as they reveal, or else the statement of an ideal than floats above actual politics."[17] No single approach, qualitative or quantitative, can fully capture the recent history of integration. Nor can we render any simple thumbs up or thumbs down verdict.

Certainly, since 1972, African Americans have entered the mainstream of political life as never before. In 1947, there were two African American members of Congress. In 1972, there were eleven Black members of the House and one senator. The Congress elected in 2024 included sixty-two African American members of the House and five senators, or about 12.5 percent of membership of Congress, roughly equal to the percentage of persons who identify as African American in the United States. In 1958 only 38 percent of Americans were willing to vote for a Black presidential candidate. By 2020 that number was up to 98 percent.[18] This of course is no longer a hypothetical question. In four out of the last five presidential elections, an African American was either a presidential or vice presidential candidate, on tickets that won three victories.

Some taboos have been effectively shattered. In 1944, in *An American Dilemma,* Myrdal speculated that the psychosexual dynamics of interracial liaisons would remain the most difficult racial problem to address.[19] As many have pointed out, it took thirteen long years following the *Brown/Briggs* decision for the Supreme Court to rule on *Loving v. Virginia* and declare antimiscegenation laws unconstitutional. In 1958, only 4 percent of Americans approved of interracial marriages. A survey in 2021 saw that number rise to 94 percent.[20] Newlyweds in interracial marriages increased from 3 percent in 1967, the year of the *Loving* decision, to 17 percent by 2015. (Of course, not all these marriages involved whites and Blacks.) In the end, for all the psychosexual anxiety and trauma this once provoked, interracial marriage and liaisons have proven to be one of the easier racial barriers to cross.

However, the real racial barrier has been economic, not sexual. Class divisions among African Americans are not new, of course, but they have expanded in recent decades, as the rise of a growing Black middle class coexists alongside the stubborn persistence of multigenerational Black poverty.

The middle class can work, live, and go to school where poorer Blacks cannot follow, and these Americans remain clustered and trapped in inner-city neighborhoods. In 1972, after decades of white citydwellers moving to the suburbs, many urban areas had become intensely segregated, in what has been described as an "American apartheid."[21] One way to measure neighborhood segregation is through a dissimilarity index. If the dissimilarity index is 0.00, the racial distribution across tracts is completely uniform. If completely segregated, the dissimilarity index is 1.00. Dissimilarity is decreasing. One study finds the dissimilarity index for major metropolitan areas decreasing from .79 in 1980, to .63 in 2000, to .55 in 2020.[22] Another study, using a somewhat different methodology, found higher figures, with the dissimilarity indices for major metropolitan areas declining from .92 in 1970, to .80 in 1980, to .73 in 2000, to .70 in 2010, with higher figures for the metropolitan areas with the largest African American populations.[23] As one study concluded, "Segregation will continue to divide Americans well into the 21st century."[24] Many predominantly Black communities remain largely untouched by the rise of middle-class mixed neighborhoods. Many Black and Hispanic families live in neighborhoods where poverty rates exceed 40 percent.[25] In recent decades the income gap between white and Black families has somewhat narrowed. In 2017, a study put the ratio at 1.7 to 1. However, the wealth gap, which is so dependent on inheritance and the inheritance of property, is much higher, at 9.7 to 1.[26]

Integration has always been about enhancing the options and life alternatives available for African Americans and not simply an idealized commitment to interracial living. Historian Keenanga-Yamahatta Taylor, echoing what Jackie Robinson said of busing, has written of Black housing choices in the mid-twentieth century: "The reality is that many African Americans wanted to live in neighborhoods that were integrated, and not because of a particular affinity for white neighbors. White neighborhoods had access to greater resources, including houses, schools, and jobs."[27] This is a basic asymmetry of integration. As a practical matter, African Americans had more interest in integrating than white Americans, feeling that they had the most to gain, practically and materially. All too often, white families believed that they had the most to lose from integration, no matter if their concerns or fears were valid. Integration failed as a national issue. As journalist Tom Wicker wrote, integration failed because "too few white Americans wanted it or were willing to sacrifice for it."[28]

This was certainly true in an aspect of racial interaction that has always been closely tied to housing: K–12 education. There is probably no greater reason for the souring on integration among African Americans than the slow implementation of the *Brown/Briggs* decision and the rise of de facto segregation in schools in the North. Though by the early 1960s, Black radicals had dismissed integration as assimilation, as Jackie Robinson knew, most Black families wanted integrated schools, less out of idealism than because they thought that their children would fare better in schools they shared with white students. In Detroit, despite a big push by Black activists for completely Black schools, as late as 1967, a survey found that two-thirds of the African Americans polled supported integration because they thought that racial isolation was contributing to inferior education for their children. As Michelle Adams has written, Black Detroit parents *favored* integration because "they believed that it would help their children escape segregated and unequal schools."[29] Much the same can be said about Black parents in southeastern Queens who supported integrated housing and education because they thought that white residents and students would get more attention from city and state officials.[30] But this was precisely because American housing and education were fundamentally unequal and tilted toward white residents. Only by attending schools with white children might Black children perhaps share in their advantages. Yet this realization was usually accompanied in the 1960s by a sense of indignation that this was necessary and a heightened feeling of Black pride—an ambivalence shared by Jackie Robinson.

Let's return to our two models of integration. If integration is measured as inclusion, there has been advancement in the half century since Jackie Robinson's death. If integration is viewed as the quest for Black citizenship, any gains made since 1972 have been eroded, if not ended and reversed. The partial success of some measures to enhance Black citizenship, increasing and maximizing life possibilities and redressing historic and continuing injustices, has been met by a resistance that has been continuous, ferocious, and unrelenting. That resistance is succeeding.

One major way to redress racial inequalities in employment and education has been through race-conscious methods to address historical racial inequalities. From the mid-1960s on, following executive orders by Presidents Kennedy and Johnson, such programs were called "affirmative action." An example would be requiring a labor union forced to admit African Americans members for the first time to relax their seniority rules to avoid putting new Black members at the back of the seniority queue.[31]

Affirmative action was always difficult to implement and was often bitterly controversial because many white Americans thought it promoted racial minorities above equally or better-qualified whites. In 1978, in *Regents of the University of California v. Bakke*, the US Supreme Court banned the use of racial quotas in college admissions and held that the only legitimate use of race-conscious policies was not in correcting historic injustices but in creating "diversity." In subsequent decades, the scope of permissible affirmative action was further narrowed. In SFFA (*Students for Fair Admissions v. President and Fellows of Harvard College* [2023]), the Supreme Court effectively banned affirmative action as a criterion for college admissions. Left in its wake was a newer and less-well-defined program to address racial imbalances—diversity, equity, and inclusion (DEI)—which, without directly employing affirmative action, still saw the creation of racial diversity as a goal. On the first day of his second term, Donald Trump banned DEI, which he called "illegal and immoral."[32] He has rejected most accounts of Black history as representing a "divisive, race-based ideology" and criticized the national holiday of Juneteenth as unnecessary.[33] If Black citizenship is seen as the recognition of collective rights, such as the redress of historic inequalities (or even the bare acknowledgement of their existence), there has not been a time as hostile to Black citizenship since the end of Reconstruction.

Despite the Black radicalism of the 1960s, and despite the white counterrevolution against integration, most African Americans continued to support the idea of integration until it became clear that political opposition to integration by most white Americans was unalterable and unappeasable. In 1974, the US Supreme Court decision *Milliken v. Bradley* largely prevented busing across county lines to remedy racial inequalities, and this marked the end of serious efforts to implement school integration. The year 1988 marked the peak of the desegregation of public schools in the United States. Since 1990, America's schools have been gradually resegregated.[34] When integrated schools work, the results often have been impressive.[35] But successful integration is never easy to create and is even more difficult to maintain.

One consequence of the failure to integrate public schools has been a growing sense that efforts at integration have been a waste. As one Black parent complained about integrated schools: "Integration[,] what was it good for? They were just setting up our babies to fail."[36] Critical race theory developed in the 1970s in part through the perception that integration was both a practical and theoretical failure. One of its earliest proponents, Derrick Bell, argued that the Supreme Court in 1954 should have reaffirmed *Plessy v. Ferguson,* though mandating that separate Black schools must become, in every way, truly equal.[37] But equal funding for segregated Black schools in the South was impossible in the years after *Brown/Briggs* and proved nearly as impossible elsewhere in the United States. As civil rights lawyer Lani Guinier once stated, there has been in recent decades "an enormous nostalgia for a pre-Brown world."[38] As with nostalgia for the Negro Leagues, a proper appreciation for what was lost with the end of segregation should not lead us to sentimentalize the limitations of segregated institutions.

From our contemporary vantage, two paramount changes must be considered when viewing the last half century of integration. The United States now, as opposed to the United States in 1972, is again a nation of immigrants. The heyday of the civil rights movement—which happened during the decades between the immigration restriction act of 1924 and its loosening in 1965—coincided with the lowest numbers of immigrants in American history. In 1970, the foreign-born population was about 9.6 million, or 4.7 percent. In 2023, 47.8 million foreign-born persons lived in the United States, or about 14.3 of the total population. One consequence of this is that the notion of "race" has become more complicated. It's no longer (and really never was) a simple Black-white dyad. In 1970, approximately 88 percent of the US population identified as white. In 2021, only 59 percent of Americans identify as "white, non-Hispanic," while within the other 41 percent, only about 12.5 percent identify as African American; the rest identify with another ethnicity or see themselves as mixed-race.

As a consequence, we are no longer a nation of citizens. We are a country with many different levels of belonging: a hierarchy in which the top rung is occupied by native-born white persons, with everyone else below them and with their right to call themselves Americans (or "real Americans") suspect. About half of the foreign-born persons in the country are naturalized citizens; a quarter have a variety of legal statuses; and about a quarter (around 12 million persons) are undocumented. The presence of so many noncitizens has profoundly changed the nature of American citizenship. When Robinson, King, and others were calling for African American citizenship, they knew that African Americans were, formally and technically, native-born citizens who didn't have the same rights as white citizens. During the civil rights era, the call for citizenship was inclusive, a demand for equality. The demand for citizenship is now often a call for exclusion, a cudgel used to beat, isolate, and dehumanize others. Integration is no longer just about full citizenship. It is a demand to recognize our common personhood and a recognition that everyone who makes their permanent home in the United States of America is an American and deserves to be respected and treated as an American.

The other inescapable reality of race and integration in American life is that we are living amid the fury of what Jackie Robinson would have called a white counterrevolution. Although its forces have been gathering for decades, it reached a new height on 20 January 2025 when Donald Trump resumed the presidency and immediately began an assault on the legal and citizenship rights of persons of color. Since then, he and his administration have waged an unrelenting campaign against immigrants, against racial minorities, against any remaining DEI programs. The Trump administration has started a massive program to arrest and deport undocumented noncitizens and has tried to abridge the unambiguous constitutional right of birthright citizenship.[39] Writing about dramatic historical change while it is ongoing, writing from within the whirlwind, is always a fool's errand. Trends are easily under- or overestimated, and sudden historical swerves can render even the most careful speculation irrelevant. But it is true that many of the most significant accomplishments of the civil rights era, such as the Voting Rights Act of 1965 (the latter already greatly weakened by recent US Supreme Court decisions) are on the chopping block.[40] Any sense that African Americans and other racial minorities have collective rights that must be respected by governmental agencies and the courts has been ruthlessly repressed. It seems remarkably sudden, all in a historical blink. Of course, it is not. Jackie Robinson might say it is the culmination of the counterrevolution that he warned about during his lifetime—his worst nightmares fulfilled.

Given this, it's hardly surprising that the second Trump administration has Jackie Robinson in its sights. In March 2025, the Department of Defense (DOD), in a supposed effort to purge all instances of DEI from its website (but really part of a wider war against African American history), eliminated a section on Robinson that discussed his troubled time in the army and his court-martial. It was removed because, according to a spokesperson from the DOD, while the department "loves Jackie Robinson," it cannot "highlight [him] through the prism of immutable characteristics such as race." Discussing Jackie Robinson or his court-martial without reference to his racial background is of course an impossibility.[41] After a brief furor, the story about Robinson was restored, but the damage was done.

In March 2025, major-league baseball responded to the new executive orders banning DEI by removing all references to "diversity" from its website. To appease the Trump administration, Commissioner of Baseball Rob Manfred further commented that "Jackie Robinson transcends any debate that is going on in today's society about issues surrounding DEI. What Jackie Robinson stands for was moving us past an overt kind of segregation that I don't believe anybody actually supports today. He's a symbol of that, and he's an important part of our history. We will continue to celebrate him as we always have."[42] One can perhaps understand Manfred's motivation in his actions and statements, as craven as they are. But trying to celebrate Jackie Robinson for what is no longer controversial is not to celebrate Robinson at all. Jackie Robinson would have seen Donald Trump as the final degradation of the Republican Party.

In 1969, James Baldwin testified before a House select subcommittee supporting a bill to establish a national commission on "Negro History and

Culture." Baldwin spoke of the myriad problems that Black Americans still faced in becoming full and productive citizens. Their accomplishments meant nothing to "the cat . . . at the bottom of the barrel." Above all, he did not want his literary achievements to be viewed as an American success story, an example of what was possible for Black people in America to achieve. He added, "I am not a witness nor a hope. I am proof of what the country does to you if you are black. That is true even if I am Jackie Robinson."[43]

Jackie Robinson felt the same way about being Jackie Robinson. He did not want to be seen as a hope, to be held up as an example of what was possible for Black people to achieve in the United States. Instead, he often spoke of the barriers that remained intact and said that by itself, his success meant little. No hungry person would be fed or homeless person housed because of his years with the Dodgers. There was no phrase more important to Robinson, or one that he more wanted to be remembered by, than "I never had it made." In June 1959, he spoke to an overflow crowd at a meeting of the Tuskegee Civic Association in Alabama. They had gathered to celebrate the second anniversary of a boycott of white-owned stores in the area to protest a gerrymander intended to greatly reduce Black voting strength. He called out the "Uncle Tomists" who argued that African Americans were pressing too quickly. "If we slow down any, we'd be going backwards." He added, "Nothing angers me more, than to see a Negro succeed, then sit back and say 'I've got it made.'" As reported in an article titled "Nobody Has It Made," this is the earliest use of the phrase by Robinson that I can find, but he'd probably used it previously.[44]

In Chicago the following year, he again lambasted those who urged patience to civil rights protesters. He condemned Eisenhower's "go slow tactics" and said of Harry Truman, who had criticized the sit-in demonstrations, that he was a "phony liberal."[45] He also took aim at critics such as Malcolm X, who had suggested that Robinson was perhaps too well-off and too well-connected to understand the realities of Black Americans, saying that Robinson "had made it, and that white men [had] put him into baseball making possible a good job, money, and a fine home. These possessions gave him less of a right to protest." Robinson angrily rejected this. "None of us have it made until the most underprivileged Negro in the South is enjoying full citizenship."[46]

In late 1967, as the Fair Housing Act was slowly making its way through Congress, Robinson published one of his strongest columns, "[They] Only Think That They Have it Made," on how some prosperous African Americans, who had purchased homes for $20,000 and up (in 1967 dollars) in an unnamed midwestern city, had joined with their white neighbors in trying to stop the building of a large public housing project that would primarily house African Americans adjacent to their neighborhood. The news, wrote Robinson, made him "almost literally ill" because "Negroes who have been fortunate enough to acquire choice property, were displaying the same sort of selfishness which we have seen in whites over the years." They were adopting the "old and phony slogan about the reduction in property values that has bedeviled the black man in his fight for open housing." And then he set forth the Jackie Robinson theory of justice: always imagine how you would prosper if, from the veil of ignorance, you had to exchange your comfortable situation with the least fortunate. "Truthfully, none of us—however rich and famous—has it made until the least of us has it made, has it made it terms of equal opportunity in every aspect of life."[47]

In 1972, he titled his autobiography and his final testament *I Never Had It Made*. Why? "Because I refuse to kid myself about the value of a comfortable home, about having a little money," about his celebrity, when "so many of my black brothers and sisters are hungry, inadequately housed, insufficiently clothed, [and] denied their dignity." Moreover, "I cannot say I have it made while our country drives full speed ahead to deepen rifts between men and women of different colors, speeds along a course toward more and more racism."[48]

What did "having it made" mean for Robinson? It didn't mean that every person had to become wealthy and famous. It meant that "every man can rent and lease and buy according to his money and desires; [that] every child can have an equal opportunity in youth and manhood," until "racism and sexism are conquered"; until, if they are citizens, "every man can vote and any man can be elected." This is the final statement of Robinson's understanding of integration as effective citizenship: each of us having the full right to choose our own way in life for ourselves and our children, the right to participate and the right not to participate in any arena or institution of American life. It meant to be unafraid. In the words of the prophet Micah—words that have a deep resonance in African American history and religion—it meant that each of us shall sit contented beneath our own vine and own fig tree, "with none to make [us] tremble."[49] It is perhaps the oldest illustration of the real meaning of equal citizenship. Comfort is the goal of effective citizenship. Complacency is its enemy. And if Jackie Robinson was speaking specifically of African Americans, he was in fact addressing all of us. Perhaps it required the present crisis of democracy to fully understand his message. Without democracy, without confidence in the rule of law, none of us are full citizens. All we hold dear can be taken from us. None of us have it made.

"Making it" is about having a sense of safety and security. Economic security, certainly. Those lacking the wherewithal to choose their own futures are not free, and Robinson worked toward a society in which economic security could be the reality for all. But it also means making it in terms of political safety and security: freedom from fear of arbitrary arrest or confinement; confidence that if someone or something menaces you, you can take your concerns to the proper authorities and be listened to, that the police are working for you and not against you.

For Robinson, the conviction that he never had it made meant a connection to the least of us, a connection to all of us. "I cannot as an individual, rejoice in the good things I have been permitted to work for and learn while the humblest of my brothers is down hollering for help and not being heard."[50] After he joined the Dodgers, Jackie Robinson was forever thereafter famous for being first. But integration is not about being first. Integration is a team sport. The race only ends when the last straggler crosses the finish line. If Robinson is to be remembered for any of his many accomplishments, perhaps it is not for being the first but for his insistence that none of us have it made until the last and least of us have made it. Otherwise, our achievements are hollow, and our security is in perpetual danger of being taken from us. The Gospel of Matthew says the first shall be last, and the last shall be first. Jackie Robinson knew the importance of both.

ACKNOWLEDGMENTS

Why this book? I have long wanted to write more on the subject of integration, which I feel is one of the most important and one of the most misunderstood social and political ideals in recent American history. But I never warmed to prospects of writing a book just about an abstraction. So why this book? I have written extensively about the Rev. Howard Thurman, the extraordinary mid-twentieth-century religious teacher and thinker, who was one of leading advocates for the social and spiritual necessity of integration. I was very intrigued when I discovered that the Rev. Karl E. Downs was both the key facilitator of the lectures that became Thurman's masterwork, *Jesus and the Disinherited,* and was also the most important mentor to a fatherless, troubled teenager in Pasadena, California, named Jackie Robinson. (Downs, as well as Robinson, are the book's two heroes.) Could I write a history of integration through a retelling of the life and thoughts of Jackie Robinson? Well, gentle reader, this is that book. It is neither a full history of integration nor a complete biography of Jackie Robinson.

To the extent that this book fulfills its intention, I was crucially assisted by many. Pride of place belongs to Keith Crook, who showed incredible generosity in sharing research materials and insights with me. If you are interested in the topic of this book, please check out his recently published book on Jackie Robinson, *Opening the Door for Jackie.* Peter Dreier, another eminent Robinsonian, gave an earlier draft of this work a thorough critical reading that was extremely helpful, as did the three anonymous outside readers. I again have had the immense privilege of having the peerless Nadine Zimmerli editing one of my books, and once again, thanks to Nadine and the entire staff at the University of Virginia Press. Rob Snyder, as always, read portions of the book, and I had many discussions with him, Vernon Burton, and Daniel Soyer about its subjects. I have been sustained and bolstered by my friends, especially when my confidence and patience was faltering. Among them are Julie Miller, Vernon and Georganne Burton, Alison Parker, Ayala Emmett, Steve Marks, Marc Korpus, T. J. Thames, and Benjamin White. The librarians at Clemson University kept the books coming amid floods, pandemics, and other disasters. The spirit of the late Harold Wechsler, the world's greatest baseball fan, hovers over this project. How I wish I had been able to talk to him about it! And, of course, most importantly, through thick and thin, Jane DeLuca has been my companion, my light, my life's co-conspirator, co-editor, and co-navigator. Keeping us company has been our cat, Sparafucile. My love to them and to you all. They have all helped to make this a far better book. For its strikeouts, infield flies, and errors, I alone am responsible.

A brief story. I finished this book while living in the Franklin Residences, in Center City Philadelphia. The building was originally opened a century ago as the Benjamin Franklin Hotel. It is a few short blocks from Independence Hall, where the Declaration of Independence and the US Constitution were debated and ratified. Both documents contain a raft of noble sentiments, but neither document condemned the institution of slavery. By 21 February 1861, it was clear to all that the problem of slavery had brought the country to the brink of civil war. On that date, president-elect Abraham Lincoln, on his progression from Illinois to Washington, stopped in Philadelphia and stayed in the Continental Hotel, the city's grandest. When a crowd gathered, Lincoln offered a few remarks from the hotel's balcony, telling them what they already knew all too well: that "there is great anxiety amongst the citizenry of the United States at this time," but he still hoped war could be averted. In this, of course, he was incorrect. But he was not wrong to hope that what he would call a few weeks later the "the better angels of our nature" would not be defeated or destroyed by what was worst about the United States.

The tests would continue. In the 1920s, the old Continental Hotel was torn down to make way for the Benjamin Franklin. In the new hotel, the Lincoln Balcony preserves the spot where he spoke to the crowd on Chestnut Street. But the new proprietors were more neglectful of his message. Until 1947, the Brooklyn Dodgers stayed in the Benjamin Franklin when they were in town to play the Phillies. But that year, the hotel's management refused to accommodate Jackie Robinson. Branch Rickey found a different hotel for the Dodgers.

It's been odd to sleep every night in a building whose onetime owners didn't allow Jackie Robinson to sleep on its premises. And it has been strange, in a different way, to know that Abraham Lincoln once did sleep in a building at this location. Once again, "there is great anxiety amongst the citizenry of the United States." We are again fighting Abraham Lincoln's and Jackie Robinson's old demons. Once again, at least metaphorically, we are engaged in a great civil war. We are again doing furious battle against bigotry, ignorance, intolerance, and racial supremacy. And I know, with courage, resilience, and knowledge of the justness of our cause, we will again prevail. It is my fondest hope that this book might in some small way aid in our eventual victory.

November 2025

NOTES

Introduction

1. Peter Dreier and Robert Elias, *Baseball Rebels: The Players, People, and Social Movements That Shook Up the Game and Changed America* (Lincoln: University of Nebraska Press, 2022), 111.
2. Adam Clayton Powell Jr., *Marching Blacks: An Interpretive History of the Rise of the Common Man* (New York: Dial Press, 1945), 3.
3. "Mayor Stops Anti-Jim Crow Baseball Meet," *New York Amsterdam News*, 25 August 1945.
4. For Parker as baseball fan, see David Waldstein, "The Mets, the Royals, and Charlie Parker, Linked by Autumn in New York," *New York Times*, 30 October 2015.
5. See, for example, James Fleming, "Preacher at Large to Universities," *The Crisis*, August 1939, 233, 251, 289.
6. "21,000 Sign Anti-Lynch Paper," *New York Times*, 24 September 1947.
7. Of the five cases combined in *Brown v. Board of Education*, the first case argued, the case with the most important trial record, and the first case alphabetically, was the South Carolina case *Briggs v. Elliott*, 342 U.S. 350 (1952). The landmark Supreme Court case was given a misleading name. The plaintiffs in *Briggs* faced armed attacks on their persons and homes. It was in a dissent to the opinion of the three-judge panel in *Briggs* that Judge J. Waites Waring first made the judicial finding that would be the main holding in *Brown:* that "segregation is *per se* inequality." Whatever was wrong with segregated schools in Topeka, Kansas, there needs to be a reminder that the conditions in segregated schools in rural Clarendon County, South Carolina, were far worse. Following the lead of South Carolina civil rights activists, in this book I am calling the case

Brown/Briggs. On *Brown/Briggs*, see Richard Gergel, *Unexampled Courage: The Blinding of Sgt. Isaac Woodard and the Awakening of President Truman and Judge J. Waites Waring* (New York: Sarah Crichton Books, 2019), 224–65; Orville Vernon Burton, "Confronting Lost Cause Memorialization in South Carolina," in Christopher Fennell, *Grappling with Oppression: Moving from Analysis to Activism* (New York: Routledge, 2025), 141–56.

8. Rob Ruck, *Raceball: How the Major Leagues Colonized the Black and Latin Game* (Boston: Beacon Press, 2011), 110.
9. Cornel West, introduction to *I Never Had It Made,* by Jackie Robinson, as told to Alfred Duckett (1972; repr. New York: Harper Collins, 1995), ix.
10. John "Buck" O'Neil quoted in John B. Holway, *Black Diamonds: Life in the Negro Leagues from the Men Who Lived It* (Westport, CT: Meckler Books, 1989), 103.
11. Jules Tygiel, *Extra Bases: Reflections on Jackie Robinson, Race, and Baseball History* (Lincoln: University of Nebraska Press, 2002), 36.
12. Martin Luther King Jr., "Hall of Famer," *New York Amsterdam News,* 4 August 1962. King's history was a little off. The first well-publicized sit-in against segregation, organized by the Congress of Racial Equality, was in Chicago in May 1943. The first freedom riders, participants in CORE's Journey of Reconciliation, embarked on their travels on 9 May 1947, a week before Robinson made his debut with the Dodgers.
13. Arnold Rampersad, *Jackie Robinson* (New York: Ballantine Books, 1997), 313.
14. Second base was the position Robinson played during his best seasons with the Dodgers, but over the course of his major league career, he played a number of games at all the infield positions as well as in the outfield. In the end, he played only slightly more than 50 percent of his games at second base.
15. Bill James, *The New Bill James Historical Baseball Abstract* (New York: Free Press, 2001), 1044–46. James, writing a quarter century ago, rated Robinson the fourth-best second baseman of all time.
16. Jackie Robinson, "Racial Unity Essential During Negro Revolution," *Chicago Defender,* 6 July 1963.
17. Raymond Willliams, *Keywords: A Vocabulary of Culture and Society* (New York: Oxford University Press, 1985).
18. See Ryan S. Balot, "Revisiting the Classical Ideal of Citizenship," and Iseult Honahan, "Liberal and Republican Conceptions of Citizenship," in *The Oxford Handbook of Citizenship,* eds. Ayelet Shachar, Rainer Baubock, Irene Bloemraad, and Maarten Vink (Oxford: Oxford University Press, 2017), 16, 89–91; Dominique Leydet, "Citizenship," *Stanford Encyclopedia of Philosophy* (rev. 2023), https://plato.stanford.edu/entries/citizenship/.
19. The models of integration used in this book—integration as inclusion and integration as nonexclusion and Black citizenship—are meant to be suggestive, a helpful way of thinking about the subject rather than a rigorous typology. Not every statement about integration can be neatly placed in either camp.

20. E. Franklin Frazier, *The Integration of the Negro into American Life* (Philadelphia: Women's International League for Peace and Freedom, 1945).
21. Martin Luther King Jr, *The Essential Writings and Speeches of Martin Luther King Jr.*, ed. James M. Washington (San Francisco: Harper Collins, 1986), 217–21.
22. Howard Thurman, "The Will to Segregation" (1943), in *The Papers of Howard Washington Thurman*, 5 vols., ed. Walter Earl Fluker (Columbia: University of South Carolina Press, 2009–19), 2:337–44.
23. Benjamin Elijah Mays and Joseph William Nicholson, *The Negro's Church* (New York: Institute of Social and Religious Research, 1933), 154–67.
24. Thurman, "The Will to Segregation," 2:339–40.
25. Seth S. Tannenbaum, "The Desegregation of Sportsman's Park in St. Louis: Black Baseball Fans Use of the National Pastime to Fight White Supremacy," *Journal of African American History* 109, no. 3 (2024): 224.
26. "Jackie Tells Churchmen About Intermarriage," *Cleveland Call and Post*, 27 July 1963. Despite the gendered language, presumably Robinson was also speaking for Black women.
27. See Ruth Bogin, "'Liberty Further Extended': A 1776 Antislavery Manuscript by Lemuel Haynes," *William and Mary Quarterly*, 3rd series, vol. 40, no. 1 (1983): 85–105. For the African American identification and argument with the Declaration, see Mia Bay, "See Your Declaration Americans!!! Abolitionism, Americanism, and the Revolutionary Tradition in Free Black Politics," in *Americanism: New Perspectives on the History of an Idea*, eds. Michael Kazin and Joseph A. McCartin (Chapel Hill: University of North Carolina, 2006), 25–52.
28. Stephen Kantrowitz, *Citizens of a Stolen Land: A Ho-Chunk History of the Nineteenth Century United States* (Chapel Hill: University of North Carolina Press, 2023), 71–72.
29. For Black voting rights in the antebellum North, see Kate Masur, *Until Justice Be Done: America's First Civil Rights Movement: From the Revolution to Reconstruction* (New York: Norton, 2021); and Van Gosse, *The First Reconstruction: Black Politics from the Revolution to the Civil War* (Chapel Hill: University of North Carolina Press, 2021).
30. Eric Foner, *The Second Founding: How the Civil War and Reconstruction Remade the Constitution* (New York: Norton, 2019).
31. See Jonathan Scott Holloway, *Confronting the Veil: Abram Harris, Jr., E. Franklin Frazier, and Ralph Bunche, 1919–1941* (Chapel Hill: University of North Carolina Press, 2002).
32. "Johnson Views Race Problem at NAACP Meet," *New York Amsterdam News*, 16 July 1938.
33. "Exclusion Wrong Policy for Negroes in America," *Philadelphia Tribune*, 16 November 1939.
34. Rachel Robinson, with Lee Daniels, *Jackie Robinson: An Intimate Portrait* (New York: Harry N. Abrams, 1996), 33.

35. Since 2021, major-league baseball has considered the Negro Leagues, from 1920 to 1948, as major leagues.
36. Jules Tygiel, *Baseball's Great Experiment: Jackie Robinson and His Legacy* (New York: Oxford University Press, 2008), 246–64.
37. Robert S. Browne and Bayard Rustin, *Separatism or Integration: Which Way America?* (New York: A. Philip Randolph Educational Fund, 1969), 10. The comment is by Browne.
38. James Farmer, "Integration or Desegregation," ch. 5 in Farmer, *Freedom—When?* (1965), National Humanities Center Toolbox Library, https://nationalhumanitiescenter.org/pds/maai3/segregation/text7/text7read.htm.
39. Martin Luther King Jr., *Where Do We Go from Here: Chaos or Community* (Boston: Beacon Press, 1967), 62.
40. Chester Hartman and Gregory D. Squires, "Integration Exhaustion, Race Fatigue, and the American Dream," in *The Integration Debate: Competing Futures for American Cities*, eds. Chester Hartman and Gregory D. Squires, (New York: Routledge, 2010), 1–8.
41. Jackie Robinson, as told to Wendell Smith, *Jackie Robinson: My Own Story* (New York: Greenberg Publishers, 1949).
42. Jackie Robinson, with Alfred Duckett, *I Never Had It Made* (New York: Putnam's, 1972), 273. Robinson wrote an earlier biography, *Jackie Robinson: My Own Story* (1949), but all references to Robinson's autobiography, unless otherwise noted, are to the 1972 edition of *I Never Had It Made.*

1. Coming of Age in Pasadena

1. NAACP, *Thirty Years of Lynching in the United States* (1919; repr. New York: Arno Press, 1969), cited in Thomas Aiello, *Mary Turner and the Mob: The Brooks-Lowndes Race Riot of 1918 in History and Memory* (Columbia: University of South Carolina Press, 2025), 89.
2. The standard story, until very recently, was that one of the lynching victims, Mary Turner, was murdered when pregnant and near her delivery date, and the fetus was ripped from her abdomen and stomped on: see Julie Buckner Armstrong, *Mary Turner and the Memory of Lynching* (Athens: University of Georgia, 2011). However, Thomas Aiello has convincingly argued that the gruesome story was invented by NAACP field secretary Walter White to bolster the chances of the passage of federal antilynching legislation: see Aiello, *Mary Turner and the Mob*.
3. The literature on Robinson could metaphorically fill the seats in Pasadena's Rose Bowl. For a sample, see Arnold Rampersad, *Jackie Robinson: A Biography* (New York: Ballantine Books, 1997); Jackie Robinson, with Alfred Duckett, *I Never Had It Made* (New York: Putnam's, 1972); Jules Tygiel, *Baseball's Great Experiment: Jackie Robinson and His Legacy* (New York: Oxford University Press, 2008); Michael G. Long, ed., *42 Today: Jackie Robinson and His Legacy* (New York: NYU Press, 2021); Bill Nowlin and Glen Sparks, eds., *Jackie: Perspectives on 42* (Phoenix, AZ: Society For American Baseball

Research, 2021); Ralph Carhart, ed., *Not An Easy Tale to Tell: Jackie Robinson on the Page, Stage, and Screen* (Phoenix, AZ: Society for American Baseball Research, 2022).

4. “Kelly Miller Says the Outlook Is Hopeful,” *Chicago Defender,* 27 September 1918.
5. Robert Whitaker, *On the Laps of Gods: The Red Summer and the Struggle for Justice That Remade a Nation* (New York: Three Rivers Press, 2009).
6. Adrienne Petty and Mark Schultz, “Breaking New Ground: African American Landowners and the Pursuit of the ‘American Dream,’” in *Lincoln’s Unfinished Work: From Generation to Generation,* eds. Orville Vernon Burton and Peter Eisenstadt (Baton Rouge: Louisiana State University, 2022), 133–73.
7. For rural life in post-Reconstruction Georgia for Black landowners, see Mark Schultz, *The Rural Face of White Supremacy: Beyond Jim Crow* (Urbana: University of Illinois Press, 2005).
8. Rampersad, *Jackie Robinson* 11.
9. Robinson and Duckett, *I Never Had It Made,* 16. According to his sister, Willa Mae Robinson Walker, Jerry Robinson showed up “one time” after his son had become famous, but “Jack didn’t have anything to do with him, and that was it.” Quoted in Danny Peary, *Jackie Robinson in Quotes* (Salem, MA: Page Street Publishing, 2016), 9.
10. For Black migration to Southern California in the interwar years, see Douglas Flamming, *Bound for Freedom: Black Los Angeles in Jim Crow America* (Berkeley: University of California Press, 2005), 17–91.
11. Jackie Robinson, *Baseball Has Done It,* ed. Charles Dexter (Philadelphia: Lippincott, 1964), 30.
12. Rampersad, *Jackie Robinson,* 16–17.
13. Rampersad, *Jackie Robinson,* 25.
14. Carl T. Rowan, *Wait till Next Year: The Life Story of Jackie Robinson* (New York: Random House, 1960), 203.
15. Peter Dreier, “The Battle over School Funding: The View from Pasadena,” *California Journal of Politics and Policy* 2, no. 1 (2010): 9.
16. American Guide Series, *California: A Guide to the Golden State* (New York: Hastings House, 1939), 245–49.
17. American Guide Series, *California: A Guide to the Golden State,* 245–49.
18. Dreier, “The Battle over School Funding,” 9.
19. Rowan, *Wait till Next Year,* 21; Peary, *Jackie Robinson in Quotes,* 17.
20. James E. Crimi, “The Social Status of the Negro in Pasadena, California” (MA thesis, University of Southern California, Los Angeles, 1941), 48.
21. One defender of Black Pasadenans allowed that “for the most part they are good citizens, some superior to whites. I think there is more cause for real concern over Jews than Negroes.” Quoted in Crimi, “Social Status of the Negro,” 68–72.
22. Crimi, “Social Status of the Negro,” 68–72.
23. Rampersad, *Jackie Robinson,* 27.

24. Edwin A. Cottrell, *Pasadena Social Agencies Survey* (Pasadena, CA: [City of Pasadena?], 1940), 322. The same study suggested that African Americans were also not really suited to the low-level, often menial positions in the "type of which for which [the Negro] had been trained and enjoyed for generations," such as domestic worker, because new technical advances in these jobs "demand a higher type of intelligence," which "most Negroes did not possess," 322.
25. Crimi, "Social Status of the Negro," 27–28, 39, 75–79.
26. Rampersad, *Jackie Robinson,* 31–32, 42–43.
27. Rampersad, *Jackie Robinson,* 23.
28. Robinson and Duckett, *I Never Had It Made,* 17; Peary, *Jackie Robinson in Quotes,* 13.
29. Communication from Peter Dreier.
30. Crimi, "Social Status of the Negro," 19.
31. Cottrell, *Pasadena Social Agencies Survey,* 16–22.
32. Crimi, "Social Status of the Negro," 49.
33. Crimi, "Social Status of the Negro," 49, 72–73, 74, 50.
34. Crimi, "Social Status of the Negro," 79–80.
35. Crimi, "Social Status of the Negro," 113.
36. Rampersad, *Jackie Robinson,* 26; Cottrell, *Pasadena Social Agencies Survey,* 40.
37. Rampersad, *Jackie Robinson,* 21.
38. Rampersad, *Jackie Robinson,* 26; Robinson, *Baseball Has Done It,* 30. Robinson singles out his kindergarten or first grade teacher, Beryl Haney, for her kindness; see Peary, *Jackie Robinson in Quotes,* 324.
39. Peter Golenbock, *An Oral History of the Brooklyn Dodgers* (New York: G. P. Putnam's, 1984), 117–18. For Robinson's Japanese and Mexican (and white) friends, see Rampersad, *Jackie Robinson,* 33.
40. Crimi, "Social Status of the Negro," 79–80.
41. Rampersad, *Jackie Robinson,* 27.
42. Crimi, "Social Status of the Negro," 82–83.
43. Rampersad, *Jackie Robinson,* 27; Robinson, *Baseball Has Done It,* 30–31.
44. Robinson, *Baseball Has Done It,* 31; Harvey Frommer, *Rickey and Robinson: The Men Who Broke Baseball's Color Barrier* (Lanham, MD: Rowman and Littlefield, 1982), 20.
45. Frank Finch, "Jackie Robinson Enters ULCA to Compete in Football, Track," *Los Angeles Times,* 17 February 1939.
46. "U.C.L.A. Sets Back Washington State," *New York Times,* 17 November 1940; Paul Zimmerman, "Jackie Robinson Big Threat on UCLA Eleven," *Los Angeles Times,* 27 August 1939; Randy Dixon, "Riding Prophetic Winds Across Gridiron Domains," *Pittsburgh Courier,* 9 September 1939.
47. "Sepians to Play Large Part in Nation's Football Scheme," *Cleveland Call and Post,* 28 September 1939.
48. Jackie Robinson, *Jackie Robinson,* 9.

49. Rampersad, *Jackie Robinson,* 71.
50. See James W. Johnson, *The Black Bruins: The Remarkable Lives of UCLA's Jackie Robinson, Woody Strode, Tom Bradley, Kenny Washington, and Ray Bartlett* (Lincoln: University of Nebraska Press, 2017).
51. Louis Melancholy Jones, "Slants on Sports," *Atlanta Daily World,* 3 August 1940.
52. Lucius Melancholy Jones, "Twelve Million Negroes Hoping UCLA Will Receive Rose Bowl Bid," *Atlanta Daily World,* 12 November 1939.
53. Adam Clayton Powell Jr., *New York Amsterdam News,* "Soap Box," 30 December 1939.
54. Randy Dixon, "The Sports Bugle," *Los Angeles Sentinel,* 13 July 1939; Peary, *Jackie Robinson in Quotes,* 50.
55. Peary, *Jackie Robinson in Quotes,* 111.
56. "Jackie Robinson to Romp for All-Stars," *Los Angeles Times,* 27 August 1941.
57. "Jackie Robinson of UCLA," *Atlanta Daily World,* 8 March 1940.
58. Rampersad, *Jackie Robinson,* 55.
59. "Famous Jackie Robinson to Play Here," *Chicago Defender,* 7 December 1940.
60. "Robinson Wins Title but Needs Dough, Quits College," *Baltimore Afro-American,* 5 March 1941.
61. Robinson and Duckett, *I Never Had It Made,* 23; Robinson, *Baseball Has Done It,* 32.
62. Rampersad, *Jackie Robinson,* 86–87.
63. Jackie Robinson, as told to Wendell Smith, *Jackie Robinson: My Own Story* (New York: Greenberg Publishers, 1949), 9.
64. Peary, *Jackie Robinson in Quotes,* 55.
65. Peary, *Jackie Robinson in Quotes,* 58.
66. Randy Dixon, "Exhibit A in a So-Called Democracy: The Case of Jackie Robinson," *Pittsburgh Courier,* 6 September 1941.
67. *Los Angeles Examiner,* August 1941, quoted in Peary, *Jackie Robinson in Quotes,* 58.
68. He did not think highly of the level of play in the league, batting .400 for the season and stealing seven bases in one game; see Robinson, *My Own Story,* 10.
69. Christina Rice, "Jackie Robinson: Southern California's Hometown Hero," *Huffpost,* 11 April 2013. Robinson played baseball in the 1945 and 1946 seasons in the California Winter League, an independent league that had both white and Blacks teams; he played four games for the Kansas City Royals in 1945 and two games for the Jackie Robinson All-Stars in 1946: see William F. McNeil, *The California Winter League: America's First Integrated Baseball League* (Jefferson, NC: McFarland, 2002), 224–28, 260.
70. Robinson, *Baseball Has Done It,* 34.
71. Dixon, "Exhibit A in a So-Called Democracy," *Pittsburgh Courier,* 6 September 1941.
72. Chris Lamb, *Conspiracy of Silence: Sportswriters and the Long Campaign to Desegregate Baseball* (Lincoln: University of Nebraska, 2012), 146.
73. The Mexican League during and after the war signed several Negro League players, including Nate Moreland, who pitched for Mexican League teams in 1941 and 1944 and

from 1947 to 1956. Robinson's future Dodgers teammate, Roy Campanella, played in the Mexican League in 1942 and 1943. See John Virtue, *South of the Border: How Jorge Pascal and the Mexican League Pushed Baseball Toward Racial Integration* (Jefferson, NC: McFarland, 2008).

74. "They Were Turned Down," *Pittsburg Courier,* 21 March 1942.
75. Ted Carroll, "Robinson, Star Dimmed by Bias, To Play on Army Team," *New York Amsterdam News,* 17 October 1942.
76. Robinson and Duckett, *I Never Had It Made,* 7.
77. "Jackie Urges Students to Continue Picketing," *Baltimore Afro-American,* 19 March 1960.
78. Rachel Robinson, with Lee Daniels, *Jackie Robinson: An Intimate Portrait* (New York: Harry M. Abrams, 1996), 124, 127.
79. In 1937, Frank Oppenheimer (brother of J. Robert Oppenheimer) and his wife Jackie were living in Pasadena. The couple were deeply concerned about discrimination at the pool and felt that the Communist Party "was the only political organization concerned" about said discrimination, so they decided to join the party and became active in a Black neighborhood of Pasadena. See K. C. Cole, *Something Incredibly Wonderful Happens: Frank Oppenheimer and the World He Made Up* (New York: Houghton Mifflin Harcourt, 2009), 48.
80. Crimi, "Social Status of the Negro," 27–28, 39, 75–79.
81. See Jeff Wiltsie, *Contested Waters: A Social History of Swimming Pools in the United States* (Chapel Hill: University of North Carolina Press, 2007).
82. Crimi, "Social Status of the Negro," 117–21.
83. Cottrell, *Pasadena Social Agencies Survey,* 322.
84. Cottrell, *Pasadena Social Agencies Survey,* 322. The expense of equalization strategies, such as the efforts in Southern states, after the decision in *Brown/Briggs* to build new "separate but equal" schools, similarly failed because of their expense and because of underlying white racism.
85. Crimi, "Social Status of the Negro," 117–21.
86. Robinson, *Baseball Has Done It,* 29.
87. Crimi, "Social Status of the Negro," 121–29.
88. Frommer, *Rickey and Robinson,* 20.

2. Karl Downs and the Cause of Integration

1. Babe Ruth, as told to Bob Considine, *The Babe Ruth Story* (New York: Dutton, 1948), 1.
2. Jackie Robinson, with Alfred Duckett, *I Never Had It Made* (New York: Putnam's, 1972), 7.
3. Harvey Frommer, *Rickey and Robinson: The Men Who Broke Baseball's Color Barrier* (Lanham, MD: Rowman and Littlefield, 1982), 23.

4. Robinson and Duckett, *I Never Had It Made,* 18.
5. Arnold Rampersad, *Jackie Robinson: A Biography* (New York: Ballantine Books, 1997), 33–34; Frommer, *Rickey and Robinson,* 23.
6. "Pasadena," *Chicago Defender,* 16 April 1938.
7. Peter Golenbock, *An Oral History of the Brooklyn Dodgers* (New York: Putnam's, 1984), 117–18. Although he was still living in Pasadena in early 1942 at the beginning of the Japanese internments, Robinson nowhere comments on this.
8. Robinson and Duckett, *I Never Had It Made,* 18.
9. Rampersad, *Jackie Robinson,* 50–51.
10. Jackie Robinson, *Baseball Has Done It,* ed. Charles Dexter (Philadelphia: Lippincott, 1964), 55.
11. Rampersad, *Jackie Robinson,* 50–51.
12. Danny Peary, *Jackie Robinson in Quotes* (Salem, MA: Page Street Pub., 2016), 4.
13. "Pasadena Grid Player Arrested," *Los Angeles Times,* 14 August 1939; Rampersad, *Jackie Robinson,* 65–66.
14. Rampersad, *Jackie Robinson,* 35.
15. Carl T. Rowan, *Wait till Next Year: The Life Story of Jackie Robinson* (New York: Random House, 1960), 30; Rampersad, *Jackie Robinson,* 34.
16. James E. Crimi, "The Social Status of the Negro in Pasadena, California" (MA thesis, University of Southern California, Los Angeles, 1941), 86.
17. Robinson and Duckett, *I Never Had It Made,* 19.
18. Michael Long and Chris Lamb, *Jackie Robinson, A Spiritual Biography: The Faith of a Boundary-Breaking Hero* (Louisville, KY: Westminster John Knox Press, 2017), 16.
19. "Religious Campaigns in '50," *Los Angeles Sentinel,* 9 November 1949.
20. Long and Lamb, *Jackie Robinson, Spiritual Biography,* 22.
21. Long and Lamb, *Jackie Robinson, Spiritual Biography,* 23.
22. Jackie Robinson, "Robinson Never Forgets Mother's Advice," *Washington Post,* 23 August 1949.
23. Robinson, *Baseball Has Done It,* 30.
24. Robinson, *Baseball Has Done It,* 30.
25. Jackie Robinson Papers, 1934–2012, Library of Congress Manuscript Division, https://lccn.loc.gov/mm2001084832.
26. Benjamin Elijah Mays and Joseph William Nicholson, *The Negro's Church* (New York: Institute of Social and Religious Research, 1933), 278.
27. For Black Protestant modernism, see Gary Dorrien, *The Making of American Liberal Theology: Idealism, Realism, and Modernity, 1900–1950* (Louisville, KY: Westminster John Knox Press, 2003), and *Breaking White Supremacy: Martin Luther King Jr. and the Black Social Gospel* (New Haven, CT: Yale University Press, 2018); and Peter Eisenstadt, *Against the Hounds of Hell: A Life of Howard Thurman* (Charlottesville: University of Virginia Press, 2021).

28. For other discussions of Downs, see Long and Lamb, *Jackie Robinson, A Spiritual Biography,* 27–34; Randal Maurice Jelks, "A Methodist Life," in *42 Today: Jackie Robinson and His Legacy,* ed. Michael G. Long (New York: NYU Press, 2021), 20–22.
29. The institution was named after Samuel Huston, an Iowa Methodist interested in African American education, not to be confused with Samuel Houston, the antebellum Texas politician and enslaver.
30. "Samuel Houston [*sic*] Prexy, Dr. Karl Downs, Dies," *Atlanta Daily World,* 27 February 1948. For Downs's serious interest in being a missionary to Liberia, see Karl Downs, "I Stand Committed," in *Stewart Missionary Foundation for Africa* (Atlanta: Gammon Theological Seminary, 1936), 11–15.
31. "Gammon Sky Pilots Rout Clark Frosh by 50–36 Mark," *Atlanta Daily World,* 6 March 1936.
32. Lucius Jones, "Three Atlantans Honored Smartly by Chicago Friends," *Atlanta Daily World,* 28 October 1934; "Church Missionary Speaks on West Coast," *Pittsburg Courier,* 17 July 1937.
33. Alemena Davis, "Duke's 'Symphonic' Classical Jazz," *Pittsburgh Courier,* 6 September 1941.
34. "To Stress the Value of the Ballot," *Atlanta Daily World,* 5 May 1935. He also is credited with another related catchphrase: "The man without a vote is the public's goat." See "Dr. Logan Optimistic over Franchise Gains," *Baltimore Afro-American,* 8 June 1946.
35. "We, Too, Sing America," in *The Duke Ellington Reader,* ed. Mark Tucker (New York: Oxford University Press, 1993), 146–47.
36. "We, Too, Sing America," 146–47.
37. Davis, "Duke's 'Symphonic' Classical Jazz." The Duke Ellington Orchestra was, by consensus, at its peak in the early 1940s. Oh, to have been in the audience! If Robinson had been in attendance, one of the songs from *Jump for Joy* would no doubt have had special resonance: "I've Got a Passport from Georgia (And I'm Going to the U.S.A.)."
38. Robinson, *Baseball Has Done It,* 30.
39. Long and Lamb, *Jackie Robinson, A Spiritual Biography,* 27–39; Robinson and Duckett, *I Never Had It Made,* 20–21.
40. For the Commission on Interracial Cooperation, see Mark Ellis, *Race Harmony and Black Progress: Jack Woofter and the Interracial Cooperation Movement* (Bloomington: Indiana University Press, 2013); and John Egerton, *Speak Now Against the Day: The Generation Before the Civil Rights Movement in the South* (Chapel Hill: University of North Carolina Press, 1994).
41. "Take Up Negro Problem," *New York Times,* 23 January 1921.
42. Lauren Kientz Anderson, "A Nauseating Sentiment, a Magical Device, or a Real Insight? Interracialism at Fisk University in 1930," in *Higher Education for African Americans Before the Civil Rights Era, 1900–1940,* eds. Marybeth Gassman and Roger Geiger (New Brunswick, NJ: Transaction Pub., 2012), 105n8.

43. Paul E. Baker, *Negro-White Adjustment: An Investigation and Analysis of the Methods in the Interracial Movement in the United States* (New York: Association Press, 1934), 261.
44. Karl E. Downs, "Timid Negro Students," *The Crisis* (June 1936), 171, 187; also printed in *Atlanta Daily World,* 6 April 1936.
45. Downs, "Timid Negro Students," 171, 187.
46. Robinson, *Baseball Has Done It,* 30.
47. "NAACP To Honor Carl [*sic*] Downs," *Baltimore Afro-American,* 12 November 1938.
48. Edward Phillips, *The New World of English Words* (London: E. Tyler, 1658), s.v. "integration."
49. Charles Darwin, *On the Origin of Species* (London: John Murray, 1859). It was Spencer, not Darwin, who coined evolution's catchphrase "the survival of the fittest."
50. Herbert Spencer, *First Principles* (London: Williams and Norgate, 1870), 396. Spencer's theory of evolution was present in embryo from his earliest works, such as *Social Statics* (1851).
51. W. H. Willing, "Review of L. Thomas Hopkins, *Integration: Its Meaning and Application* [D. Appleton-Century, 1937]," *Journal of Educational Research* 33, no. 1 (1939): 50.
52. Israel Zangwill, "The Position of Judaism," *North American Review* 169, no. 401 (1895): 425–39.
53. Harvard Sitkoff, *A New Deal for Blacks: The Emergence of Civil Rights as a National Issue* (New York: Oxford University Press, 1978), 35–37.
54. Peter Slade, "Howard Kester," in *Can I Get a Witness? Thirteen Peacemakers, Community Builders, and Agitators for Peace and Justice,* eds. Charles Marsh, Shea Tuttle, and Daniel P. Rhodes (Grand Rapids, MI: William B. Eerdmans Pub., 2019), 101. See also Leroy Davis, *A Clashing of the Soul: John Hope and the Dilemma of African American Leadership and Black Higher Education in the Early Twentieth Century* (Athens: University of Georgia Press, 1998), 227.
55. Kelly Miller, "Go Back to the Farm, Kelly Miller Says," *Pittsburgh Courier,* 31 December 1932.
56. "Lynchings Rose 180% in Nation Last Year," *New York Times,* 2 January 1934; "Collusion Between Law Officers and Mobs Seen as Most Ominous, Evident in 1933 Lynching Epidemic," *Norfolk Journal and Guide,* 6 January 1934; "47 Lynchings in 1933, States ILD," *Atlanta Daily World,* 3 January 1934.
57. "Another Bank Closed," *Pittsburgh Courier,* 28 May 1932.
58. Monroe K. Work, *Annual Encyclopedia of the Negro, 1931–1932* (Tuskegee Institute, AL: Negro Year Book Publishing, 1931), 118.
59. "It's Time to Be Honest," *Pittsburgh Courier,* 14 May 1932.
60. "The Negro College" (1933), in W. E. B. Du Bois, *Writings,* ed. Nathan I. Huggins (New York: Library of America, 1986), 1015.
61. Ernest Calloway, "The Trade Union Movement and Negro Integration," *Bags and Baggage* 1, no. 1 (1937).

62. "Resolutions of the Second Amenia Conference," in *Black Protest Thought in the Twentieth Century,* eds. August Meier, Francis L. Broderick, and Elliot M. Rudwick (Indianapolis, IN: Bobbs-Merrill, 1971), 154–58. For the Second Amenia Conference, see Eben Miller, *Born Along the Color Line: The 1933 Amenia Conference and the Rise of a National Civil Rights Movement* (New York: Oxford University Press, 2012).
63. "On Being Ashamed of Oneself: An Essay in Race Pride" (1933), in Du Bois, *Writings,* 1024.
64. W. E. B. Du Bois, "Observations," *The Crisis* 41, no. 1 (1934).
65. W. E. B. Du Bois "Segregation in the North," *The Crisis* 41, no. 4 (1934): 115–16.
66. W. E. B. Du Bois, "Segregation," *The Crisis* 41, no. 1 (1934).
67. For Du Bois on cooperatives, see *Writings,* 706–14. See also Victoria W. Wolcott, "Black Cooperators: Owenism and Utopia in Black America," in *Utopian Imaginings: Saving the Future in the Present,* ed. Victoria W. Wolcott (Albany: SUNY Press, 2024), 37–66; Barbara Ransby, *Ella Baker and the Black Freedom Struggle: A Radical Democratic Life* (Chapel Hill: University of North Carolina Press, 2004), 75–86.
68. Du Bois, "Segregation," *The Crisis* 41, no.1 (1934); "The N.A.A.C.P. and Race Segregation," *The Crisis* 41, no. 2 (1934): 52–53.
69. Du Bois, "Segregation in the North" (1934), in *Writings,* 1239–47.
70. Malcolm X, *The End of White World Supremacy: Four Speeches* (New York: Arcade Press, 1971), 75.
71. Charles F. Lane, "Is Dr. DuBois Growing Weary? Has He Quit?," *Chicago Defender,* 24 March 1934; Rev. A. Wayman Ward, "He Fought in Vain," *Chicago Defender,* 24 March 1934; Dewey R. Jones, "Why Fight Segregation—Dr. DuBois: Distinguished Race Leader Sees Nothing to be Gained by Opposing Jim Crow System in the United States, Tells Chicago Audience We Should Make Best of Situation, No Relief in Sight, Is He a Quitter?," *Chicago Defender,* March 24, 1934; "Calls Du Bois a Traitor to His Race," *Chicago Defender,* 14 April 1934; Samuel Williams, "An Elegy to Dr. Du Bois," *Pittsburgh Courier,* 14 April 1934.
72. William Hastie, "Oh, Mr. Du Bois! How Could You?," *Baltimore Afro-American,* 25 January 1934.
73. "Was He Right After All?," *Chicago Defender,* 24 March 1934.
74. Carter G. Woodson, "DuBois's Segregation Views Irk Woodson, Who Tells You Why," *Baltimore Afro-American,* 21 April 1934.
75. Walter White, "Segregation—A Symposium," *The Crisis* 41, no. 3 (1934): 80–81.
76. James Weldon Johnson, *Negro Americans, What Now?* (New York: Viking Press, 1934), 12–18.
77. Johnson, *Negro Americans, What Now?,* 12–18.
78. Mary McLeod Bethune, "Weekly Chats," *Pittsburgh Courier,* 6 February 1937.
79. George Schuyler, "Must Negro Lose Himself Racially?," *New York Amsterdam News,* 5 June 1937; "No! Claude McKay, Noted Author, Argues," ibid. See also the follow-up

letters, "That Heated Debate on Integration Is Still Being Argued," *New York Amsterdam News*, 19 June 1937.

80. Dizzy Gillespie, with Al Fraser, *To Be or Not to Bop . . . Memoirs* (Garden City, NY: Doubleday, 1979), 30.
81. Edwin D. Hoffman, "The Genesis of the Modern Movement for Equal Rights in South Carolina, 1900–1939," *Journal of Negro History* 44, no. 4 (1959): 346–69. See also Peter F. Lau, "Mr. NAACP: Levi G. Byrd and the Remaking of the NAACP in State and Nation," in *Toward a Meeting of the Waters: Currents in the Civil Rights Movement of South Carolina During the Twentieth Century*, eds. Winnifred B. Moore Jr. and Orville Vernon Burton (Columbia: University of South Carolina Press, 2008), 146–55.
82. Rebecca Stiles Taylor, "Integration Versus Disintegration Is the Question of the Hour," *Chicago Defender*, 13 September 1941.
83. HLM, "Tragedy: Fauset Style," *New York Amsterdam News*, 6 December 1933.
84. Harvey Klehr, *The Heyday of American Communism: The Depression Decade* (New York: Basic Books, 1984), 348. See also Mark Solomon, *The Cry Was Unity: Communists and African Americans, 1917–36* (Jackson: University of Mississippi Press, 1998).
85. Robert A. Hill, ed., *The FBI's RACON: Racial Conditions in the United States During World War II* (Boston: Northeastern University Press, 1995), 33–34, and passim. If Scottsboro became a rallying cry for the Communist Party, so too for some Black nationalist organizations. In 1933, Elijah Karriem wrote the following letter to the *Baltimore Afro-American:* "Nine poor brothers are in jail today even after one of their accusers came into the court and acknowledged that these innocent boys had not touched her or her mate. But the wicked enemies of the black man cried for the righteous blood of these boys as they always have, for more than three hundred years. But thanks be to *Allah*, vengeance is his. He will repay." See Karriem, "Moslems Are Misrepresented by Caucasians" [Letter to Editor], *Baltimore Afro- American*, 6 May 1933. The following year, he adopted a new name, Elijah Muhammad, and became leader of the Nation of Islam.
86. Oscar C. Brown Sr., *By a Thread* (New York: Vantage Press, 1983), 56; Christopher Robert Reed, *The Chicago NAACP and the Rise of Black Professional Leadership, 1910–1966* (Bloomington: Indiana University Press, 1997), 114–15. The dream of the forty-ninth state is not to be confused with the proposal for African American self-determination in the Southern "Black Belt." This was an official policy of the Communist Party USA after 1928, though it was deemphasized after 1935 and terminated in 1942.
87. Thomas H. R. Clarke, "Use of Word 'Negro' is Bitterly Resented," *Pittsburgh Courier*, 14 October 1933. Clarke did not practice what he preached, and throughout his long life he remained a pillar of Washington's Black elite. See "Thomas H. R. Clarke" [obituary notice], *Washington Post*, 18 July 1947. George Schuyler, the mercurial African American columnist and author of the satirical novel *Black No More* (1931) did not pass or advocate for passing but called for racial amalgamation through interracial marriage, couplings, and mixed-race offspring as the surest way of solving America's

racial problems. See George Schuyler, "Must Negro Lose Himself Racially? Yes, Caustic George S. Schuyler Maintains," *New York Amsterdam News,* 5 June 1937.

88. Gunnar Myrdal, *An American Dilemma: The Negro Problem and Modern Democracy* (New York: Harper and Brothers, 1944), 129, 1208.
89. Quoted in George Schuyler, "Views and Reviews," *Pittsburgh Courier,* 14 May 1938.
90. M. S. Stuart, *An Economic Detour: A History of Insurance in the Lives of American Negroes* (New York: Wendell Malliet, 1940), 335.
91. "'Minority Jingo,'" *Pittsburgh Courier,* 30 October 1937.
92. Mallie Robinson had attended an AME church in Georgia; Rachel Robinson attended an AME church in her childhood. See Long and Lamb, *Jackie Robinson, A Spiritual Biography,* 35.
93. "Methodist Youth Oppose Plan of Church," *Pittsburgh Courier,* 19 September 1936. For the Central Jurisdiction, see Peter C. Murray, *Methodists and the Crucible of Race, 1930–1975* (Columbia: University of Missouri Press, 2004); Grant S. Shockley, ed. *Heritage and Hope: The African American Presence in United Methodism* (Nashville: Abingdon Press, 1991).
94. Karl E. Downs, "Did My Church Forsake Me? A Negro Methodist Asks a Question," *Zion's Herald,* 9 March 1938.
95. Lee Lowenfish, *Branch Rickey: Baseball's Ferocious Gentleman* (Lincoln: University of Nebraska Press, 2007), 289–90.
96. Downs, "Did My Church Forsake Me?"
97. Downs, "Did My Church Forsake Me?"
98. Johnson, *Negro Americans, What Now?,* 103.
99. Rampersad, *Jackie Robinson,* 114; Eric Enders, "'A Disciplinarian Coach': Jackie Robinson's Little-Known Stint Coaching College Basketball," in *Jackie: Perspectives on 42,* 115.
100. Karl E. Downs, *Meet the Negro* (Los Angeles: Methodist Youth Fellowship Southern California–Arizona Annual Conference, 1943), 21, 24.
101. Langston Hughes, "Here to Yonder," *Chicago Defender,* 16 December 1944.
102. For contributionism, see Stephen G. Hall, *A Faithful Account of the Race: African American Historical Writing in Nineteenth-Century America* (Chapel Hill: University of North Carolina Press, 2009).
103. Downs, *Meet the Negro,* 21, 27.
104. Quoted in Eisenstadt, *Against the Hounds of Hell,* 226.
105. "Just Browsing," *People's Voice,* 31 July 1943.
106. Enders, "Disciplinarian Coach," in *Jackie: Perspectives on 42,* 114.
107. Rampersad, *Jackie Robinson,* 113–14.
108. Rampersad, *Jackie Robinson,* 114.
109. "Jackie Robinson, Baseball Star, Married on Coast," *Chicago Defender,* 23 February 1946.
110. Karl E. Downs, "All the Negro Asks!," *Zion's Herald,* 12 February 1947, 158–59.

111. "Role of Women Explained to 73 College Graduates," *Baltimore Afro-American,* 14 June 1947.
112. "Just Browsing," *People's Voice,* 31 July 1943.
113. Rampersad, *Jackie Robinson,* 193; Robinson and Duckett, *I Never Had It Made,* 82–83.
114. Robinson, *Baseball Has Done It,* 30.
115. Robinson and Duckett, *I Never Had It Made,* 82–83.
116. R. E. Dixon, "Skipper's Southwest Sports-o-Graph," *Atlanta Daily World,* 3 March, 1948.
117. For Thurman, see Eisenstadt, *Against the Hounds of Hell.*
118. Eisenstadt, *Against the Hounds of Hell,* 261–62.
119. Howard Thurman, *Jesus and the Disinherited* (1949; repr., Boston: Beacon Press, 1996).
120. Thurman, *Jesus and the Disinherited,* 34.
121. Thurman, *Jesus and the Disinherited,* 15.
122. Eisenstadt, *Against the Hounds of Hell,* 132.
123. "America in Search of a Soul" (1976), in Howard Thurman, *Democracy and the Soul of America,* eds. Peter Eisenstadt and Walter Earl Fluker (Maryknoll, NY: Orbis Books, 2022), 114–24.
124. In a critique of modern notions of freedom, Sophia Rosenfeld has recently argued that "choice went from being a benefit of freedom to freedom's very essence"; see *The Age of Choice: A History of Freedom in Modern Life* (Princeton, NJ: Princeton University Press, 2025), 340. The ability to make crucial life choices without fear, without coercion, was for Thurman and advocates of integration a benefit of freedom, a byproduct of real citizenship.
125. Eisenstadt, *Against the Hounds of Hell,* 271–72.
126. Eisenstadt, *Against the Hounds of Hell,* 284.
127. Thurman, *Jesus and the Disinherited.* For Thurman on fear, see Peter Eisenstadt, "We Are Not Afraid: Howard Thurman and the Casting Out of Fear," in *The Unfinished Search for Common Ground: Reimagining Howard Thurman's Life and Work,* ed. Walter Earl Fluker (Maryknoll, NY: Orbis, 2023), 139–56.
128. James Baldwin, "My Dungeon Shook" (1962), in Baldwin, *The Price of the Ticket: Collected Nonfiction, 1948–1985* (New York: St. Martin's, 1985), 334.

3. Integration Controversies

1. In 1945, Jackie Robinson signed a minor-league contract with the Brooklyn Dodgers, a major-league team. Minor-league teams affiliated with the major leagues were for all intents and purposes subsidiaries of the major leagues and followed the same policy of racial exclusion. When discussing the major-league color line, the minor-league color line is always implied.
2. "Baseball Ban Draws Pickets at First Game," *New York Amsterdam News,* 21 April 1945.

3. Howard Thurman, "The Will to Segregation," in *The Papers of Howard Washington Thurman*, 5 vols., ed. Walter E. Fluker (Columbia: University of South Carolina Press, 2009), 3:337–44.
4. Kevin M. Kruse and Stephen Tuck argue that the impact of World War II on the civil rights movement has been exaggerated, see "Introduction: The Second World War and the Civil Rights Movement," in *The Fog of War: The Second World War and the Civil Rights Movement*, eds. Kevin M. Kruse and Stephen Tuck (New York: Oxford University Press, 2019), 3–14.
5. "Bitter and Disillusioned," *Pittsburgh Courier*, 25 August 1934; "Dean Houston Hits J. Crow in U.S. Army," *Atlanta Daily World*, 15 August 1934; "Houston Attacks Army Jim Crowism," *Pittsburgh Courier*, 25 August 1934.
6. "Bitter and Disillusioned," *Pittsburgh Courier*, 25 August 1934.
7. For more on African Americans during World War II, to touch on a vast literature, see Neil A. Wynn, *The African American Experience in World War II* (Lanham, MD: Rowman and Littlefield, 2010); and Kruse and Tuck, *Fog of War.*
8. "Courier Winning for Race Men in Army," *Pittsburgh Courier*, 21 September 1940.
9. Gordon Blaine Hancock, "Defends Negro Divisions as Means to Desirable End," *Pittsburgh Courier*, 4 June 1938.
10. "Race Leaders Oppose Interference in Europe," *Pittsburgh Courier*, 13 May 1939.
11. Hancock, "Defends Negro Divisions," *Pittsburgh Courier*, 4 June 1938.
12. "Price of Segregation," *Pittsburgh Courier*, 28 December 1940.
13. "Price of Segregation," *Pittsburgh Courier*, 28 December 1940.
14. Philip McGuire, *He, Too, Spoke for Democracy: Judge Hastie, World War II, and the Black Soldier* (New York: Greenwood Press, 1988), 38, 9.
15. McGuire, *He, Too, Spoke for Democracy*, 29.
16. FDR had told A. Philip Randolph in a meeting in September 1940 that though African Americans would start in segregated units, during the course of war, the segregation would be modified: see FDR Presidential Library and Museum, Transcript, 27 September 1940, http://docs.fdrlibrary.marist.edu/transcr4.html.
17. Robinson and Duckett, *I Never Had It Made*, 12.
18. Peter Golenbock, *Bums: An Oral History of the Brooklyn Dodgers* (New York: Putnam's, 1984), 132; Arnold Rampersad, *Jackie Robinson: A Biography* (New York: Ballantine Books, 1997), 93.
19. Rampersad, *Jackie Robinson*, 95.
20. Rampersad, *Jackie Robinson*, 97.
21. From 2023 to 2025, the base was renamed Fort Cavazos, after Richard E. Cavazos, a Medal of Honor winner and the first Hispanic four-star general. However, in June 2025, the base's name reverted to Fort Hood, ostensibly to honor an obscure and far less distinguished soldier named Hood who was a veteran of World Wars I and II. So with a wink and a nod, it is still named after a Confederate traitor.

22. McGuire, *He, Too, Spoke for Democracy,* 56.
23. Rampersad, *Jackie Robinson,* 97–109.
24. Charlie Cherokee, "National Grapevine," *Chicago Defender,* 12 August 1944.
25. Rampersad, *Jackie Robinson,* 108. Robinson's understanding of the historical meaning of the word follows the best understanding of its development: see Elizabeth Stroudeur Pryor, "The Etymology of 'Nigger': Resistance, Language, and the Politics of Freedom in the Antebellum North," *Journal of the Early Republic* 36, no. 2 (2016): 203–45.
26. Jackie Robinson, as told to Wendell Smith, *Jackie Robinson: My Own Story* (New York: Greenberg Publishers, 1949), 32.
27. Some contemporary reports claimed that it was his chronically injured ankle, rather than his court-martial, that kept him from serving overseas: Bob Stone, "Yank: The Army Weekly," cited in Danny Peary, *Jackie Robinson in Quotes* (Salem, MA: Page Street Pub., 2016), 69.
28. Jackie Robinson, with Alfred Duckett, *I Never Had It Made* (New York: Putnam's, 1972), 34.
29. Robinson and Duckett, *I Never Had It Made,* 23.
30. In *Jackie Robinson and the Integration of Baseball* (Hoboken, NJ: Wiley, 2007), author Scott Simon claims that Robinson received a general rather than an honorable discharge that did not carry benefits (23), but he doesn't document this, and no other source makes this claim.
31. Kruse and Tuck, introduction to *Fog of War.*
32. Robinson and Smith, *Jackie Robinson,* 33.
33. "The Sports," *Baltimore Afro-American,* 1 September 1945; Eric Enders, "'A Disciplinarian Coach': Jackie Robinson's Little-Known Stint Coaching College Basketball," in *Jackie: Perspectives on 42,* eds. Bill Nowlin and Glen Sparks (Phoenix, AZ: Society for American Baseball Research, 2021), 114.
34. "Coast Professional Football Barrier," *Pittsburgh Courier,* 18 November 1944; J. Cullen Fentress, "Sepia Stars Sparkle in Pro League on Coast," *Pittsburgh Courier,* 11 November 1944.
35. See James W. Johnson, *The Black Bruins: The Remarkable Lives of UCLA's Jackie Robinson, Woody Strode, Tom Bradley, Kenny Washington, and Ray Bartlett* (Lincoln: University of Nebraska Press, 2017), 140; Alan H. Levy, *Tackling Jim Crow: Racial Segregation in Professional Football* (Jefferson, NC: McFarland, 2003).
36. Robinson and Duckett, *I Never Had It Made,* 35.
37. Robinson and Duckett, *I Never Had It Made,* 35.
38. Michael Carter, "It's a Press Victory, Says Jackie Robinson," *Baltimore Afro-American,* 3 November 1945.
39. Peter Golenbock, *Bums: An Oral History of the Brooklyn Dodgers* (New York: Putnam's, 1984), 134.
40. Peary, *Jackie Robinson in Quotes,* 80.

41. Joe Posnanski, "The Amazing Jackie Robinson," 15 April 2019, https://www.joeposnanski.com/p/the-amazing-jackie-robinson.
42. "Satchel Paige to Pitch," *New York Times.*
43. Golenbock, *Bums,* 134.
44. "Monarchs Invade Gotham for Three Days," *New Journal and Guide,* 14 July 1945; "The Sports," *Baltimore Afro-American,* 24 March 1945; "Monarchs Praised by School Youngsters," *Cleveland Call and Post,* 21 April 1945.
45. Rampersad, *Jackie Robinson,* 130.
46. Moses Fleetwood Walker (1856–1924), the first self-identified African American to play major-league baseball, like Robinson had an abiding interest in racial politics. Both men shared a deep commitment to racial equality: "There can be no division of American citizenship by classes," Walker wrote in his political tract *Our Home Country* (Steubenville, OH: Herald Printing Co., 1908), 17. However, their remedies were very different. Walker concluded that obtaining full citizenship for American Blacks was impossible in the United States and called for racial separation and a return to Africa. See David Zang, *Fleet Walker's Divided Heart: The Life of Baseball's First Black Major Leaguer* (Lincoln: University of Nebraska Press, 1995).
47. "A Color Line in Baseball," *New York Times,* 17 September 1887.
48. Sol White, *Sol White's History of Colored Base Ball, with Other Documents on the Early Black Game, 1886–1936,* ed. Jerry Malloy (1907; repr., Lincoln: University of Nebraska Press, 1995), 74. There probably were some successful attempts at "passing," especially by light-skinned Cuban ballplayers on the Washington Senators in the 1930s and 1940s; see Rick Swaine, *The Integration of Major League Baseball: A Team by Team History* (Jefferson, NC: McFarland, 2009), 13–15.
49. For the early history of Black baseball, see George B. Kirsch, *Baseball in Blue and Gray: The National Pastime During the Civil War* (Princeton, NJ: Princeton University Press, 2003), 82, 122–29; Michael E. Lomax, *Black Baseball Entrepreneurs, 1860–1901: Operating by Any Means Necessary* (Syracuse, NY: Syracuse University Press, 2003.) For the later history, see Neil Lanctot, *Negro League Baseball: The Rise and Fall of a Black Institution* (Philadelphia: University of Pennsylvania Press, 2004).
50. See Jonathan Scott Holloway, *Confronting the Veil: Abram Harris, Jr., E. Franklin Frazier, and Ralph Bunche, 1919–1941* (Chapel Hill: University of North Carolina Press, 2002).
51. See Keith Crook, *Before The "Great Experiment": Opening the Doors for Jackie Robinson* (Jefferson, NC: McFarland, 2025), 90–101.
52. Lucius Harper, "A Chinese Gives Us a Tip on His Race Pride," *Chicago Defender,* 21 May 1938.
53. "Naziism [*sic*] in Baseball," *New York Amsterdam News,* 15 April 1939. See also Lucius Harper, "Dustin' Off the News," *Chicago Defender,* 21 May 1938.
54. Golenbock, *Bums,* 124.
55. Violet Moten Foster, "Plea for More Segregation," *Chicago Defender,* 6 July 1940.

56. Foster, "Plea for More Segregation," *Chicago Defender,* 6 July 1940.
57. "What's Wrong with Baseball," *New York Daily News,* 1 February 1933.
58. "Haywood Broun Flays Color Bar in Baseball," *Pittsburgh Courier,* 18 February 1933.
59. "A Young Negro Looks at Life," *Pittsburgh Courier,* 23 October 1933.
60. Carroll, *When to Stop the Cheering?,* 86–87.
61. See Lanctot, *Negro League Baseball,* 209–14; Sam Lacy, with Moses J. Newson, *Fighting for Fairness: The Life Story of Hall of Fame Sportswriter Sam Lacy* (Centreville, MD: Tidewater Pub., 1998); Irwin Silber, *Press Box Red: The Communist Who Helped Break the Color Line in Baseball* (Philadelphia: Temple University Press, 2003); Henry D. Fetter, "The Party Line and the Color Line: The American Communist Party, the *Daily Worker,* and Jackie Robinson," *Journal of Sports History* 28, no. 3 (2001): 375–402.
62. "Segregation by Major Leagues Hit by 'Post,'" *Cleveland Call and Post,* 6 May 1937 (reprinted editorial from the *New York Post*).
63. George V. Kelly, "Catholic Paper Demands: End Baseball's Jim Crow," *New York Amsterdam News,* 28 May 1942; "Father Campion Again Urges Negro Players in Majors," *New York Amsterdam News,* 26 December 1942.
64. "White Sports Writers Again Ask for Negroes in Big Leagues," *New York Amsterdam News,* 11 December 1937.
65. Dan Parker, "Negroes Not Barred but Not Admitted Either," *New Journal and Guide,* 25 July 1942 (reprinted editorial from *New York Daily Mirror*).
66. "Josh Gibson Better Catcher than Bill Dickey . . . Walter Johnson," *Atlanta Daily World,* 20 April 1939.
67. Wendell Smith, "Fifth Columners in Baseball," *Pittsburgh Courier,* 25 May 1940.
68. Joe Bostic, "In Re Negroes in Big Leagues," *People's Voice,* 11 July 1942.
69. Joe Bostic, "C'mon Let's Slug on the Baseball Issue," *People's Voice,* 8 August 1942; Lucius (Melancholy) Jones, "Satchel Paige (West), Josh Gibson (East) in Dream Game Today," *Atlanta Daily World,* 16 August 1942; Joe Bostic, "The Judge Spoke, But He Did He Say Anything," *People's Voice,* 25 July 1942; Joe Bostic, "Father Campion Is Really Fine for Baseball Equality," *People's Voice,* 12 September 1942.
70. Joe Bostic, "Is Negro Baseball Worth Saving?," *People's Voice,* 17 October 1942; Joe Bostic, "Reform or Die," *People's Voice,* 8 May 1943.
71. Cum Posey, "Posey's Points," *Pittsburgh Courier,* 26 March 1938.
72. John Foster, "'Come and Get 'Em,' says Dr. Martin, Mrs. Manley," *Cleveland Call and Post,* 8 August 1942.
73. Lem Graves Jr., "Some Views on the Major League Question," *Norfolk Journal and Guide,* 24 April 1943.
74. Wendell Smith, "Smitty's Sports Spurts," *Pittsburgh Courier,* 18 December 1943; Brian Carroll, *When to Stop the Cheering? The Black Press, the Black Community, and the Integration of Professional Baseball* (New York: Routledge, 2007), 91.
75. Dan Burley, "Confidentially Yours," *Amsterdam News,* 22 December 1943.

76. Lem Graves Jr., "Some Views on the Major League Question," *Norfolk Journal and Guide,* 24 April 1943.
77. Robert H. Kinzer and Edward Sagarin, *The Negro in American Business: The Conflict Between Separatism and Integration* (New York: Greenberg Pub., 1950), 11.
78. Sam Lacy, "Players Indifferent About Entering Major Leagues," *Baltimore Afro-American,* 12 August 1939.
79. Graves, "Views on the Major League Question," *Norfolk Journal and Guide,* 24 April 1943.
80. Dan Burley, "Purely Baseball and Satchel Paige," *New York Amsterdam News,* 15 August 1942. Influencing Paige's views might well have the fact that between his salary and well-compensated participation in barnstorming tours, he was by far the most highly compensated player in the Negro Leagues.
81. John Holway, "How to Score from First on a Sacrifice," *American Heritage* 21, no. 5 (1970), https://www.americanheritage.com/how-score-first-sacrifice.
82. Joe Posnanski, *The Baseball 100* (New York: Simon and Schuster, 2021), 377.
83. Donn Rogosin and Monte Irvin, *Invisible Men: Life in Baseball's Negro Leagues* (1983; repr., Lincoln: University of Nebraska Press, 2007), 219.
84. Jones, "Paige, Gibson in Dream Game Today," *Atlanta Daily World,* 16 August 1942.
85. Dan Burley, "Confidentially Yours," *New York Amsterdam News,* 29 December 1945.
86. Quoted in Dan Burley, "Confidentially Yours," *New York Amsterdam News,* 15 August 1942.
87. Robinson and Smith, *Jackie Robinson,* 34.
88. Jackie Robinson, "What's Wrong with Negro Baseball," *Ebony* (June 1948): 16–18.
89. Fay Young, "End of Baseball's Jim Crow Seen with the Signing of Robinson," *Chicago Defender,* 3 November 1945.
90. "Will Appeal to Chandler," *New York Times,* 24 October 1945; "Rickey Takes Slap at Negro Leagues," *New York Times,* 25 October 1945.
91. Alvin Moss, "Negro League Baseball Must Survive," *Atlanta Daily World,* 5 February 1948.
92. Carroll, *When to Stop the Cheering?,* 167.
93. Bill James, "The Negro Leagues," in *The New Bill James Historical Baseball Almanac* (New York: Free Press, 2001), 356–416.
94. Carroll, *When to Stop the Cheering?,* 149.
95. Jules Tygiel, *Baseball's Great Experiment: Jackie Robinson and His Legacy* (New York: Oxford University Press, 2008), 246–52.
96. Amiri Baraka, *The Autobiography of Leroi Jones* (Chicago: Lawrence Hill Books, 1997), 51.
97. For a discussion, see Tygiel, *Baseball's Great Experiment,* 347–49.
98. Tygiel, *Baseball's Great Experiment,* 348.
99. Peary, *Jackie Robinson in Quotes,* 190.
100. Peary, *Jackie Robinson in Quotes,* 348.

101. Ralph J. Bunche, "A Critique of New Deal Social Planning as It Affects Negroes," *Journal of Negro Education* 5, no. 1 (1936): 59–65.
102. Sol White, "The Grand Old Game," *New York Amsterdam News,* 18 December 1930, reprinted in White, *Sol White's History of Colored Base Ball,* 153.
103. White, *Sol White's History of Colored Base Ball,* 67.
104. Dan W. Dodson, "Tentative Proposal for Report of the Mayor's Committee on Baseball," 28 September 1945, Arthur Mann papers, Library of Congress. I would like to thank Keith Crook for sharing this document with me.
105. Carroll, *When to Stop the Cheering?,* 93.

4. Integration's Test Case

1. Keith Crook, *Before the Great Experiment: Opening the Door to Jackie Robinson* (Jefferson, NC: McFarland, 2025), 38. Crook was referring to the so-called Goldilocks Zone, the collection of conditions that make life on Earth possible.
2. He said this as early as 1915; see Fred R. Shapiro, ed., *The New Yale Book of Quotations* (New Haven, CT: Yale University Press, 2021), 683.
3. Randy Dixon, "Exhibit A in a So-called Democracy: The Case of Jackie Robinson," *Pittsburgh Courier,* 6 September 1941.
4. Chris Lamb, *Conspiracy of Silence: Sportswriters and the Long Campaign to Desegregate Baseball* (Lincoln: University of Nebraska Press, 2012), 189–90.
5. "Organized baseball" is an outdated term for the major leagues and affiliated minor leagues and is only used in direct quotations.
6. Lucius C. Harper, "Landis Would Make Baseball Interracial, But," *Chicago Defender,* 1 August 1942.
7. "Cleveland Agrees to Give Negro Players a Tryout," *New York Amsterdam News,* 1 August 1942; "Negro Leagues Resent 'Raids' MacPhail Says," *Washington Post,* 28 July 1942; Irwin Silber, *Press Box Red: The Story of Lester Rodney, the Communist Who Helped Break the Color Line in American Sports* (Philadelphia: Temple University Press, 2003), 82. For the credulousness of the *Daily Worker* after Landis's statement, see ibid., 84. John Fisher, "Landis Ruling May Open Way for Negroes Into Majors," *Cleveland Call and Post,* 25 July 1942; "Commissioner's Landis' Emancipation Proclamation," *Pittsburgh Courier,* 25 July 1942.
8. Dan Parker, "Negroes Not Barred but Not Admitted Either," *New York Daily Mirror,* 25 July 1942.
9. Quoted in Jimmy Breslin, *Branch Rickey: A Life* (New York: Penguin, 2011), 55.
10. John Thorn, "When Paul Robeson and Judge Kenesaw Mountain Landis Met," mlb.com, 19 December 2024, https://www.mlb.com/news/featured/paul-robeson-met-judge-landis-to-end-baseball-segregation.
11. "Cleveland Agrees to Give Tryouts to Negro Players," *New York Amsterdam News,*

1 August 1942; Jules Tygiel, *Baseball's Great Experiment: Jackie Robinson and His Legacy* (New York: Oxford University Press, 2008), 39–40.

12. "CIO Backing League Fight," *New York Amsterdam News,* 8 August 1942.
13. Dan Burley, "Confidentially Yours," *New York Amsterdam News,* 24 October 1942; "Plea for Negro Players," *New York Times,* 13 October 1942.
14. "How New York Sportswriters Viewed Big League Attitudes on Admitting Colored Baseball Aces," *New York Amsterdam News,* 11 December 1942; "Robeson Relates Plea for Newsmen," *Atlanta Daily World,* 4 January 1944.
15. Wendell Smith, "Publishers Place Case of Negro Players Before Big League Owners," *Pittsburgh Courier,* 11 December 1943; "Judge Landis, Leagues, Hear Negro Publishers Plea," *New York Amsterdam News,* 12 November 1944; "How New York Sportswriters Viewed Big League Attitudes," *New York Amsterdam News,* 11 December 1942.
16. Herman Hill, "Connie Mack Vague on When Negroes Will Crash Majors," *Pittsburgh Courier,* 12 December 1944.
17. Connie Mack to Larry MacPhail, 29 October 1945, private collection of Keith Crook, whom I would like to thank for making this letter available to me.
18. "Rickey Claims 15 Clubs Voted to Bar Negroes from the Majors," *New York Times,* 18 February 1948.
19. David Levering Lewis, *The Improbable Wendell Wilkie: The Businessman Who Saved the Republican Party and Conceived a New World Order* (New York: Liveright Pub., 2018), 200.
20. Roi Ottley, *'New World A-Coming': Inside Black America* (Boston: Houghton, Mifflin, 1943).
21. Roi Ottley, "New World A-Coming," *New York Amsterdam News,* 1 April 1944.
22. Ottley, *New World A-Coming,* 211.
23. For the best biography of Powell, see Charles V. Hamilton, *Adam Clayton Powell Jr.: The Political Biography of an American Dilemma* (New York: Atheneum, 1991).
24. Krishnahal Shridharani's *War Without Violence: A Study of Gandhi's Method and Its Accomplishments* (New York: Harcourt, Brace, 1939) opens with a nonviolent call to arms, invoking, "We, the vociferants of the 20th century," xxiii.
25. Dominic J. Capeci Jr., *The Harlem Riot of 1943* (Philadelphia: Temple University Press, 1977), 99–115; Nat Brandt, *Harlem at War: The Black Experience in World War II* (Syracuse, NY: Syracuse University Press, 1996), 183–207; Clarence Taylor, *Fight the Power: African Americans and the Long History of Police Brutality in New York City* (New York: NYU Press, 2019), 9–34.
26. Matthew F. Delmont, *Half American: The Epic Story of African Americans Fighting for Democracy at Home and Abroad* (New York: Viking, 2022), 156.
27. "Race Bias Denied as Rioting Factor," *New York Times,* 3 August 1943; "We Want Action Now!," *New York Amsterdam News,* 4, September 1943.
28. "Powell Declares 'Negro First' Aim," *New York Times,* 9 April 1944.

29. Gamewell Valentine, "Theme and Variations," *Atlanta Daily World,* 16 February 1940.
30. Adam Clayton Powell Jr., *Marching Blacks: An Interpretive History of the Rise of the Common Black Man* (New York: Dial Press, 1945), 3.
31. Danny Peary, *Jackie Robinson in Quotes* (Salem, MA: Page Street Pub., 2016), 82.
32. Powell, *Marching Blacks,* 204.
33. See Daniel Soyer, *Left in the Center: The Liberal Party and the Rise and Fall of American Social Democracy* (Ithaca, NY: Cornell University Press, 2022).
34. "Harlem Editors Endorse Ben Davis Bill," *New York Age,* 7 April 1945; "Democrats Endorse Ben Davis," *New York Age,* 12 May 1945.
35. Henry Lee Moon, *Balance of Power: The Negro Vote* (Garden City, NY: Doubleday, 1948).
36. For the best account of this movement, see Martha Biondi, *To Stand and Fight: The Struggle for Civil Rights in Postwar New York City* (Cambridge, MA: Harvard University Press, 2003).
37. "Mixed Dancing Closed Savoy Ballroom," *New York Amsterdam News,* 1 May 1943; "Savoy Ballroom Opens Friday Night," *New York Amsterdam News,* 23 October 1943.
38. "Mixed Housing Hindered Here by Jim Crow," *New York Amsterdam News,* 20 January 1945; Peter Eisenstadt, *Rochdale Village: Robert Moses, 6,000 Families, and New York City's Great Experiment in Integrated Housing* (Ithaca, NY: Cornell University Press, 2010), 76–77.
39. "New Blood Bank Bars Jim Crow," *New York Amsterdam News,* 13 October 1945; "Medics Frown on Jim Crowed Vet Hospitals," *New York Amsterdam News,* 20 October 1945. Sydenham Hospital, in Harlem, was celebrating its second anniversary as the "country's first inter-racial hospital."
40. Lillian Smith, "Segregation Not Limited to the South," *Pittsburgh Courier,* 22 December 1945; S. W. Garlington, "YMCA Directors Picketed by Group as 'Un-Christian,'" *New York Amsterdam News,* 31 March 1945; Earl Conrad, "Statue of Liberty Ferry Loses Jim Crow Lavatory," *Chicago Defender,* 24 March 1945.
41. Julius J. Adams, "Discriminatory Injustice in New York Can Be Halted," *New York Amsterdam News,* 3 February 1945.
42. Ruth Danenhowser Wilson, "Negroes in Greater New York," *New Republic* 113 (1945): 72–75.
43. D. B. Richards, "Ives Bill Exempts Educational Institutions," *Baltimore Afro-American,* 24 March 1945; "AFRO Story Eases Library Jim Crow," *Baltimore Afro-American,* 15 July 1945.
44. Taylor, *Fight the Power,* 9–34.
45. See Joshua B. Freeman, "Here Comes the CIO," and Martha Biondi, "Labor and the Fight for Racial Equality," in *City of Workers, City of Struggle: How Labor Movements Changed New York,* ed. Joshua B. Freeman (New York: Columbia University Press, 2019), 106–16, 129–41.
46. Merl E. Reed, *Seedtime for the Modern Civil Rights Movement: The President's Committee*

on Fair Employment Practices, 1941–1946 (Baton Rouge: Louisiana State University Press, 1992).

47. Delmont, *Half American,* 59–62, 133–35.
48. Erik Loomis, *A History of America in Ten Strikes* (New York: New Press, 2018), 140.
49. James Wolfinger, *Philadelphia Divided: Race and Politics in the City of Brotherly Love* (Chapel Hill: University of North Carolina Press, 2008), 142–77.
50. New York was the first state to pass such a bill, but the Territory of Alaska had passed a similar bill a month earlier, primarily designed to address discrimination against indigenous communities; see "The Anti-Discrimination Act of 1945 and Elizabeth Peratrovich," Alaska State Archives, accessed 22 August 2025, https://archives.alaska.gov/education/peratrovich.html.
51. Tod M. Ottman, "'Government That Has Both a Heart and a Head': The Growth of New York State Government During the World War II Era, 1930–1950" (PhD diss., SUNY, Albany, 2001), 136, and 127–93, passim.
52. John A. Davis, *How Management Can Integrate Negroes into War Industries* (Albany: New York State War Council, Committee on Discrimination in Employment, 1942).
53. Ottman, "Government That Has Heart and Head," 176.
54. Ottman, "Government That Has Heart and Head," 181.
55. Leo Egan, "Ives Report Urges Permanent Ban to Bar Bias in Jobs," *New York Times,* 29 January 1945.
56. "Dewey Asks Study of Race Prejudice," *New York Times,* 18 March 1944; Ottman, "Government That Has Heart and Head," 168–72.
57. Leo Egan, "Bias Bill Battle Waged at Hearing," *New York Times,* 21 February 1945.
58. "90 Groups to Urge Anti-Racial Bias Bill," *New York Times,* 19 February 1945.
59. "The Anti-Discrimination Bill," *New York Times,* 22 February 1945.
60. Mason B. Williams, *City of Ambition: FDR, La Guardia, and the Making of Modern New York* (New York: Norton, 2013), 310.
61. For La Guardia's support of the FEPC, see LaGuardia, "Poletti Score Job Bias as FEPC Opens Probe," *Norfolk Journal and Guide,* 21 February 1942; Edgar T. Rouzeau, "FEPC Threatens to Revoke Biased Union Charters," *Norfolk Journal and Guide,* 28 February 1942. For criticism of La Guardia for his support of discrimination at the Stuyvesant Town project and his tensions with Adam Clayton Powell Jr., see Domenic J. Capeci Jr., *The Harlem Riot of 1943* (Philadelphia: Temple University Press, 1977), 13–18, 23–25.
62. "La Guardia All Out for FEPC Bill," *New York Amsterdam News,* 24 February 1945. La Guardia was referring to the antidiscrimination provisions in New York State's 1938 liberal constitutional revision.
63. "La Guardia All Out for FEPC Bill," *New York Amsterdam News,* 24 February 1945.
64. "The Anti-Discrimination Bill," *New York Times,* 22 February 1945.
65. Egan, "Bias Bill Battle," *New York Times,* 21 February 1945.

66. Eisenstadt, *Rochdale Village,* 77–78. For quotas in college admissions, see Harold S. Wechsler, *The Qualified Student: A History of Selective College Admissions in America* (New Brunswick, NJ: Transaction Publishers, 2014).
67. "Faults Found in Ives Bill" [letter to the editor], *New York Times,* 13 February 1945. For Burlingham, see George Martin, *CCB: The Life and Century of Charles C. Burlingham, 1858–1959* (New York: Hill and Wang, 2005). Burlingham's opposition to the Ives-Quinn Act is not mentioned.
68. Anthony S. Chen, *The Fifth Freedom: Jobs, Politics, and Civil Rights in the United States, 1941–1972* (Princeton, NJ: Princeton University Press, 2009), 102, 329n20.
69. Richard Norton Smith, *Thomas E. Dewey and His Times* (New York: Simon and Schuster, 1982), 445–48. In *Branch Rickey,* Jimmy Breslin not only offers undue praise for Dewey but unloads an unwarranted rant against Tallulah Bankhead and other Dewey detractors (74).
70. Ottman, "Government that Has Heart and Head," 181–82.
71. "Ives Assails Foes of Anri-Bias Bill as Disfavor Rises," *New York Times,* 13 February 1945; Leo Egan, "After Bias Bill Foes Admit Defeat by 'a Highly Organized Minority," *New York Times,* 22 February 1945.
72. Nat Low, "Work FEPC Heralds End of Baseball Jimcrow," *Daily Worker,* 7 March 1945. After the signing of Robinson, Don Deleigbuhr Jr. suggested that because of the Ives-Quinn Act (whose penalties he considerably exaggerated), every club would have Black players at their training camps the following spring: "Negro Club Owners to Fight Robinson Deal," *Cleveland Call and Post,* 3 November 1945.
73. Nat Low, "Work FEPC Heralds End of Baseball Jimcrow," *Daily Worker,* 7 March 1945.
74. Tygiel, *Baseball's Great Experiment,* 69.
75. "NY Assemblyman Raps Baseball JC," *Baltimore Afro-American,* 14 July 1945.
76. Bob Williams, "Sports Rambler," *Cleveland Call and Post,* 21 April 1945.
77. "The Baseball Situation," *Pittsburgh Courier,* 28 April 1945.
78. "La Guardia All Out for FEPC Bill," *New York Amsterdam News,* 24 February 1945.

5. Branch Rickey and Integration

1. Llewellyn Ransom, "Head of African Film Gets Poletti's Help," *People's Voice,* 7 November 1942.
2. Roscoe McGowen, "Rickey Named Dodger President and General Manager," *New York Times,* 31 October 1942.
3. Branch Rickey to Fred Ankerman, 15 November 1942, Branch Rickey Papers, Library of Congress, Digital Collections. I would like to thank Keith Crook for making this document available to me.
4. Arthur Daley, "The Dodger Deacon Discourses," *New York Times,* 12 February 1943.
5. Murray Polner, *Branch Rickey* (New York: Atheneum, 1982), 65.

6. See Barbara Gannon, *The Won Cause: Black and White Comradeship in the Grand Army of the Republic* (Chapel Hill: University of North Carolina Press, 2011).
7. Polner, *Branch Rickey,* 116; Rickey to Herman H. Lahnworthy, 21 September 1939; Homer B. Mann to Rickey, 15 September 1939; Rickey to Homer B. Mann, 19 September 1939, Branch Rickey Papers, LoC.
8. Polner, *Branch Rickey,* 47–48.
9. Polner, *Branch Rickey,* 46–47.
10. Rickey to A. M. Curtis, 22 October 1937, Branch Rickey Papers, LoC. For early twentieth-century progressives who opposed the New Deal, see Otis L Graham, *An Encore for Reform: The Old Progressives and the New Deal* (New York: Oxford University Press, 1967).
11. "Appeal Made for U.S. to Mobilize for War" *New York Times,* 3 January 1941; "An Open Letter to Congress," *New York Times,* 5 January 1941. For Rickey's support of the latter, see Polner, *Branch Rickey,* 116.
12. Branch Rickey to Bill Harman, 28 December 1943, Branch Rickey Papers, LoC.
13. David Levering Lewis, *The Improbable Wendell Wilkie: The Businessman Who Saved the Republican Party and Conceived a New World Order* (New York: Liveright Pub., 2018), 213–22.
14. David A. Hollinger, *Christianity's American Fate: How Religion Became More Conservative and Society More Secular* (Princeton, NJ: Princeton University Press, 2022), 72–80. For samples of the statement of the Federal Council of Churches, see "Christians Asked to End Race Bias," *New York Times,* 22 June 1942; "Christians Urged to Fight Race Bias," *New York Times,* 6 December 1943.
15. Edward Davidson Soper, *Racism, A World Issue* (New York: Abingdon-Cokesbury, 1947).
16. Branch Rickey, with Robert Riger, *The American Diamond: A Documentary of the Game of Baseball* (New York: Simon and Schuster, 1965), 47.
17. Soper, *Racism,* 290.
18. Polner, *Branch Rickey,* 147.
19. Henry B. Jameson, "The 'Daddy' of Baseball Farm System," *Washington Post,* 31 March 1940.
20. John Collins, "Something New Has Been Added," *Montreal Star,* 27 October 1945. I would like to think Keith Crook for sharing this cartoon with me.
21. Jimmy Powers, "Powerhouse," *New York Daily News,* 12 March 1946.
22. Branch Rickey to Larry MacPhail, 22 August 1941, Branch Rickey Papers, LoC. I would like to thank Keith Crook for making this document available to me.
23. Howard Thurman, "The Sources of Power for Christian Action," in *The Papers of Howard Washington Thurman,* 5 vols., ed. Walter Earl Fluker (Columbia: University of South Carolina Press, 2012), 2:93–101.
24. Lee Lowenfish, *Branch Rickey: Baseball's Ferocious Gentleman* (Lincoln: University of Nebraska Press, 2007), 325.

25. Arthur Mann, "The Negro in Baseball," (unpublished article, 1947), in *The Jackie Robinson Reader,* ed. Jules Tygiel (New York: Dutton, 1997), 74–75.
26. Arthur Mann, *Branch Rickey: American in Action* (Boston: Houghton Mifflin, 1957), 214–15.
27. Quoted in Polner, *Branch Rickey,* 144.
28. Polner, *Branch Rickey,* 145; Crook, *Before the Great Experiment,* 15.
29. Mann, *Rickey: American in Action,* 213; Arthur Mann, *The Jackie Robinson Story* (New York: Grosset & Dunlap), 11.
30. Mann, *Rickey: American in Action,* 216–18.
31. Harold Parrott, *The Lords of Baseball: A Wry Look at a Side of the Game the Fan Seldom Sees—The Front Office* (Atlanta: Longstreet Press, 2001), 232–34.
32. Jimmy Breslin, *Branch Rickey: A Life* (New York: Penguin, 2011), 13.
33. Mann, *Rickey: American in Action,* 214.
34. Roscoe McGowen, "Rickey Suggests Majors Pool Players if 4-F Men Are Put in Essential Jobs," *New York Times,* 31 March 1944; Roscoe McGowen, "Owen Will Catch, Dodger Chief Says," *New York Times,* 17 March 1944.
35. Roscoe McGowen, "Sukeforth, Veteran Scout, Signs Contract as Player for Dodgers," *New York Times,* 5 April 1945.
36. "NY Assemblyman Raps Baseball JC," *Baltimore Afro-American,* 14 July 1945.
37. Gerald Holland, "Mr. Rickey and the Game," *Sports Illustrated,* 7 March 1955.
38. Jim Kreuz, "The Dodgers' First Choice Wasn't Jackie Robinson," *Black Ball* 7 (2014): 114–26.
39. "Brooklyn Dodgers Go Liberal," *Pittsburgh Courier,* 4 September 1943.
40. Jules Tygiel, *Baseball's Great Experiment: Jackie Robinson and His Legacy* (New York: Oxford University Press, 1983), 80.
41. Chandler is generally characterized as a racial "moderate," though in the Senate he supported the poll tax, opposed the FEPC, voted against a federal antilynching bill, and, several decades later, in 1968, was seriously considered by George Wallace to be his vice presidential running mate: see Wikipedia, "Happy Chandler," last updated 21 June 2025.
42. Lowenfish, *Branch Rickey: Ferocious Gentleman,* 359–60. Rickey told his family and close Dodgers associates about the plan in early 1945; they were not enthusiastic. See Parrott, *Lords of Baseball,* 232–36.
43. John Thorn, "When Paul Robeson and Judge K Kenesaw Mountain Landis Met," mlb.com, 19 December 2024, https://www.mlb.com/news/featured/paul-robeson-met-judge-landis-to-end-baseball-segregation.
44. Breslin, *Branch Rickey: A Life,* 73–78.
45. In 1936, Rickey was appointed to the Methodist Church's Board of Temperance, Prohibition, and Public Morals. See Lowenfish, *Branch Rickey: Ferocious Gentleman,* 324.
46. Mann, *Rickey: American in Action,* 217.

47. Branch Rickey, speech made 28 July 1945, Branch Rickey Papers, LoC. I would like to thank Keith Crook for making this document available.
48. "Rickey Takes Slap at Negro Leagues," *New York Times*, 25 October 1945.
49. Dan Daniel, "All Met Teams Soon Must Sign Negro Players—Rickey," *New York World-Telegram*, 25 October 1945.
50. Mann, *Rickey: American in Action*, 254–55; Mann, *Jackie Robinson Story*,162–65.
51. See Evelyn Brooks-Higginbotham, *Righteous Discontent: The Women's Movement in the Black Baptist Church, 1880–1920* (Cambridge, MA: Harvard University Press, 1993).
52. Lucius C. Harper, "Dustin' Off the News," *Chicago Defender*, 23 December 1945.
53. Fay Young, "Through the Years," *Chicago Defender*, 17 May 1947.
54. Jackie Robinson, with Alfred Duckett, *I Never Had It Made* (New York: Putnam's, 1972), 6.
55. Larry MacPhail et al., "Report of the Major League Steering Committee for Submission to the National and American Leagues on 27 August, 1946," 18–21. I would like to thank Keith Crook for making this document available to me.
56. Jules Tygiel, *Extra Bases: Reflections on Jackie Robinson, Race, and Baseball History* (Lincoln: University of Nebraska Press, 2002), 37.
57. Branch Rickey, "One Hundred Percent Wrong Club Speech," Atlanta, 20 January 1956, Branch Rickey Papers, LoC.
58. Lowenfish, *Branch Rickey: Ferocious Gentleman*, 358.
59. Joe Bostic, "What Was Gained at Bear Mountain," *People's Voice*, 19 May 1945; "That Conversation Between McDuffie and Rickey," *Pittsburgh Courier*, 14 April 1945; Tygiel, *Baseball's Great Experiment*, 45–46; Lowenfish, *Branch Rickey: Ferocious Gentleman*, 361–63.
60. See Bostic's 1944 attacks on Rickey in the *People's Voice* issues of 27 May; 27 July; 12 August; 16 September; 30 September.
61. Tygiel, *Baseball's Great Experiment*, 45–46.
62. Tygiel, *Baseball's Great Experiment*, 45–46; "Negro Stars Don't Impress Bums Boss," *Atlanta Daily World*, 13 April 1945; W. Rollow Wilson, "Brooklyn Situation Raises Furor Among Sportswriters," *Philadelphia Tribune*, 14 April 1945.
63. Neil Lanctot, *Negro League Baseball: The Rise and Fall of a Black Institution* (Philadelphia: University of Pennsylvania Press, 2004), 254.
64. "Dodger Boss Sees Two Colored Stars in Drill," *Baltimore Afro-American*, 14 April 1945.
65. Lanctot, *Negro League Baseball*, 255.
66. Polner, *Branch Rickey*, 158.
67. Wendell Smith, "Players Get Tryouts: Red Sox Consider Negroes," *Pittsburgh Courier*, 21 April 1945; Bob Wilson, "Dodgers' Tryout May Pave Way for Negroes in Majors!," *Cleveland Call*, 14 April 1945; Sam Lacy, "Lookin' 'Em Over," *Baltimore Afro-American*, 14 April 1945; Tygiel, *Baseball's Great Experiment*, 44–45.
68. Fenway's high left-field wall, commonly called the "green monster," was first painted green in 1947. Previously it had been covered with advertisements.

69. Crook, *Before the Great Experiment,* 45.
70. Carl T. Rowan, *Wait till Next Year: The Life Story of Jackie Robinson* (New York: Random House, 1960), 99.
71. "Wendell Smith," in *No Cheering in the Press Box,* ed. Jerome Holtzman (New York: Henry Holt, 1995), 312–24.
72. Wendell Smith, "Smitty's Sports Spurts," *Pittsburgh Courier,* 28 April 1945.
73. Fay Young, "Through the Years," *Chicago Defender,* 26 May 1945.
74. Lanctot, *Negro League Baseball,* 263–70.
75. Fay Young, "Through the Years," *Chicago Defender,* 26 May 1945.
76. Tygiel, *Baseball's Great Experiment.*
77. Arnold Rampersad, *Jackie Robinson: A Biography* (New York: Ballantine Books, 1997), 123.
78. Roscoe McGowen, "Sukeforth, Veteran Scout, Signs Contract as Player for Dodgers," *New York Times,* 5 April 1945.
79. See Eisenstadt, *Against the Hounds of Hell,* 216.
80. Rampersad, *Jackie Robinson,* 123–24; Tygiel, *Baseball's Great Experiment,* 64–65.
81. Neil Lanctot, *Campy: The Two Lives of Roy Campanella* (New York: Simon and Schuster, 2011), 118.
82. Rampersad, *Jackie Robinson.*
83. Giovanni Papini, *Life of Christ,* trans. Dorothy Canfield Fisher (New York: Harcourt, Brace, 1925), 106. Over the course of his life, Italian philosopher Giovanni Papini (1881–1956) moved from militant atheism to right-wing Catholicism. By the 1920s, he had embraced Fascism. In 1945, he was living under an assumed name in a Franciscan monastery: Wikipedia, s.v. "Giovanni Papini," accessed 4 August 2025.
84. Papini, *Life of Christ,* 106.
85. Jackie Robinson, "Negroes Tired of Turning Other Cheek," *New York Amsterdam News,* 15 September 1964.
86. Robinson and Duckett, *I Never Had It Made,* 211.
87. Peter Dana, "Dr. Thurman Speaks on Indian Question," *Pittsburgh Courier,* 29 August 1942.
88. Lowenfish, *Branch Rickey: Ferocious Gentleman,* 515.
89. Jackie Robinson, "Jackie Robinson," *Chicago Defender,* 12 May 1960.
90. Robinson and Duckett, *I Never Had It Made,* 59.
91. Carl Prince, *Brooklyn's Dodgers: The Bums, the Borough, and the Best of Baseball* (New York: Oxford University Press, 1996), 45, has a choice selection of Robinson's misogynistic and homophobic taunts.
92. Danny Peary, *Jackie Robinson in Quotes* (Salem, MA: Page Street Pub., 2016), 81.
93. Branch Rickey to Dick Young, 5 February 1952, Branch Rickey Papers, LoC.
94. "Rickey Admits Calling in Jackie Robinson," *Pittsburgh Courier,* 1 September 1945.
95. Fay Young, "We Won't Stand for Any Bunk," *Chicago Defender,* 1 September 1945. See

also Dan Burley, "Confidentially Yours," *New York Amsterdam News,* 29 September 1945; Bill Mardo, "In This Corner," *Daily Worker,* 3 October 1945.

96. Burley, "Confidentially Yours," *New York Amsterdam News,* 29 September 1945.
97. But there had been picketing before a Pacific Coast League game in Los Angeles in 1943: see Herman Hill, "Los Angeles Site of Protest as Pickets March," *Pittsburgh Courier,* 29 May 1944.
98. Wendell Smith, "Plan to Boycott Yankees," *Pittsburgh Courier,* 14 April 1945; Joe Cummiskey, "Those Picket Lines Won't Do Any Good," *PM,* 22 April 1945; "Pickets Protest Baseball Bigotry," *Chicago Defender,* 25 April 1945.
99. "The Big Leagues Won't Play Ball," *Chicago Defender,* 12 May 1945.
100. Jerome Mehlman, "Council Battling Jim Crow Baseball," *New York Amsterdam News,* 30 June 1945.
101. For the best account of the Committee to End Jim Crow in Baseball, see Keith Crook, *Before the Great Experiment,* 76–81, 83–85, 100–118.
102. "Notables Open Drive on Jimcrow Baseball," *Daily Worker,* 30 July 1945.
103. Crook, *Before the Great Experiment,* 86–88.
104. Crook, *Before the Great Experiment,* 86–88.
105. "Experts to Be Hired by Unity Committee," *New York Times,* 7 March 1944.
106. Crook, *Before the Great Experiment,* 65.
107. Dan W. Dodson, "The Mayor's Committee on Unity of New York City," *Journal of Educational Sociology* 19, no. 5 (1946): 289–98. For a brief overview of Dodson's career, see his obituary: Robert Thomas Jr., "Dan W. Dodson, 88, Foe and Scholar of Racism," *New York Times,* 19 August 1995.
108. Dan W. Dodson, "The Integration of Negroes in Baseball," *Journal of Educational Sociology* 28, no. 2 (1954): 82.
109. Joe Blow, "La Guardia Seen Beclouding Ball Race Ban Issue," *New York Amsterdam News,* 18 August 1945.
110. Dodson, "Integration of Negroes in Baseball."
111. Dodson, "Integration of Negroes in Baseball."
112. "Branch Rickey to Study Ball Bias," *New York Amsterdam News,* 1 September 1945.
113. "No Colored Players to Be Hired by Yankees Declares McPhail [*sic*]," *Baltimore Afro-American,* 22 September 1945.
114. Branch Rickey to Elmer Carter, 15 August 1950, Branch Rickey Papers, LoC.
115. "Tentative Proposal for Report of the Mayor's Committee on Baseball," 28 September 1945. The report suggested that because of its interstate nature, the committee was not sure that Ives-Quinn was applicable to major-league baseball.
116. Bill Mardo, "Drive for Negroes in Big Leagues Started in 'Daily,'" *Daily Worker,* 25 October 1945.
117. Dan Burley, "New York Giants to Hunt Negro Players Next Year," *New York Amsterdam News,* 27 October 1945.

118. Burley, "Giants to Hunt Negro Players," *New York Amsterdam News,* 27 October 1945.
119. Terry Lichtash, "Ives-Quinn Act—The Law Against Discrimination," *St. John's Law Review* 19, no. 2 (1945): 170–76.
120. Jennifer Delton, *Racial Integration in Corporate America, 1940–1990* (Cambridge: Cambridge University Press, 2009), 165–75.
121. Eisenstadt, *Rochdale Village,* 79–80.
122. Biondi, *To Stand and Fight.*
123. "N.Y. Anti-Bias Commission Considered Effective Despite Widespread Criticism," *Baltimore Afro-American,* 26 January 1946.
124. Paul D. Moreno, *From Direct Action to Affirmative Action: Fair Employment Law and Policy, 1932–1977* (Baton Rouge: Louisiana State University Press, 1997), 117.
125. "N.Y. Anti-Bias Commission Considered Effective," *Baltimore Afro-American,* 26 January 1946.
126. Rickey also corresponded with the African American author J. Sanders Redding, whose *No Day of Triumph* (New York: Harper and Brothers, 1942) tried to dispel common stereotypes: see Polner, *Branch Rickey,* 147.
127. Gunnar Myrdal, *An American Dilemma: The Negro Problem and American Democracy* (New York: Harper and Brothers, 1944).
128. Lowenfish, *Branch Rickey: Ferocious Gentleman,* 351.
129. Myrdal, *An American Dilemma,* li.
130. Wendell Smith, "Why I Signed Jackie Robinson," *Pittsburgh Courier,* 3 November 1945.
131. Myrdal, *An American Dilemma,* 928.
132. Mann, *Jackie Robinson Story,* 17–18.
133. Myrdal, *An American Dilemma,* 69.
134. Polner, *Branch Rickey,* 196.
135. Karl E. Downs, *Meet the Negro* (Los Angeles: Methodist Youth Fellowship Southern California–Arizona Annual Conference, 1943), 27.
136. Lowenfish, *Branch Rickey: Ferocious Gentleman,* 354.
137. Gerald Holland, "Mr. Rickey and the Game," *Sports Illustrated,* 7 March 1955.
138. Frank N. Tannenbaum, *Slave and Citizen: The Negro in the Americas* (New York: Knopf, 1947), 127–28.
139. See Barbara Weinstein, "How to Become a Historian of Latin America: The Extraordinary Career of Frank Tannenbaum," *The Americas* 80, no. 3 (2023): 383–93.
140. Brazil was another Latin American country that was seen as having less toxic race relations than the United States, an opinion shared by the eminent sociologist E. Franklin Frazier: see "Says Brazil Is Almost Without Racial Prejudice," *New York Amsterdam News,* 27 March 1945. Much of this optimism (or over-optimism) was based on the work of Brazilian sociologist Gilberto Freyre, whose major work, *The Masters and the Slaves* (published in English in 1946), Rickey deemed "eminently useful": see Polner,

Branch Rickey, 149. Freyre argued that race relations in Brazil were less binary and brutal than in the United States and offered a possible model to emulate.

141. Peary, *Jackie Robinson in Quotes,* 128, 130.
142. Lowenfish, *Branch Rickey: Ferocious Gentleman,* 417.
143. Polner, *Branch Rickey,* 169–70.
144. Polner, *Branch Rickey,* 169–70.
145. "1,300 Hear Harriman, Rickey, Ellington Plead for NAACP Aid," *Atlanta Daily World,* 1 December 1957.
146. John Golightly, "We Must Get Rid of Colonization in Our Own Land," *Norfolk Journal and Guide,* 2 February 1957.
147. "Jackie Blasts Patience Talk," *Chicago Defender,* 7 May 1960.
148. Rickey to Robinson, 21 February 1964; Rickey to Citizens for Goldwater, 30 September 1964, Branch Rickey Papers, LoC.
149. Bob Nightengale, "Branch Rickey," *Los Angeles Times,* 31 March 1997.
150. In the *New York Times* between 1939 and 1945, there were forty-eight articles that contained both the words "racism" and "Nazi," and nineteen articles with both "racism" and "Negro."
151. Daryl Michael Scott, "Black Personality in the Integrationist Era," in *The Oxford Handbook of African American Citizenship, 1865–Present,* ed. Henry Louis Gates Jr. et al. (Oxford: Oxford University Press, 2012), 745.
152. "Why I Signed Jackie Robinson," *Pittsburgh Courier,* 3 November 1945.
153. Michael Carter, "It's a Press Victory, Says Jackie Robinson," *Baltimore Afro-American,* 3 November 1945.

6. At Bat During the Cold War

1. Arnold Rampersad, *Jackie Robinson: A Biography* (New York: Ballantine Books, 1997), 139–43, 153.
2. "Woodard Stars in Drama Staged by United Vets," *Norfolk Journal and Guide,* 14 June 1947.
3. Michael Carter, "It's a Press Victory, Says Jackie Robinson," *Baltimore Afro-American,* 3 November 1945.
4. Horace R. Cayton, "Barber Shop Talk," *Pittsburgh Courier,* 19 October 1946.
5. Langston Hughes, "Here to Yonder," *Chicago Defender,* 9 August 1947.
6. Roscoe McGowen, "Double by Reiser Beats Boston, 5–3," *New York Times,* 16 April 1947; Arthur Daley, "Opening Day at Ebbets Field," *New York Times,* 16 April 1947.
7. Rampersad, *Jackie Robinson,* 185.
8. Polner, *Branch Rickey,* 201–2.
9. Carl E. Prince, *Brooklyn's Dodgers: The Bums, the Borough, and the Best of Brooklyn, 1947–1957* (New York: Oxford University Press, 1996), 4–18.

10. Peter Dreier and Robert Elias, *Baseball Rebels: The Players, People, and Social Movements That Shook Up the Game and Changed America* (Lincoln: University of Nebraska Press, 2022), 87; Jackie Robinson, "Now I Know Why They Boo Me" (*Look* magazine, January/February 1955), reprinted in Jules Tygiel, ed., *The Jackie Robinson Reader* (New York: Penguin, 1997), 193–202.
11. Said on *The Ingraham Angle,* Fox News, February 2018.
12. For Robinson on Mays, see "My 'Unbiased' Friend," *Norfolk Journal and Guide,* 6 June 1964.
13. Robinson, "Now I Know Why They Boo Me," 195.
14. The most comprehensive account of the game is Dennis VanLangen, "June 2, 1954: Jackie Robinson Ejected in Brooklyn's Rain-Shortened Win Over Milwaukee," in *From the Braves to the Brewers: Great Games and Exciting History at Milwaukee's County Stadium,* ed. Gregory H. Wolf (Phoenix, AZ: Society of American Baseball Research, 2016), 35–38.
15. "Tossed Bat Hits Usher," *New York Times,* 3 June 1954; Jackie Robinson, "Now I Know Why They Boo Me," 196.
16. "Tossed Bat Hits Usher," *New York Times,* 3 June 1954; "Stanky Says Robinson Got Off Easy," *Philadelphia Tribune,* 12 June 1954.
17. Although it does not appear to directly figure into this incident, the Milwaukee Braves, especially Lew Burdette and Warren Spahn, were notorious for their racism and for beanballing Black Dodgers batters: see Prince, *Brooklyn's Dodgers,* 16–18.
18. Robinson, "Now I Know Why They Boo Me," 196.
19. Van Langen, "June 2, 1954."
20. Robinson, "Now I Know Why They Boo Me," 196.
21. Josh Levin, "The Story Behind Jackie Robinson's Damning Kiss-Off to a White Sportswriter," *Slate,* 12 February 2021.
22. But some people had a much better 2 June 1954, than Jackie Robinson. For some it was the most important and probably the best day of their lives. Like me. On that day, in a maternity ward in an upper Manhattan hospital, I entered the world and promptly started to cry.
23. "Two New York Scribes on Same Paper Take Different Views on Jackie," *Baltimore Afro-American,* 19 June 1954.
24. "Bum's Fiery Star Riled by Umpire," *Philadelphia Tribune,* 5 June 1954.
25. Cal Jarox, "Robinson's Dilemma," *Norfolk Journal and Guide,* 26 June 1954.
26. "Bum's Fiery Star Riled by Umpire," *Philadelphia Tribune,* 5 June 1954.
27. Danny Peary, *Jackie Robinson in Quotes* (Salem, MA: Page Street Pub., 2016), 171, 192, 252.
28. "George Weiss Denies Yankees Prejudiced," *Washington Post,* 1 December 1952; John Klima, "The True Story of Willie Mays's Signing," Society for American Baseball Research, 2017, accessed 22 August 2025, https://sabr.org/research/article/the-true-story-of-willie-mayss-signing/.

29. Rampersad, *Jackie Robinson,* 253–54; Earl Brown, "Are Yankees Kidding?," *New York Amsterdam News,* 13 December 1952; Joe Bostic, "An Open Letter to Jackie Robinson," *New York Amsterdam News,* 6 December 1952.
30. Keefe quoted in Levin, "Behind Robinson's Damning Kiss-Off," *Slate,* 12 February 2021.
31. Levin, "Behind Robinson's Damning Kiss-Off," *Slate,* 12 February 2021.
32. Jackie Robinson to William Keefe, 23 July 1956, in Jackie Robinson, *First Class Citizenship: The Civil Rights Letters of Jackie Robinson,* ed. Michael G. Long (New York: Times Books, 2007), 15–16.
33. "Excerpts from Transcripts of 25th Day of Senate Testimony," *New York Times,* 3 June 1954; Anthony Leviero, "Eisenhower Posts His Anti-Red Score," *New York Times,* 3 June 1954; "Text of Statement on Reds," *New York Times,* 3 June 1954; James Reston, "Dr. Oppenheimer Is Barred from Security Clearance," *New York Times,* 2 June 1954.
34. W. H. Lawrence, "Exchange Bitter: Counsel Is Near Tears as Audience Applauds," *New York Times,* 10 June 1954.
35. Paul P. Kennedy, "Plot Still Fought by Guatemalans," *New York Times,* 3 June 1954.
36. Henry R. Lieberman, "Vietnam's Army to Get a Big Role," *New York Times,* 3 June 1954.
37. "Racial Ban Retained," *New York Times,* 3 June 1954.
38. "Byrnes Firm on Bias Ban," *New York Times,* 3 June 1954. There is one more news event in early June 1954 that needs to be mentioned. Starting on June 9 and 10, the US government commenced what became known as "Operation Wetback." ("Wetback" is a derogatory term for Mexican immigrants.) Starting in Arizona and California and later extending to Texas, the Immigration and Naturalization Service, the US Border Patrol, and other US agencies used quasi-military tactics to round up and deport undocumented Mexicans to Mexico. Estimates for the numbers deported vary widely, but at least 300,000 persons were deported from the United States. It has often been called the "largest mass deportation in American history," though this record is likely to be challenged in the near future. See Kelly Lytle Hernandez, *Migra! A History of the US Border Patrol* (Berkeley: University of California Press, 2010).
39. E. Washington Rhodes, "Pioneer's Role Difficult, Thankless, Jackie Learns," *Philadelphia Tribune,* 22 June 1954; Neil Lanctot, *Campy: The Two Lives of Roy Campanella* (New York: Simon and Schuster, 2011), 307–12.
40. Prince, *Brooklyn's Dodgers,* 23–44.
41. Prince, *Brooklyn's Dodgers,* 6–7; Jackie Robinson, "Free Minds and Hearts at Work," This I Believe, https://thisibelieve.org/essay/16931/.
42. "Jackie Robinson Urges Race Integration Care," *Los Angeles Times,* 16 February 1954.
43. Arthur Daley, "Teapot Tempest," *New York Times,* 7 April 1955; Arthur Daley, "Foot in Mouth Disease," *New York Times,* 15 January 1957.
44. Jackie Robinson, with Alfred Duckett, *I Never Had It Made* (New York: Putnam's, 1972), 79.

45. "Rookie of the Year," *Time,* 22 September 1947, reprinted in Jules Tygiel, ed., *The Jackie Robinson Reader* (New York: Penguin, 1997), 145–54.
46. Mark Bzomowski "He Held His Temper," *New York Times,* 13 April 1997.
47. See Mary L. Dudziak, *Cold War Civil Rights: Race and the Image of American Democracy* (Princeton, NJ: Princeton University Press, 2000).
48. Karl E. Downs, *Meet the Negro* (Los Angeles: Methodist Youth Fellowship Southern California–Arizona Annual Conference, 1943), 162–63.
49. "Harlem Fraternal Center," International Workers Order flyer, November 1946. I'd like to thank Keith Crook for sharing this document with me.
50. "'Communist Front' Award to GI Red Veteran," *Washington Post,* 22 November 1946.
51. "Robeson to Sing for Carolina Veterans," *New Journal and Guide,* 27 November 1946; Conrad Clark, "UNAVA Plans to Fight Blot on Red Tag," *New York Amsterdam News,* 7 February 1948.
52. "Jackie to Accept Vets' Portfolio," *Philadelphia Tribune,* 1 June 1946.
53. "UNAVA, NNC, Placed on Subversive List," *New Journal and Guide,* 13 December 1947.
54. "Robeson to Sing for Carolina Veterans," *New Journal and Guide,* 27 November 1946.
55. Chester L. Washington, "Sez Chez," *Pittsburgh Courier,* 27 December 1941.
56. Bill Mardo, "Robinson—Robeson," in *Jackie Robinson: Race, Sports and the American Dream,* eds. Joseph Dorinson and Joram Warmund (Armonk, NY: M. E. Sharpe, 1998), 98–105.
57. "Publisher's 1943 Plea to Landis Caused Lift of Baseball's Jim Crow," *Chicago Defender,* 3 November 1945.
58. For recordings of "Ballad for Americans" and the "Anthem of the USSR," see Paul Robeson, *Songs for Free Men, 1940–1945,* Pearl, Gemm CD 9264, 1997.
59. Sam Lacy, "Looking 'Em Over," *Baltimore Afro-American,* 8 January 1944.
60. Polner, *Branch Rickey,* 148.
61. As an example of why Rickey might have worried about being tagged with communist ties, when the left-wing United Negro Veterans and Allied Veterans of America awarded both Robinson and Rickey Freedom Awards, another recipient was Shirley Graham, a member of the Communist Party who was soon to marry W. E. B. Du Bois: see "Woodard Stars in Drama Staged by United Vets," *Norfolk Journal and Guide,* 22 June 1947.
62. "Rickey Claims 15 Clubs Voted to Bar Negroes from the Majors," *New York Times,* 18 February 1948.
63. Sam Maltin, "Paul Robeson, Canadian Press Hails Signing," *Pittsburgh Courier,* 27 October 1945.
64. Martin B. Duberman, *Paul Robeson: A Biography* (New York: Knopf, 1988), 338.
65. Duberman, *Paul Robeson,* 342.
66. Duberman, *Paul Robeson,* 342.
67. "'Ol' Man River' Retained," *New York Times,* 13 June 1949; "Robeson as Speaker for

Negroes Denied," *New York Times,* 25 April 1949; "Hold Public May 'Freeze' Robeson," *New York Amsterdam News,* 30 April 1949.

68. "Connecticut Official Asks for Ban on Robeson," *New York Times,* 24 April 1949.
69. Kostya Kennedy, *True: The Four Seasons of Jackie Robinson* (New York: St. Martin's Press, 2022), 11. Kennedy's book is authoritative but unfortunately not footnoted.
70. Lee Lowenfish, *Branch Rickey: Baseball's Ferocious Gentleman* (Lincoln: University of Nebraska Press, 2007), 471–74.
71. "Text of Jackie Robinson's Statement to House Unit," *New York Times,* 19 July 1949.
72. Rampersad, *Jackie Robinson,* 211.
73. Harold Roettger, "Draft of Robinson Statement Before HUAC, July 1949," Branch Rickey Papers, Library of Congress Digital Collections. I would like to thank Keith Crook for making this document available to me.
74. Roettger, "Draft of Robinson Statement Before HUAC," Branch Rickey Papers, LoC.
75. C. P. Trussell, "Red Failures Here Told by Minorities," *New York Times,* 14 July 1949; "'Black Stalin' Aim Laid to Robeson," *New York Times,* 15 July 1949.
76. "Text of Jackie Robinson's Statement to House Unit," *New York Times,* 19 July 1949.
77. "Robinson's Statement to House Unit," *New York Times,* 19 July 1949.
78. "Robinson's Statement to House Unit," *New York Times,* 19 July 1949.
79. "Communist Shutout," *New York Times,* 20 July 1949.
80. Prince, *Brooklyn's Dodgers,* 40.
81. Gordon Hancock, "Jackie Robinson, Interracialist," *Los Angeles Sentinel,* 4 August 1949.
82. "Drop That Gun, Jackie," *Baltimore Afro-American,* 16 July 1949.
83. James L. Hicks, "Robeson Praises Jackie, Refuses to Be Drawn into Personal Feud," *Atlanta Daily World,* 27 July 1949.
84. "Du Bois Says Handle Our Own Problems First," *Baltimore Afro-American,* 20 August 1949.
85. Lanctot, *Campy,* 192.
86. "That Robeson Riot," *Chicago Defender,* 10 September 1949.
87. Mardo, "Robinson—Robeson," 98–105.
88. Allen McMillian, "Memo to Muriel, My Best Girl," *New York Amsterdam News,* 6 August 1949; "Biggest Benefit Ball in the History of Harlem" [advertisement], *New York Amsterdam News,* 2 October 1949; Barney Josephson and Terry Trilling-Josephson, *Cafe Society: The Wrong Place for the Right People* (Urbana: University of Illinois Press, 2009), 223–54; "Loves Soviet Best, Robeson Declares," *New York Times,* 20 June 1949.
89. Sam Lacy, "Jackie Again Swings at Reds for Attempting to Make Issue of Ump's Ejection," *Baltimore Afro-American,* 8 October 1949.
90. "Jackie Denies He Merited Ejection," *Baltimore Afro-American,* 1 October 1949.
91. After a lengthy and heated trial, the defendants were convicted for their supposed violation of the 1940 Smith Act, which made it a crime to advocate for the violent overthrow of the American government. For Robinson's award, see William G. Weart,

"Freedoms Group Honors Our Way," *New York Times,* 22 November 1949. Other honorees included the ardent segregationist James F. Byrnes, conservative Republicans such as Herbert Hoover and Robert F. Taft, and future Secretary of State John Foster Dulles. In 1952, Walter O'Malley invited Medina to a Dodgers game, and a highlight was a handshake and exchange of banter between Robinson and Medina: see Meyer Berger, "Medina Overruled by Giants," *New York Times,* 24 May 1952.

92. Alice A. Dunnigan, "US Needs to Clean Up Mississippi, Alabama," *Pittsburgh Courier,* 23 June 1956.
93. Tygiel, *Jackie Robinson Reader,* 217.
94. Prince, *Brooklyn's Dodgers,* 40.
95. Robinson and Duckett, *I Never Had It Made,* 94–98.
96. "Robinson's Statement to House Unit," *New York Times,* 19 July 1949.
97. For the influence of members of the Communist Party on the civil rights movement, see the many books of Gerald Horne, among them *Black and Red: W. E. B. Du Bois and the Afro-American Response to the Cold War, 1944–1963* (Albany: SUNY Press, 1986); and *Black Liberation/Red Scare: Ben Davis and the Communist Party* (Newark: University of Delaware Press, 1993).
98. Martha Biondi, *To Stand and Fight: The Struggle for Civil Rights in Postwar New York City* (Cambridge, MA: Harvard University Press, 2003).
99. Peter Eisenstadt, *Rochdale Village: Robert Moses, 6,000 Families, and New York City's Great Experiment in Integrated Housing* (Ithaca, NY: Cornell University Press, 2010), 162.
100. For a spirited defense of the NAACP during the 1940s and early 1950s as a progressive civil rights organization domestically and internationally, see Carol Anderson, *Bourgeois Radicals: The NAACP and the Struggle for Colonial Liberation, 1940–1960* (Cambridge: Cambridge University Press, 2015). For the anti-Communist Liberal Party's excellent record on civil rights, see Daniel Soyer, *Left in the Center: The Liberal Party of New York and the Rise and Fall of American Social Democracy* (Ithaca, NY: Cornell University Press, 2021), 94–98.
101. "Malcolm X Answers Jackie Robinson," *Chicago Defender,* 7 December 1963; "Jackie Robinson Writes Again to Malcolm X," *New York Amsterdam News,* 14 December 1963.
102. Jackie Robinson, as told to Wendell Smith, *Jackie Robinson: My Own Story* (New York: Greenberg Publishers, 1949), 118–19.

7. White Brooklyn, Black Brooklyn

1. Leo Durocher, "Los Angeles Will Love the Dodgers!," *New York Herald Tribune,* 9 March 1958, cited in Thomas J. Campanella, *Brooklyn: The Once and Future City* (Princeton, NJ: Princeton University Press, 2019), 445.
2. Ray McCarey, dir., *It Happened in Flatbush,* 20th Century Fox (1942). Not to be confused

with the somewhat better film, *It Happened in Brooklyn,* a 1947 MGM musical starring Frank Sinatra, another film concerned with the metaphysics of true Brooklynness.

3. James Agee, *Brooklyn Is Southeast of the Island: Travel Notes* (New York: Fordham University Press, 2005), 5, 6. The essay was originally commissioned by *Fortune* in 1939 but was deemed too harsh to publish.
4. *The WPA Guide to New York City: The Federal Writers Project Guide to 1930s New York* (1939; repr., New York: Pantheon, 1982), 432.
5. Agee, *Brooklyn Is Southeast,* 5.
6. See Ronald H. Bayor, *Neighbors in Conflict: The Irish, Germans, Jews, and Italians of New York City, 1929–1941* (Baltimore: Johns Hopkins University Press, 1988).
7. Carl E. Prince, *Brooklyn's Dodgers: The Bums, the Borough, and the Best of Baseball, 1947–1957* (New York: Oxford University Press, 1996), 102–18.
8. Alfred Kazin, *A Walker in the City* (New York: Harcourt, Brace, 1951), 12.
9. Neal Gabler, *Barbra Streisand: Redefining Beauty, Femininity, and Power* (New Haven, CT: Yale University Press, 2016), 13.
10. Craig Steven Wilder, *A Covenant with Color: Race and Social Power in Brooklyn* (New York: Columbia University Press, 2000), 185–95.
11. Geoffrey D. Needler, "King's English: Fact and Folklore of Brooklyn Speech," in *Brooklyn USA: The Fourth Largest City in America,* ed. Rita Selden Miller (New York: Brooklyn College Press, 1979), 173–88.
12. "How To Speak Brooklynese," *Brooklyn Eagle,* 27 March 1929. This is the earliest article I could find in the *Brooklyn Eagle* on "Brooklynese."
13. Needler, "King's English," 173.
14. "Three-Layer Cake Cut by Brooklyn," *New York Times,* 13 June 1946. The "nowhere—this is Brooklyn" unfunny joke serves as a frontispiece in John Richmond and Abril Lamarque, *Brooklyn, USA* (New York: Creative Age Press, 1946).
15. Alfred Hitchcock, dir., *Lifeboat,* 20th Century Fox (1944).
16. Arthur Daley, "The Dodger Deacon Discourses," *New York Times,* 12 February 1943.
17. Daley, "The Deacon Discourses," *New York Times,* 12 February 1943.
18. James Rubin, "The Brooklyn Dodgers and Ebbets Field—Their Departure," in Miller, *Brooklyn USA,* 160–72.
19. Kostya Kennedy, *True: The Four Seasons of Jackie Robinson* (New York: St. Martin's Press, 2022,), 88–89, 102–4.
20. Peter Golenbock, *Bums: An Oral History of the Brooklyn Dodgers* (New York: Putnam's, 1984), 153.
21. Wilder, *Covenant with Color,* 212.
22. "Curbs on Crime in Brooklyn Sought," *New York Times,* 25 November 1941.
23. Robert Gruber, "It Happened in Brooklyn: Reminiscences of a Fan," in *Jackie Robinson: Race, Sports and the American Dream,* eds. Joseph Dorinson and Joram Warmund

(Armonk, NY: M. E. Sharpe, 1998), 43–48; Danny Peary, *Jackie Robinson in Quotes* (Salem, MA: Page Street Pub., 2016), 133.

24. Irwin Silber, *Press Box Red: The Story of Lester Rodney, the Communist Who Helped Break the Color Line in American Sports* (Philadelphia: Temple University Press, 2003), 27.
25. Golenbock, *Bums,* 156.
26. Wilder, *Covenant with Color,* 196–97.
27. Jimmy Breslin, "And Proud of It," *New York Times,* 20 August 1975.
28. Peter Eisenstadt, *Rochdale Village: Robert Moses, 6,000 Families, and New York City's Great Experiment in Integrated Housing* (Ithaca, NY: Cornell University Press, 2010), 56.
29. See Ira Katznelson, *When Affirmative Action Was White: An Untold Story of Racial Inequality in Twentieth-Century America* (New York: Norton, 2005).
30. Earl Conrad, "Statue of Liberty Ferry Closes Jim Crow Lavatory," *Chicago Defender,* 17 March 1945; "'Strange Fruit' Author Finds N.Y. Hotels Bar Negroes," *Chicago Defender,* 22 December 1945; "Many Downtown Hotels Welcome Negro Visitors," *New York Amsterdam News,* 4 September 1948.
31. The Dodgers often did business with the McAlpin Hotel: see Rampersad, *Jackie Robinson,* 168.
32. Jackie Robinson, as told to Wendell Smith, *Jackie Robinson: My Own Story* (New York: Greenberg Publishers, 1949), 88.
33. Rampersad, *Jackie Robinson,* 220.
34. Eisenstadt, *Rochdale Village,* 50.
35. Eisenstadt, *Rochdale Village,* 48. The Klan rally in downtown Jamaica on Memorial Day in 1927 has become notorious because some Klan supporters were arrested, among them Fred Trump, father of Donald.
36. "Court Grants Writ Barring Sale of a Home in Queens to a Negro," *New York Amsterdam News,* 14 February 1947; "St. Albans Ban Outlawed," *New York Amsterdam News,* 8 May 1948; "Ruling Is Acclaimed Here," *New York Times,* 4 May 1948.
37. Carl T. Rowan, with Jackie Robinson, *Wait till Next Year: The Life Story of Jackie Robinson* (New York: Random House, 1969), 306. Jackie Robinson, as told to Ed Reid, "Robeson Has the Wrong Attitude," *Washington Post,* 30 August 1949.
38. "St. Albans Ban Outlawed," *New York Amsterdam News,* 8 May 1948; "Queens Swankiest Section" [advertisement], *New York Amsterdam News,* 30 May 1955; Floyd Shelson, "St. Albans Becomes Finest Home Section," *New York Amsterdam News,* 17 February 1955; Eisenstadt, *Rochdale Village,* 50; "Launch Fight Against Negro Home Ban," *New York Amsterdam News,* 8 May 1948; Betty Granger, "P.O. Changeover Threatens St. Albans' Property Values," *New York Amsterdam News,* 15 December 1951.
39. For a discussion of blockbusting in St. Albans, see "L.I. Brokers Promote Anti-Negro Bias," *New York Amsterdam News,* 30 May 1953.
40. Rampersad, *Jackie Robinson,* 272.

41. Al Moses, "Beating the Gun," *Philadelphia Tribune,* 27 December 1949.
42. "City Lists Conditions at Schools," *New York Times,* 1 November 1959. Two St. Albans schools were listed as needing replacement or requiring serious improvement.
43. Rowan, *Wait till Next Year,* 306.
44. Rowan, *Wait till Next Year,* 306.
45. Robinson and Smith, *Jackie Robinson,* 129.
46. Luis Virgil Overbea, "Beating the Gun," *Philadelphia Tribune,* 5 December 1954; "Jackie Robinson Accepted by Whites in New Mansion," *Philadelphia Tribune,* 16 July 1955.
47. "Robinson Signs '55 Contract," *Pittsburgh Courier,* 22 January 1955; "Family Income in the United States: 1954 and 1953," US Census Bureau, https://www.census.gov/.
48. "Robinsons to Buy House," *New York Times,* 17 December 1953.
49. Rampersad, *Jackie Robinson,* 271–75; Overbea, "Beating the Gun," *Philadelphia Tribune,* 5 December 1954.
50. Jews played a key role in facilitating the Robinson's move to Stamford. Andrea Simon, wife of the head of the Simon and Schuster, helped to find sympathetic realtors and became one of Rachel Robinson's best friends. The only bank that would provide them with a mortgage was owned by two Jewish brothers: see Peter Dreier, "Jackie Robinson and the Jews," *Jewish Journal,* 30 March 2022.
51. Rampersad, *Jackie Robinson,* 271–55; "Robinson Rouses Home-Sale Dispute," *New York Times,* 12 December 1953; Lydia T. Brown, "Jackie Robinson, Family, Welcomed by Neighbors," *Baltimore Afro-American,* 26 December 1953.
52. Robinson, *Jackie Robinson,* 132.
53. Brown, "Robinson, Family, Welcomed by Neighbors," *Baltimore Afro-American,* 26 December 1953.
54. Henry G. Stelter, *Racial Integration in Private Residential Neighborhoods in Connecticut* (Hartford, CT: Commission on Civil Rights, 1957), v, 16, 19.
55. John Barrington, "Robinson's 'Dream Home' May Help Him Forget Those Days as a Pioneer," *Pittsburgh Courier,* 22 January 1955. Accusations of this sort would linger. In 1964, Elombe Brath, a Black nationalist activist would write of Robinson: "When more black people moved to St. Albans, Jackie moved out . . . to Connecticut . . . From his home in Connecticut, he tries to tell the masses in Harlem how happy they should be" [ellipses in original]. Elombe Brath, *The Artistic Activism of Elombe Brath,* ed. Thomas Aiello (Jackson: University of Mississippi Press, 2021), 140.
56. Rampersad, *Jackie Robinson,* 272.
57. "Jackie Robinson Accepted by Whites in New Mansion," *Philadelphia Tribune,* 16 July 1955.
58. "Robinson Accepted by Whites," *Philadelphia Tribune,* 16 July 1955.
59. Rachel Robinson, *Jackie Robinson: An Intimate Portrait* (New York: Harry N. Abrams, 1996), 131.
60. Rowan, *Wait till Next Year,* 30.

61. Robert H. Kinzer and Edward Sagarin, *The Negro in American Business: The Conflict Between Separatism and Integration* (New York: Greenberg Publishers, 1950), 11.
62. Robinson and Duckett, *I Never Had It Made,* 108.
63. Thomas Sugrue, *Sweet Land of Liberty: The Forgotten Struggle for Civil Rights in the North* (New York: Random House, 2008), 211.
64. "Robby Hits Levittown Bias Plan," *New York Amsterdam News,* 16 February 1952.
65. Dorothy Anderson, "Politicians Leading Campaign to Chase Myers Out of Levittown," *Philadelphia Tribune,* 7 September 1957.
66. "Protest Action May Return to City Hall," *New York Amsterdam News,* 16 November 1957.
67. Wendell Pritchett, "Where Shall We Live? Class and the Limitations of Fair Housing," *Urban Lawyer* 35, no. 3 (2002): 399–470, esp. 418–41.
68. James Booker, "Cardinal Spellman Backs Housing Bill," *New York Amsterdam News,* 2 November 1957.
69. "Honor Three Housing Proponents," *New York Amsterdam News,* 20 December 1958.
70. Jackie Robinson, "An Unholy Proposition," *Chicago Defender,* 24 October 1964; Jackie Robinson, "Help of Citizens Needed to Pass Fair Housing Bill," *Philadelphia Tribune,* 28 February 1967; Jackie Robinson, "The GOP Party and the Negro Vote," *Chicago Defender,* 18 March 1967; Jackie Robinson, "Senator Percy and the Housing Issue," *Chicago Defender,* 29 April 1967.
71. James Hicks, "No Interpreter Needed When Germany Met Brooklyn," *Baltimore Afro-American,* 1 August 1953.
72. Sid Frigand, "Brooklyn's Negroes Have Risen Steadily Since 1633," *Brooklyn Eagle,* 25 July 1954.
73. Sid Frigand, "Church Attendance Among Negroes Soars," *Brooklyn Eagle,* 31 July 1954.
74. Sid Frigand, "Negroes in Search of Decent Housing Caught in Squeeze," *Brooklyn Eagle,* 1 August 1954.
75. Sid Frigand, "Families of Negroes Living Amicably in White Neighborhoods," *Brooklyn Eagle,* 3 August 1954.
76. Sig Frigand, "Brooklyn, With its Climate of Freedom, Haven to Negroes," *Brooklyn Eagle,* 8 August 1954.
77. Agee, *Brooklyn Is,* 37. Italics in quote from the original.
78. Frigand, "Brooklyn's Negroes Have Risen Steadily," *Brooklyn Eagle,* 25 July 1954.
79. *WPA Guide to New York City,* 501–2; Richmond and Lamarque, *Brooklyn, USA,* 82; Jonathan Rieder, *Canarsie: The Jews and Italians of Brooklyn Against Liberalism* (Cambridge, MA: Harvard University Press, 1985), 14.
80. Agee, *Brooklyn Is,* 40.
81. Rieder, *Canarsie,* 16.
82. Rieder, *Canarsie,* 63.
83. Rieder, *Canarsie,* 90. In the end, it was to little avail. Most whites left Canarsie, as they

left most "non-Brownstone" neighborhoods in Brooklyn. By the 2020s, Canarsie's population was three-quarters nonwhite, with a large Caribbean population.

84. Wendell E. Pritchett, *Brownsville, Brooklyn: Blacks, Jews, and the Changing Nature of the Ghetto* (Chicago: University of Chicago Press, 2002), 84.
85. Pritchett, *Brownsville, Brooklyn,* 43.
86. Pritchett, *Brownsville, Brooklyn,* 149.
87. Nathan Glazer, "Is 'Integration' Possible in New York Schools?," in *American Race Relations Today,* ed. Earl Raab (Garden City, NY: Doubleday, 1962), 135–63, 148.
88. Eisenstadt, *Rochdale Village,* 159.
89. Eisenstadt, *Rochdale Village,* 159.
90. Jackie Robinson, "Calls 'Cry for Freedom' a 'Jingle,'" *Chicago Defender,* 4 January 1964.
91. Jackie Robinson, "Donovan Must Go!," *New York Amsterdam News,* 15 February 1964.
92. See Clarence A. Taylor, *Knocking at Our Door: Milton A. Galamison and the Struggle to Integrate New York City's Schools* (Lanham, MD: Lexington Books, 2001); Eisenstadt, *Rochdale Village,* 159. The supporters of the boycott included myself, proudly representing Mrs. Elman's fourth-grade class from PS 57 in the Bronx.
93. Robinson, "Donovan Must Go!," *New York Amsterdam News,* 15 February 1964.
94. Simon Anweke, "Big Flare Up Avoided," *New York Amsterdam News,* 10 August 1963.
95. Jackie Robinson, "There Must Be a Better Way," *New York Amsterdam News,* 30 January 1965.
96. Jackie Robinson, "Counter-Revolt Is On," *Chicago Defender,* 11 April 1964.
97. Robinson, "Counter-Revolt Is On," *Chicago Defender,* 11 April 1964.
98. Jerald Podair, *The Strike That Changed New York: Blacks, Whites, and the Ocean Hill–Brownville Strike* (New Haven, CT: Yale University Press, 2002); Eisenstadt, *Rochdale Village,* 191–214.
99. Podair, *Strike That Changed New York;* Eisenstadt, *Rochdale Village,* 191–214.
100. Jackie Robinson, "Donovan Must Go!," *New York Amsterdam News,* 15 February 1964.
101. Alfred Duckett, "Jackie in Hot Answer to Rustin," *New York Amsterdam News,* 10 May 1969.
102. See Michael Shapiro, "Forgiving the Demon of the Dodgers," *New York Times,* 16 March 2003.
103. See Suleiman Osman, *The Invention of Brownstone Brooklyn: Gentrification and the Search for Authenticity in Postwar New York* (New York: Oxford University Press, 2011).
104. For an account of an effort to create an integrated school in contemporary Brooklyn, see Clara Hemphill, *A Brighter Choice: Building a Just School in an Unequal City* (New York: Teacher's College Press, 2023).

8. After the Dodgers

1. Gary Scott Smith, *Strength for the Cause: The Life and Faith of Jackie Robinson* (Grand Rapids, MI: Eerdmans, 2022), 164.
2. Wayne Phillips, "Negro Pastors Press Boycott by Preaching Passive Resistance," *New York Times,* 26 February 1956.
3. "Battle Against Tradition," *New York Times,* 21 March 1956. Robinson's and King's paths first crossed no later than June 1957, when both men were awarded honorary degrees from Howard University: see "Jackie Robinson Gets Honorary Degree from Howard University," *Atlanta Daily World,* 11 June 1957.
4. Martin Luther King Jr., *A Testament of Hope: The Essential Writings and Speeches of Martin Luther King, Jr.,* ed. James M. Washington (1956; repr., New York: HarperCollins, 1986), 76.
5. Martin D. Jenkins, "Problems Incident to Racial Integration and Some Suggested Approaches to These Problems," *Journal of Negro Education* 21, no. 3 (1952): 411–21.
6. "Laws Can Change Hearts," *Norfolk Journal and Guide,* 21 January 1961.
7. A. H. Raskin, "Negro Labor Unit Founded By 1,000," *New York Times,* 28 May 1960.
8. William Walker, "'Tokenism,' the New Opiate for Negroes," *Cleveland Call and Post,* 7 May 1960.
9. King, "The Ethical Demands of Integration" (1963), in *Testament of Hope,* 117–25.
10. See "Desegregation, Integration, and the Beloved Community," in Howard Thurman, *The Papers of Howard Washington Thurman,* 5 vols., ed. Walter Earl Fluker (Columbia: University of South Carolina Press, 2019), 5:147–58.
11. See Peter Eisenstadt, *Rochdale Village: Robert Moses, 6,000 Families, and New York City's Great Experiment in Integrated Housing* (Ithaca, NY: Cornell University Press, 2010), 156–58.
12. For an early appearance of the term "de facto segregation," see Benjamin Fine, "Northern Cities Confront the Problem of De Facto Segregation in the Schools," *New York Times,* 10 February 1957.
13. Langston Hughes, "No Civil War Without an Atomic Bomb," *Chicago Defender,* 28 May 1958.
14. "Jackie Robinson vs. Bob Kennedy," *Baltimore Afro-American,* 3 September 1960; also Patrick Henry, "Kareem's Omission? Jackie Robinson, Black Profile in Courage," in *Jackie Robinson: Race, Sports, and the American Dream,* eds. Joseph Dorinson and Joram Warmund (Armonk, NY: M. E. Sharpe, 1998), 209.
15. Jackie Robinson, "Disunity Is No Memorial," *New York Amsterdam News,* 6 July 1962.
16. Jackie Robinson, "'Adam Powell' Is My Friend," *New York Amsterdam News,* 20 April 1962.
17. Jackie Robinson, "Could Never Live with 'Uncle Tom,'" *Pittsburgh Courier,* 27 January

1968; "Jackie Robinson Blasts 'Uncle Tom' Like Negroes," *Pittsburgh Courier,* 7 February 1959.

18. Howard Thurman, *The Search for Common Ground* (New York: Harper and Row, 1971), 93.
19. Les Matthews, "Mr. 1-2-5," *New York Amsterdam News,* 21 July 1962; Fred Shapiro, editor of *The New Yale Book of Quotations* (New Haven, CT: Yale University Press, 2021), attributes the quote to the English author Evelyn Beatrice Hall (801).
20. Jackie Robinson to Roy Wilkins, in Jackie Robinson, *First Class Citizenship: The Civil Rights Letters of Jackie Robinson,* ed. Michael G. Long (New York: Henry Holt, 2007), 244–46.
21. Samuel Haynes, "High Point of My Career—Jackie on Spingarn Award," *Baltimore Afro-American,* 15 December 1956.
22. Arnold Rampersad, *Jackie Robinson* (New York: Ballantine Books, 1997), 302–3.
23. Jackie Robinson, as told to Wendell Smith, *Jackie Robinson: My Own Story* (New York: Greenberg Publishers, 1949), 124.
24. Rampersad, *Jackie Robinson,* 320–23.
25. Juliet E. K. Walker, *The History of Black Business in America: Capitalism, Race and Entrepreneurship* (New York: Macmillan Reference/Prentice Hall International, 1998), 341.
26. William R. Conklin, "Jackie Robinson, Chock Full O' Poise, as Executive," *New York Times,* 9 March 1958.
27. George Davis and Glegg Watson, *Black Life in Corporate America: Swimming in the Mainstream* (Garden City, NY: Doubleday, 1982), 17, 20.
28. Jackie Robinson, with Alfred Duckett, *I Never Had It Made* (New York: Putnam's, 1972), 279.
29. Sadie Stein, "A Millionaire's Money Can't Buy," *Paris Review Daily,* 26 February 2014; Andrew F. Smith, "Chock full o'Nuts," in *Savoring Gotham: A Food Lover's Companion to New York City,* ed. Andrew F. Smith (New York: Oxford University Press, 2015).
30. "From Cents to Millions: William Black," *New York Times,* 4 January 1960.
31. "Chock Full O'Nuts Needs New Workers," *New York Amsterdam News,* 26 September 1942.
32. Joe Bostic, "Band Stars on Showboat," *New York Amsterdam News,* 16 August 1943.
33. Conklin, "Jackie Robinson, Chock Full O' Poise," *New York Times,* 9 March 1958.
34. "Bias Case Is Won by Lunch Chain," *New York Times,* 3 October 1963.
35. "My Experiences" [Letter Writer], in "Word Game," *New York Times,* 21 July 1969.
36. Rampersad, *Jackie Robinson,* 321.
37. Conklin, "Jackie Robinson Chock Full O' Poise"; "From Cents to Millions," *New York Times,* 4 January 1960.
38. "Jackie Robinson Wins Labor Case," *New York Times,* 6 June 1958.
39. Jackie Robinson to William Black, 14 August 1963, in Robinson, *First Class Citizenship,* 175–76; "Deny Chock Full Six Fired for Union Bid," *New York Amsterdam News,*

10 August 1963. One of the disputes was that the company was trying to avoid unionization by hiring only African Americans: see "Chock Full O'Nuts Picketed by Whites," *New York Times,* 20 July 1963; "Bias Case Is Won by Lunch Chain," *New York Times,* 4 October 1963.

40. Rampersad, *Jackie Robinson,* 322. Robinson strongly supported efforts to unionize major-league baseball and was one of the few ex-ballplayers to testify on behalf of Curt Flood's challenge to the reserve clause: see ibid., 455. Robinson opposed so-called right to work laws and criticized racist practices in major unions in the AFL-CIO such as the ILGWU. Jackie Robinson, "An Unholy Proposition," *Chicago Defender,* 24 October 1964; Jackie Robinson, "Labor Leaders Should Shed More Light Than Heat on the Charges of Bias," *Philadelphia Tribune,* 6 November 1962.
41. Jackie Robinson, "Why I Left Chock Full O'Nuts," *New York Amsterdam News,* 28 March 1964.
42. Robinson, "Why I Left Chock Full O'Nuts," *New York Amsterdam News,* 28 March 1964.
43. Rampersad, *Jackie Robinson,* 322.
44. James L. Hicks, "Waring Quits CCJ over Segregation," *Baltimore Afro-American,* 16 April 1955. Distinguished retired federal judge J. Waites Waring, the first judge to rule that segregation was unconstitutional, left the National Conference of Christians and Jews because it did not have a policy of nonsegregation in its Southern branches.
45. "Nation Needs NAACP, Jackie Robinson Asserts," *Atlanta Daily World,* 23 January 1957.
46. Marion E. Jackson, "Sports of the World," *Atlanta Daily World,* 11 July 1958; Jackie Robinson, "Jackie Robinson," *Chicago Defender,* 9 December 1959.
47. "Jackie Robinson to Martin Luther King Jr., 5 May 1960," in Robinson, *First Class Citizenship,* 92–93. Jackie Robinson, "An Open Letter to Paul Zuber," "Paul Zuber Answers Jackie Robinson," "Jackie Robinson Answers Paul Zuber," *New York Amsterdam News,* 21 April, 28 April, 12 May 1962. Zuber, who played a key role in winning a landmark desegregation case in New Rochelle, New York, accused the NAACP and Governor Rockefeller of foot-dragging in support of the plaintiffs and had a strong case. In some ways, Zuber, a fiery Black Republican, had much in common with Robinson. For Zuber, see Martin J. Siegel, *Judgment and Mercy: The Turbulent Life and Times of the Judge Who Condemned the Rosenbergs* (Ithaca, NY: Cornell University Press, 2023), 167–83.
48. "Jackie Hits Weak NAACP Leadership," *Philadelphia Tribune,* 12 July 1958; Rampersad, *Jackie Robinson,* 334.
49. Edward Peeks, "10,000 in Youth March Say 'Integrate,'" *Baltimore Afro-American,* 1 November 1958; "65 Busloads Bolster Youth March to DC," *Baltimore Afro–American,* 25 October 1958; Rampersad, *Jackie Robinson,* 336; "Jackie Robinson Raps New York NAACP Head," *Pittsburgh Courier,* 6 December 1958.
50. "Expect 5,000 at Student Rally," *New York Amsterdam News,* 26 March 1960.
51. "We Are Going to Cause Trouble," *Baltimore Afro-American,* 7 May 1960.

52. "Jackie Urges Students to Continue Picketing," *Baltimore Afro-American,* 19 March 1960.
53. "Jackie Blasts Patience Talk," *Chicago Defender,* 7 May 1960.
54. For the NAACP in the 1950s, see Patricia Sullivan, *Lift Every Voice: The NAACP and the Making of the Civil Rights Movement* (New York: New Press, 2009); Manfred Berg, *The Ticket to Freedom: The NAACP and the Struggle for Black Political Integration* (Gainesville: University of Florida Press, 2005); Manfred Berg, "Black Civil Rights and Liberal Anti-Communism: The NAACP in the Early Cold War," *Journal of American History* 94, no. 1 (2007): 75–95; Eric Arnesen, "The Traditions of African American Anti-Communism," *Twentieth-Century Communism* 6, no. 6 (2014): 124–48. For a defense of the NAACP's combination of anti-communism and anti-imperialism, see Carol Anderson, *Bourgeois Radicals: The NAACP and the Struggle for Colonial Liberation, 1941–1960* (New York: Cambridge University Press, 2015).
55. Theodore C. Stone, "Raise $20Gs at NAACP Dinner," *Chicago Defender,* 16 July 1957.
56. Rampersad, *Jackie Robinson,* 200–221. For more on Robinson's friendly relations with Jews, see Peter Dreier, "Jackie Robinson and the Jews," *Jewish Journal,* 30 March 2022.
57. Joshua Leifer, *Tablets Shattered: The End of an American Jewish Century and the Future of Jewish Life* (New York: Dutton, 2024), 343.
58. "Jackie Robinson Makes First Speech Since Quitting Baseball," *Baltimore Afro-American,* 9 February 1957.
59. "Robinson Makes First Speech," *Baltimore Afro-American,* 9 February 1957.
60. Jackie Robinson, "Jackie Robinson," *Baltimore Afro-American,* 23 January 1960.
61. See, for instance, Cheryl Greenberg, *Troubling the Waters: Black-Jewish Relations in the Twentieth Century* (Princeton, NJ: Princeton University Press, 2006); Jack Salzman and Cornel West, eds., *Struggles in the Promised Land: Toward a History of Black-Jewish Relations in the United States* (New York: Oxford University Press, 1997).
62. Although as we saw in chapter 7, during the 1968 New York City Teacher's Strike, when Robinson perceived a conflict between African Americans and Jews, he supported what he thought was the "Black side" and stridently criticized African Americans such as Bayard Rustin who thought differently.
63. "They Don't Believe They Can Fill Powell's Shoes," *New York Amsterdam News,* 12 December 1959.
64. Jackie Robinson, "Jackie Robinson," *New York Amsterdam News,* 30 January 1960.
65. "The Way I See It," *New York Amsterdam News,* 10 July 1959.
66. Rampersad, *Jackie Robinson,* 336–37.
67. Rampersad, *Jackie Robinson,* 338–39.
68. Rampersad, *Jackie Robinson,* 352; James Wechsler to Jackie Robinson, 4 November 1960, in Robinson, *First Class Citizenship,* 115–17. From 1962 to 1968, his column was syndicated in the Black press.
69. Robinson was quite angry at the *Post*'s decision and later wrote of it that "there is a

peculiar parallel between some of our great Northern 'liberals' and some of our outstanding Southern liberals. . . . They both inevitably say the same thing: 'We know the Negro and what is best for him.'" Jackie Robinson, "Jackie Robinson Says," *New York Amsterdam News,* 6 January 1962. Robinson still wished to be a columnist for a white newspaper, and in 1964 wrote to the president of the (soon to cease independently publishing) *New York Herald Tribune* asking about the possibility of a column, to no avail: see Robinson, *First Class Citizenship,* 192.

70. Louis Lautier, "Hubert, Nixon Heavy Favorites," *Baltimore Afro-American,* 5 September 1959.
71. Jackie Robinson, "Negroes Know Their Enemies," *New York Amsterdam News,* 24 February 1962.
72. Jackie Robinson, "Robinson Blasts Home Rule Enemies," *New York Amsterdam News,* 15 October 1966.
73. Geoffrey Kabaservice, *Rule and Run: The Downfall of Moderation and the Destruction of the Republican Party* (New York: Oxford University Press, 2012), 26. See also Joshua D. Farrington, *Black Republicans and the Transformation of the GOP* (Philadelphia: University of Pennsylvania Press, 2016); Leah Wright Rigeur, *The Loneliness of the Black Republican: Pragmatic Politics and the Pursuit of Power* (Princeton, NJ: Princeton University Press, 2015).
74. Jackie Robinson, "A Negro First," *New York Amsterdam News,* 7 July 1964.
75. Jackie Robinson, "Some Republicans," *New York Amsterdam News,* 2 November 1963.
76. Jackie Robinson to Richard Nixon, December 1971, in Robinson, *First Class Citizenship.*
77. Jackie Robinson, "Jackie Robinson," *Chicago Defender,* 10 September 1959.
78. See Kevin M. Kruse, "The Southern Strategy," in *Myth America: Historians Take on the Biggest Legends and Lies About Our Past,* eds. Kevin M. Kruse and Juliam E. Zelizer (New York: Basic Books, 2022), 169–96.
79. Julian Duscha, "Jackie Robinson Joins Humphrey, Hopes for DC Primary Homers," *Washington Post,* 10 March 1960.
80. Rampersad, *Jackie Robinson,* 260–61.
81. "Jackie, NAACP Leaders Clash Over Ike's Stall," *Chicago Defender,* 4 May 1957; "Satch Blast Echoed by Top Performers," *Chicago Defender,* 29 September 1957.
82. Jackie Robinson, "The President and Civil Rights," *New York Amsterdam News,* 27 January 1962.
83. Rampersad, *Jackie Robinson,* 341–42.
84. Jackie Robinson, "Jackie Robinson," *New York Amsterdam News,* 20 June 1960.
85. Jackie Robinson to Chester Bowles, 26 August 1959, in Robinson, *First Class Citizenship,* 70–72.
86. Jackie Robinson, "Jackie Robinson," *Chicago Defender,* 26 May 1960.
87. Richard Nixon to Jackie Robinson, 16 January 1960, in Robinson, *First Class Citizenship,* 84.

88. Jackie Robinson, "Jackie Robinson," *Chicago Defender,* 26 May 1960.
89. Jackie Robinson, "Jackie Robinson," *Los Angeles Sentinel,* 20 September 1960.
90. "Nixon Is Criticized by Jackie Robinson," *New York Times,* 10 March 1961; "Negro Vote Beat Nixon, Jackie Robinson Insists," *Norfolk Journal and Guide,* 25 March, 1961; Robinson and Duckett, *I Never Had It Made,* 135–40.
91. Philip Benjamin, "Then and Now," *New York Times,* 15 April 1962.
92. Jackie Robinson, "An Open Letter to Dick Nixon," *New York Amsterdam News,* 4 May 1963.
93. Jackie Robinson, "Kennedy Is No Lincoln," *New York Amsterdam News,* 26 February 1962; Jackie Robinson, "Open Letter to JFK," *New York Amsterdam News,* 5 May 1963; Jackie Robinson, "The President Is Re-Elected," *New York Amsterdam News,* 22 June 1963; Jackie Robinson, "JFK Snubs Negro Clergy," *New York Amsterdam News,* 15 October 1963.
94. Jackie Robinson, "It's the Principle, Not the Party," *Chicago Defender,* 29 September 1964; Jackie Robinson, "We Must Look at the Record," *New York Amsterdam News,* 8 June 1968. But he lavished praise on Robert Kennedy for his antipoverty efforts in Bedford-Stuyvesant: see Jackie Robinson, "A Giant Step in the Right Direction," *New York Amsterdam News,* 24 December 1966.
95. Jackie Robinson, "A Negro First," *New York Amsterdam News,* 7 July 1964.
96. Robinson, "A Negro First," *New York Amsterdam News,* 7 July 1964.
97. Kabaservice, *Rule and Ruin,* 118.
98. Robinson, "Did Goldwater Promise Nixon?," *New York Amsterdam News,* 21 November 1964; Jackie Robinson to Nelson Rockefeller, 27 March 1968, in Robinson, *First Class Citizenship,* 275–76; Jackie Robinson, "New Challenge," *New York Amsterdam News,* 26 February 1966.
99. For Rockefeller Republicanism, see Marsha E. Barrett, *Nelson's Rockefeller's Dilemma: The Fight to Save Moderate Republicanism* (Ithaca, NY: Cornell University Press, 2024).
100. Jackie Robinson to John Lindsay, 10 February 1966, in Robinson, *First Class Citizenship,* 228–29; Jackie Robinson, "New Challenge," *New York Amsterdam News,* 26 February 1966; Jackie Robinson, "Negro Business in Harlem," *New York Amsterdam News,* 27 August 1967.
101. C. B. Powell, "Rockefeller Didn't Pull Any Punches," *New York Amsterdam News,* 30 July 1960.
102. "YMCA Leaders Praised," *New York Times,* 1 December 1949; "Rocky in Harlem Saturday," *New York Amsterdam News,* 29 October 1960; "Rockefeller Meets with Harlemites," *New York Amsterdam News,* 16 April 1961; Jackie Robinson, "Death of a President," *New York Amsterdam News,* 2 December 1963.
103. Martin Luther King, "The Presidential Nomination," *New York Amsterdam News,* 25 April 1964.

104. Powell, "Rockefeller Didn't Pull Any Punches," *New York Amsterdam News,* 30 July 1960; Marsha Barrett, "Defining Rockefeller Republicanism," *Journal of Policy History* 34, no. 3 (2022): 335–70, at 347.
105. "New York Yields Florida Fugitive," *New York Times,* 24 November 1959; Jackie Robinson, "Jackie Robinson," *Baltimore Afro American,* 5 December 1959. Also see Gilbert King, *Devil in the Grove: Thurgood Marshall, the Groveland Boys, and the Dawn of a New America* (New York: Harper, 2011); "New York Refuses to Block Minister's Extradition," *Baltimore Afro-American,* 1 July 1961.
106. James Booker, "Rocky's Vetoes Draw Protests," *New York Amsterdam News,* 2 May 1964.
107. Robinson, *First Class Citizenship,* 204–5.
108. Jackie Robinson, "In Praise of 2 Brave Senators," *New York Amsterdam News,* 10 September 1966; Barrett, *Nelson Rockefeller's Dilemma,* 119. Robinson had bitterly opposed Robert Kennedy's senatorial bid in 1964 but wrote that he was wrong to doubt his commitment to civil rights, though he opposed his presidential bid in 1968.
109. Jackie Robinson to Richard Nixon, December 1971, in Robinson, *First Class Citizenship.*
110. Robinson, *First Class Citizenship,* 314–15. Robinson's sharp criticism of Rockefeller, somewhat surprisingly, did not include the New York state police assault at the Attica Correctional Facility in September 1971. Although he had criticisms of Rockfeller's handling of this terrible incident, he later wrote that Rockefeller "used his best judgment" and that his decisions "did not take the full measure of the man." See Robinson and Duckett, *I Never Had it Made,* 208–10. Robinson evidently felt that at Attica, Rockefeller was acting under great pressure, which to some extent might excuse his misjudgments. In his deliberate turn against civil rights, there could be no excuse and no exculpation.
111. Robinson, *First Class Citizenship,* 315–16.
112. David S. Broder, "Rocky Takes a Hard Right," *Washington Post,* 28 August 1975.
113. Barrett, "Defining Rockefeller Republicanism," 337.
114. Robinson and Duckett, *I Never Had It Made,* 78.
115. Benjamin, "Then and Now," *New York Times,* 15 April 1962.
116. See Wendell E. Pritchett, *Robert Clifton Weaver and the American City: The Life and Times of an Urban Reformer* (Chicago: University of Chicago Press, 2008), 211–32.
117. Jackie Robinson, "The President and Civil Rights," *Chicago Defender,* 27 January 1962.
118. Jackie Robinson, "What Role Should Bob Weaver Play?," *New York Amsterdam News,* 17 March 1962.
119. Albert O. Hirschman, *Exit, Voice, Loyalty: Response to Decline in Firms, Organizations, and States* (Cambridge, MA: Harvard University Press, 1970).
120. "Jackie Robinson Speaks for the NAACP," *Baltimore Afro-American,* 20 April 1961.

9. The Business of Integration

1. Rex Lardner, "Success" (1950), in *The Fun of It: Stories from the Talk of the Town,* ed. Lillian Ross (New York: Modern Library, 2001), 153–54.
2. Arnold Rampersad, *Jackie Robinson: A Biography* (New York: Ballantine Books, 1997), 224–25.
3. Rampersad, *Jackie Robinson,* 251–53.
4. Rampersad, *Jackie Robinson,* 398; Val Adams, "Jackie Robinson Is Back in Baseball as a Commentator," *New York Times,* 18 March 1965; James Tuite, "Old and New: Jackie Robinson Joins the Dodgers," *New York Times,* 3 May 1966.
5. Jackie Robinson, "More Than One Way," *Chicago Defender,* 20 June 1964.
6. Robinson, "More Than One Way," *Chicago Defender,* 20 June 1964.
7. Robinson, "More Than One Way," *Chicago Defender,* 20 June 1964.
8. Jackie Robinson, "Buck and Ballot," *New York Amsterdam News,* 2 November 1963.
9. "Negro Business in Harlem," *New York Times,* 27 August 1967.
10. Rampersad, *Jackie Robinson,* 411.
11. Jackie Robinson, "A Shattered Dream," *New York Amsterdam News,* 30 December 1967.
12. Jackie Robinson, "Dreams Do Come True," *New York Amsterdam News,* 2 July 1966.
13. Robinson, "Dreams Do Come True," *New York Amsterdam News,* 2 July 1966.
14. "Jackie Robinson Joins Insurer as Stockholder and Director," *New York Times,* 23 June 1966.
15. Rampersad, *Jackie Robinson,* 396.
16. Jackie Robinson, "More Than One Way," 10 July 1965; "Join the Mainstream," *Chicago Defender,* 20 June 1964.
17. Marcia Chatelain, *Franchise: The Golden Arches in Black America* (New York: Liveright Pub., 1972), 13.
18. Paul Delany, "Jackie Robinson Scores Nixon on Black Capitalism Problems," *New York Times,* 21 January 1970.
19. Rampersad, *Jackie Robinson,* 421.
20. "Jackie Robinson to Build Project," *New York Amsterdam News,* 24 February 1951.
21. Rampersad, *Jackie Robinson,* 395.
22. "2 Negro Athletes Plan a Community," *New York Times,* 10 May 1963.
23. Rampersad, *Jackie Robinson,* 395.
24. "$14 Million Fulton Housing Announced," *New York Amsterdam News,* 17 June 1972; "Jackie Robinson's Firm President," *Norfolk Journal and Guide,* 4 November 1972. Robinson was a friend of prominent developer Samuel LeFrak and, surprisingly, defended him against accusations of bias in renting to African Americans: see "Blacks Back Lefrak Against Changes," *New York Amsterdam News,* 17 October 1970; "Blacks Back Lefrak in US Bias Case," *New York Times,* 14 October 1970. See also Peter Eisenstadt,

Rochdale Village: Robert Moses, 6,000 Families, and New York City's Great Experiment in Integrated Housing (Ithaca, NY: Cornell University Press, 2010), 17.

25. Robinson and Smith, *Jackie Robinson*, 208.
26. Rampersad, *Jackie Robinson*, 437–38.
27. Merhsa Baradaran, *The Color of Money: Black Banks and the Racial Wealth Gap* (Cambridge, MA: Harvard University Press, 2017), 196.
28. Jackie Robinson, with Alfred Duckett, *I Never Had It Made* (New York: Putnam's, 1972), 184.
29. Rampersad, *Jackie Robinson*, 394.
30. "Freedom Bank Shows Tremendous Growth," *New York Amsterdam News*, 1 April 1967; 28 March 1970.
31. Cathy White, "UN Official Hails Freedom Natl. Bank," *New York Amsterdam News*, 9 January 1965.
32. Jackie Robinson, "A Bank That Is Color Blind," *New York Amsterdam News*, 4 January 1965.
33. Robinson, "Bank That Is Color Blind," *New York Amsterdam News*, 4 January 1965.
34. Rampersad, *Jackie Robinson*, 392–94.
35. Rampersad, *Jackie Robinson*, 394.
36. Robinson and Duckett, *I Never Had It Made*, 196.
37. Robinson and Duckett, *I Never Had It Made*, 196.
38. Robinson and Duckett, *I Never Had It Made*, 193.
39. When the bank failed, the Federal Deposit Insurance Corporation (FDIC) made the unusual decision to combine all accounts of a depositor and apply a cap of $100,000; a special act of Congress was required to pay off all depositors. See Baradaran, *Color of Money*, 241.
40. What eventually transformed Harlem's economy was not Black capitalism but the infusion of white capital as Harlem gentrified in the late twentieth and early twenty-first centuries: see Lance Freeman, *There Goes the Neighborhood: Views of Gentrification from the Ground Up* (Philadelphia: Temple University Press, 2006); Brian D. Goldstein, *The Roots of Urban Renaissance: Gentrification and the Struggle Over Harlem* (Princeton, NJ: Princeton University Press, 2017).
41. Robinson and Smith, *Jackie Robinson*, 156.
42. "TV Show Hits Black Group," *New York Amsterdam News*, 27 July 1959; "Moslems Fight Back," *New York Amsterdam News*, 1 August 1959.
43. Robinson and Smith, *Jackie Robinson*, 156.
44. "A Switch—Muslims to Admit Whites to Rally," *New York Amsterdam News*, 30 July 1960; Jackie Robinson, "On the Right and Morality of Hating," *Norfolk Journal and Guide*, 25 August 1963.
45. Jackie Robinson, "The Riddle of Malcolm X," *New York Amsterdam News*, 18 July 1964.

46. Jackie Robinson, "Mysterious Malcolm," *New York Amsterdam News,* 2 March 1964.
47. Jackie Robinson, "Who Is Behind Muslims?," *Norfolk Journal and Guide,* 13 July 1963.
48. Robinson, "Who Is Behind Muslims?," *Norfolk Journal and Guide,* 13 July 1963.
49. Jackie Robinson, "Malcolm X and Adam Powell," *New York Amsterdam News,* 16 November 1963. Although the Nation of Islam's mosques—in New York City, in Los Angeles, and elsewhere—were hardly free from police violence.
50. Malcolm X, "Malcolm X's Letter," *New York Amsterdam News,* 30 November 1963.
51. Jackie Robinson, "Jackie Robinson Writes Again to Malcolm X," *New York Amsterdam News,* 14 December 1963.
52. Robinson, "Riddle of Malcolm X," *New York Amsterdam News,* 18 July 1964.
53. Jackie Robinson, "The Right to Hate," *New York Amsterdam News,* 25 August 1962.
54. Jackie Robinson, "Bobby Kennedy—Guy with Style," *New York Amsterdam News,* 9 June 1962; Robinson, "Right to Hate," *New York Amsterdam News,* 25 August 1962.
55. John Bland, "Working Together" [Letter to Editor], *New York Amsterdam News,* 1 September 1962.
56. Jackie Robinson, "Martyr Malcolm," *Norfolk Journal and Guide,* 20 March 1965.
57. Jackie Robinson, "Deacons Here to Stay," *Norfolk Journal and Guide,* 7 July 1965. See also Lance Hill, *The Deacons for Defense: Armed Resistance and the Civil Rights Movement* (Chapel Hill: University of North Carolina Press, 2004).
58. Adam Clayton Powell, "Soap Box," *New York Amsterdam News,* 30 December 1939.
59. "I'll Keep a-Talking: A. Powell," *New York Amsterdam News,* 30 March 1963.
60. Robinson, "Jackie Robinson: His Answer to Adam Powell," *New York Amsterdam News,* 30 March 1963.
61. Jackie Robinson, "Powell and the Power Structure," *New York Amsterdam News,* 21 January 1969.
62. James F. Clarity, "Jackie Robinson Condemns Party over Meredith," *New York Times,* 9 March 1967.
63. Murray Illson, "Jackie Robinson Assails Powell," *New York Times,* 12 March 1967. In 1970, Robinson was one of many backers who supported Charles Rangel in his victorious race against Powell in the Democratic primary, ending Powell's long congressional career: see Jessie H. Walker, "Rangel Makes It Official," *New York Amsterdam News,* 21 February 1970.
64. Jackie Robinson, "Praises Powell Stand on Power," *New York Amsterdam News,* 22 October 1966.
65. Jackie Robinson, "Mr. Celler Sounds Off Again," *New York Amsterdam News,* 6 May 1967; "Extremists Aid Segregationists, Says Robinson," *Chicago Defender,* 29 August 1968; Clayton Willis, "Draft Arrests Aimed at Stokely," *New York Amsterdam News,* 13 January 1968.
66. Jackie Robinson, "Cassius Did More Than Just Win," *New York Amsterdam News,* 14 March 1964.

67. Jackie Robinson, "In Defense of Cassius Clay," 11 March 1967; "Heroism and Tragedy of Muhammad Ali," 14 October 1967, both in *New York Amsterdam News.*
68. Jackie Robinson, "Dr. Martin L. King," *New York Amsterdam News,* 13 May 1967.
69. Jackie Robinson, "Defeat the Home-Style Enemy."
70. Jackie Robinson, "What I Think of Dr. Martin King," *New York Amsterdam News,* 8 July 1967.
71. Jackie Robinson, "Some Resolutions for the New Year," *New York Amsterdam News,* 6 January 1968.
72. "Eartha Kitt Denounces War Policy to Mrs. Johnson," *New York Times,* 19 January 1968; Jackie Robinson, "Negroes' Scars" [Letter to the Editor], *New York Times,* 27 January 1968.
73. Cal Jacobs, "Press Box," *Pittsburgh Courier,* 20 July 1968.
74. Jackie Robinson, "After Emotions Die Down," *New York Amsterdam News,* 13 April 1968.
75. Jackie Robinson, "Violent Society: The American Way," *Pittsburgh Courier,* 22 June 1968.
76. Jackie Robinson, "More Thoughts About Dr. King," *New York Amsterdam News,* 18 May 1968.
77. Jackie Robinson, "Dr. Martin L. King," *New York Amsterdam News,* 13 May 1967.
78. Jackie Robinson, "Violent Society: The American Way," *Pittsburgh Courier,* 22 June 1968; Jackie Robinson, "Nixon Candidacy Imperils America," *New York Amsterdam News,* 13 August 1968.
79. Jackie Robinson, "Mixed Emotions on Boycott," *New York Amsterdam News,* 16 December 1967.
80. "Exclude South Africa from Olympics, US Group Says," *Chicago Defender,* 8 May 1967. In a tribute to Robinson's range of contacts and organizing skills, the signers ranged from Stokely Carmichael to Ed Sullivan.
81. Robinson, "Mixed Emotions on Boycott," *New York Amsterdam News,* 16 December 1967. The OPHR called off the boycott in June, and Tommie Smith participated in the games and won the gold medal in the men's 200-meter run. When he and the bronze-medal winner John Carlos each raised a black-gloved fist from the winners' podium during the national anthem, they set off a furor.
82. Alfred Duckett, "Rustin Gets a 'Duster' from Jackie Robinson," *New York Amsterdam News,* 10 May 1969.
83. "Toward a Black Middle Class: Sea Host, Inc. [interview with Jackie Robinson]" (1969), in Jackie Robinson, *Beyond Home Plate: Jackie Robinson on Life After Baseball,* ed. Michael G. Long (Syracuse, NY: Syracuse University Press, 2013), 63–64.
84. Jackie Robinson, "The Police and the Black Panthers," *New York Amsterdam News,* 12 April 1968; Robinson, "West Coast Action! Reaction in New York?," *New York Amsterdam News,* 21 September 1968; Robinson and Duckett, *I Never Had It Made,* 280–82.

85. Jackie Robinson, "The Police and the Panthers" [Letter to the Editor], *New York Amsterdam News,* 12 April 1969; Robinson, "West Coast Action!," *New York Amsterdam News,* 21 September 1969.
86. Jackie Robinson, "A Reply to Bill Buckley," *New York Amsterdam News,* 7 September 1968.
87. Jackie Robinson, "A Negro First," *New York Amsterdam News,* 4 July 1964.
88. Alfred Duckett, "Jackie in Hot Answer to Rustin," *New York Amsterdam News,* 10 May 1969.
89. Matthew F. Delmont, *Why Busing Failed: Race. Media, and the Resistance to School Desegregation* (Berkeley: University of California Press, 2016.) Among those who campaigned against busing and were elected to the Senate for the first time in 1972, beginning long senatorial careers, were Jesse Helms (R-NC) and Joseph Biden (D-DE).
90. Jackie Robinson to Richard Nixon, 21 March 1972, in Robinson, *First Class Citizenship.*
91. Jackie Robinson to Richard Nixon, 21 March 1972, in Robinson, *First Class Citizenship.*
92. Danny Peary, *Jackie Robinson in Quotes* (Salem, MA: Page Street Pub., 2016), 177.
93. Jon Nordheimer, "Flag on July 4th: Thrill to Some, Threat to Others," *New York Times,* 4 July 1971.
94. Norman O. Unger, "'Jackie' The Legend, Lives On," *Chicago Defender,* 26 October 1972.
95. When Roger Kahn's famous book about the Robinson years of the Brooklyn Dodgers, *The Boys of Summer,* was published in the summer of 1972, Robinson was unable to read the print: see Peary, *Jackie Robinson in Quotes,* 380.
96. Kenneth N. Sherwood, "The Legacies of Jackie Robinson," *New York Amsterdam News,* 18 November 1972.
97. "All-American," *New York Times,* 25 October 1972.
98. Wendell Smith, "The Jackie I Knew," *Pittsburgh Courier,* 11 November 1972.
99. Unger, "'Jackie' Legend Lives On," *Chicago Defender,* 26 October 1972.
100. Jackie Robinson, *Baseball Has Done It,* ed. Charles Dexter (Philadelphia: Lippincott, 1964), 9–10.
101. Robinson and Duckett, *I Never Had It Made,* 279–80.

Epilogue

1. Peter Dreier, "Jackie Robinson's Legacy: Baseball, Race, and Politics," in *Baseball and the American Dream: Baseball, Race and Politics,* ed. Robert Elias (Armonk, NY: M. E. Sharpe, 2001), 9.
2. T. A. Frail, "Meet the 100 Most Significant Americans," *Smithsonian Magazine,* 17 November 2014.
3. "University of Washington Students Honor 100 Greatest Americans," 10 December 2009, https://www.washington.edu/news/2009/12/10/100-greatest-americans; Little Sis, "The 100 Most Influential People in American History, 2015," https://littlesis

.org/lists/1040-the-100-most-influential-figures-in-american-history-2015/members; Ranker, "The Greatest Americans Ever," 1 April 2014, https://www.ranker.com/list/top-100-most-influential-men-and-women-in-american-history/junior53.

4. Peter Dreier, *The 100 Greatest Americans of the Twentieth Century: A Social Justice Hall of Fame* (New York: Nation Books, 2012).
5. "Mount Rushmore: Trump Denounces 'Angry Mobs' Tearing Down Statues," BBC, 4 July 2020.
6. Donald J. Trump, Executive Order 13934, "Building and Rebuilding Monuments to American Heroes," 3 July 2020.
7. Sharon Robinson, *Testing the Ice: A True Story About Jackie Robinson* (New York: Scholastic Press, 2009).
8. Myron Uhlberg, *Dad, Jackie, and Me* (Atlanta: Peachtree, 2005).
9. Betty Bao Lord, *In the Year of the Lord and Jackie Robinson* (New York: HarperCollins, 1984).
10. Graham Hays, "More Than a Number: ECU's Morgan Jackson Still Guided by Jackie Robinson's Example," *D1Softball*, 2 April 2024, https://d1softball.com/more-than-a-number-ecus-morgan-johnson-still-guided-by-jackie-robinsons-example/.
11. Fred R. Shapiro, ed., *The New Yale Book of Quotations* (New Haven, CT: Yale University Press, 2021), 106.
12. Steve Sailer, "How Jackie Robinson Desegregated America," *National Review*, 8 April 1996, 42–44.
13. Sharon A. Stanley, *An Impossible Dream? Racial Integration in the United States* (New York: Oxford University Press, 2017), 1.
14. Ibram X. Kendi, *Stamped from the Beginning: The Definitive History of Racist Ideas in America* (New York: Nation Books, 2016), 231, 340.
15. See, for example, the scant coverage of integration in the comprehensive collection *African American Political Thought*, eds. Melvin L. Rogers and Jack Turner (Chicago: University of Chicago Press, 2021).
16. Rebecca Stiles Taylor, "Integration Versus Disintegration Is the Question of the Hour," *Chicago Defender*, 13 September 1941.
17. Judith Stein, "History of an Idea," *The Nation*, 14 December 1998.
18. Lydia Saab, "Socialism and Atheism Still U.S. Political Liabilities," Gallup Poll, 11 February 2020, https://news.gallup.com/poll/285563/socialism-atheism-political-liabilities.aspx.
19. Gunnar Myrdal, *An American Dilemma: The Negro Problem and American Democracy* (New York: Harper and Brothers, 1944), 62–67.
20. Matthew Ygelsias, "The Troubling Rise of Hitler Revisionism," Substack (blog), 14 April 2025, https://www.slowboring.com/p/the-troubling-rise-of-hitler-revisionism.
21. Douglas S. Massey, *American Apartheid: Segregation and the Making of the Underclass* (Cambridge, MA: Harvard University Press, 1993).

22. John R. Logan and Brain J. Stults, "Metropolitan Segregation: No Breakthrough in Sight," US Census Bureau, working paper CES-22–14, 12 August 2021.
23. Richard H. Sander, Yana A. Kucheva, and Jonathan M. Zaslow, *Moving Toward Integration: The Past and Future of Fair Housing* (Cambridge, MA: Harvard University Press, 2018).
24. Logan and Stults, "Metropolitan Segregation."
25. Matthew Desmond, *Poverty, By America* (New York: Crown, 2023), 22.
26. Orville Vernon Burton and Armand Derfner, *Justice Deferred: Race and the Supreme Court* (Cambridge, MA: Harvard University Press, 2021), 296.
27. Keenanga-Yamahatta Taylor, *Race for Profit: How Banks and the Real Estate Industry Undermined Black Home Ownership* (Chapel Hill: University of North Carolina Press, 2019), 256.
28. Tom Wicker, *Tragic Failure: Racial Integration in America* (New York: William Morrow, 1996), 3.
29. Michelle Adams, *The Containment: Detroit, the Supreme Court, and the Battle or Racial Justice in the North* (New York: Farrar, Straus, and Giroux, 2025), 24–25.
30. Peter Eisenstadt, *Rochdale Village: Robert Moses, 6,000 Families, and New York City's Great Experiment in Integrated Housing* (Ithaca, NY: Cornell University Press, 2010), 106–73.
31. For affirmative action, see Burton and Derfner, *Justice Deferred,* 296–319; Eisenstadt, *Rochdale Village,* 92–93.
32. Donald J. Trump, "Ending Radical and Wasteful Government DEI Programs and Preferencing," The White House, Presidential Actions, 20 January 2025. The acronym DEI first appeared in the *New York Times* in 2018.
33. See, for instance, Clyde McGrady, "Trump's Order to Sanitize Black History Meets Institutional Resistance," *New York Times,* 6 May 2025; Erica L. Green, "How Trump Treats Black History Different from Other Parts of America's Past," *New York Times,* 20 June 2025; Fallon Roth, "More Than a Dozen Slavery Displays in Philly, Including Washington's Former House, Have Been Flagged for a Trump Administration Review," *Philadelphia Inquirer,* 28 July 2025.
34. Adams, *The Containment,* 360.
35. See Rucker C. Johnson, *Children of the Dream: Why School Integration Works* (New York: Basic Books, 2019); Clara Hemphill, *A Brighter Choice: Building a Just School in an Unequal City* (New York: Teacher's College Press, 2023).
36. Greg Winter, "Long After Brown v. Board of Education, Sides Switch," *New York Times,* 16 May 2004.
37. Derrick A. Bell Jr., "*Brown v. Board of Education* and the Interest-Convergence Dilemma," *Harvard Law Review* 93 (1980): 518–33. For other critiques of integration, see Leslie T. Fenwick, *Jim Crow's Pink Slip: The Untold Story of Black Principal and Teacher Leadership*

(Cambridge, MA: Harvard Educational Press, 2022); Noliwe Rooks, *Integrated: How America's Schools Failed Black Children* (New York: Pantheon, 2025).

38. Winter, "Long After Brown v. Board of Education," *New York Times,* 16 May 2004.
39. See American Immigration Council, "Analyzing the Trump's Administration's Attacks on Immigration, Democracy, and America," July 2025, https://www.americanimmigrationcouncil.org/report/mass-deportation-trump-democracy/.
40. See Burton and Defner, *Justice Deferred,* 223–93; Abbie VanSickle, "Supreme Court, for Now, Pauses Court Decision on Limiting Voting Rights Act," *New York Times,* 24 February 2025.
41. Jeff Passan, "Defense Dept. Restores Story on Jackie Robinson's Military Service," ESPN, 19 March 2025.
42. Jack Mintz, "Jackie Robinson Day Is Pure Celebration—and That's the Problem," Yahoo Sports, 15 April 2025.
43. James Baldwin, "The Nigger We Invent," in Baldwin, *The Cross of Redemption: Uncollected Writings,* ed. Randall Kenan (1969; repr., New York: Vintage, 2010), 90.
44. William Fowler, "Nobody Has It Made!," *Atlanta Daily World,* 23 June 1959; Harmon G. Perry, "Robinson Lauds Tuskegee Group," *Atlanta Daily World,* 25 June 1959. For the history of the Tuskegee boycott, see Robert J. Norrell, *Reaping the Whirlwind: The Civil Rights Movement in Tuskegee* (Chapel Hill: University of North Carolina Press, 1998). The boycott ended when the US Supreme Court, in the landmark *Gomillion v. Lightfoot* decision (1960), declared the gerrymander unconstitutional.
45. Lee D. Jenkins, "Jackie Robinson Blasts Civil Rights Patience Talk," *Chicago Defender,* 7 May 1960. The following year, Robinson would call Truman a "senile old man" for claiming the Freedom Riders were inspired by communists: see Jackie Robinson, "HST—Man from Nowhere Going Home," *New York Amsterdam News,* 10 June 1961.
46. Jenkins, "Robinson Blasts Patience Talk," *Chicago Defender,* 7 May 1960.
47. Jackie Robinson, "They Only Think They Got It Made," *Chicago Defender,* 12 November 1967.
48. Jackie Robinson, with Alfred Duckett, *I Never Had It Made* (New York: Putnam's, 1972), 269.
49. Micah 4:4.
50. Robinson and Duckett, *I Never Had It Made,* 269.

INDEX

Illustrations in the gallery are indicated by the word "photo."

Recent books in the

CARTER G. WOODSON INSTITUTE SERIES

Black Studies at Work in the World

Grievous Entanglement: Consumption, Connection, and Slavery in the Atlantic World
Erin Pearson

Unleashing Black Power: Grassroots Organizing in Harlem and the Advent of the Long, Hot Summers
Peter D. Blackmer

The Evolution of a Rural Free Black Community: Goochland County, Virginia, 1728–1832
Reginald D. Butler, edited by Peter S. Onuf

Roses in December: Black Life in Hanover County from Civil War to Civil Rights
Jody Lynn Allen

The Struggle for Change: Race and the Politics of Reconciliation in Modern Richmond
Marvin T. Chiles

A Little Child Shall Lead Them: A Documentary Account of the Struggle for School Desegregation in Prince Edward County, Virginia
Brian J. Daugherity and Brian Grogan, editors

We Face the Dawn: Oliver Hill, Spottswood Robinson, and the Legal Team That Dismantled Jim Crow
Margaret Edds

Keep On Keeping On: The NAACP and the Implementation of Brown v. Board of Education in Virginia
Brian J. Daugherity

Schooling Jim Crow: The Fight for Atlanta's Booker T. Washington High School and the Roots of Black Protest Politics
Jay Winston Driskell Jr.

The Punitive Turn: New Approaches to Race and Incarceration
Deborah E. McDowell, Claudrena N. Harold, and Juan Battle, editors

Freedom Has a Face: Race, Identity, and Community in Jefferson's Virginia
Kirt von Daacke

Gabriel's Conspiracy: A Documentary History
Philip J. Schwarz, editor

Rambles of a Runaway from Southern Slavery
Henry Goings, edited by Calvin Schermerhorn, Michael Plunkett, and Edward Gaynor

Whispers of Rebellion: Narrating Gabriel's Conspiracy
Michael L. Nicholls

Word, Like Fire: Maria Stewart, the Bible, and the Rights of African Americans
Valerie C. Cooper

Strategies for Survival: Recollections of Bondage in Antebellum Virginia
William Dusinberre

Criminal Injustice: Slaves and Free Blacks in Georgia's Criminal Justice System
Glenn McNair

Segregation's Science: Eugenics and Society in Virginia
Gregory Michael Dorr

The Segregated Scholars: Black Social Scientists and the Creation of Black Labor Studies, 1890–1950
Francille Rusan Wilson

Bitter Fruits of Bondage: The Demise of Slavery and the Collapse of the Confederacy, 1861–1865
Armstead L. Robinson

Migrants against Slavery: Virginians and the Nation
Philip J. Schwarz

Black Prisoners and Their World, Alabama, 1865–1900
Mary Ellen Curtin

Rituals of Race: American Public Culture and the Search for Racial Democracy
Alessandra Lorini

"Rearing Wolves to Our Own Destruction": Slavery in Richmond, Virginia, 1782–1865
Midori Takagi

Enterprising Southerners: Black Economic Success in North Carolina, 1865–1915
Robert C. Kenzer

Free Blacks in Norfolk, Virginia, 1790–1860: The Darker Side of Freedom
Tommy L. Bogger

A House Divided: Slavery and Emancipation in Delaware, 1638–1865
Patience Essah

A New Plantation South: Land, Labor, and Federal Favor in Twentieth-Century Arkansas
Jeannie M. Whayne

Limits of Anarchy: Intervention and State Formation in Chad
Sam C. Nolutshungu